Backpacking in
Alaska

a Lonely Planet walking guide

Jim DuFresne

Backpacking in Alaska

1st edition

Published by
    Lonely Planet Publications
    Head Office: PO Box 617, Hawthorn, Vic 3122, Australia
    Branches: 155 Filbert St, Suite 251, Oakland, CA 94607, USA
                  10 Barley Mow Passage, Chiswick, London W4 4PH, UK
                  71 bis rue du Cardinal Lemoine, 75005 Paris, France

Printed by
    Colorcraft Ltd, Hong Kong

Photographs by
    Alaska Discovery (AD), Jim DuFresne (JD), Carl Palazzola (CP), Donna Pietsch (DP),
    Deanna Swaney (DS), Jeff Williams (JW)

    Front cover: Pinnell Mountain Trail (Jim DuFresne)
    Title page: Hikers on White Thunder Ridge, Glacier Bay (Jeff Sloss)
    Back cover: Setting up camp, Wrangell-St Elias National Park (Jim DuFresne)

    Black & white photos on pages 171, 205 & 229 by Jim DuFresne

First Published
    April 1995

National Library of Australia Cataloguing in Publication Data

DuFresne, Jim
    Backpacking in Alaska

    1st ed.
    Includes index.
    ISBN 0 86442 266 0.

    1. Hiking – Alaska – Guidebooks. 2. Alaska –
    Guidebooks I. Title. (Series: Lonely Planet walking
    guide).

917.98045

Jim DuFresne

Jim is a former sports and outdoors editor of the *Juneau Empire* and the first Alaskan sportswriter to win a national award from Associated Press. He is presently a freelance writer, specializing in outdoor and travel writing. His previous books include Lonely Planet's *Tramping in New Zealand* and *Alaska – a travel survival kit*, and wilderness guides to Isle Royale, Voyageurs and Glacier Bay national parks.

From the Author

Sandy Graham gave me his pair of hiking boots (actually he sold them to me). Fine leather boots 'already broken in' he said. They weren't! Not for my feet anyway and I endured an excruciating blister on the back of my heel in the middle of the Wrangell Mountains. But during an endless summer of backpacking in Alaska, that was the only real inconvenience I suffered. And Sandy's advice, a trekker himself of few equals, has never cost me anything.

The best piece of advice Sandy has ever given me, or anybody else, is this: grab your backpack, toss in some extra bandages and moleskins and just go. Don't worry about bears, the cost of the trip or your job back home. If you do, you'll never pack your bags. Just go and experience land that has yet to be bulldozed into a shopping mall. The world is changing but backpacking in the wilds is one small way to postpone the inevitable.

I deeply appreciate the considerable assistance I received from Carla Sullivan of the Fairbanks Convention & Visitor Bureau, Connie Taylor of the Cordova Chamber of Commerce, Suzi Bock of the Matanuska-Susitna Visitor Bureau and Ken Morris of the Anchorage Convention & Visitor Bureau.

Also lending me a hand were Dave Vickery of the Bureau of Land Management, Linda Mickle of the Alaska Marine Highway System, Carol Waddell of Reeve Aleutian Airways, John Beiler of the Alaska Division of Tourism, Bill Ehrlich of Alaska Airlines, Janet Swanson of The Alaska Railroad and Ike Waits of Wild Rose Guidebooks. I deeply appreciate my equipment sponsors MSR, Patagonia, Kelty, Vasque Boots, Dana Packs, Benchmark stores of Michigan and Ohio, and John Barton and Carl Walter of Klepper Kayaks.

Most of all I thank my traveling partners and those Alaskans who put me up for the night: Tim and Racheli Feller of Anchorage, Lisa Taylor and Peter Brondz of Bird Creek and Phoebe Riches of Australia. There were also Jack and Eileen Hughes and their wonderful sauna in Homer, Sandra Stimson, Rita Gittins and Ed Fogels in Anchorage and Gary Benson of Sourdough Outfitters in Bettles. An extra dose of appreciation goes out to Carl Palazzola of California and Donna Pietsch of Minnesota.

Finally there were those people back home that I didn't worry too much while I was backpacking in Alaska. My editors at both the *Saginaw News* and Booth News Service covered for me while I was gone, even though they couldn't understand why anybody would want to spend two months in a tent – especially Dennis Tanner whose idea of paradise is 99c breakfasts and 50c slot machines. Each to his own, huh Dennis?

From the Publisher

This first edition of *Backpacking in Alaska* was edited at the Lonely Planet office in Australia by Samantha Carew. The proofreader was Frith Pike, who also provided valuable editorial guidance. Mapping was done by Matt King. David Kemp was responsible for the design, layout and some mapping. The illustrations are by David,

Trudi Canavan and Tamsin Wilson. Valerie Tellini designed the cover.

Disclaimer

Although the author and publisher have done their utmost to ensure the accuracy and currency of all information in this guidebook, they cannot accept responsibility for any loss, injury or inconvenience sustained by any person using this book. In particular, we cannot guarantee that paths described have not been destroyed in the interval between research and publication.

All hiking times given *exclude* rest stops and, unless otherwise stated, assume the trail is unobstructed by snow. The fact that a trip or area is described in this guidebook does not mean that it is necessarily a safe one for you or your group. The maps included are only to help you understand the trail descriptions – you'll need the proper topographical maps before setting out.

You are finally responsible for judging your own capabilities in the light of the conditions you encounter.

Warning & Request

Things change – prices go up, schedules change, good places go bad and bad places go bankrupt – nothing stays the same. So if you find things better or worse, recently opened or long since closed, please write and tell us and help make the next edition better!

Your letters will be used to help update future editions and, where possible, important changes will also be included as a Stop Press section in reprints.

We greatly appreciate all information that is sent to us by travelers. Back at Lonely Planet we employ a hard-working readers' letters team to sort through the many letters we receive.

The best ones will be rewarded with a free copy of the next edition or another Lonely Planet guide if you prefer. We give away lots of books, but, unfortunately, not every letter/ postcard receives one.

Contents

Map Legend

BOUNDARIES

━ ·· ━ ·· ━ ·· ━ ·· ━ ·· ━	International Boundary
━ · · ━ · · ━ · · ━ · · ━	State Boundary
━ ━ ━ ━ ━ ━ ━ ━	Regional Boundary
• • • • • • • • • • • • • • •	Arctic Circle

ROUTES

	Freeway
	Highway
	Major Road
━ ━ ━ ━ ━ ━ ━	Unsealed Road or Track
	City Road
	City Street
┼┼┼┼┼┼┼┼┼┼┼┼	Railway
━ ━ ━ ━ ━ ━ ━	Walking Track
• • • • • • • • • • • • • •	Unmarked Trail
━ ━ ━ ━ ━ ━ ━ ━	Ferry Route
┼━┼━┼━┼━┼━┼━┼	Cable Car or Chairlift

AREA FEATURES

	Park, Gardens
	National Park & Forest
	Built-Up Area
	Pedestrian Mall
	Market
+ + + + + +	Cemetery
	Glacier
	Beach or Desert
	Rocks

HYDROGRAPHIC FEATURES

	Coastline
	River, Creek
━ ━ ━ ━	Intermittent River or Creek
	Lake, Intermittent Lake
	Canal
	Swamp

SYMBOLS

✪ CAPITAL		National Capital	✚	★	Hospital, Police Station
◉ Capital		State Capital	✈	✝	Airport, Airfield
CITY		Major City	☞	✿	Swimming Pool, Gardens
● City		City	❖	🐘	Shopping Centre, Zoo
● Town		Town	⚲	⩊	Winery or Vineyard, Picnic Site
● Village		Village	←	A25	One Way Street, Route Number
■		Place to Stay		∴	Archaeological Site or Ruins
▼		Place to Eat	🏛	⚱	Stately Home, Monument
☗		Pub, Bar	⌁	⛽	Golf Course, Gas Station
✉	☎	Post Office, Telephone	⌒	⌂	Cave, Hut or Cabin
❶	❸	Tourist Information, Bank	▲	�※	Mountain or Hill, Lookout
⊖	Ⓟ	Transport, Parking	⚲	⚓	Lighthouse, Shipwreck
🏛	⌂	Museum, Youth Hostel	)(	✕	Pass, Spot Height
⌸	⚒	Caravan Park, Campground			Ancient or City Wall
✝	▱ ✝	Church, Cathedral			Rapids, Waterfalls
☖	✡	Mosque, Synagogue			Cliff or Escarpment, Tunnel
⚖	♨	Buddhist Temple, Hindu Temple			Railway Station

Note: not all symbols displayed above appear in this book

Introduction

You can visit Alaska, you can tour Alaska, or you can experience Alaska. The best way to really appreciate this magnificent land is by foot; get off the bus, get out of the car, get away from the road and get on a trail. More than any other activity, trekking allows you to escape the crowds, dodge those monstrous recreational vehicles on George Parks Hwy, and sneak away from the cities with their fast-food chains and high prices, to really see, and experience, what Alaska is all about – wilderness, pristine and pure.

Alaska draws trekkers, backpackers, hikers and other wilderness-seekers like few other places in the world. This 'Final Frontier' is the first place that comes to mind for those tempted by the North Country. It evokes images of mountains, icy-blue glaciers, brown bears feeding on a salmon run and treeless tundra valleys, uncluttered by buildings, billboards or other signs of so-called 'progress'.

Alaska is home to the highest peak in North America (Mt McKinley, 20,320 feet), has a glacier (Malaspina) 50% larger than the US state of Delaware, boasts an inland lake with a surface area of 1000 sq miles (Iliamna) and has more coastline than the rest of the US states put together. At 591,004 sq miles (a fifth of the size of the USA), Alaska is a vast land of extraordinary dimensions.

More than three-quarters of Alaska is 'land locked up' as parks, wildlife preserves, wild rivers and national forests. The National Park Service (NPS) alone oversees 45 million acres, including Denali and Wrangell-St Elias national parks. Within these and other parks there are endless trekking and roaming possibilities.

This book is a detailed guide to 32 trails and routes that extend from Ketchikan in the Southeast to near the Arctic Circle, north of Fairbanks. The trails include an afternoon day hike along the edge of the Mendenhall Glacier in Juneau, a 10-day journey across the Kenai Peninsula on the Resurrection trail

system, and an adventure in Denali Wilderness where there are no trails at all.

Dozens of other trails throughout the six regions of the state – Southeast, Anchorage, Kenai Peninsula, Wrangell-St Elias, Denali and Fairbanks – are mentioned and briefly described, and include information on transport to the area and the trailheads, special concerns, permits and places to stay off the trail.

Each trek is rated in terms of difficulty. 'Easy' trails are well maintained with bridges over all major streams and planking over many bog areas. Paths are easy to locate and follow, primarily because they are well used by both trekkers and other groups like mountain bikers and equestrians. Often junctions are posted with mileage signs or sometimes even maps. Some climbing may be necessary, but switchbacks make the ascents considerably less difficult than expected.

'Moderate' trails are still beaten paths in the woods but they are not posted as often as the easy trails. They require you to ford small streams or negotiate short stretches along ridges or other alpine areas. The trekking is more demanding, involving greater elevation gains, longer days and 'bouldering' (stepping from one large rock to the next) rocky slopes around peaks.

'Challenging' treks are often a combination of several hiking trails, often following the natural routes of a ridge line or the gravel bars of a river. You'll often use animal trails to help make your way from one valley to another in an area that may not have any maintained trails. The challenging treks in this guidebook often involve fording rivers – a difficult, if not impossible task when water levels are high – as well as alpine crossings where there is little protection from weather that suddenly turns foul. These treks demand that you be in good walking condition, have previous backcountry experience and possess a sound understanding of maps and compasses.

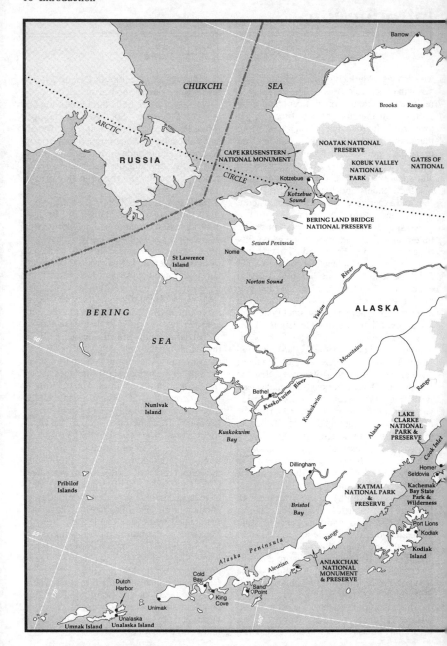

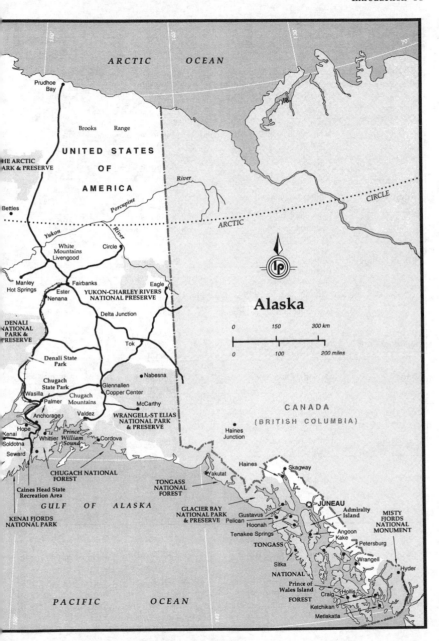

Region	Trail Name	Rating	Distance (miles)
Southeast	Deer Mountain & John Mountain	Moderate	11.9
	Gavan Hill/Harbor Mountain	Moderate	11
	Mt Edgecumbe	Moderate-Challenging	13.4 (RT)
	Perseverance	Easy-Moderate	10
	Dan Moller	Easy	6.6 (RT)
	West Glacier	Easy	6.8 (RT)
	Montana Creek & Windfall Lake	Moderate	13
	Amalga	Moderate	15 (RT)
	Mt Riley	Easy	10.7
	Chilkoot	Moderate-Challenging	33
	Upper Dewey Lake	Challenging	6.5 (RT)
Anchorage	Flattop Mountain	Easy	3.4 (RT)
	Williwaw Lakes	Moderate	18
	McHugh & Rabbit Lakes	Moderate	16.4
	Historic Iditarod	Challenging	26
	Eklutna Lakeside	Easy	31
Kenai Peninsula	Johnson Pass	Moderate	23
	Resurrection Pass	Easy	38.5
	Russian Lakes	Easy	21.6
	Primrose & Lost Lake	Moderate	15
	Coastal	Easy	16 (RT)
	Grewingk Glacier & Lagoon	Moderate	16.5-30
Wrangell-St Elias National Park	Dixie Pass	Challenging	22
	Nugget Creek	Moderate	29
	Bonanza Mine	Moderate	8 (RT)
Denali	Mt Healy Overlook	Moderate	5 (RT)
	Polychrome Pass Circuit	Moderate	8
	East Branch of the Toklat River	Moderate	12-16 (RT)
	Mt Eielson Loop	Moderate	14 (RT)
	Little Coal Creek	Moderate-Challenging	16-27.3
Fairbanks	Pinnell Mountain	Moderate	27.3
	Granite Tors	Easy	15

Don't let the fear of bears and bugs dictate where or when you go trekking in Alaska. These are minor concerns; the great dangers in the Alaska wilderness are hypothermia, underestimating swollen rivers and getting lost. Eliminate these risks by being properly equipped, choosing the right trek for your ability and scheduling enough days so that exhaustion doesn't lead to an accident.

Be prepared, and you will enjoy your trekking in Alaska. Only through the soles of your boots will you unlock the wonders of this land and experience the wilderness and wildlife that has been so carefully protected.

Number of Days	Cabins	Transport	Features	Page Numbers
D/O	Y	Bus/Taxi	Alpine terrain	80-83
D/O	Y	Taxi	Alpine terrain	89-90
2-3	Y	Boat	Volcanic landscape	90-92
D/O	N	Walking	Mining ruins & alpine terrain	99-101
D/O	Y	Bus	Alpine terrain	101-103
D	N	Bus	Glacier	103-105
2	N	Bus	Rainforest & fishing	104-106
D/O	Y	Taxi/Rental Car	Glacier	106-107
D/O	N	Walking	Coastline	110-112
4-5	N	Taxi	Mining ruins & alpine pass	115-120
D/O	Y	Walking	Waterfalls & alpine lakes	120-121
D	N	Bus/Van Service	Alpine terrain	132-133
2	N	Bus/Van Service	Lakes & mountains	133-135
2	N	Van Service	Lakes & alpine terrain	135-137
3	N	Van Service	Mining ruins & glaciers	137-140
3-4	Y	Van Service	Lake & glacier	140-143
2	N	Bus	Alpine pass	150-151
4-5	Y	Bus	Lakes & alpine pass	152-156
2	Y	Bus	Lakes & fishing	156-159
2	Y	Bus	Lake & alpine terrain	159-161
2-3	N	Walking	Ruins & coastline	165-168
3-4	Y	Boat	Coastline & glacier	173-177
4-5	N	Van Service	Alpine pass	184-187
3-4	Y	Van Service	Mining ruins	186-189
D/O	N	Van Service	Mining ruins & alpine terrain	189-192
D	N	Walking	Alpine terrain	206-207
2	N	Bus	Mountains	207-209
2	N	Bus	Glaciated river	209-210
2-3	N	Bus	Mt McKinley	210-212
2-4	N	Van Service	Alpine terrain & Mt McKinley	215-218
3	Y	Private	Alpine traverse	225-230
2	Y	Van Service/Rental Car	Granite pinnacles	230-232

RT – *round trip*
D/O – *day/overnight hike (backcountry camping)*
Cabin – *rental cabins or free-use shelters (not necessarily one for every night of the hike)*

Facts about Alaska

HISTORY

Alaska's history is a strange series of spurts and sputters, booms and busts. Although today Alaska is viewed as a wilderness paradise and an endless source of raw materials, it has often in the past been regarded as frozen wasteland, a suitable home only for Inuits and polar bears. Whenever some natural resource was uncovered, however, a short period of prosperity and exploitation followed. Firstly there was sea-otter skins, then gold salmon and oil, and most recently, untouched wilderness. After each resource was exhausted, some would say raped, the land slipped back into oblivion.

The First Alaskans

The first Alaskans migrated from Asia to North America 30,000 to 40,000 years ago during an ice age that lowered the sea level and gave rise to a 900-mile land bridge spanning Siberia and Alaska. The nomadic groups were not bent on exploring the new world but on following the animal herds that provided them with food and clothing. Although many tribes wandered deep into North and South America, four ethnic groups – the Athabascans, Aleuts, Inuits and the coastal tribes of Tlingits and Haidas – remained in Alaska and made the harsh wilderness their homeland.

The First Europeans

The first written record of the state was made by Virtus Bering, a Danish navigator sailing for the czar of Russia. Bering's trip in 1728 proved that America and Asia were two separate continents, and 13 years later, commanding the ship *St Peter*, he went ashore near Cordova to become the first European to set foot in Alaska.

Bering and many of his crew died from scurvy during that journey, but his lieutenant (aboard the ship *St Paul*) sailed all the way to Sitka before turning around. Despite all the hardships, the survivors brought back fur pelts and tales of fabulous seal and otter colonies – Alaska's first boom was under way. Russian fur merchants wasted little time in overrunning the Aleutian Islands and quickly established a settlement on Kodiak Island. Chaos followed as bands of Russian hunters robbed and murdered each other for furs while the peaceful Aleutian Indians, living near the hunting grounds, were almost annihilated.

By the 1790s, Russia had organized the Russian-American Company to regulate the fur trade and ease the violent competition. However, tales of the enormous wealth in the Alaskan wildlife trade brought several other countries to the frigid waters. Spain claimed the entire North American west coast, including Alaska, and sent several explorers to the Southeast region. These early visitors took boat loads of furs, but left neither settlers nor forts, only a few Spanish names.

The British arrived when Captain James Cook began searching the area for the mythical Northwest Passage between the Pacific and Atlantic oceans. From Vancouver Island, Cook sailed north to Southcentral Alaska in 1778, anchoring at Cook Inlet for a spell, before continuing on to the Aleutian Islands, Bering Sea, even the Arctic Ocean. The French sent Jean de La Perouse, who in 1786 made it as far as Lituya Bay on the southern coast of Alaska. But it was Cook's shipmate, George Vancouver, returning on his own in the 1790s who finally charted the complicated waters of the Southeast's Inside Passage. Aboard his ship HMS *Discovery*, Vancouver surveyed the coastline from California to Alaska's Panhandle, producing maps so accurate they were still being used a century later.

When the fur colonies in the Aleutians were depleted, Alexander Baranof, who headed the Russian-American Company, moved his territorial capital from Kodiak to Sitka in the Southeast. After subduing the Tlingit Indians in his ruthless manner, he proceeded to build a stunning city, 'an American Paris in Alaska' with the immense profits from furs. At one point, Baranof oversaw, or some would say ruled, a fur empire that stretched from Bristol Bay to northern California but when the British began pushing north into Southeast Alaska, he built a second fort near the mouth of the Stikine River in 1834. That fort eventually evolved into the small lumbering and fishing town of Wrangell.

When a small trickle of US adventurers began to arrive, four nations had a foot in the Panhandle of Alaska: Spain and France were squeezed out of the area by the early 1800s while the British were reduced to leasing selected areas from the Russians.

The Sale of Alaska

By the 1860s, the Russians found themselves badly overextended. Their involvement in Napoleon's European wars, a declining fur industry and the long lines of shipping between Sitka and the heartland of Russia were draining their national treasury. The country made several overtures to the USA for the sale of Alaska, and fishers from Washington State pushed for it.

The American Civil War delayed the negotiations and it wasn't until 1867 that US Secretary of State William H Seward, with extremely keen foresight, signed a treaty to purchase the state for $7.2 million – less than two cents an acre.

Gold

What brought Alaska into the world limelight was gold. The promise of quick riches and the adventure of the frontier became the most effective lure Alaska ever had. Gold was discovered in the Gastineau Channel in the 1880s and the towns of Juneau and Douglas sprang up overnight, living off the very productive Treadwell and Alaska-Juneau mines. Circle City in the Interior suddenly emerged in 1893 when gold was discovered in nearby Birch Creek. Three years later, one of the world's most colorful gold rushes took place in the Klondike of the Yukon Territory (Canada).

Often called 'the last grand adventure', the Klondike Gold Rush took place when the country and much of the world was suffering a severe recession. Thousands of people quit their jobs and sold their homes to finance a trip through Southeast Alaska to the newly created boom town of Skagway. From this tent city, almost 30,000 prospectors tackled the steep Chilkoot Trail to Lake Bennett, where they built crude rafts to float the rest of the way to the gold fields; an equal number returned home along the route, broke and disillusioned.

The number of miners who made a fortune was small, but the tales and legends that emerged were endless. The Klondike stampede, though it only lasted from 1896 to the early 1900s, was Alaska's most colorful era and earned the state the reputation of the country's last frontier.

Statehood

The USA experienced its only foreign invasion on home soil when the Japanese attacked the Attu Islands and bombed Dutch Harbor in the Aleutian Islands during WW II. Congress and military leaders panicked and rushed to develop and protect the rest of Alaska. Large army and air-force bases were built throughout the state in places including Anchorage, Fairbanks, Sitka, Whittier and Kodiak, and thousands of military personnel were sent to run them. But it was the famous Alcan (also known as the Alaska Hwy) that was the single most important project of the military build-up. The 1520-mile road was a major engineering feat and became the only overland link between Alaska and the rest of the USA.

The road was built by the military but it was the residents who benefited as it stimulated the development of Alaska's natural resources. The growth lead to a new drive for statehood to fix what many felt was Alaska's status of '2nd-class citizenship' in Washington DC. Early in 1958, Congress approved a statehood act which Alaskans quickly accepted, and on 3 January 1959, President Dwight Eisenhower proclaimed the land the 49th State of the Union.

The Modern State

Alaska entered the 1960s full of promise and then disaster struck: the most powerful earthquake ever recorded in North America (9.2 on the Richter scale) hit Southcentral Alaska on Good Friday morning in 1964. If the natural catastrophe left the newborn state in a shambles, then it was a gift from nature that rushed it to recovery and beyond. Alaska's next boom took place in 1968 when Atlantic Richfield discovered massive oil deposits underneath Prudhoe Bay in the Arctic Ocean.

Oil has given Alaska an economic base that is the envy of many other states; its residents enjoy the highest per-capita income in the country. The state's budget is in the billions and legislators in Juneau have transformed Anchorage into a stunning city with sports arenas, libraries and performing-arts centers, while virtually every Bush town has a million-dollar school.

Alaskans, however, had a rude awakening in March 1989 when the biggest oil spill in US history occurred in their state: the *Exxon Valdez*, a 987-foot Exxon Oil supertanker rammed Bligh Reef a few hours out of the port of Valdez. The ship spilled almost 11 million gallons of North Slope crude into the bountiful waters of Prince William Sound and then the oil quickly spread 600 miles from the grounding.

Many Alaskans felt betrayed by Big Oil, the very companies that had fed them so well in the past. The unfortunate event may be just the latest round in Alaska's greatest debate – that concerning the exploitation of the wilderness. The issue moved to center stage when industry, conservationists and the government came head to head over a single paragraph in the Native Claims Settlement Act, known simply as 'd-2', that called for the preservation of 80 million acres of Alaskan wilderness. Most residents used it to cover the entire issue of federal interference with the state's resources and future.

The resulting battle was a tug of war about how much land the US Congress would preserve, to what extent industries such as mining and logging would be allowed to develop, and what permanent residents would be allowed to purchase. The fury over wilderness reached a climax when on the eve of his departure from office in 1980, President Jimmy Carter signed the Alaska Lands Bill into law, setting aside 106 million acres for national parks and preserves with a single stroke of the pen.

The problems of how to manage the USA's remaining true wilderness are far from over. Oil-company officials, already preparing for the day the Prudhoe Bay fields run dry, have been eyeing other wilderness areas such as the Arctic National Wildlife Refuge (ANWR) and Bristol Bay, home of Alaska's greatest salmon runs. The ANWR also fell victim to the Persian Gulf War and President George Bush's background as a Texas oilman. The Bush administration pushed hard to open up a portion of this 1.5-million acre refuge to drilling after the Gulf War with Iraq made gas prices sky rocket. But environmentalists, especially the National Wildlife Federation, held their ground until the US Senate killed a bill in November 1991 that would have allowed offshore drilling in the ANWR and made it easier to build a gas pipeline across the refuge.

All this alarms environmentalists who say pipelines, oil drills and the activity associated in removing the oil will forever disrupt one of the last true wilderness areas on earth – not just a park or a bay but a complete ecosystem. Others doubt that environmentalists can continue to win this battle, not in a state where 85% of the revenue comes from the oil industry.

GEOGRAPHY

Southeast

Also known as the Panhandle, Southeast Alaska is a 500-mile coastal strip that extends from Dixon Entrance, north of Prince Rupert, to the Gulf of Alaska. In between are the hundreds of islands (including Prince of Wales Island, the third largest island in the USA) of the Alexander Archipelago and a narrow strip of coast separated from Canada's mainland by the glacier-filled Coastal Mountains.

Winding through the middle of the region is the Inside Passage waterway, the lifeline for the isolated communities, including Juneau, the state capital of Alaska, as the rugged terrain prohibits road building. High annual rainfall and mild temperatures have turned the Southeast into rainforest which is broken up by majestic mountain ranges, glaciers and fjords that surpass those in Norway.

The major parks and preserves of the Southeast are Glacier Bay National Park, Admiralty Island National Monument and Misty Fjord National Monument. Nearly every town in this region has trails that go into the surrounding mountains or remote wilderness-like valleys. By hopping from one town to the next, on the State Marine Ferry, you can easily spend a month or an entire summer just day hiking and never need to shoulder a pack that weighs more than a parka, your camera and lunch.

Southcentral

This region curves 650 miles from the Gulf of Alaska, past Prince William Sound to Kodiak Island. Like the Southeast, it is a mixture of rugged mountains, glaciers, steep fjords and virgin forests, and includes the Kenai Peninsula – a superb recreational area for backpacking, day hiking and escaping into the wilderness.

The weather along the coastline can often be rainy and stormy but the summers are usually mild and have their share of sunshine. You can reach the peninsula by bus or rental car from Anchorage, and by the State Marine Ferry which crosses Prince William Sound and stops at Seward and Homer before heading onto Kodiak.

The major parks and preserves include Chugach National Forest, Kenai Fjords National Park, Kenai National Wildlife Refuge and Kachemak Bay State Park & Wilderness. Like the Southeast, you'll find the Kenai Peninsula crisscrossed with foot trails that are easy to reach and well-marked and maintained. Many lend themselves to overnight treks or longer backpacking trips.

It's even possible to trek from Homer to Seward. This explains why at times the area becomes overrun by RVers (those who travel in recreational vehicles), tourists and trekkers.

The trails on Kodiak Island are for the most part for experienced trekkers because they are not maintained or marked as well as those in the national forests.

Anchorage

With almost half the state's population living in the Anchorage Bowl region, you'd expect a good system of hiking trails and there are. Only Juneau rivals this big city for the number of trails and diversity of hiking opportunities. Anchorage has the luxury of mountains above it skyline and wilderness at its doorstep. The city itself is practically surrounded by Chugach State Park while surrounding the state park is Chugach National Park.

You can reach most of the trailheads by either People Mover, the city bus service, or Backpacker Shuttle, a relatively new van service for trekkers and backpackers. You'll also find a variety of accommodations, outfitters and backpacking shops and a tour guide who can arrange just about anything you want to do in Alaska. You can spend a week or longer hiking in the Anchorage area and also arrange the rest of your trekking plans from here, including campground bookings and shuttle-bus permits for Denali National Park in the Interior.

The Interior

This area includes three major roads – the George Parks, Glenn and Richardson highways – that cut across the center of the state and pass a number of forests, state parks and recreational areas, including Denali National Park & Preserve, Alaska's number one attraction, Denali State Park and Wrangell-St Elias National Park & Preserve.

The heartland of Alaska offers warm temperatures in the summer and ample opportunities for outdoor activities in some of the state's most scenic and accessible areas. With the Alaska Range to the north, the Wrangell and Chugach mountains to the south and the Talkeetna Mountains cutting through the middle, the Interior has a rugged appearance matching that of either Southeast or Southcentral Alaska but without much of the rain and cloudy weather.

Fairbanks

The boom town of both the gold-rush days and later the pipeline construction to Prudhoe Bay, Fairbanks, Alaska's second-largest city, is often a disappointment to most travelers as it is very spread out. Fairbanks is in the flat valley floor formed by the Tanana and Chena rivers; the Alaska Range and Mt McKinley are off in the distance.

Fairbanks is a major departure point for those who want to venture north of the Arctic Circle into the Brooks Range. Unfortunately it lacks those close-to-town trekking opportunities offered by Anchorage and Juneau, but there are a number of outstanding trails for both day hiking and longer adventures.

Transportation to the trailheads is challenging and often costly. The exception is the Chena River State Park, especially now that Fairbanks is becoming more affected by the tourist boom sweeping the state. There are several trails in the park, reached by a paved road that rental car companies actually allow you to drive vehicles on. Off and on there has also been a van service to Chena Hot Springs, a delightful resort at the end of Chena Hot Springs Rd.

The Bush

This region covers a vast area that includes the Brooks Range, Arctic Alaska, Western Alaska on the Bering Sea, the Alaska Peninsula and also the Aleutian Islands which make up the out-reaching western arm of the state. The Bush is larger than the other five regions put together and is separated from them by great mountains and mighty rivers.

Occasionally, there are ways of beating the high cost of getting to the far reaches of the state, but for the most part traveling to the Bush involves chartering small, expensive aircraft called 'bush planes'. Most trekkers are drawn to Katmai National Park & Preserve on the Alaska Peninsula and the Gates of the Arctic National Park & Preserve in the Brooks Range north-west of Fairbanks.

The climate in the summer can range from a chilly 40°F in the treeless and nightless arctic tundra to the wet and fog of the Bering Sea coast, where the terrain is a flat land of lakes and slow-moving rivers.

CLIMATE & THE 24-HOUR DAY

It makes sense that a place as large and diverse as Alaska would have a climate to match. The effects of oceans surrounding 75% of the state, the mountainous terrain and the low angle of the sun give Alaska an extremely variable climate and daily weather that is famous for being unpredictable.

Temperatures in the Interior can top 90°F during the summer, yet six months later in the same region can drop to -60°F. Fort Yukon holds the state record for maximum temperature at 100°F in June 1915, yet it once recorded a temperature of -78°F.

For the most part, Southeast and Southcentral Alaska have high rainfall with temperatures that only vary 40°F during the year. Anchorage, shielded by the Kenai Mountains, has an annual rainfall of 15 inches and averages from 60°F to 70°F from June to August. Juneau averages 57 inches of rain or snow annually, while Ketchikan gets 154 inches a year, most of which is rain, as the temperatures are extremely mild even in the winter.

A good week in Southcentral and Southeast Alaska during the summer will include three sunny days, two overcast ones and two when you will have to pull your rain gear out or duck for cover.

In the Interior and up around Fairbanks, precipitation is light but temperatures can fluctuate by more than 100°F during the year. In the summer, the average daytime temperature can range from 55°F to 75°F with a brief period in late July to early August where it will top 80°F or even 90°F. At night, temperatures can drop sharply to 45°F or even lower, and freak snowfalls can occur in the valleys during July or August, with the white stuff lasting a day or two.

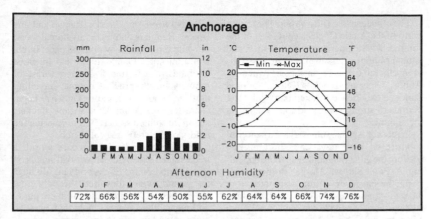

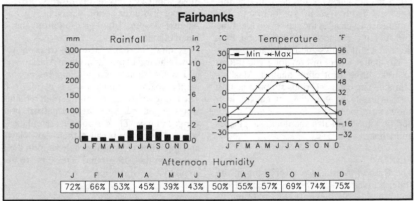

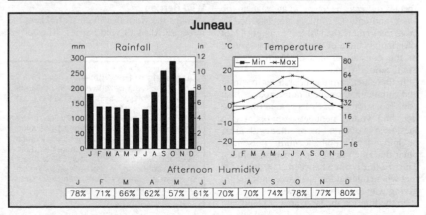

The climate in the Bush varies. The region north of the Arctic Circle is cool most of the summer with temperatures around 45°F, and annual rainfall is less than four inches. This far north, fall colors begin appearing in mid-August. Other areas such as Katmai National Park can experience a mixed bag, with long periods of strong winds and foul weather in the summer.

In most of Alaska, summers are a beautiful mixture of long days and short nights, making the great outdoors even more appealing. At Point Barrow, Alaska's northernmost point, the sun never sets for 2½ months from May to August. The longest day is on June 21 (equinox), when the sun sets for only two hours in Fairbanks, for four hours in Anchorage and from five to six hours in the Southeast. Even after the sun sets in late June and July, it is replaced not by night, but by a dusk that still allows good visibility.

No matter where or how long you intend to trek, bring protection against Alaska's climate. You can get serious sunburn in July just as easily as you can get caught in a snowstorm in August. Pack warm clothing and rain gear, and also sunblock, sunglasses and a hat.

FLORA

The flora of Alaska, like everything in the state, is diverse, changing dramatically from one region to the next. There are 33 native species of trees, the fewest of any state in the USA, and only 12 of these are classified as large trees (more than 70 feet in height). Not surprisingly, nine of these species are found in the coastal regions of Southeast and Southcentral Alaska.

In these areas, mild temperatures in winter and summer and frequent rains produce lush coniferous forests of Sitka spruce (the state tree) and western hemlock. Any opening in the forest is often a bog or filled with alder or spiny devil's club, a mildly poisonous plant that often results in a rash on contact. The tree line is often between 2000 and 3000 feet where thick alder takes over until finally giving way to alpine meadows.

In the Interior, the large area of plains and hills between the Alaska Range and the Brooks Range is dominated by boreal forest of white spruce, cottonwood and paper birch, while on north-facing slopes and in moist lowlands you'll find a stunted forest of scrawny black spruce. Continue travelling north and you'll enter a zone known as taiga, characterized by muskeg, willow thickets and more stunted spruce, before entering the tundra of the arctic coastal region.

The arctic tundra is a bizarre world, a treeless area except for a few small stands on gravel flood plains of rivers. Plant life hugs the ground; even willow trees that only grow six inches in height still produce pussy willows. Other plants, including grasses, mosses and a variety of tiny flowers, provide a carpet of life for a short period in July and August despite little precipitation and a harsh climate.

Tundra can make for tough trekking for those who travel this far north in Alaska. Wet and moist tundra is underlain by permanently frozen ground known as permafrost. The tundra thaws in the summer but remains waterlogged because the permafrost prevents drainage. The caribou get around these soggy conditions because their dew claws and spreading cleft hooves help support their weight on the soft ground. Trekkers are not so lucky.

Wild Berries

Perhaps the flora that interests trekkers the most are Alaska's wild berries. Blueberries

---

Diamonds in the Willow

One of the most prized woods in Alaska is diamond willow, so-called because the grain of the wood has a distinctive diamond pattern. There are 33 species of willow in the state and at least five of these can develop diamond patterns (caused by fungus) which is easy to see when you strip the bark. Diamond willows can be found throughout Alaska, particularly in river valleys, and in gift shops where the wood has been carved into lamps and walking sticks. ■

are found throughout much of the state while in the Southeast you'll encounter huge patches of huckleberries and salmonberries. Other species include blackberries, raspberries, high-bush cranberries and strawberries. If you plan to feast on berries, take the time to learn which ones are inedible. The most common poisonous one is the baneberry, found in the Southeast and the Interior, which often appears as a white berry.

FAUNA

From the road, most visitors see more wildlife in Alaska than they do in a lifetime elsewhere. From the trails, such encounters are often the highlight of an entire trip.

Moose & Deer

Moose are an improbable-looking mammal: long-legged to the extreme, short-bodied, with a huge rack and drooping nose. Standing there, they look uncoordinated until you watch them run, or better yet, swim – then their speed and grace is astounding. They are the largest member of the deer family in the world; the Alaskan species is the largest of all moose. A newborn weighs in at 35 pounds and can grow to more than 300 pounds within five months. Cows range from 800 to 1200 pounds and bulls from 1000 to more than 1500 pounds.

In the wild, moose may reach more than 20 years in age and often range 20 to 40 miles in their effort to find their main forage of birch, willow, alder and aspen saplings. In the spring and summer, you often encounter them feeding in lakes and ponds with that huge nose below the water as they grab for aquatic plants and weeds.

The population ranges from an estimated 120,000 to 160,000 animals and historically moose have always been the most important game animal in Alaska. Athabascan Indians survived by utilizing the moose as a source of food, clothing and implements while market hunting boomed in the 19th century with professional hunters supplying moose meat to mining camps. Today some 35,000 Alaskans and nonresidents annually harvest

9000 moose (a total of five million pounds of meat) during the hunting season.

Moose are widespread throughout the state and range from the Stikine River in the Southeast to the Corville River on the Arctic slope. They're most abundant in the second-growth birch forests, timber-line plateaus and along major rivers of Southcentral and the Interior. Moose are frequently sighted in most of the parks and Denali National Park is an excellent place to watch them.

The Sitka black-tailed deer is a native to the coastal rainforests of Southeast Alaska but its original range has since been expanded to Prince William Sound and Kodiak Island. The deer is a favorite target of hunters but is not the source of meat that the moose is. The largest black-tailed deer can weigh 212 pounds but most average 100 pounds, bucks 150 pounds. The summer coat is reddish-brown and replaced by grey in the winter. The antlers are small, normal development is three points on each side, and its tail is indeed black. Sitka black-tailed deer respond readily to calls. Most 'calls' are a thin strip of rubber or plastic between two pieces of wood held between the teeth and blown on. This produces a high-pitch note simulating a fawn's cry and can stop a deer in its tracks and turn it around. Some old-time hunters can make the call by simply blowing on a leaf.

Caribou

Caribou, of which there are an estimated 600,000 living in Alaska's 13 herds, are more difficult to view because they travel from the Interior north to the Arctic Sea. Often called the 'nomads of the north', caribou range in weight from 150 pounds to more than 400 pounds for a large bull. They migrate hundreds of miles annually between their calving grounds, rutting areas and winter area. In the summer, they feed on grasses, grass-like sedges, berries and small shrubs of the tundra. In the winter, they eat a significant amount of lichen called 'reindeer moss'.

The principal predators of caribou are wolves and some packs on the North Slope have been known to follow caribou herds throughout the years, picking off the young, old and victims of disabling falls caused by running in tightly massed herds. Bears, wolverines, foxes and eagles will also prey on calves, while every year several thousand nonresident hunters come to Alaska in search of a bull.

The place most trekkers see caribou is Denali National Park. But perhaps one of the greatest wildlife encounters left in the world today is the migration of the Western Arctic herd of barren-ground caribou, North America's largest at 300,000 animals. The calving ground of the herd is along the North Slope and in late August many of the animals begin to cross the Noatak River in their journey southward. During that time the few visitors lucky enough to be on the river are often rewarded with an awesome experience of watching 20,000 or more caribou crossing the tundra towards the Brooks Range.

Mountain Goats & Dall Sheep

The mountain goat is the single North American species of the widespread group of goat-antelopes. All are characterized by short horns and a fondness for the most rugged alpine terrain. Although Captain Cook obtained goat hides in the 1700s, very little was known about the animal due to its remote habitat.

Although goats are often confused with dall sheep, they are easily identified by their longer hair, black horns and deep chest. They are quite docile, making them easy to watch in the wilds, and their gait, even when they're approached too closely, is a deliberate pace. In the summer, they are normally found in high alpine meadows, grazing on grasses and herbs, and in the winter they often drop down to the tree line. In Alaska, they range throughout most of the Southeast, north and west into the coastal mountains of Cook Inlet as well as the Chugach and Wrangell mountains. Good places to spot them include Glacier Bay National Park, Wrangell-St Elias National Park and from many of the alpine trails in Juneau. But you have to climb to spot them.

Dall sheep are more numerous and widespread than mountain goats. They number close to 80,000 in Alaska and are found principally in Wrangell, Chugach and the Kenai mountain ranges. Often sheep are spotted in Denali National Park when the bus crosses Polychrome Pass on the way to Wonder Lake.

Rams are easy to spot by their massive curling horns which grow throughout the life of the sheep, unlike deer antlers which are shed and regrown annually. The horns, like claws, hooves and your fingernails, grow from the skin. As rams mature, the horns continue their ever-increasing curl, reaching a three-quarters curl in four to five years and a full curl in seven years.

It's spectacular to watch two rams in a horn-clashing battle, but contrary to popular belief they are not fighting over a female, just demonstrating social dominance. Dall sheep do not clash as much as their big-horn cousins to the south but you can spot the activity throughout the summer and into fall. The best time to spot rams and see them clash is right before the rut, which begins in November. At that time they are moving among bands of ewes and often encountering other unfamiliar rams.

Bears

There are three species of bears in Alaska – brown, black and polar bears – with brown bears having the greatest range.

At one time, brown and grizzly bears were listed as separate species but now both are classified as *Ursus arctos*. The difference isn't so much genetics but size. Browns live along the coast where abundant salmon runs help them reach a large size (often exceeding 800 pounds), while the famed Kodiak brown bear has been known to stand 10 feet tall and tip the scales at 1500 pounds. Grizzlies are browns found inland, away from the rich salmon runs, and normally a male ranges in weight from 500 to 700 pounds. Females weigh half to three-quarters as much.

The color of a brown bear can be anything from an almost black through to blond and resemble a black bear in appearance. One way biologists tell them apart is to measure

Brown Bear or Black Bear?

In the backcountry, it's easy to get brown and black bears confused from a distance, especially if both species are found in the region you're trekking through.

The first thing you should look at to determine whether it is a brown bear or a black bear is the animal's profile. Brown bears have a distinct hump on their back that is formed by the muscles in their forelegs. Black bears, on the other hand, have a straighter back. If you have high-powered binoculars, study the head. The head of a brown bear is massive in relation to its body and its profile is concave, or 'dished'. The black bear has a much straighter facial profile, a tapered nose and longer nostrils.

If you come across the tracks of a bear, measure them for size. Brown-bear prints are large, usually ranging from five to 10 inches wide; black-bear prints range from 3.5 to seven inches. The claws on the front feet of a brown bear are long and appear further away from the toes (which are close together and less arced). Often you won't see the claw marks on the print of a black bear but when you do, they'll be shorter, more arched and closer to the toes.

Ironically, the least dependable trait of each species is the color of their fur. A black bear can vary tremendously in color, from blond to brown. Some brown bears can be almost black in color. ∎

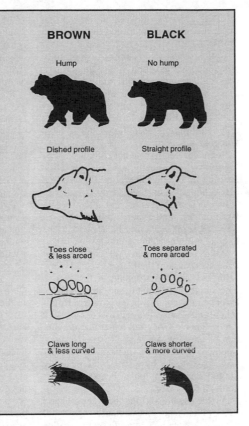

BROWN — BLACK

Hump — No hump

Dished profile — Straight profile

Toes close & less arced — Toes separated & more arced

Claws long & less curved — Claws shorter & more curved

the upper rear molar. The length of the crown of this tooth in a brown is always more than an inch and a quarter. Perhaps a better way is to look for the prominent shoulder hump, easily seen behind the neck when a brown bear is on all fours.

Brown bears occur throughout Alaska except for some islands in the Frederick Sound in the Southeast, the islands west of Unimak in the Aleutian chain and some Bering Sea islands. There are more than 40,000 brown bears in Alaska and the most noted place to watch them is at Brooks River in Katmai National Park. Brown bears are also common in Denali National Park, on Admiralty Island in the Southeast and in Wrangell-St Elias National Park.

Though black bears are the most widely distributed of the three bear species in the USA, their range is more limited in Alaska than that of their brown cousin. They usually are found in most forested areas of the state but not on the Seward Peninsula, or north of the Brooks Range or on many large islands like Kodiak and Admiralty.

The average male weighs from 180 to 250 pounds and can range in color from black to a rare creamy-white color. A brown or cinnamon black bear is often seen in Southcentral, leaving many backpackers confused as to what the species is. Beyond measuring that upper rear molar, look for the straight facial profile to confirm it's a black bear.

Both species are creatures of opportunity when it comes to eating. Bears are omnivorous and common foods include berries, grass, sedge, salmon runs and any carrion they happen to find in their travels. Browns occasionally fill the role of a predator but only in the spring when the young are most vulnerable.

Bears don't hibernate but enter a stage of 'dormancy' – basically a deep sleep while denning up during the winter. Browns and black bears enter their dens usually in November or December and re-emerge in April or May. In the more northern areas of the state, some bears may be dormant for as long as seven or eight months a year.

Polar bears have always captured our interest because of their large size and white color but plan on stopping at the zoo in Anchorage if you want to see one in Alaska. Polar bears occur only in the Northern Hemisphere and almost always in association with Arctic Sea ice. They fall under the jurisdiction of only five nations – Russia, Norway, Denmark (Greenland), Canada and the USA – and past studies have shown there is only limited denning of polar bears along the north Alaska Coast.

A male usually averages between 600 and 1200 pounds but occasionally tops 1400 pounds. Adaptations to a life on the sea ice by polar bears include a white coat with water-repellent guard hairs and dense under fur, specialized teeth for its carnivorous diet (primarily seals), and hair almost completely covering the bottom of their feet

Wolves

While the wolf is struggling in numbers throughout most of the USA, its natural distribution and numbers still seem to be unaffected by human undertakings in Alaska. There are roughly 8000 wolves scattered in packs throughout the state except for some islands in the Southeast, Prince William Sound and the Aleutian chain.

Unlike the hunters, who seek out the outstanding physical specimens, wolves can usually only catch and kill the weak, injured or young, thus strengthen the herd they are stalking. A pack of wolves is no match for a healthy 1200-pound moose.

Most adult males weigh between 85 and 115 pounds. Their pelts can range in color from grey, black, off-white, brown, yellow, or even have tinges approaching red. Wolves travel, hunt, feed and operate in the social unit of a pack and are very much carnivores. In the Southeast their principal food is deer, in the Interior it's moose and in Arctic Alaska it's caribou.

Even when trekking, your chances of seeing wolves are rare. You might, however, find evidence of them either in their dog-like tracks, their howls at night or the remains of a wild kill

Other Mammals

In the lowlands, trekkers have a chance to view red fox, beaver, pine marten, snowshoe hare, red squirrel and on very rare occasions wolverines. Around lakes and rivers you have a good chance of spotting land otters and beavers. Both are found throughout the state, except on the North Slope, and are large animals. Otters weigh between 15 and 35 pounds, beavers between 40 and 70 pounds – though 100-pound beavers have been recorded in Alaska. In alpine areas, look for the ever curious marmot, a large ground squirrel

Salmon

The salmon runs are another of Alaska's most amazing sights and are common throughout much of the state. From late July to mid-September, many coastal streams are choked with salmon swimming upstream to spawn. You won't see just one here and there, but thousands – so many that they have to wait their turn to swim through narrow gaps of shallow water. The salmon are famous for their struggle against the current, their magnificent leaps over waterfalls, and for covering stream banks with carcasses afterwards. There are five kinds of salmon in Alaska: sockeye (also referred to as red salmon), king (chinook), pink (humpie), coho (silver) and chum

Birds

More than anything, Alaska is a haven for winged wildlife. Biologists have identified 437 species of birds in the state and only 65 of them are accidental visitors. The Pribilof Islands in the Bering Sea attracts birders (they no longer call themselves bird-watchers) from around the world. If you can't afford that, just visit Potter Marsh south of Anchorage, a sanctuary that attracts more than 100 species annually.

The most impressive bird in Alaska's wilderness is the bald eagle, whose white tail and head, and wingspan that often reaches eight feet has become the symbol of a nation. While elsewhere the bird is on the endangered list, in Alaska it thrives. The eagle can be sighted almost daily in most of the Southeast and is common in Prince William Sound. It also migrates once a year in a spectacle that exceeds even the salmon runs. As many as 1500 bald eagles gather along the Chilkat River north of Haines from late October to December. They come to feed on the late chum-salmon run and create an amazing scene during the bleakness of early winter. Bare trees support 80 or more bald eagles, four or five to a branch.

The state bird of Alaska, however, is the ptarmigan, a cousin of the prairie grouse. The species is found through the state in high treeless country and the birds are easy to spot during the summer as their wings remain white while their head and chest turn brown. In the winter they have pure white plumage.

If you're serious about birding while traveling the state, the best bird book to pick up is *Guide to the Birds of Alaska* by Robert H Armstrong (Alaska Northwest Books, 22026 20th Ave, SE, Bothell, WA 98021; 344 pages, $19.95). The guide indexes 372 species with color photos and field identification marks.

NATIONAL PARKS, FORESTS & REFUGES

With almost three-quarters of the state locked up as public land, it can be a little confusing at times who controls what land in Alaska and if you need trekking permits. Almost all of the recreational areas, parks and forests, including the campgrounds and trails in them, are controlled by one of five organizations.

National Parks

These are the crown jewels of the US park system. In Alaska, national parks tend to be large, contain the best natural scenery and are listed in every travel brochure and guide. They attract many visitors, especially Denali National Park & Preserve which becomes so crowded at its entrance that it's a logistic nightmare arranging a backcountry permit in the middle of the summer.

The National Park Service (NPS) in Alaska also administers Glacier Bay and Katmai national parks and preserves, which are accessible by an Alaska Airlines flight, and Kenai Fjords and Wrangell-St Elias, which have roads leading into them. These parks are well known but do no receive the crush of summer tourism like Denali because their facilities are not nearly as well developed and they are expensive to reach.

There are three other national parks (Gates of the Arctic, Kobuk Valley and Lake Clark) and three national preserves (Aniakchak, Noatak and Yukon-Charley Rivers) that are administered by the NPS. Access is by bush plane or boat; most visitors use guide companies to venture into the wilderness areas by raft, kayak or on foot. The parks offer no facilities.

Apart from a few nature paths around the visitors' centers, there are no maintained trails in Alaska's national parks. All trekking is cross-country (in Wrangell-St Elias you follow old miners' roads). Without a doubt the most popular park for trekkers is Denali but in recent years Wrangell-St Elias has been attracting a greater number of trekkers as have Gates of the Arctic and Lake Clark.

At Gates of the Arctic, trekkers are now able to access the park from the Dalton Hwy and avoid the high cost of bush planes.

For information on all parks, contact the main NPS offices: Alaska Public Lands Information Center (☎ (907) 271-2737), 605 West 4th Ave, Suite 105, Anchorage, AK 99501-2231; NPS (☎ (907) 586-7137), 709 West 9th St, Juneau, AK 99801.

National Forests

Most of the Southeast and practically all of the eastern Kenai Peninsula, including Prince William Sound, is preserved as Tongass and Chugach national forests. Some of the best trails in Alaska are in the national forests where trekking is free and permits are not required.

The US Forest Service (USFS) provides trekking information and maintains 190 public-use cabins and campgrounds. Most USFS campgrounds charge from $5 to $8 per day, depending on the facilities, and have a 14-day limit. Many of the cabins are on the trail system and are only $25 a night. They are heavily booked throughout the summer, however, so advanced reservations are recommended.

The Tongass National Forest maintains more than 150 cabins in the Southeast and trails in almost every major town including the extensive systems in Juneau and Sitka. For more information about the Tongass National Forest contact the office in the area you plan to visit:

Chatham Area Supervisor
    204 Siginaka Way, Sitka, AK 99835 (☎ (907) 747-6671)
Forest Service Information Center
    PO Box 1628, Juneau, AK 99802 (☎ (907) 586-8751)
Ketchikan Area Supervisor
    Federal Building, Ketchikan, AK 99901 (☎ (907) 225-3101)
Stikine Area Supervisor
    PO Box 309, Petersburg, AK 99833 (☎ (907) 772-3871)

The Chugach National Forest in Southcentral has 39 cabins, including seven along the Resurrection Trail and two on the Russian Lakes Trail. There are also a couple of cabins in the Cordova area that you can reach by foot. For a complete list of cabins and trails in the Chugach National Forest, write to the following USFS district offices in Alaska:

Anchorage Ranger District
    201 East 9th Ave, Suite 206, Anchorage, AK 99501 (☎ (907) 271-2500)
Cordova Ranger District
    PO Box 280, Cordova, AK 99574 (☎ (907) 424-7661)
Seward Ranger District
    PO Box 390, Seward, AK 99664 (☎ (907) 224-3374)

State Parks

The Alaska Division of Parks & Outdoor Recreation controls more than 100 areas in the Alaska state park system, ranging from the 1.5-million acre Wood-Tikchik State Park, north of Dillingham on Bristol Bay, to the small wayside parks along the highways. The areas also include state trails, campgrounds, wilderness parks and historical sites.

The more popular parks for trekkers are Chugach which surrounds Anchorage, Denali State Park south of Mt McKinley, Nancy Lake Recreational Area just south of Willow, and Chilkat State Park south of Haines. Trekking is free. Most campgrounds cost $6 a night; the more popular ones cost $10 a night. The State Parks Division also rents out recreational cabins in some Southeast, Southcentral and Interior parks for $20 to $25 a night.

For trekkers planning to spend a summer camping in Alaska, a state park camping pass, allowing unlimited camping for a year, is a wise investment at $75. To obtain an annual Alaska Camping Pass in advance, send a check or money order to one of the following Alaska Division of Parks offices: PO Box 7001, Anchorage, AK 99510 (☎ (907) 561-2020) or 400 Willoughby Center, Juneau, AK 99801 (☎ (907) 465-4563).

National Refuges

The US Fish & Wildlife Service (USF&WS) is an arm of the Department of the Interior that administers 16 wildlife refuges in Alaska that total more than 77 million acres. The largest, Yukon Delta surrounding Bethel in Western Alaska, is almost 20 million acres.

The purpose of wildlife refuges is to protect habitats; visitor use and developed recreational activities are strictly an after-thought. Most of the refuges are in remote areas of the Bush and are poorly developed. The one exception is Kenai National Wild-life Refuge, which can be reached by road from Anchorage. It has more than 200 miles of maintained trails and water routes, and 15 campgrounds.

For information contact the regional office of the USF&WS (☎ (907) 786-3487), 1011 East Tudor Rd, Anchorage, AK 99503.

Bureau of Land Management

The Bureau of Land Management (BLM) is the federal agency that maintains much of the wilderness around and north of Fairbanks. It has developed 25 campgrounds and a dozen public-use cabins in the Interior as well as two popular trails, Pinnell Mountain and White Mountain, both located off the high-ways north of Fairbanks.

For more information contact the BLM district office (☎ (907) 474-2200), 1150 University Ave, Fairbanks, Alaska 99709 or (☎ (907) 822-3217), PO Box 147, Glenn-allen, AK 99588.

POPULATION

Alaska, the largest state in the USA, has the second smallest population, behind only Wyoming, and is the most sparsely popu-lated. Permanent residents, not including the large influx of seasonal workers in the fishing and tourist industries, number 550,043 in a state of 586,412 sq miles. There is more than a sq mile for every resident but Alaska is even less sparse when you consider more than half of its population lives in the Anchorage Bowl area.

It is estimated that only 30% of the state's population were born in Alaska while 25% have moved there in the last five years. This means that the average resident is young

(aged between 26 and 28), mobile and mostly from the US west coast. Inuits and other indigenous groups make up only 15% of the total population while ethnic groups of Japanese, Filipinos and Blacks represent less than 5%.

The five largest cities in Alaska are Anchorage (population 237,907) Fairbanks (77,720), Juneau (30,000), Kodiak (15,575) and Ketchikan (13,828).

PEOPLE & CULTURE
Native Alaskans

Long before Bering's journeys to Alaska, other groups of people had made their way there and established a culture and lifestyle in one of the world's harshest environments. The first major invasion, which came across the land bridge from Asia, was by the Tlingits and the Haidas (who settled throughout the Southeast and British Colum-bia), and the Athabascans (a nomadic tribe which lived in the Interior). The other two major groups were the Aleuts of the Aleutian

Inuit child

Islands and the Inuits, who settled on the coast of the Bering Sea and the Arctic Ocean. Both groups are believed to have migrated only 3000 years ago but were well established by the time the Europeans arrived.

The Tlingit and Haida cultures were advanced, as the tribes had permanent settlements including large clan houses. They were noted for their excellent woodcarving, most notably poles, called *totems*, that can still be seen today in most Southeast communities. The Tlingits were spread throughout the Southeast in large numbers and occasionally went as far south as Seattle in their large dugout canoes. Both groups had few problems gathering food as fish and game were plentiful in the Southeast.

Not so for the Aleuts and the Inuits. With much colder winters and cooler summers, both groups had to develop a highly effective sea-hunting culture to sustain life in the harsh regions of Alaska. This was especially true for the Inuits, who could not have survived the winters without their skilled ice-hunting techniques. In the spring, armed with only jade-tipped harpoons, the Inuits stalked and killed 60-ton bowhead whales in skin-covered kayaks called *bidarkas* and *umikaks*.

The Aleuts were known for some of the finest basket weaving in North America, using the highly prized Attu grass of the Aleutian Islands. The Inuits were unsurpassed carvers of ivory, jade and soapstone; many support themselves today by continuing the art.

The indigenous people, despite their harsh environment, were numerous until the White people brought guns, alcohol and disease that destroyed the Native Alaskans' delicate relationship with nature and wiped out entire villages. At one time, there were an estimated 20,000 Aleuts living on almost every island of the Aleutian chain. It took the Russians only 50 years to reduce the population (mainly through forced labor) to less than 2000.

The whalers who arrived at Inuit villages in the mid-1800s were similarly destructive, introducing alcohol that devastated the lifestyles of entire villages. Even when the 50th anniversary of the Alcan was celebrated in October 1992, many indigenous people in Alaska and Canada called the event a 'commemoration' and not a 'celebration' due to the things that the highway brought (disease, alcohol and a cash economy) that further changed a nomadic lifestyle.

Today, there are more than 85,000 indigenous people living in Alaska of which half are Inuits. They are no longer tribal nomads but live in permanent villages ranging in size from less than 30 people to 3200 in Barrow, the largest center of indigenous people in Alaska.

Most indigenous people in the Bush still depend on some level of subsistence, but today their houses are constructed of modern materials and often heated by electricity or oil. Visitors are occasionally shocked when they fly hundreds of miles into a remote area only to see TV antennas sticking out of cabins, community satellite dishes, people drinking Coca-Cola or children listening to the latest songs on their boom box.

Facts for the Backpacker

VISAS & EMBASSIES

If you are traveling to Alaska from overseas there are one or two things you need depending on your nationality: a passport (except for USA and Canadian citizens who only need a driver's license or voter registration card) and at least one visa, possibly two. Obviously a US visa is needed, but if you're taking either the Alcan (also called the Alaska Hwy) or the State Marine Ferry from Prince Rupert in British Columbia then you will also need a Canadian visa. The Alcan begins in Canada, requiring travelers to pass from the USA into Canada and back into the USA again.

Travelers from Western Europe and most Commonwealth nations do not need a Canadian visa and can get a six-month travel visa to the USA without too much paperwork or delay. Visitors from the UK, Australia and New Zealand don't even need a visa to enter the USA if they plan to stay less than 90 days, have a return ticket and complete a visa wavier form and an arrival/departure card. All visitors must have an onward or return ticket to enter the USA and sufficient funds to pass into Canada. Those arriving at the Canadian border with less than $250 will most likely be turned back.

Foreign Consulates

There are no embassies in Alaska but there are more than a dozen foreign consulates offices in Anchorage to assist overseas travelers with unusual problems. They include:

Belgium, 1031 West 4th Ave, Suite 400, Anchorage, AK 99501-5995 (☎ (907) 276-5617)

Britain, 3211 Providence Drive, Room 362, Anchorage, AK 99508-4614 (☎ (907) 786-4848)

Canada, 3512 Campbell Airstrip Rd, Anchorage, AK 99504-3838 (☎ (907) 333-1400)

Denmark, 3111 C St, Suite 100, Anchorage, AK 99503-3915 (☎ (907) 279-7611)

Finland, 1529 P St (☎ (907) 274-6607)

France, 3111 C St, Suite 100 (☎ (907) 261-7680)

Germany, 425 G St, Suite 650, Anchorage, AK 99501-2176 (☎ (907) 274-6537)

Italy, 12840 Silver Spruce Drive, Anchorage, AK 99516-2603 (☎ (907) 762-7664)

Japan, 550 West 7th Ave, Suite 701, Anchorage, AK, 99510-3559 (☎ (907) 279-8428)

Korea, 101 West Benson Blvd, Suite 304, Anchorage, AK 99503-3997 (☎ (907) 561-5488)

Norway, 333 M St, Suite 405, Anchorage, AK 99501-1902 (☎ (907) 274-4900)

DOCUMENTS
Backpacking Permits

For the most part trekking and backpacking is free in Alaska. Denali National Park charges an entrance fee and a few popular state parks have recently instituted daily parking fees but that's rare.

In most national parks including Denali, Wrangell-St Elias and Katmai, you must register and obtain a backcountry permit. The permits allow you to spend the night in the parks; they're free and easy to obtain from ranger stations near the trailheads.

There is no need for a backcountry or trekking permit for trails in state parks and national forests. However, at most trailheads there is an 'intentions book' and it is a wise practice to add your name, address, the number of days you plan to trek and your route.

CUSTOMS

Vaccinations are not required for either the USA or Canada and you'll only be detained by immigration officials if you've been on a farm during the past 30 days (to make sure you're not bringing in some unusual or unwanted live insects, or animal or seed-borne plant diseases). Travelers are allowed to bring all personal goods (including camping gear or hiking equipment) into the USA and Canada free of duty, along with food for two days and up to 50 cigars, 200 cigarettes and 40 ounces of liquor or wine.

There are no forms to fill out if you are a foreign visitor bringing any vehicle into

Alaska whether it is a bicycle, motorcycle or a car; nor are there forms for hunting rifles or fishing gear. Hunting rifles (handguns and automatic weapons are prohibited) must be registered in your own country and you should bring proof of this. There is no limit to the amount of money you can bring into Alaska but anything over $5000 must be registered with customs officials. A limited amount of fresh fruits and vegetables can be carried into Canada, except to British Columbia where peaches, apricots, nectarines and any apple grown east of the Rockies are not permitted. If you're driving into Canada, be prepared to produce evidence that your vehicle has liability insurance.

Overseas travelers should be aware of the procedures to re-enter the USA. Occasionally visitors get stuck in Canada without the necessary papers to enter Alaska after passing through the Lower 48. Canadian immigration officers often caution people who they feel might have difficulty returning to the USA.

MONEY & COSTS

Alaskans use the same currency as the rest of the USA, American dollars (US$) – only they tend to use a little more of it. The state is traditionally known for having the highest cost of living in the country, though places like southern California, San Francisco and New York City have caught up with Alaska if not surpassed it.

A rule of thumb for Alaskan prices is that they are lowest in Ketchikan and increase gradually as you go north. Overall, the Southeast is generally cheaper than most towns in the Interior or elsewhere because barge transportation from Seattle (the supply center for the area) is only two days away.

Anchorage and to a lesser extent Fairbanks are the exceptions to the rule as they have competitive prices due to their large populations and business communities. Anchorage, which also receives most of its goods on ocean-going barges, can be extremely affordable if you live there, outrageous if you are a tourist. Gas is often hovering around $1.15 a gallon and apples

in a supermarket could cost less than 90c a pound. But it's hard to find a motel room under $80 and prices of other tourist-related services, such as taxis and restaurants, seem to be inflated as well.

When entering remote parks, be prepared; stock up on supplies before reaching such places as McCarthy in the Wrangell-St Elias National Park or even Denali National Park. You'll save a bundle by hauling in a week's worth of Lipton noodle dinners, instant oatmeal and a six-pack of beer.

The National Bank of Alaska (NBA) is the largest bank in the state with offices in almost every village and town on the heavily traveled routes. The NBA can meet the needs of most visitors and, though hours vary from branch to branch, you can usually count on them being open from 10 am to 5 pm Monday through Friday with evening hours on Wednesday and Friday. The popular brands of travelers' checks are widely used around the state and many merchants also accept Canadian money, though they usually burn you on the exchange rate.

Note: All prices quoted in this book are in US dollars unless otherwise stated. The following currencies convert at these approximate rates:

A$1   = $0.76
C$1   = $0.73
DM1   = $0.64
NZ$1 = $0.62
UK£1 = $1.56

WHEN TO GO

The trekking season in Alaska generally runs from May through September, possibly later in some regions. Beginning in October, a steady drizzle in the Southeast lasts until late November or December. The weather also deteriorates in Southcentral at this time of year while further north, especially in Fairbanks, it begins snowing, and doesn't stop until April.

Because most trekkers like to avoid minus-degree temperatures, the peak season for trekking is early July through mid-

August, a time when places like Denali National Park or the Kenai Peninsula can be a dismal experience because of crowds.

There are an awful lot of tourists trying to see Alaska in a very short period of time so consider traveling during the 'shoulder season'. May and September offer not only mild weather but also off-season discounts on motels and transportation. At this time the backcountry in most parks is usually empty of trekkers and other travelers. If you arrive early or stay late, just make sure you equip yourself for some cold, rainy weather.

WHAT TO BRING
Day-Hike Equipment
Equip yourself not only for a week-long expedition but also for a spur-of-the-moment, three-hour day hike. In addition to your large backpack, take a soft day pack or rucksack. Some expedition packs, such as Dana Designs, allow you to convert the top pouch and hip belt into a fanny pack that is ideal for an afternoon trek up a mountain trail. Otherwise, carry a small, compressible, nylon knapsack.

On all-day hikes you should carry a water-proof parka, woollen mittens and a hat if you are climbing above the tree line. Also pack a knife, high-energy food (chocolate), matches, maps and a compass, insect repellent and a water bottle.

Expedition Equipment
For longer treks into the wilderness you will need to have suitable equipment such as the appropriate clothing, a tent, sleeping bag, camp stove, maps and a compass. Buy these before you leave home because while most towns in Alaska will have at least one store with a wall full of camping supplies, prices will be high and by mid to late summer certain items will be out of stock.

Clothing The only way to dress for a climate as varied as Alaska's is in layers: underwear, insulating layer and shell layer.

Synthetic underwear, as opposed to wool, silk or cotton, will do the best job of 'wicking' moisture away from the skin to the surface of the garment. In the summer, an increasingly common form of dress in the backcountry is synthetic underwear under baggy hiking shorts. Such an outfit, though it might seem strange, provides comfort in cold temperatures and protection from too much sun and bugs, and also maximum freedom of movement.

On any trip longer than two days you should have two to three pairs of woollen socks, a pair of woollen mittens, a knitted hat, spare shirt, walking shorts and long pants – preferably light wool or supplex nylon, never blue jeans.

For your insulating layer, use a pile fabric jersey as opposed to a wool sweater. Like wool, the pile will keep you warm when wet but dries much faster. At all costs, avoid a cotton, hooded sweatshirt.

The final layer must protect you against wind, snow or rain. Some overpants and parkas are windproof and water resistant but will not hold up in an all-day rain. Water-proof but 'breathable' garments will provide the most protection and comfort. Gore-Tex is the best known of the breathable materials, but others are available. A parka and pants set can range from $300 to $500, but will be a worthwhile investment.

Boots The traditional footwear is the heavy leather hiking boot that has been smeared on the outside with half a can of beeswax. It's rarely seen these days; today, many recreational backpackers opt for the new lightweight nylon boots made by sporting-shoe companies like Nike, Vasque or Hi-Tech. These are 'day-hiking boots' designed for hiking on easy terrain and carrying light loads.

Backpacking boots, on the other hand, offer more support with a stiff leather upper, a more durable sole and protective shanks. These boots are suitable for trekking on rocky and unstable ground (like you find in trail-less areas) and for carrying heavier packs over longer treks in the backcountry. Which style of boot you bring to Alaska will depend on where and how long you're planning to trek.

You should also pack a spare pair of shoes for fording rivers or to wear once you have reached camp. Most trekkers still choose tennis shoes but a growing number now use rafter sandals. These heavy rubber soled sandals, held onto your foot by straps, are lighter to carry, dry quicker and can be just as comfortable and warm as tennis shoes when worn with wool socks. They also strap on nicely to the outside of your pack.

Tent

Your tent is probably the most essential item you'll carry in your pack. Generally in Alaska, trekkers use one of three shapes or models. The most popular by far is the dome tent. Its curved design and crisscrossed poles provide plenty of room and it's light to carry. More importantly, these tents are freestanding so they don't have to be staked out to be set up.

Tunnel tents are an elongated variation of the dome tent. They usually require two or three stakes but are lighter than dome tents and are far more stable in strong winds or heavy storms – important if you plan to spend a great deal of time above the tree line. Bivy or ultralight tents are extremely small units that provide shelter for one person, and are often used by cyclists and rock climbers.

Your choice of tent will be depend on how much space you need and your budget. Some models exceed $500, providing such features as a vestibule for your equipment, drying lofts for wet clothes and ultralight aluminum poles (instead of the heavier

Dome tents

fibreglass type). Whatever you spend, the tent have should have a good rain fly which can double as a shade provider during those long Alaskan summer days when the sun is still shining long after you've gone to bed. Make sure the netting around the doors and windows is bug proof to prevent you from turning into a nightly smorgasbord for any mosquito that passes by. If your present tent is more than four years old, waterproof the floor and the rain fly before you leave home.

Sleeping Bag There has been many an all-night discussion among backpackers about the qualities of down versus synthetic fibres. What can't be argued about though is down's quality of clumping when wet – in rainy Southeast and Southcentral Alaska this means trouble during most wilderness trips. Synthetics are also easier to wash and dry; an advantage if you plan to spend the summer trekking in Alaska.

Try to choose a three-season bag which suits temperatures between -10°F and 40°F. A mummy-shaped bag will fit closer to your body. If you like to roll around in your bag, the slightly wider modified mummy bag is more suitable, but weighs more.

Along with a sleeping bag, bring an insulated foam pad to sleep on – it will reduce much of the ground chill. In the Interior, you will often be sleeping just inches away from permafrost, or permanently frozen ground. If you'll be spending a considerable amount of time sleeping in the wilderness, skip the foam and invest in a self-inflating sleeping pad such as the Thermarest. It may cost $60 but once you're out there you'll be thankful for having purchased it.

Also consider packing one of the new backpacker's pillows. It's one more thing to carry but if it helps you get a good night's sleep, it might be worth it.

Camp Stove Cooking dinner over a crackling campfire may be a romantic notion while you're planning your trip, but it is an inconvenience and often a major headache when you're actually on the trail. Bring a reliable stove and make life simple in the

View from the Alpine Trail, Kachemak Bay State Park (DP)

Top: Fall, Denali National Park (JD)
Bottom Left: Blueberries (JD)
Bottom Right: Fireweed (JD)

woods. Rain, strong winds and a lack of available wood will hamper your efforts to build a fire, while some preserves like Denali National Park won't even allow campfires in the backcountry. There are many brands on the market today but stoves like MSR Whisper Lite, that can be 'field repaired', are the most dependable.

Remember, you cannot carry white gas or other camp-stove fuels on an airline flight, however, just about every small town or park visitors' center will stock them.

Map & Compass Trekkers should not only carry a compass into the wilderness but should know how to use it correctly. Also pack the correct US Geological Survey (USGS) map for the area in which you are planning to travel. (See Maps later in this chapter for more information.)

Sun Protection Alaska has long hours of sunlight during the summer and the sun's rays are even more intense when they are reflected off snow or water. Bring a cap with a visor on it and a small tube of sunblock to save at least one layer of skin on your nose. If you plan to do any alpine hiking around snowfields, you should also plan on bringing a pair of dark sunglasses, known by many locals as 'glacier goggles'.

Food You can buy food in almost any town or village at the start of most treks, though the smaller and more remote the town, the more you'll have to pay. (See the Food section later in this chapter for more information.)

TOURIST OFFICES
The first place to write to when planning your adventure is the Alaska Division of Tourism (Dept 901, PO Box 110801, Juneau, AK 99811; ☎ (907) 465-2010, fax 586-8399) to request a copy of the *Alaska State Vacation Planner*, a free 120-page annually updated magazine.

The visitors' bureaus of the three main cities that are entry points to Alaska are also useful. In Anchorage write to the Anchorage

Camp stove

Visitors' Bureau, 1600 A St, Suite 200, Anchorage, AK 99501-5162 or visit the Log Cabin Visitor Information Center downtown at the corner of 4th Ave and F St. In Fairbanks write to or visit the Fairbanks Visitors' Bureau, 550 1st Ave, Fairbanks, AK 99701, and in Juneau, write to the Davis Log Cabin Visitor Center, 134 3rd St, Juneau, AK 99801.

Travel information is easy to obtain once you are on the road as almost every city, town and village has a tourist contact center whether it be a visitors' bureau, chamber of commerce or a hut near the ferry dock. They are good sources of free maps, information on local accommodations and directions to the nearest campground or hiking trail.

USEFUL ORGANIZATIONS
There are a number of useful organizations in Alaska, details follow.

National Audubon Society
Birders can contact the regional office in Anchorage for a local bird list or schedule of field trips during the summer. Contact the society at 308 G St, Suite 219, Anchorage, AK 99501-2134 or call ☎ (907) 276-7034.

Mountaineering Club of Alaska
For information about scaling peaks or other climbs, contact this Anchorage-based club. If they cannot help you, they will know the

outfitter who can. Write to PO Box 102037, Anchorage, AK 99501 or leave a message on ☎ (907) 272-1811.

Arctic Bicycle Club

Alaska's largest bicycle club can provide information on rides, routes and tours. Call their hot-line number (☎ (907) 566-0177) for details on road conditions, mountain bike races and organized bike tours. Or write to PO Box 140269, Anchorage, AK 99514.

Knik Canoers & Kayakers

This paddlers club is based in Southcentral Alaska. Write to PO Box 101935, Anchorage, AK 99510; ☎ (907) 272-9351.

Wolf Song of Alaska

Dedicated to understanding the wolf, this group offers education programs that promote wolf awareness. Contact them at PO Box 110309, Anchorage, AK 99511-0309 or call ☎ (906) 346-3073.

Alaska Natural History Association (ANHA)

ANHA promotes a better understanding of Alaska's natural, cultural and historical resources by working with the agencies that manage them. This group runs most of the bookstores in the national parks and the other 30 located around the state. By joining the association, you can get a 10% discount on their books and on goods at Public Lands Information Centers that sell, among other things, USGS topos. Write to 605 West 4th Ave, Suite 85, Anchorage, AK 99501.

Southeast Alaska Conservation Council (SEACC)

This group is the environmental watchdog of Southeast Alaska. There would be a lot more clear cuts and strip mines without them (PO Box 21692, Juneau, AK 99802; ☎ (907) 586-6942).

The Sierra Club

The oldest and best known environmental group in the country today can be contacted at 241 East 5th Ave, Suite 205, Anchorage, AK 99501; ☎ (907) 276-4048.

The Wilderness Society

A national organization, the Society lobbies for the preservation of the remaining wilderness areas in the USA. Contact their Alaska office, 430 West 7th Ave, Suite 205, Anchorage, AK 99501; ☎ (907) 272-9453.

Lynn Canal Conservancy

Want to help protect the Tatshenshini and Alsek? These two rivers flow through British Columbia and Southeast Alaska and are considered by many to be North America's wildest river system. This Southeast group is dedicated to keeping miners and loggers away from the pristine waters. Write to PO Box 964, Haines, AK 99827.

BUSINESS HOURS

Banks and post offices in Alaska are generally open from 9 am to 5 pm Monday through Friday with reduced hours or drive-in window service (banks) on Saturday. Other business hours vary but most shops are open until 9 or 10 pm during the week, from 10 am to 6 pm Saturday and from noon to 5 pm on Sunday.

POST & TELECOMMUNICATIONS

When writing home or to friends send your mail 1st class by sticking a 32c stamp on the envelope or by using a 45c airgram for overseas destinations. Surface mail, slow anywhere in the USA, can take up to a month moving to or from Alaska.

To receive mail while traveling in Alaska, have it sent c/o General Delivery to a post office along your route. Although everybody passes through Anchorage (zip code (post code) 99510), it's probably better to choose smaller towns like Juneau (99801), Ketchikan (99901), Seward (99664), Tok (99780) or Delta Junction (99737). Post offices are supposed to keep letters for 10 days before returning them, although smaller places may keep letters longer, especially if your letters have 'please hold' on the front written in big red letters. If you are planning to stay at youth hostels, those are the best addresses to leave with letter writers.

Telephone area codes are simple in Alaska: the entire state shares 907 except Hyder which uses 604.

TIME

With the exception of four Aleutian Island communities and Hyder, a small community on the Alaska/British Columbia border, the entire state shares the same time zone, Alaska Time, which is one hour earlier than Pacific Standard Time which applies to Seattle.

When it is noon in Anchorage, it is 9 pm in London, 4 pm in New York and 7 am the following day in Melbourne.

ELECTRICITY

Voltage in Alaska is 110/120 V – the same as everywhere else in the USA.

WEIGHTS & MEASURES

Alaska uses the imperial system of measurement. Weight is measured in ounces (oz) and pounds (lb), volume is measured in pints and gallons, and length in inches, feet and yards.

BOOKS

The following publications will aid travellers heading north to Alaska. A few of the more popular ones can be found in any good bookstore but most are available only in Alaska or by writing to the publisher. A good alternative, however, is to write to Wild Rose Guidebooks, an Anchorage-based distributor of more than 50 Alaskan guides and maps on travel, fishing, camping and natural history as well as recreational books for trekkers, backpackers and kayakers. Send for their catalogue by writing to Wild Rose Guidebooks, PO Box 240047, Anchorage, AK 99524.

General

Alaska by James A Michener (Fawcett Books, New York, NY) gives an overview of the state's history that few books can provide. Whether you love or hate Michener as an author, just about everybody agrees that he leaves no stone unturned in writing about a place. He usually begins with the creation of the mountains and rivers, and 1000 pages later brings you to the present day. This wordy but popular novel is treated no differently and is the result of three of summers of research in Sitka.

Coming into the Country by John McPhee (The Noonday Press, 19 Union Square West, New York, NY 10003; 438 pages, $9.96) takes a mid-1970s look at Alaska in a book that is 600 pages shorter and considerably lighter than Michener's effort. McPhee's experiences included a kayaking down the Kobuk River in the Brooks Range, living in the town of Eagle and spending time in Juneau during the height of the capital move issue. All of the stories provide an excellent insight into the state and the kind of people who live there.

Alaska's Brooks Range by John Kauffmann (Mountaineer-Books, 1011 SW Klickitat Way, Suite 107, Seattle, WA 98134; 192 pages, $14.95) is a guidebook profiling the world's last, great unspoiled wilderness area. Kauffmann, who spent 20 years with the National Park Service and was chief planner for the Gates of the Arctic National Park, explores the geography, history, natural inhabitants and the conservation effort to protect this untamed territory.

Facts About Alaska (Alaska Northwest Books, 22026 20th Ave SE, Bothell, WA 98021; 224 pages, $8.95) is an Alaska almanac, covering just about every topic imaginable, from what a 'potlach' is, to the state's heaviest snowfall (974.4 inches). Topics are arranged alphabetically and each subject has a snippet of background information and interesting facts.

Travel Guides

Alaska – a travel survival kit by Jim DuFresne (Lonely Planet Publications, PO Box 617, Hawthorn, Victoria 3122, Australia; 448 pages, maps, photos, $14.95) is the Lonely Planet companion to visiting Alaska. This comprehensive guidebook has extensive details on accommodations, places to eat, sights, transportation, and activities such as hiking and paddling.

The Milepost (Alaska Northwest Books, 22026 20th Ave SE, Bothell, WA 98041; 640 pages, $16.95), unquestionably the most popular travel guide, is put out every year. While it has good information, history and maps of Alaska and western Canada, its drawbacks include its large size – at eight by 11 inches it is impossible to slip into the side pocket of a backpack – and that it is written for travellers who are driving. Listings of restaurants, hotels and other businesses are also limited to advertisers.

The Alaska Wilderness Milepost (Alaska Northwest Books, 22026 20th Ave SE, Bothell, WA 98041; 454 pages, $14.95) used to be a slim section in *The Milepost* but it has now been split into a guidebook of its own by the publisher. Perhaps the most comprehensive guide to Bush Alaska, the parts of Alaska that can't be reached by road, as it covers more than 250 remote towns and villages. Its smaller format, six by nine inches, also makes it easier to store in a pack.

Adventuring in Alaska by Peggy Wayburn (Sierra Club Books, 530 Bush St, San Francisco, CA 94108; 375 pages, $10.95) is a good general guidebook to the many new national parks, wildlife preserves and other remote regions of Alaska. It also contains excellent 'how-to' information on undertaking wilderness expeditions in the state, whether the mode of travel is canoeing, kayaking or hiking.

Alaska's Southeast: Touring the Inside Passage by Sarah Eppenbach (Globe Pequot Press, PO Box 833, Old Saybrook, CT 06475; 308 pages, $12.95) offers some of the most comprehensive accounts of the Southeast's history and culture, although it lacks detailed travel information. It does a superb job giving you a feeling for each town and area of the Panhandle.

The Inside Passage Traveler by Ellen Searby (Windham Press, Box 1332, Juneau, AK 99802; 208 pages, $12.95) is another travel guide devoted to the Southeast as written by a former State Marine Ferry crew member. It is mediocre overall and offers little more than what you can get from brochures and the US Forest Service's *Opportunity & Recreation Guide* on every state ferry.

Alaska's Parklands, The Complete Guide by Nancy Simmerman (Mountaineer-Books, 1011 SW Klickitat Way, Suite 107, Seattle, WA 98134; 336 pages, $16.95) is the encyclopedia of Alaska wilderness, covering over 110 state and national parks and wilderness areas. It lacks detailed travel information and guides to individual canoe and hiking routes but does a thorough job of covering the scenery, location, wildlife and activities available in each preserve.

The Alaska Highway: An Insider's Guide by Ron Dalby (Fulcrum Publishing, 350 Indiana St, Golden, CO 80401; 204 pages, $15.95) is a personal alternative to *The Milepost*. Dalby, a former editor of *Alaska Magazine*, is shallow with his travel details (where's the next gas station!!!) but long on stories he has gathered driving the legendary road to the north.

Hiking Guides

55 Ways to the Wilderness in Southcentral Alaska by Nancy Simmerman & Helen Nienhueser (Mountaineer-Books, 1011 SW Klickitat Way, Seattle, WA 98134; 1994, 208 pages, $12.95) is a hiking guide with information covering popular trails, canoe trips and winter outings around the Kenai Peninsula, the Anchorage area and from Palmer to Valdez. It includes maps, distances and estimated trekking times.

15 Hikes in Denali by Don Croner (Trans-Alaska Publishing Company, 200 West 34th Ave, Anchorage, AK; 1989, 42 pages, $7.95) is a large-format guide which outlines 15 hikes in Denali National Park, ranging from short day hikes to 40-mile (64 km) treks. This second edition also contains additional information and drawings of plants, birds and the geology of the park. It's a good purchase if you plan an extended trip to the park.

Alaska Wilderness: Exploring the Central Brooks Range by Robert Marshall (Wild Rose Guidebooks, PO Box 240047, Anchorage, AK, 99524; 1989, 175 pages, $12.95) was written and published in the 1930s and then republished in 1989 for the simple reason that the mountains, rivers, passes and terrain of the Central Brooks Range have not changed. What Marshall saw and many of the routes he explored are still the popular ones today.

Juneau Trails by the US Forest Service (1985, 60 pages, $3), a little green book, is a bible for Juneau hikers as it describes 26 trails around the capital city – perhaps the best area for hiking in Alaska. The guidebook includes maps, distances, rating of the trails and the location of trailheads, along with brief descriptions of the route. The book can be obtained at the USFS Information Center in the Centennial Building on Egan Drive in Juneau, but you have to ask for it.

Sitka Trails also by the US Forest Service (72 pages, $3) is similar to *Juneau Trails* and covers 30 hiking trails around Sitka and its nearby coastline. Each trail has a one paragraph description, rough map and information on access and special features. Either write to or visit the Sitka Ranger District, 204 Siginaka Way, AK 99835.

Discover Southeast Alaska with Pack & Paddle by Margaret Piggott (Mountaineer-Books, 306 2nd Ave West, Seattle, WA 98119; 1990, 238 pages, $12.95), is a guidebook to the water routes and hiking trails of the Southeast which was out of print for years until the author finally updated the first edition in 1990. The guide thoroughly covers the hiking and paddling routes from Ketchikan to Skagway. Its downfall is the weak hand-drawn maps. Make sure you pack the topos.

Backcountry for Denali National Park by Jon Nierenberg (Alaska Natural History Association, 605 West 4th Ave, Anchorage, AK 99501; 94 pages, maps, photos, $8.95), is a general guide to wilderness trekking in the popular national park. Not a trail guide, it provides short synopses to each of Denali's backcountry zones to help trekkers pick the most suitable area to travel.

Katmai by Jean Bodeau (Alaska Natural History Association, 605 West 4th Ave, Anchorage, AK 99501; 1992, 206 pages, photos, $14.95), is a general guide to Katmai National Park on the Alaska Peninsula. It will help you understand this special park and arrange a trip here but it's not adequate to lead you through the Valley of 10,000 Smokes.

Nature Guides

Guide to the Birds of Alaska is by Robert Armstrong (Alaska Northwest Books, 130 2nd Ave South, Edmonds, WA 98020; 1990, 332 pages, $19.95). To ornithologists, Alaska is the ultimate destination. More than 400 species of birds have been spotted in the state and this guide has information on identification, distribution and the habitat of 335 of them. The book contains color photographs, drawings and a bird check list.

A Guide to Alaskan Seabirds by the Alaska Natural History Association, 2525 Gambell St, Anchorage, AK 99501 (1982, 40 pages, $4.95) is a slim guide to the birds that thrive along coastal Alaska. It has excellent drawings for easy identification.

Wild, Edible & Poisonous Plants of Alaska by Dr Christine Heller (Alaska Natural History Association; 88 pages, $2.50), a handy little guide, is an excellent companion on any trek, as it contains both drawings and color photos of Alaskan flora, including edible plants, berries and wild flowers.

A Guide to Wildlife Viewing in Alaska (Wild Rose Guidebooks; 1983, 170 pages, $12.95) is an Alaska Department of Fish & Game sponsored guide which covers the best opportunities to view wildlife by regions and seasons. The first chapter explains how to find wildlife and the subsequent chapters cover Alaska's 14 different types of wildlife habitats.

MAPS

A good topographical map, known to trekkers as simply a 'topo' or 'quad', is indispensable when trekking in Alaska. For most trails, especially multi-day treks, you should have the corresponding topos.

US Geological Survey (USGS) topographical maps come in a variety of scales but trekkers prefer the smallest scale that is available for most of Alaska (1:63,360) where each inch equals a mile. The free maps

of Tongass and Chugach national forests sent by the USFS will not do for any wilderness adventure, as they cover too much and lack the detail that trekkers rely on. *The maps in this book will not suffice either; they are meant only as a reference guide to help you understand the trail descriptions.*

USGS maps cost $2.50 a section for 1:63,360 and $4 for 1:250,000 and can generally be purchased at bookstores, sports shops or camping stores in the last Alaskan town from which you enter the backcountry. However, it is not uncommon for the stores to have sold out of the maps covering popular areas. If possible, order your maps ahead of time from the main office (USGS Western Distribution Branch, Denver Federal Center, PO Box 25286 Denver, CO 80225). Write first and ask for a free index of the maps for Alaska.

You can also purchase topos for the entire state in both Anchorage and Fairbanks. In Anchorage, the USGS map center is in Grace

---

Finding Your Way with a Compass

When following a well-maintained and posted trail, it's often not necessary to have a compass. However, in wilderness areas like Denali and Wrangell-St Elias national parks, where you follow natural routes, it's necessary to determine your direction of travel, or bearing, from one point to the next (especially if you cannot judge your location from land formations alone). To take a compass bearing from a map follow these steps:

Step 1 Draw a straight line on the map from your location to your destination and extend it across any one of the borders on a USGS quad. Borders on the topos are oriented in true north-south and east-west directions.

Step 2 Center the compass on the line where it intersects the border and then align the compass housing north-south or east-west to whichever border you chose. Read the true bearing of your drawn line from the compass circle.

Step 3 To use the bearing, you must compensate for magnetic declination – a compass never points to true north. The needle shows magnetic north because it is attracted by a magnetic force (which varies in different parts of the world). In Alaska, the difference between true north and magnetic north ranges from 12° in the Aleutian Islands to almost 30° in the Southeast.

On all USGS quads there is a magnetic declination diagram showing the difference between true north and magnetic north. If the magnetic north arrow is to the right of the true north line as it is on Alaska maps, subtract the degrees from the figure on the compass circle. If it is to the left, then you add it.

Step 4 You can now set the direction-of-travel arrow on the compass to the bearing. Keep the magnetic needle inside the house on 'N' and the arrow will point to the proper line of travel. ■

Hall at Alaska Pacific University at the east end of Providence Drive. Hours are from 8.30 am to 4.30 pm weekdays. In Fairbanks, the USGS office is in the Federal Building at 101 12th St, east of Cushman St. Hours are from 8 am to 5 pm weekdays.

There are a growing number of commercial trekker maps on the market that are much more up to date than USGS quads but aren't as detailed. Trails Illustrated Topo Maps, a Colorado mapping company, publishes more than 40 that cover US national parks. Among them are Alaska's Denali and Kenai Fjords, which also includes the southern half of the Chugach National Forest. Printed on waterproof paper the maps cost $7.95. Call Trails Illustrated at ☎ (800) 962-1643 for a complete list.

FILM & PHOTOGRAPHY

Take a camera to Alaska! Even if you have never toted one, the scenery here is too overwhelming not to capture it on film.

A small, fixed-lens, so-called 'no-brain' (just point and shoot!) 35 mm camera is OK for a summer of trekking in the north country. A better camera is a 35 mm with a fixed zoom lens. The Nikon Zoom-Touch 500 series, for example, provides a lens that zooms from a 35 mm wide angle to an 80 mm telephoto. The camera is still compact and easy to use but will greatly increase your variety of shots.

If you want to get serious about photography you need a full 35 mm camera with two interchangeable lenses. To photograph wildlife in its natural state, a 135 mm or larger telephoto lens is needed to make the animal the main object in the picture. Just remember any lense larger than 135 mm will probably also require a tripod to eliminate camera shake, especially during low-light conditions. A wide-angle lens of 35 mm, or better yet a 28 mm, adds considerable dimension to scenic views while a fast (f1.2 or f1.4) 50 mm 'normal' lens will provide more opportunities for pictures during weak light. If you want simplicity, check out today's zoom lenses. They are much smaller and compact than they have been in the past and provide

a sharpness that's more than acceptable to most amateur photographers. A zoom from 35 mm to 105 mm would be ideal.

Keep in mind the rainy weather you'll encounter during your trip; a waterproof camera bag·is an excellent investment. When flying to and around Alaska, pack your film in your carry-on luggage and have it hand-inspected. Security personnel are required by law at US airports to honor such requests and are usually very accommodating if you have the film out and ready. Scanning machines are supposed to be safe for film, but why take the chance? Remember the higher the speed of film, the more susceptible it is to damage by scanners.

Many photographers find that Kodachrome (ASA 64 or 100) is the best all-around film, especially when photographing glaciers or snowfields where the reflection off the ice and snow is strong. A few rolls of high-speed film (ASA 200 or 400) are handy for nature photography as most wildlife will be encountered at dusk and dawn, periods of low light.

FISHING
Equipment

If you plan to undertake a few wilderness trips, and enjoy fishing, by all means pack a rod, reel and some tackle. It's now possible to purchase a rod that breaks down into five sections and has a light reel; it takes up less room than soap, shaving cream and wash rag. In the Southeast and Southcentral regions, you can catch cutthroat trout, rainbow trout and the similar Dolly Varden. Further north, especially around Fairbanks, you'll get grayling, with its sail-like dorsal fin, and arctic char; during August, salmon seem to be everywhere.

If angling is just a second thought, load an open-face spinning reel with a light line, something in the four to six-pound range, and take along a small selection of spinners and spoons. After you arrive, you can always purchase the lures used locally, but in most wilderness streams I've rarely had a problem catching fish on Mepps spinners Nos 1 to 3.

Other lures that work well are Pixies, Dardevils and Krocodiles.

For fly fishing a No 5 or No 6 rod with a matching floating line or sinking tip is well suited for Dolly Varden, rainbow and grayling. For species of salmon a No 7 or No 8 rod and line is a better choice. For ease of travel, rods should break down and be in a case.

A nonresident's fishing license is $50 a year (compared to only $15 for residents) or you can purchase a three-day license for $15 or a 14-day license for $30; every bait shop in the state sells them. The Alaska Department of Fish & Game puts out a variety of material including the *Recreational Fishing Guide*. You can obtain the 72-page guide ($5) by writing to the Department of Fish & Game (☎ (906) 465-4285), PO Box 3-2000, Juneau, AK 99802-2000.

Following is a brief synopsis of the most common non-salmon species you'll find in lakes and streams throughout summer while you're roaming the backcountry.

Rainbow Trout

This is without a doubt the best fighting fish and thus the most sought after. Fishing from shore in lakes is best in late spring and early summer, just after ice break-up, and again in the fall when water temperatures are cooler. During the height of the summer, rainbows move into deeper water in lakes and you usually need a boat to fish for them.

The best time to fish for them is at dawn and dusk; on calm days they can be seen surfacing for insects. Use spinners No 1 through No 3 and flashy spoons, but avoid treble hooks (or clip one or two of the hooks together) as it makes releasing fish hard. The

workhorse fly is the lake leech, in either purple or olive, fished with a slow retrieve on sinking-tip lines.

Cutthroat Trout

The cutthroat picks up its name from the reddish-orange slash along the inner edge of its lower jaw. Outside of Southeast Alaska, most traveling anglers end up casting for resident cutthroats that spend their entire lives in the streams and lakes as opposed to larger anadromous cutthroats that migrate to saltwater where food is more abundant. This trout likes to stay submerged under logs, aquatic vegetation or other cover, and is an aggressive feeder.

In most lakes, you can take them on small spinners, No 0 up to No 2, but also will hit on larger spoons, especially red-and-white Dardevils. For fly fishing, a floating line with a nine-foot leader and a slowly twitching mosquito larva fly can be very effective. The best time to fish is early morning and at dusk – the light is low and cutthroats often cruise the shallows for food.

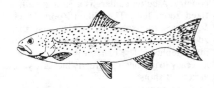

Cutthroat trout

Dolly Varden

This is one of the most widespread fish in Alaska and their aggressive behavior makes them easy to catch. Dolly Varden are often

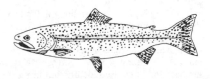

Rainbow trout

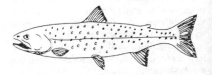

Dolly Varden

caught near the entrances of streams or along weed beds near shore, making them accessible to anglers. Use spinners in sizes No 1 and No 2 or small spoons. Fly fishers often use a blue smolt fly on a sinking-tip line and a short leader and use an erratic strip retrieve. Other streamers work as well while a pinhead muddler and a floating line is often used in shallow rivers or when Dolly Varden are holding in shallow water.

Arctic Char

A closely related cousin to the Dolly Varden, the arctic char is not quite as widespread in Alaska. Often anglers will confuse the two species. Arctic char are found predominantly in the Alaska Peninsula and Bristol Bay areas, on Kodiak Island, in some lakes in the Kenai Peninsula and in the Brooks Range and to the north. Spawning male char turn brilliant red or gold with red or orange spots while Dolly Varden are just as brightly colored but only on their lower body. For the most part, anglers use the same tackle and techniques for both species.

Grayling

The grayling's long dorsal fin allows you to identify the fish even if you have never hooked one. Grayling in streams feed at the surface or mid-water drift and almost exclusively on insects or larva – they are a fly fisher's dream. Extremely receptive to dry flies they rarely choose one pattern over another. Generally small flies, No 16 to No 18, will produce more raises than larger ones. Even if you have spinning gear, tie on a clear plastic bubble four to six feet above a dry fly.

HEALTH

Travel health depends on your predeparture preparations, your day-to-day health care while traveling and how you handle any medical problem or emergency that does develop. While the list of potential dangers can seem quite frightening, with a little luck, some basic precautions and adequate information, few travellers experience more than upset stomachs.

Travel Health Guides

Books on travel health include:

Travellers' Health (Dr Richard Dawood, Oxford University Press) is comprehensive, easy to read, authoritative and also highly recommended, although it's rather large to lug around.

Where There is No Doctor (David Werner, Hesperian Foundation) is a very detailed guide intended for someone planning to work in an undeveloped country, rather than for the average traveler.

Travel with Children (Maureen Wheeler, Lonely Planet Publications) includes basic advice on travel health for younger children.

Wilderness Medicine (Dr William W Forgey, ICS Books) is a detailed but easy-to-use guide to basic first aid as well as more complicated procedures for injuries that occur on expeditions in the backcountry of parks or wilderness areas.

First Aid Pamphlet (Mountaineer-Books) is a handy 36-page booklet with quick information that covers the basics plus life-threatening emergencies for those mountaineering or trekking in remote backcountry areas.

Predeparture Preparations

Health Insurance The cost of health care in the USA is extremely high and in Alaska it's no different. A travel insurance policy to cover theft, loss and medical problems is therefore a wise idea. There are a wide variety of policies and your travel agent will have recommendations. The international student travel policies handled by the Student Travel Association (STA) or other student travel organizations are usually good value. Some policies offer lower and higher medical expense options: the higher one is chiefly for countries like the USA which have extremely high medical costs. Check the small print:

• Some policies specifically exclude 'dangerous activities' which can include scuba diving, motorcycling, even trekking. If such activities are on your agenda you don't want that sort of policy. A locally acquired motorcycle license may not be valid under your policy.

• You may prefer a policy which pays doctors or hospitals direct rather than you having to pay on the spot and claim later. If you have to claim later make sure you keep all documentation. Some policies ask you to call back (collect) to a center in your home country where an immediate assessment of your problem is made.

- Check if the policy covers ambulances or an emergency flight home. If you have to stretch out you will need two seats and somebody has to pay for them!

Medical Kit A small, straightforward medical kit is a wise thing to carry. A possible kit list includes:

- Aspirin or Panadol – for pain or fever
- Antihistamine (such as Benadryl) – useful as a decongestant for colds, allergies, to ease the itch from insect bites or stings or to help prevent motion sickness. Antihistamines may cause sedation and interact with alcohol so care should be taken when using them.
- Antibiotics – useful if you're traveling well off the beaten track, but they must be prescribed and you should carry the prescription with you. Some individuals are allergic to commonly prescribed antibiotics such as penicillin or sulfa drugs – always carry information of such allergies with you.
- Kaolin preparation (Pepto-Bismol), Imodium or Lomotil – for stomach upsets
- Rehydration mixture – for treatment of severe diarrhoea. This is particularly important if traveling with children, but is recommended for everyone.
- Antiseptic such as Betadine, which comes as impregnated swabs or ointment, and an antibiotic powder or similar 'dry' spray – for cuts and grazes.
- Calamine lotion – to ease irritation from bites or stings.
- Bandages and Band-aids – for minor injuries
- Scissors, tweezers and a thermometer (note that mercury thermometers are prohibited by airlines)
- Insect repellent, sunblock, chap stick and water purification tablets

Ideally antibiotics should be administered only under medical supervision and should never be taken indiscriminately. Take only the recommended dose at the prescribed intervals and continue using the antibiotic for the prescribed period, even if the illness seems to be cured earlier. Antibiotics are quite specific to the infections they can treat. Stop taking them immediately if there are any serious reactions and don't use the antibiotic at all if you are unsure that you have the correct one.

Health Preparations Make sure you're healthy before you start traveling. If you are

embarking on a long trip make sure your teeth are OK.

If you wear glasses take a spare pair and your prescription. Losing your glasses can be a real problem.

If you require a particular medication take an adequate supply, as it may not be available locally.

Basic Rules

Care in what you eat and drink is the most important health rule; stomach upsets are the most likely travel health problem (between 30% and 50% of travelers in a two-week stay experience this) but the majority of these upsets will be relatively minor.

Water Purification Tap water in Alaska is safe to drink but it is wise to purify surface water that is to be used for cooking and drinking. The simplest way of purifying water is to boil it thoroughly. Vigorously boiling for five minutes should be satisfactory; however, at high altitude water boils at a lower temperature, so germs are less likely to be killed.

Simple filtering will not remove all dangerous organisms, so if you cannot boil water it should be treated chemically. Chlorine tablets (Puritabs, Steritabs or other brand names) will kill many but not all pathogens, including giardia and amoebic cysts. Iodine is very effective in purifying water and is available in tablet form (such as Potable Aqua), but follow the directions carefully and remember that too much iodine can be harmful.

If you can't find tablets, tincture of iodine (2%) or iodine crystals can be used. Four drops of tincture of iodine per quart of clear water is the recommended dosage; the treated water should be left to stand for 20 to 30 minutes before drinking. Iodine crystals can also be used to purify water but this is a more complicated process, as you have to first prepare a saturated iodine solution. Iodine loses its effectiveness if exposed to air or damp so keep it in a tightly sealed container. Flavored powder will disguise the taste of treated water and is a good idea if you are traveling with children.

If you are trekking in the wilderness, all this can be handled more easily with a high-quality filter. Filters such as First Need or MSR's Waterworks are designed to take out whatever you shouldn't be drinking, including *giardia lamblia* (see the following Dangers & Annoyances section). The filters cost $45 to $80 and are well worth it.

Water from glacial rivers may appear murky but it can be drunk, if necessary, in small quantities. The murk is actually fine particles of silt scoured from the rock by the glacier and drinking too much of it has been known to clog up internal plumbing

Food If a place looks clean and well run, then the food is probably safe to eat. In general, places that are packed with travelers or locals will be fine, while empty restaurants are questionable. Busy restaurants mean the food is being cooked and eaten quite quickly with little standing around and is probably not being reheated.

Nutrition If your food is poor or limited in availability, if you're traveling hard and fast and therefore missing meals, or if you simply lose your appetite, you can soon start to lose weight and place your health at risk.

Make sure your diet is well balanced. Eggs, tofu, beans, lentils and nuts are all safe ways to get protein. Fruit is a good source of vitamins. Try to eat plenty of grains (rice) and bread. If your diet isn't well balanced or if your food intake is insufficient, it's a good idea to take vitamin and iron pills.

During those Alaskan summer days with 19 hours of daylight or more, make sure you drink enough – don't rely on feeling thirsty to indicate when you should drink. Not needing to urinate or very dark yellow urine is a danger sign. At the start of each trekking day, drink at least a quart of water. Excessive sweating can lead to loss of salt and therefore muscle cramping – salt tablets are not a good idea as a preventative, but in places where salt is not used much, adding salt to food can help.

Everyday Health A normal body temperature is 37°C (98.6°F); more than 2°C higher is a 'high' fever. A normal adult pulse rate is 60 to 80 beats per minute (children 80 to 100, babies 100 to 140). You should know how to take a temperature and a pulse rate. As a general rule the pulse increases about 20 beats per minute with every °C rise in fever.

Respiration (breathing) rate is also an indicator of illness. Count the number of breaths per minute: between 12 and 20 is normal for adults and older children (up to 30 for younger children, 40 for babies). People with a high fever or serious respiratory illness (like pneumonia) breathe more quickly than normal. More than 40 shallow breaths a minute usually means pneumonia.

Medical Problems & Treatment

Sunburn Sunburn and windburn are primary concerns for anyone planning to spend time trekking or traveling over snow and ice. The sun will burn you even if you feel cold, and the wind will cause dehydration and skin chafing. Use a good sunblock and a moisture cream on exposed skin, even on cloudy days. A hat provides added protection and zinc oxide or some other barrier cream for your nose and lips is recommended.

Reflection and glare off the ice and snow can cause snow blindness; high-protection sunglasses are essential for any glacier visit.

Hypothermia Perhaps the most dangerous health threat in the arctic regions is hypothermia. Hypothermia occurs when the body loses heat faster than it can produce it and the core temperature of the body falls. It is surprisingly easy to progress from very cold to dangerously cold due to a combination of wind, wet clothing, fatigue and hunger, even if the air temperature is above freezing. It is best to dress in layers; silk, wool and some of the new artificial fibres are all good insulating materials. A hat is important, as a lot of heat is lost through the head. A strong, waterproof outer layer is essential, because

Medical Problems & Medications
Diarrhoea & Vomiting
  norfloxacin
  tinidazole
  Imodium or Lomotil
  rehydration salts
  metoclopramide
  promethazine suppositories
Colds
  throat lozenges
  Actifed
  codeine phosphate
  amoxicillin
  erythromycin
Blisters & Skin Infection
  antiseptic (eg Betadine)
  cephalexin
  erythromycin
Rashes & Insect Bites
  diphenhydramine
  miconazole cream
  hydrocortisone 1% cream
Traumatic Injuries
  Ibuprofen
  codeine
Altitude Sickness
  acetazolamide
  dexamethasone
  nifedipine
Other Medical Problems
  gastritis – antacids
  constipation – dulcolax pills
  urinary tract infection – norfloxacin
  vaginitis – mycostatin vaginal tabs
  conjunctivitis – sodium sulamyd eye
    drops
  internal ear infection – amoxicillin,
    cephalexin, erythromycin or
    azithromycin

out of the wind and/or rain, remove their clothing if it's wet and replace it with dry, warm clothing. Give them hot liquids – not alcohol – and some high-kilojoule, easily digestible food. Do not rub victims but place them near a fire or in a warm (not hot) bath. This should be enough for the early stages of hypothermia, but if it has gone further it may be necessary to place victims in a warm sleeping bag and get in with them.

Altitude Sickness Acute Mountain Sickness, or AMS, occurs at high altitudes and can be fatal. The lack of oxygen at high altitudes affects most people to some extent. A number of measures can be adopted to prevent Acute Mountain Sickness:

* Ascend slowly – have frequent rest days, spending two to three nights at each rise of 3280 feet (1000 meters). If you reach a high altitude by trekking, acclimatization takes place gradually and you are less likely to be affected than if you fly direct.
* Drink extra fluids. The mountain air is dry and cold and you lose moisture as you breathe.
* Eat light, high-carbohydrate meals for more energy.
* Avoid alcohol as it may increase the risk of dehydration.
* Avoid sedatives.

Even with acclimatization (the term we use to describe the process by which the body adapts to altitude) you may still have trouble adjusting. Mild altitude problems will generally abate after a day or so but if the symptoms persist or become worse the only treatment is to descend – even 1640 feet (500 meters) can help. Breathlessness, a dry, irritative cough (which may progress to the production of pink, frothy sputum), severe headaches, loss of appetite, nausea, and sometimes vomiting are all danger signs. Increasing tiredness, confusion, and lack of coordination and balance are real danger signs. Any of these symptoms individually, even just a persistent headache, can be a warning.

There is no hard and fast rule as to how high is too high. Although more common at higher altitudes, AMS has occurred at 5900 feet (1800 meters). It has been fatal at altitudes

keeping dry is vital. Carry basic supplies, including food containing simple sugars to generate heat quickly and lots of fluid to drink.

Symptoms of hypothermia are exhaustion, numb skin (particularly toes and fingers), shivering, slurred speech, irrational or violent behavior, lethargy, stumbling, dizzy spells, muscle cramps and violent bursts of energy. Irrationality may take the form of sufferers claiming they are warm and trying to take off their clothes.

To treat hypothermia, first get the person

of 9840 feet (3000 meters), although 11,480 to 14,760 (3500 to 4500 meters) is the usual range. It is always wise to sleep at a lower altitude than the greatest height reached during the day.

Motion Sickness Since a great deal of travel in Alaska is by boat and much of the overland travel is over rough, unsurfaced roads, motion sickness can be a real problem for those prone to it. Eating lightly before and during a trip will reduce the chances of motion sickness. If you are prone to motion sickness try to find a place that minimizes disturbance – near the wing on aircraft, close to midships on boats, near the center on buses. Fresh air usually helps, reading or cigarette smoke doesn't. Commercial anti-motion-sickness preparations, which can cause drowsiness, have to be taken before the trip commences; when you're feeling sick it's too late. Ginger is a natural preventative and is available in capsule form.

Jet Lag Jet lag is experienced when a person travels by air across more than three time zones (each time zone usually represents a one-hour time difference). It occurs because many of the functions of the human body (such as temperature, pulse rate and empty-ing of the bladder and bowels) are regulated by internal 24-hour cycles called circadian rhythms. When we travel long distances rapidly, our bodies take time to adjust to the 'new time' of our destination, and we may experience fatigue, disorientation, insomnia, anxiety, impaired concentration and loss of appetite. These effects will usually be gone within three days of arrival, but there are ways of minimizing the impact of jet lag:

• Rest for a couple of days prior to departure; try to avoid late nights and last-minute dashes for travelers' checks, passport etc.
• Try to select flight schedules that minimize sleep deprivation; arriving late in the day means you can go to sleep soon after you arrive. For very long flights, try to organize a stopover.
• Avoid smoking, as this reduces the amount of oxygen in the airplane cabin even further and causes greater fatigue.

• Avoid excessive eating (which bloats the stomach) and alcohol (which causes dehydration) during the flight. Instead, drink plenty of noncarbonated, non-alcoholic drinks such as fruit juice or water.
• Make yourself comfortable by wearing loose-fitting clothes and perhaps bringing an eye mask and ear plugs to help you sleep.

Diarrhoea A change of water, food or climate can all cause the runs; diarrhoea caused by contaminated food or water is more serious. Despite all your precautions you may still have a bout of mild travelers' diarrhoea but a few rushed toilet trips with no other symptoms is not indicative of a serious problem. Moderate diarrhoea, involving half-a-dozen loose movements in a day, is more of a nuisance. Dehydration is the main danger with any diarrhoea, partic-ularly for children where dehydration can occur quite quickly. Fluid replacement remains the mainstay of management. Weak black tea with a little sugar, soda water, or soft drinks allowed to go flat and diluted 50% with water are all good. With severe diarrhoea a rehydrating solution is necessary to replace minerals and salts. Commercially available ORS (oral rehydration salts) are very useful; add the contents of one sachet to a quart of boiled or bottled water. In an emergency you can make up a solution of eight teaspoons of sugar to a quart of boiled water. You should stick to a bland diet as you recover.

Lomotil or Imodium can be used to bring relief from the symptoms, although they do not actually cure the problem. Only use these drugs if absolutely necessary. For children Imodium is preferable, but under all circum-stances fluid replacement is essential. Do not use these drugs if you have a high fever or are severely dehydrated.

Giardiasis The parasite causing this intesti-nal disorder is present in contaminated water. The symptoms are stomach cramps, nausea, a bloated stomach, watery, foul-smelling diarrhoea and frequent gas. Giardiasis can appear several weeks after you have been exposed to the parasite. The symptoms may disappear for a few days and then return; this can go on for several weeks. Tinidazole, known as Fasigyn, or metronidazole (Flagyl) are the recommended drugs for treatment. Either can be used in a single treatment dose. Antbiotics are of no use. (See Dangers & Annoyances later in this chapter for more information.)

Viral Gastroenteritis This is caused not by bacteria but, as the name suggests, by a virus. It is characterized by stomach cramps, diarrhoea, and sometimes by vomiting and/or a slight fever. All you can do is rest and drink lots of fluids.

Rabies Rabies is found in Alaska, especially among small rodents such as squirrels and chipmunks in wilderness areas; and is caused by a bite or scratch by an infected animal. Any bite, scratch or even lick from a warm-blooded, furry animal should be cleaned immediately and thoroughly. Scrub with soap and running water, and then clean with an alcohol solution. If there is any possibility that the animal is infected medical help should be sought immediately. Even if the animal is not rabid, all bites should be treated seriously as they can become infected or can result in tetanus. A rabies vaccination is now available and should be considered if you are in a high-risk category.

Sexually Transmitted Diseases Sexual contact with an infected sexual partner spreads these diseases. While abstinence is the only 100% preventative, using condoms is also effective. Gonorrhoea and syphilis are the most common of these diseases; sores, blisters or rashes around the genitals, discharges or pain when urinating are common symptoms. Symptoms may be less marked or not observed at all in women. Syphilis symptoms eventually disappear completely but the disease continues and can cause severe problems in later years. Antibiotics are used to treat gonorrhoea and syphilis.

There are numerous other sexually transmitted diseases, most of which have effective treatments. However, there is no cure for herpes and there is also currently no cure for AIDS.

HIV/AIDS HIV, the Human Immunodeficiency Virus, may develop into AIDS, Acquired Immune Deficiency Syndrome. HIV is a major problem in many countries. Any exposure to blood, blood products or bodily fluids may put the individual at risk. In many developing countries transmission is predominantly through heterosexual sexual activity. This is quite different from industrialized countries where transmission is mostly through contact between homosexual or bisexual males or contaminated needles in IV drug users.

Apart from sexual abstinence, the most effective preventative is always to practise safe sex using condoms. It is impossible to detect the HIV-positive status of an otherwise healthy-looking person without a blood test.

HIV/AIDS can also be spread through infected blood transfusions and by dirty needles – vaccinations, acupuncture, tattooing and ear or nose piercing can potentially be as dangerous as intravenous drug use if the equipment is not clean.

Fear of HIV infection should never preclude treatment for serious medical conditions. Although there may be a risk of infection, it is very small indeed.

Cuts & Scratches Skin punctures can easily become infected making them much more difficult to heal. Treat any cut with an antiseptic such as Betadine. Where possible avoid bandages and Band-aids, which can keep wounds wet.

Bites & Stings Bee and wasp stings are usually painful rather than dangerous. Calamine lotion will give relief or ice packs will reduce the pain and swelling.

Women's Health
Gynecological Problems Poor diet, lowered resistance due to the use of antibiotics for stomach upsets and even taking contraceptive pills can lead to vaginal infections

when traveling. Keeping the genital area clean, and wearing skirts or loose-fitting trousers and cotton underwear will help to prevent infections.

Yeast infections, characterized by a rash, itch and discharge, can be treated with a vinegar or even lemon-juice douche or with yoghurt. Nystatin suppositories are the usual medical prescription. Trichomonas is a more serious infection; symptoms are a discharge and a burning sensation when urinating. If a vinegar-water douche is not effective medical attention should be sought. Male sexual partners must also be treated; metronidazole (Flagyl) is the prescribed drug.

Pregnancy Most miscarriages occur during the first three months of pregnancy, so this is the most risky time to travel as far as your own health is concerned. Miscarriage is not uncommon, and can occasionally lead to severe bleeding. The last three months should also be spent within reasonable distance of good medical care. A baby born as early as 24 weeks stands a chance of survival. Additional care should be taken to prevent illness and particular attention should be paid to diet and nutrition. Alcohol and nicotine, for example, should be avoided.

Women travellers often find that their periods become irregular or even cease while they're on the road. Remember that a missed period in these circumstances doesn't necessarily indicate pregnancy. There are health posts or Family Planning clinics in many small and large urban centres, where you can seek advice and have a urine test to determine whether you are pregnant or not.

DANGERS & ANNOYANCES
Drinking Water
Alaska's water is affected by *giardia lamblia*, or 'beaver fever' as it is known among trekkers. The parasite is found in surface water, particularly beaver ponds, and is transmitted between humans and animals. Giardia is an intestinal parasite that causes stomach cramps, nausea, a bloated stomach, watery, foul-smelling diarrhoea and frequent

gas. Giardiasis can appear several weeks after you have been exposed to the parasite. The symptoms may disappear for a few days and then return; this can go on for several weeks. Metronidazole, known as Flagyl, is the recommended drug, but it should only be taken under medical supervision. Antibiotics are of no use. See the Health section for ways of purifying your drinking water.

Often in the backcountry you'll encounter glacially fed streams, distinguished by a grey, sluggish color. Glacial water may be drunk, if necessary, in small quantities, although drinking too much of it tends to clog up the internal plumbing. The murk is actually fine particles of silt scoured from the rock by the glacier. Avoid it if possible and if you have to drink from such a stream, let the water sit overnight in a bottle to allow the particles to settle at the bottom.

Insects
Alaska is notorious for its biting insects. In the cities and towns you'll have few problems, but out in the woods you'll have to contend with a variety of insects, including mosquitos, black flies, white-socks, 'no-see-ums' and deer flies. Coastal areas, with their cool summers, have smaller numbers of insects than the Interior. Generally, camping on a beach where there is some breeze is better than pitching a tent in the woods. In the end, just accept the fact that you will be bitten.

Mosquitos can often be the most bothersome pest. They emerge from hibernation before the snow has entirely melted away, peak in late June and are around until the first frost. It's the female of the species which is after your blood, and they're most active early in the morning and at dusk. Luckily, even a slight wind grounds them. You can combat mosquitos by wearing light colors, a snug-fitting parka and by tucking the legs of your pants into your socks or boots.

The best protection by far is a high-potency insect repellent; the best choice a high percentage of Deet (diethyltoluamide), the active ingredient. A little bottle of Musk Oil or Cutters can cost $6 or $7 (they contain

100% Deet) but it's one of the best investments you will make.

Unfortunately, repellents are less effective, and some people say useless, against black flies and no-see-ums. Their season runs from June to August and their bite is far more annoying. The tiny no-see-um bite is a prolonged prick after which the surrounding skin becomes inflamed and itches intermittently for up to a week or more. Unlike the mosquito, these insects will crawl into your hair and under loose clothing in search of bare skin.

Thus, the best protection and a fact of life in Alaska's backcountry are long-sleeved shirts, socks that will allow you to tuck your pants into them and a snug cap or woollen hat. You also see many backcountry travelers packing head nets. They're not something you wear a lot, it drives you crazy looking through mesh all day, but when you really need one they are a lifesaver. Being relatively light to pack and inexpensive, you might as well pack one if you are doing extensive wilderness travel in areas like the Brooks Range or Katmai National Park.

Other items you might consider are bug jackets and an after-bite medication. The mesh jackets are soaked in insect repellent and kept in a zip-lock bag until you wear them and some people say they are the only effective way to keep no-see-ums at bay. After-bite medications contain ammonia and are rubbed on; while it might drive away your tent partner, it does soothe the craving to scratch the assortment of bites on your arms and neck.

Bears

Bears are a fact of life in the Alaska backcountry and wilderness areas and the best way to avoid them is to follow a few common-sense rules. Bears do not roam the backcountry looking for trekkers to maul; they only charge when they feel trapped, when a trekker comes between a sow and her cubs or when they are enticed by food. It is a good practice to sing or clap when traveling through thick bush so you don't bump into a bear. It has happened, and usually the bear

feels threatened and has no choice but to defend itself. Don't camp near bear food sources or in the middle of an obvious bear path. Stay away from thick berry patches, streams choking with salmon or beaches littered with bear scat.

Other people attach 'bear bells' all over their backpacks, boots and clothing. Bells will alert any bear in the immediate area, but unfortunately will also scare all other wildlife, even the species you want to see. The constant ringing not only eliminates the chances to view animals but blocks out the natural sounds of the woods that ease the mind and fill the soul with wonder.

Leave the pet at home; a frightened dog only runs back to its owner and most dogs are no match for a bear. Set up your 'kitchen' – the spot where you will cook and eat – 30 to 50 yards away from your tent. In coastal areas, many trekkers eat in the tidal zone, knowing that when the high tide comes in all evidence of food will be washed away.

At night, try to place your food sacks 10 feet or more off the ground by hanging them in a tree, placing them on top of a tall boulder or putting them on the edge of a rock cliff. In a treeless, flat area, cover up the food sacks with rocks. A bear is not going to see the food bags, it's going to smell them. By packaging all food items in zip-lock plastic bags, you greatly reduce the animal's chances of getting a whiff of your next meal. Avoid odoriferous foods such as bacon or sardines in areas of high concentrations of bears.

And please, don't take food into your tent at night. Don't even take toothpaste, hand lotion, suntan oils or anything with a smell. If a bear smells a human, it will leave; anything else might encourage it to investigate.

If you do meet a bear on the trail, *do not* turn and run. Stop, make no sudden moves and begin talking calmly to it. Bears have extremely poor eyesight and speaking helps them understand that you are there. If it doesn't take off right away, back up slowly before turning around and departing the area. A bear standing on its hind legs is not on the verge of charging, only trying to see you better. When a bear turns sideways or begins a series of woofs, it is only challenging you for space – just back away slowly and leave. But if the animal follows you, *stop* and hold your ground.

Most bear charges are bluffs, with the animal veering off at the last minute. Experienced trekkers handle a charge in different ways. Some throw their packs three feet in front of them, as this will often distract the bear long enough for them to back away. Others fire a hand-held signal flare over the bear's head (but never at it) in an attempt to use the noise and sudden light to scare it away. If an encounter is imminent, drop into a fetal position, place your hands behind your neck and play dead.

Some people carry a gun to fend off bear charges. This is a skilled operation if you are a good shot, a foolish one if you are not. With a gun, you must drop a charging bear with one or two shots as the animal will be extremely dangerous if only wounded. Others are turning to defensive aerosol sprays which contain capsicum (red pepper extract) that cost $40 a piece and have been used with some success for protection against bears. These sprays are effective at a range of six to eight yards but must be discharged downwind. If not, you will just disable yourself.

Be extremely careful in bear country, but don't let the bears' reputation keep you out of the woods.

Poisonous Plants

The one plant you should learn to recognize and then avoid at all costs is devil's club, or *Opolopanax horridus*. Devil's club is found throughout the Southeast and in parts of Southcentral Alaska and can grow to 10 feet in height. It has huge maple-shaped leaves and stems covered with sharp barbed spines.

When a spine touches your skin, it feels like a bee sting and often swelling occurs. Due to its barb, the spines are difficult to remove. Wear gloves and long-sleeved shirts when you encounter heavy areas of devil's club.

There are also a few poisonous berries found in Alaska and the most common one,

Devil's club

the baneberry (*Acteaea rubra*), is also the most poisonous. As few as six berries can cause dizziness, burning in the stomach and colicky pains. Baneberries are usually found in forests and thickets of the Southeast, Southcentral Alaska, including the Kenai Peninsula and Kodiak, and some areas of the Yukon River and Bristol Bay. The plant ranges in height from two to three feet, its leaves are large, lobed and coarsely toothed and its berries can be either white or red.

For a complete guide to all the edible plants and poisonous ones, purchase the excellent *Wild, Edible & Poisonous Plants of Alaska* (see the earlier Books section).

Shellfish Poisoning

Alaska has a significant problem with poisonous shellfish, commonly referred to as Paralytic Shellfish Poisoning (PSP). When the toxin is present, symptoms may appear soon after the clams are eaten, sometimes in less than two hours. They often include a tingling of numbness of the lips, tongue and fingertips followed by loss of muscular coordination and incoherence.

Trekking without Bridges

More so in Alaska than in other more developed areas of the USA, backpackers must know how to ford a river correctly. Crossing unbridged rivers is inevitable in a region as wild as Alaska. Ford a river haphazardly and you're courting a potential disaster that has probably claimed more lives in the wilderness than bear attacks.

River crossing involves picking the best time and the right place, and using the proper technique. Knowing when to ford is especially important. In the summer, glacial rivers are usually at their lowest levels in the early morning before the heat of the sun has made them swell. Be aware of approaching storms – cross before heavy rainfall turns a stream into a raging river. If a stream has turned into white water, simply wait for it to drop to its normal level.

Never cross a river barefoot. The cold temperatures of a mountain stream can cause numbness in your feet, and you're likely to stub a toe on rocks and boulders and slip. Carry a pair of tennis shoes for fording rivers, or neoprene booties with hard soles. Sport sandals with thick rubber soles are becoming popular. Just remember that many sandals use Velcro to hold the straps in place and in water Velcro quickly loosens and releases. If you don't have a spare pair of shoes take off your socks and wear your boots.

Before crossing the river, release all the waist belts and chest straps on your pack. If you fall, you must be able to ditch your pack as it will fill with water and become a deadly anchor. If you are making a solo crossing you might also want to use a long sturdy stick.

Choosing the right place to cross a river is the key to fording it safely. Wide sections of a river are the shallowest. Avoid areas of cut banks, a deep current will be eroding the shoreline. Look for a spot where the river is braided, having divided into several manageable channels. If you are unsure about the depth of the river, toss a big rock into it. A hollow 'kathump' indicates deep water.

When you cross the river, look at the shore opposite, never at the mesmerizing rushing current. Face slightly downstream and move diagonally in that direction, probing each step as you cross. This is where a sturdy stick is useful. If you are in a group, put the largest and strongest person at the upstream end and then sandwich the smaller people in between. Link arms and enter the river all together.

If the water is deeper than your thighs, turn back and look for another place to cross. If the stream is especially swift, turn back when it reaches your knees. If you do fall, ditch your pack and roll over on your back, pointing your feet downstream. This will allow you to fend off approaching boulders. Swim towards the shore by waving or 'flippering' with your arms. ■

PSP is serious and can cause death from respiratory muscle paralysis. If you are unsure about the quality of a beach or shoreline, don't eat the clams. For the latest warnings on PSP and a list of approved clamming beaches in the state contact Alaska Division of Agriculture (☎ (907) 745-3236), PO Box 1088, Palmer, AK 99645.

BACKCOUNTRY CONDUCT

It is wise to check in with the US Forest Service (USFS) office or National Park headquarters before entering the backcountry. By letting them know your intentions, you'll get peace of mind knowing that someone knows you're out there. If there is no ranger office in the area, advise the air charter service responsible for picking up your party of your travel plans.

Do not harass wildlife while traveling in the backcountry. Avoid startling an animal, as it will most likely flee, leaving you with a short and forgettable encounter. If you flush a bird from its nest, leave the area quickly, as an unattended nest leaves the eggs vulnerable to predators. Never attempt to feed wildlife; it is not healthy for you or the animal.

Choosing a spot to pitch a tent in a campground is easy, but in the wilderness the choice is more complicated and should be made carefully to avoid problems in the middle of the night. Throughout much of Alaska, especially the Interior, river bars are the best place to pitch a tent. Strips of sand or small gravel patches along rivers provide good drainage and a smoother surface on which to pitch a tent than tussock grass.

Take time to check out the area before unpacking your gear. Avoid animal trails (whether the tracks be moose or bear), areas with bear scat, and berry patches with ripe fruit. In late summer, it is best to stay away from streams choked with salmon runs.

In the Southeast and other coastal areas of Alaska, search out beaches and ridges with southern exposures; they provide the driest conditions in these rainy zones. Old glacier and stream outwashes (sand or gravel deposits) make ideal campsites as long as you stay well above the high-tide line. Look for the last ridge of seaweed and debris on the shore and then pitch your tent another 20 to 30 yards above that to avoid waking up with saltwater flooding your tent. Tidal fluctuations along Alaska's coast are among the largest in the world – up to 30 feet in some places.

Finally, be thoughtful when in the wilderness as it is a delicate environment. Carry in your supplies and carry out your trash; never litter or leave garbage to smoulder in a fire pit. Always put out your fire and cover it with natural materials or better still don't light a fire in heavily traveled areas. Use biodegradable soap and do all washing away from water sources. In short, practice low-impact no-trace camping and leave no evidence of your stay. Only then can these areas remain true wilderness.

ACCOMMODATIONS
Camping
Alaska is a camper's paradise. The motels might be expensive, the hostel system limited and B&Bs often unpractical for those without transportation but there are state, federal and private campgrounds from Ketchikan to Fairbanks. Nightly fees range from $6 for most state campgrounds to $15 per tent in some of the more deluxe private campgrounds.

Campgrounds Some trails begin or end along campgrounds that can be reached by vehicles and usually feature drinking water, toilets, tables and fire grills.

Free-Use Shelter This can be a three-sided shelter, an old miner's hut or a new, completely enclosed cabin with windows and a wood stove. They vary greatly but are used on a first-come-first-use basis and are free. In many areas, such as on the Pinnell Mountain Trail, the shelters are designed as emergency shelter during foul weather and as an escape from the wind when cooking – they are not free lodging for the night. Even if there is a shelter on the trail, you should always plan on packing along a tent.

Backcountry Campsites Along some trails, like Resurrection Pass and the Historic Iditarod Trail, there are posted campsites which may feature tent pads and fire grills.

Backcountry Camping This refers to an area that is good for camping but sites are not posted and there are no facilities such as tables, fire rings or vault toilets (outhouses).

Forest Service Cabins
The most affordable accommodations in the Alaska wilderness are Forest Service cabins. Built and maintained by the USFS, the cabins are scattered throughout the Tongass National Forest (practically the entire Southeast), the Chugach National Forest on the Kenai Peninsula, and different islands and bays in Prince William Sound. For the most part, the cabins are rustic log cabins or A-frames with wood-burning stoves, plywood bunks, pit toilets and often a rowboat if there is a lake nearby.

Some of the cabins can be reached on foot but for most, a bush plane or chartered boat has to drop you off and then return for you.

At $25 per night for the whole cabin, these are accommodations you can afford in Alaska. You can reserve them 179 days in advance by sending the total payment and the dates you want to stay in the cabins to the relevant Forest Service offices which administer them.

During the summer, the cabins are heavily used by both locals and travelers, and stays are limited to seven consecutive nights per party. In the Chugach National Forest, there is a three-day limit on hike-in cabins from May to August. Some cabins are so popular that the USFS holds a lottery among all the reservation requests sent 179 days in advance, in order to determine who will be allowed to occupy them during peak periods of the summer.

Of the 190 USFS public-use cabins, almost 150 of them are in the Southeast and are accessible from Ketchikan, Petersburg, Juneau or Sitka. If you don't make reservations but have a flexible schedule, it is still possible to rent one. During the summer, USFS offices in the Southeast maintain lists of the cabins and dates still available. There are always a few cabins available for a couple of days in the middle of the week, although they are most likely to be the remote ones requiring more flying time (and thus money) to reach. The most accessible ones, including those along the popular trails, are usually booked solid by the time June rolls around.

For a complete list of cabins in the Southeast, write to the following USFS offices in Alaska for a booklet describing each cabin in its district, the surrounding terrain and the best way to travel to it.

Chatham Area Supervisor
    204 Siginaka Way, Sitka 99835 (☎ (907) 747-6671)
Forest Service Information Center
    PO Box l628, Juneau 99802 (☎ (907) 586-8751)
Ketchikan Area Supervisor
    Federal Building, Ketchikan 99901 (☎ (907) 225-3101)
Stikine Area Supervisor
    PO Box 309, Petersburg 99833 (☎ (907) 772-3871)

The Chugach National Forest in Southcentral has 39 cabins, including seven along the Resurrection Trail and three on the Russian Lakes Trail. There are also a couple of cabins in the Cordova area that can be reached by foot, but the rest are accessible only by air or boat. For a complete list of cabins and bookings in the Chugach National Forest, write to the following USFS district offices in Alaska:

Anchorage Ranger District
    201 East 9th Ave, Suite 206, Anchorage 99501 (☎ (907) 271-2500)
Cordova Ranger District
    PO Box 280, Cordova 99574 (☎ (907) 424-7661)
Seward Ranger District
    PO Box 390, Seward 99664 (☎ (907) 224-3374)

Hostels

The once-struggling Alaska Council of International Hostelling is now a lot more stable and most of its 12 hostels scattered around the state have been in operation for years at the same location. The mainstays of the system are the hostels in Anchorage, Juneau, Ketchikan, Sitka, Haines, Delta Junction and Tok. The first hostel you check into is the best source of information on which youth hostels are open and which need reservations in advance.

Perhaps the most important hostel for many budget travelers is the Anchorage International Hostel, which recently moved closer to the city center and the bus terminal.

Hostel fees range from $5 to $12 for a one-night stay, more if you are a nonmember. For more information on Alaska's youth hostels, write to or call the Alaska Council of International Hostelling (☎ (907) 276-3635 or 276-7772 for a machine message), 700 H St, Anchorage, AK 99501.

Long overdue, Alaska is finally getting some offbeat hostels that offer cheap bunkroom accommodations but without all the rules and regulations of an official youth hostel. Check them out in Anchorage, Fairbanks and Homer. More are sure to spring up in the near future.

B&Bs

It is now possible to stay in a B&B from Ketchikan to Anchorage, Cordova, Fairbanks, and all the way to Nome and Bethel. What was once a handful of private homes catering to travelers in the early 1980s is now a network of hundreds. One B&B owner estimated there are now more than 1000

B&Bs in Alaska with several hundred in Anchorage alone.

B&Bs can be an acceptable compromise between sleeping on the ground and high-priced motels and lodges. Some B&Bs are bargains and most have rates below that of major hotels. Still, they are not cheap and you should plan on spending anywhere from $50 to $100 per couple per night for a room.

All recommend reservations in advance but it is often possible, in cities like Anchorage, Juneau and Fairbanks where there are many B&Bs, to obtain a bed the day you arrive by calling around. Many visitors' centers now have sections devoted entirely to the B&Bs in their area and even courtesy phones to book a room. For more information before your trip or to make reservations, contact the following statewide B&B associations in Alaska:

Southeast Alaska
  Alaska Bed & Breakfast Association, PO Box 21890, Juneau 99802 (☎ (907) 586-2959)
Statewide
  Alaska Private Lodging, 4631 Caravelle Drive, Anchorage 99520 (☎ (907) 248-2292). Send $3 for a descriptive directory.
Stay with a Friend, 3605 Arctic Blvd, Suite 173, Anchorage 99503 (☎ (907) 278-8800). Send a SASE (self-addressed stamped envelope) for a brochure or $2 for a descriptive directory.
Accommodations in Alaska, PO Box 110624, Anchorage 99511 (☎ (907) 345-4279/4761). Send a large SASE for a brochure.
Kenai Peninsula
  Accommodations on the Kenai, PO Box 2956, Soldotna 99669 (☎ (907) 262-2139)
Fairbanks
  Fairbanks Bed & Breakfast, PO Box 74573, Fairbanks 99707 (☎ (907) 452-4967)
Kodiak
  Kodiak Bed & Breakfast Service, 308 Cope St, Kodiak 99615 (☎ (907) 486-5367)

Hotels & Motels

Hotels and motels are the most expensive lodging you can book. Although there are a few bargains, the average single room in an 'inexpensive' hotel costs from $40 to $50 and a double costs from $50 to $60; these are the places down by the waterfront with shared bathrooms. Better hotels in each town will be even more costly, with Anchorage's best places charging close to $150 per night.

The other problem with hotels and motels is that they tend to be full during much of the summer. Without being part of a tour or having advanced reservations, you may have to search for an available bed in some cities. In small villages, you could be out of luck as they may only have one or two places to choose from.

FOOD

You'll be able to stock up for your next trek from supermarkets in every major town. Occasionally fresh fruits, vegetables and dairy products might be limited or simply unavailable but there will always be a good stock of dried and canned food. Rice and noodle dinners that need only be boiled in water for 10 minutes or less, instant oatmeal and Cup-A-Soups are popular items, as are freeze-dried coffee, instant milk, non-dairy creamer, instant pudding and small tins of chicken and tuna fish.

You can create quick lunches from cheeses, meat spreads in a can, crackers, a variety of dried fruits (raisins, peaches, apricots) and trail mix (nuts, raisins, M&Ms – commonly called gorp). Also pack a good supply of Kool-Aid with Nutrasweet. The thin packets of powdered drink mix take up little space and each makes two quarts of flavored drink.

In the cities and major towns, you'll find the usual fast-food chains that have invaded the rest of the country. You can now order a Big Mac in Ketchikan, Juneau, Kodiak, Homer and Eagle River as well as in Anchorage and Fairbanks. Other chains such as Pizza Hut, Burger King, Wendy's and Taco Bell are almost as widespread. Prices in fast-food chains reflect the high cost of living in Alaska – a Big Mac will cost you between $2.25 and $2.50, a hamburger 89c and small french fries 95c.

Much of the state, however, is safe from the fast-food invasion and the smaller towns you pass through will offer only a local coffee shop or café. Breakfast, which many places serve all day, is the best bargain: a plate of eggs, toast and hash browns will cost $4 to $6 while a cup of coffee will cost from 75c to $1.

An influx of Orientals immigrating to Alaska has resulted in most mid-size towns having at least one Chinese restaurant if not two. All of these places have a lunch buffet that runs from 11 am to 3 pm or so and is an all-you-can-eat affair that costs from $5 to $7. Eat a late lunch in one of these places and you can make it to breakfast the next morning.

DRINKS
Alcohol
The legal drinking age in Alaska is 21 years, and only the churches outnumber the bars. Except for 70 native Alaskan towns like Bethel or Angoon, where alcohol is prohibited, it is never very difficult to find an open bar or liquor store. That and the long, dark winters explains why Alaska has the highest alcoholism rate per capita in the USA, especially among the indigenous people. Bar hours vary but there are always a few places that open their doors at 9 am and don't close until 5 am. All serve the usual US beer found in the Northwest (Miller, Rainier, Olympia) and usually one or two places have that fine Canadian brew, charging around $3 for a 12 ounce bottle. There is also Alaska Ambler from a Juneau brewer that is now seen all over the state. It's good, but one of the most expensive beers available.

If you like to end your long day of trekking with a glass of wine on a mountain ridge, keep in mind the 'wine-in-a-box' that most liquor stores sell in Alaska. A three-quart box is not bulky to carry, especially when you discard the cardboard box it's sold in. What you're left with is a handy plastic sack that easily fits in whatever space is left in your pack. After the wine is gone, the sack makes a great water bottle.

Getting There & Away

If you are coming from the US mainland, there are three ways of getting to Alaska: by the Alcan (also known as the Alaska Hwy), the Inside Passage waterway, or flying in from a number of cities. If you are coming from Asia or Europe, it is no longer as easy to fly direct to Anchorage, via the polar route. Many international airlines, British Airways and Japan Air Lines to name but two, have dropped their service to Anchorage in recent years. Now most international travelers come through a variety of gateway cities including Seattle, Los Angeles, Detroit and Vancouver to pick up a second flight to Anchorage.

AIR

The quickest and easiest way to reach Alaska is to fly there. Depending what your time is worth, flying to Alaska is not nearly as expensive as it was 10 to 15 years ago in comparison to taking the state ferry or driving. A number of major US domestic carriers and international airlines offer regular service to Alaska, primarily to Anchorage International Airport. A result of the deregulation of the US airline industry, fares tend to fluctuate wildly due to airline ticket wars and travel promotions. What is listed below are sample fares but it is well worth the effort to check out all possibilities before purchasing a ticket.

Tickets generally fall into two basic types: regular fares, which no budget traveler would ever be caught purchasing; and Advance Purchase Excursion (Apex) or 'Supersavers' (as they are known domestically) that require round-trip tickets to be booked 14 to 30 days in advance and have a maximum number of days you can stay. The US domestic airlines also offer a special price to passengers traveling on Tuesdays and Wednesdays – off-peak days for the airline industry – and many have off-season rates for those who travel between December and May. But in the end, if you want to fly

to Alaska during its peak season, plan on booking that ticket as far in advance as possible. Often by May and June the discount fares are long gone and some flights are booked solid.

Anchorage International Airport

The vast majority of visitors to Alaska fly into Anchorage International Airport. International flights arrive at the North Terminal, domestic ones at the South Terminal and there is a complimentary shuttle service between the two terminals and all the various parking lots. The People Mover bus departs from the South Terminal for downtown Anchorage and most of the rental car companies also have rental counters here. You'll find taxis at both of them.

The airport has the usual services of any major center, including gift shops, restaurants, bars, banks of pay phones, ATMs (automatic teller machines), currency exchange, and baggage storage at $3 a day per bag (South Terminal, ground level; ☎ (907) 248-0373).

The following airlines have scheduled services into and out of Anchorage. The numbers are either local Anchorage numbers or toll-free numbers good for anywhere in the USA.

Aeroflot	☎ 248-8400
Alaska Airlines	☎ (800) 426-0333
China Airlines	☎ 248-3603
Continental	☎ (800) 525-0280
Delta Airlines	☎ (800) 221-1212
ERA Aviation	☎ (800) 426-0333
Hawaiian Airlines	☎ (800) 367-5320
Korean Air	☎ 243-3329
MarkAir	☎ (800) 478-0800
Morris Air	☎ (800) 444-5660
Northwest Air	☎ (800) 225-2525
PenAir	☎ (800) 448-4226
Reeve Aleutian Airways	☎ 243-4700
United Airlines	☎ (800) 241-6522

To/From the USA

Domestic airfares are constantly moving up

and down and will vary greatly with the season, the days you want to travel, the length of your stay and how rigid the ticket is in terms of changes and refunds. Each airline has its own requirements and restrictions that come with discount tickets and these should be examined carefully, especially terms regarding the length of stay. Many tickets allow you to stay in Alaska from three months up to a year. Some allow a stay of 21 days or less which makes it challenging when you're planning a pair of week-long treks into the Alaska wilderness.

Occasionally you can pick up a round-trip ticket from the US Midwest or East Coast to Anchorage for under $500. But most of these 'economy fares' either have tight restrictions, are for off-season travel or have such a limited number of seats available that it's a minor miracle when you reserve one. In the end, the summer travel season in Alaska is short and demand for seats on the plane is high. This is when the airlines must make their profit and they can't do that by offering economy fares during July.

Seattle (Washington) is the traditional departure point within the USA for air travel to Alaska, but now you can book a nonstop flight to Anchorage from a number of cities including San Francisco, Salt Lake City, Detroit, Minneapolis, Portland, and Honolulu. Northwest flies round-trip nonstop between Minneapolis and Anchorage for $641 on an advance purchased ticket and $725 for a similar ticket from Detroit. The airline also has a one-stop flight out of Chicago for $640. All flights must be booked 14 days in advance and you have to stay at least one Saturday. Delta Airlines flies from Salt Lake City to Anchorage for a round-trip fare of $672 with identical requirements. Hawaiian Airlines has a nonstop flight from Honolulu on Friday for $549 round trip to Anchorage.

United Airlines also has a daily, one-stop flight but with no change of planes from Chicago to Anchorage for $650 and San Francisco to Anchorage for $593 if booked 14 days in advance. Continental offers the same service, one-stop flight from Houston to Anchorage for $1114; only $750 for a connecting flight where you change planes. On either one you must return within 30 days. Delta offers a connecting service on a 14-day advance ticket from Dallas for $704 round trip and New York City for $725 with both planes stopping in Salt Lake City. Other cities with one-stop, no-change-of-plane flights include Los Angeles, San Jose and Oakland (Alaska Airlines), Memphis (Northwest), Cincinnati (Delta), Washington DC and Philadelphia (United Airlines).

Flights that change planes in Seattle are offered from an even greater number of cities, including Boise, Atlanta, Denver, Los Angeles, Las Vegas, New Orleans, New York, Oakland, Sacramento, Reno, Boston, San Diego, Houston, Dallas and Chicago to name a few.

Alaska Airlines is by far the largest carrier of travelers to Anchorage with 12 daily flights from Seattle compared with three by United, two by Delta, two by Northwest, four by MarkAir and one by Continental. During the off and shoulder season (May and September) Alaska Airlines has non-refundable return fares from Seattle to Anchorage for as low as $393. The only requirement is that you book 14 days in advance, stay over at least one Saturday and return within a year. Similar return fares between Seattle and Juneau are $365 and between Seattle and Fairbanks $418. Keep in mind these are the lowest fares the airlines offer and the number of tickets is limited.

The US domestic airlines can be contacted on the following toll-free numbers for information on fares and schedules:

Alaska Airlines	☎ (800) 426-0333
Continental	☎ (800) 525-0280
Delta Airlines	☎ (800) 221-1212
Hawaiian Airlines	☎ (800) 367-5320
Northwest Airlines	☎ (800) 225-2525
United Airlines	☎ (800) 241-6522

To/From Canada

Canadian Airlines does not service Alaska but will fly you to Seattle where you can pick up a domestic US carrier for the second leg of your journey. A round-trip fare from Toronto to Seattle, for a ticket purchased 14 days in advance, is C$580.

The airline also has three flights a day during the summer from Vancouver to Whitehorse where you could then pick up a connecting flight on Air North to Juneau. A round-trip, advance purchase ticket from Vancouver to Juneau is C$572. You can contact Canadian Airlines toll free at ☎ (800) 663-0010 from British Columbia; ☎ (416) 798-2211 from Toronto; ☎ (800) 263-6133 from anywhere else in Ontario; and ☎ (800) 426-7000 in the USA.

Air North also has flights that connect Whitehorse with Fairbanks. A round-trip ticket purchased seven days in advance is C$410 while the airlines' Klondike Explorer Pass is C$550. This allows unlimited air travel for 21 days between the five cities it serves: Juneau, Whitehorse, Dawson City, Old Crow and Fairbanks. In Alaska, call Air North at ☎ (800) 764-0407; in northern British Columbia and Yukon Territories call ☎ (800) 661-0407 and elsewhere in Canada call ☎ (403) 668-2228.

To/From the UK

British Airways no longer flies into Anchorage. The airline does have nonstop flights from Heathrow to Seattle where you can pick up a domestic carrier to continue north. Delta Airlines also has a London-to-Anchorage flight that begins at Gatwick Airport and changes planes in Cincinnati. A round-trip Apex fare is £349. Northwest (Gatwick), Continental and United Airlines (Heathrow) offer similar flights.

To/From Europe

The most common route to Anchorage from Europe is to head west with a stop in New York and then Seattle. From Paris, Continental offers a daily flight to Anchorage that changes planes in Houston and then makes an additional stop before reaching Alaska. A round-trip fare, no advance purchase and fully refundable, is $2755. Northwest also has a daily Paris-to-Anchorage flight, that changes planes in Detroit (don't worry, the

airport is 15 miles from the city). A round-trip fare is $1384 but the ticket must be booked seven days in advance and the maximum stay in Alaska would be 30 days. You also have to travel on a week day.

Similar flights can also be arranged from Frankfurt through Delta, Northwest and United Airlines. Northwest charges $1493 for a round trip with a 21-day advance purchase ticket but allows you to stay up to three months. Travel must take place on a week day. Delta is $1484 for midweek travel, $1541 on the weekends.

To/From Asia

There are four daily flights and a variety of others from Tokyo to Anchorage. None are direct, nonstop flights but several fly into Seattle or Los Angeles and then on to Alaska. Keep in mind the fares with US-based airlines like Northwest and Delta fluctuate wildly with the rise and fall of the dollar against the yen.

Northwest flies into Seattle and onto Anchorage daily. They require you to purchase the ticket only three days in advance. Round-trip fare is A$1285. Delta offers a daily flight that changes at Salt Lake City.

Japan Air Lines (JAL) has discontinued its service to Anchorage and Seattle. On JAL the best you can do is fly to San Francisco and then pick up an Alaska Airlines flight to Anchorage.

There is also a daily service from Seoul to Anchorage which is far cheaper than departing from Tokyo. Northwest is the cheapest carrier at $1220 for a seven-day advance purchase ticket. United Airlines offers a daily flight with a change of planes at San Francisco. Or you can fly nonstop four days a week with Korean Air. Their round-trip fare is $1370 and requires only a two-day advance purchase.

There is also a nonstop service between Taipei, Taiwan and Anchorage with China Air, and a daily service with United Airlines with a change of planes in San Francisco.

To/From Australia & NZ

In Australia, STA Travel and Flight Centres are major dealers in cheap airfares. They have branches in all major cities. Otherwise, check the travel agents' ads in the Yellow Pages and ring around. Qantas Airways has flights from Sydney to Los Angeles with connections on Alaska Airlines to Anchorage. Several round-trip (excursion) fares are available. A return 21-day advance purchase ticket will cost from A$2572 return during most of the Alaskan summer (June through September) and is good for a stay of up to 60 days. The US government tax on the ticket is an additional A$32.60.

Most flights between the USA and New Zealand are to/from the USA's west coast. Most go through Los Angeles but some also arrive and depart from San Francisco. With Air New Zealand, you can arrange a 14-day advance purchase ticket from Auckland to Los Angeles with a connecting flight on either Alaska Airlines or Delta Airlines to Anchorage. The round-trip fare is NZ$2750 (US government taxes are usually incorporated in this price); maximum stay is 60 days.

OVERLAND – THE ALCAN

What began in April 1942 as an unprecedented construction project during the heat of WW II ended eight months later as the first overland link between the Lower 48 and Alaska, known formally as the Alaska-Canada Military Hwy and affectionately as the Alcan. Today, the Alcan (also known as the Alaska Hwy) is a road through the vast wilderness of north-west Canada and Alaska. It offers a spectacular drive. Each summer thousands of travelers enjoy taking their time to soak up the scenery, wildlife and the clear, cold streams along the way.

For those with the time, driving the Alaska Hwy is a unique way to travel north. The trip is an adventure in itself; the 1520-mile road is a legend among highways and completing the journey puts a feather in any traveler's cap. *Mile 0* of the Alcan is at Dawson Creek in British Columbia, while the other end is at Fairbanks (although residents of Delta Junction will debate that).

The Alcan is now entirely asphalt-paved, and although sections of jarring potholes, frost heaves (the rippling effect of the pavement caused by freezing and thawing) and loose gravel still prevail, they are nothing like the rough conditions it was famous for 10 to 15 years ago. The era of lashing spare fuel cans to the side of the car and gasoline stations every 250 miles are also gone. Food, gas and lodging can be found every 20 to 50 miles along the highway, with 100 miles being the longest stretch between fuel stops.

There are several ways to get to the Alcan: you can begin in the US states of Washington, Idaho or Montana and pass through Edmonton or Jasper in Alberta or Prince George in British Columbia, Canada. There are also several ways of traveling the highway: bus, car or a combination of State Marine Ferry and bus.

Bus

A combination of buses will take you from Seattle via the Alcan to Anchorage, Fairbanks, Skagway or Haines for a moderate cost. There are no direct bus services from the Lower 48 to Alaska; travelers have to be patient as services are more limited than those in the rest of the country. But by using buses, the cost of reaching Alaska is cheap compared to flying or taking the State Marine Ferry.

Greyhound The closest you can get to Alaska on this giant of bus companies is Whitehorse in British Columbia and this involves purchasing two tickets. You begin at the Greyhound station in the center of Seattle on the corner of 8th Ave and Stewart St where you can buy a one-way ticket to Vancouver for $22. The bus departs at least three times a day, more often if the demand is high during the summer. Call the station (☎ (206) 628-5530) to double-check exact departure days and times or the Greyhound information line (☎ (800) 231-2222). You switch to a Greyhound Lines of Canada bus at the Pacific Central Station on Main St in Vancouver, and continue your journey north with two-hour layovers at Prince George and Dawson Creek in British Columbia. The bus departs at 8 am on Monday, Wednesday and Friday and arrives in Whitehorse at 5.15 am,

48 hours later. It's hard to go any cheaper – a one-way fare from Vancouver to the Yukon capital is only C$290.

When planning your trip, keep in mind that most Greyhound special offers, such as Ameripass (unlimited travel for seven days), do not apply to Yukon or Alaska destinations. There is also a more pleasant way to reach Alaska than spending two days on a Greyhound bus. Once in Vancouver, you can also pick up a ticket to Prince Rupert, where you can then hop on the delightful Alaska state ferries. There are two buses a day, at 8 am and 8.45 pm, and they arrive in Prince Rupert 25 hours later (though the 8 pm bus is quicker due to a shorter layover in Prince George). A one-way fare is C$162. Call Greyhound of Canada (☎ (604) 662-3222) for more information.

Alaskon Express Once you've reached Whitehorse, you change to an Alaskon Express bus for the next leg of the journey. Operated by Gray Line of Alaska from May to September, you can pick up the buses either at Westmark Whitehorse, 2288 2nd Ave, or in the Greyhound Bus Terminal at the north end of 2nd Ave.

Buses depart from the Yukon capital for Anchorage on Tuesday, Wednesday, Friday and Sunday at noon, stay overnight at Beaver Creek in the Yukon and then continue to Anchorage the next day, reaching the city at 7 pm. You can also leave the bus earlier at Tok, Glennallen or Palmer. On Monday, Tuesday, Thursday and Saturday buses depart from Whitehorse at noon for Haines, reaching the Southeast Alaska town and ferry terminal port at 6.30 pm.

As testimony to the popularity of the Chilkoot Trail, an Alaskon Express bus departs daily from Whitehorse at 4.30 pm for Skagway, stopping along the way to pick up backpackers coming off the popular trek and reaching the Alaskan town two hours later.

You can also go overland to Fairbanks, something that was hard to do in the past. An Alaskon Express bus departs at noon on Tuesday, Wednesday, Friday and Sunday for Fairbanks with a stopover in Beaver Creek.

A nice thing about these buses is that you can flag them down along the road or in a small town, which is good if you have been sitting around for most of the morning trying to thumb a ride out of a town like Haines Junction. Can you imagine doing that to a Greyhound bus in the Lower 48?

The one-way fare from Whitehorse to Anchorage is $179, to Fairbanks $149, Haines $76 and to Skagway $52. Keep in mind that these fares do not include lodging at Beaver Creek. In Whitehorse, call ☎ (403) 667-2223 for current bus information. If you are still planning your trip, call Gray Line of Alaska (☎ (800) 544-2206 toll free); by January each year they can provide schedules, departure times and rates for the following summer.

Alaska Direct Busline Much smaller and slightly cheaper than Gray Line's Alaskon Express is this bus company based out of Anchorage. On Tuesday, Friday and Sunday an Alaska Direct bus departs from Whitehorse at 7 am, reaching Tok around 3 pm where you can continue on to Fairbanks or transfer to a bus for Anchorage.

The one-way fare from Whitehorse to Tok is $80, to Fairbanks $120 and to Anchorage, $145. In Alaska or the USA call Alaska Direct at ☎ (800) 770-6652; in Whitehorse call ☎ (403) 668-4833. It is very important to make sure you call to find out what hotel the pick-up point is at that summer or if the company is even still in business.

AlaskaPass

A scheme which has been hugely popular in Europe for years arrived in the North Country in 1989 when a small company in Haines (of all places) organized nine major carriers and offered an unlimited travel pass. AlaskaPass Inc, now with headquarters in Seattle, has put together the only all-inclusive ground transportation pass that will get you from Washington through Canada into Alaska and even as far north as Dawson City in the Yukon, for a set price.

You purchase your pass, choosing the number of days you want to travel, then armed with the schedules of various carriers, make your own reservations or arrangements. The carriers include Alaska State Marine Ferry, Greyhound of Canada, Island Coach Lines, British Columbia Rail and British Columbia Ferries to move you from Bellingham or Vancouver north. You can continue on Alaskon Express, Gray Line of Alaska, Norline Coaches or the Alaska Railroad to reach Alaska and travel around the state. Each time you pick up a ticket you just flip them your AlaskaPass.

On the plus side, you can save money with such a pass. On the down side you have to plan carefully to do so and the pass does not include any air travel. The passes are offered for either continuous travel or flexible travel which allows travel on a number of days during a time period. Overall, however, if you're planning to do two or three extensive treks in Alaska, this might not be such a bargain because of the time restrictions.

The best choice for trekkers is the 12/21-day pass (travel for 12 out of 21 days) for $649 or the 21/45 for $929. There are discounts for children, aged between three and 11 years, and for an off-season pass for travel from October through April. You can purchase a pass in advance from most travel agencies or directly from the company by calling ☎ (800) 248-7598 in Canada or the USA, and ☎ (0800) 89-82-85 from the UK.

Driving

Without a doubt, driving your own car to Alaska allows you the most freedom. You can leave when you want, stop where you feel like it and reach those remote trailheads without having to hitch a ride the final 12 miles. It's not exactly cheap driving to Alaska, and that's not even considering the wear and tear and thousands of miles you'll clock up on your vehicle. The final bill will depend on where you're coming from, where you stay at night (campground, cabins or a lodge) and what you eat (food prepared by yourself or from cafés along the way).

If you're contemplating this car trip, remember that the condition of your tyres is most important. The Alcan may be paved but it's constantly under repair and stretches of frost heaves and potholes are common, especially on the Canadian side; worn tyres don't last long here. Even your spare, and you *must* have one, should be fairly new. You should also avoid the newer 'space-saver' spares, and carry a full-size spare as your extra tyre.

Windshield wipers are another important item. Replace them before you depart and carry an extra set along with a gallon of solvent for the windshield-washer reservoir. Dust, dirt and mud make good visibility a constant battle while driving. Also bring a jack, wrenches and other assorted tools, spare hoses, fan belts, a quart of oil or two; even bringing an extra headlight or air filter is not being too extreme. Carry them and hope you never have to use them.

Some travelers use an insect screen, others put plastic headlight covers or a wire-mesh screen over the headlights, or place a rubber mat or piece of carpet between the gas tank and securing straps. All this is to protect the vehicle from the worse danger on the road – flying rocks that are kicked up by passing truck-and-trailer rigs.

By far the worst problem on the Alcan and many other roads in Alaska and the Yukon is dust; that's why even on the hottest days, you see most cars with their windows up. To control dust in a RV or trailer, reverse the roof vent on your rig so it faces forward. Then keep it open a few inches while driving, creating air pressure inside to combat the incoming dust.

Those traveling the route in small or compact vehicles often face another common problem – the biggest single cause of flat tyres and broken suspension systems along the Alcan is an overloaded car.

Since almost 80% of the Alcan is in Canada, it's best to brush up on the metric system (either that or have a conversion chart taped to the dashboard). On the Canada side you'll find kilometer posts (as opposed to mileposts found in Alaska) are placed every five km with the zero point in Dawson Creek, of course.

With more than 1000 vehicles passing through this town en route to Alaska daily during the summer, it's the one place where you might want to book a room or a campsite in advance. From there you'll find traffic and travelers more spread out the further north you go. Most Alcan veterans say 300 miles a day is a good pace – one that will allow for plenty of stops to check out scenery or wildlife.

The best stretch? That's tough but some will argue it's the 330 miles from Fort Nelson, British Columbia, to Watson Lake, Yukon. This is the day you cross the Rockies and along with the hairpin turns and granite peaks, you'll enjoy panoramas of the mountains, rest areas overlooking Summit Lake and a good chance of spotting wildlife, especially if you leave early in the morning.

It's always good to have Canadian currency on hand to purchase gasoline and not depend on the small stations along the way to cash your travelers' cheques for you. One or two of the major gasoline credit cards can come in handy, especially if you have a major breakdown.

Tourism Yukon operates a number of visitor reception centers that provide a wealth of information and maps for drivers. The ones along the Alcan are:

Watson Lake
    Alaska Hwy Interpretive Center, junction of the Alcan and Campbell St (☎ (403) 536-7469)
Whitehorse
    Visitor Center, near *Milepost 886*, adjacent to the Transportation Museum (☎ (403) 667-2915)
Haines Junction
    Visitor Center, shares space with Kluane National Park Headquarters (☎ (403) 634-2345)
Beaver Creek
    Visitor Center, *Mile 1202* of the Alcan in the heart of Beaver Creek (☎ (403) 862-7321)

SEA
The Inside Passage
Leaving Bellingham As an alternative to the Alcan or to avoid doubling back on the highway, you can travel the Southeast's Inside Passage, a waterway made up of thousands of islands, fjords and mountainous coastlines. To many people, the Southeast is the most beautiful area in the state and the

Alaska Marine ferries are the country's best public transport bargain.

The large 'blue canoes' of the State Marine Highway are equipped with observation decks, food services, bars, lounges and solariums with deck chairs. You can rent a stateroom for overnight trips but most trekkers head straight for the solarium and sleep in one of the deck chairs or on the floor with a sleeping pad. On long-distance hauls from Bellingham, travelers even pitch their dome tents.

With its leisurely pace, travel on the marine ferries is a delightful experience. The midnight sun is warm and apart from the scenery, the possibility of sighting whales, bald eagles or sea lions keeps most travelers at the side of the ship. This is also an excellent way to meet other independent travelers heading for a summer in the north country.

A big change in the state ferry system occurred in 1990 when Bellingham replaced Seattle as the new southern terminus of the Alaska Marine Hwy. The new terminus includes an information center, ticket office, luggage lockers and an outdoor seating area with a nice view of Bellingham Bay and the surrounding hills. It's 10 minutes north of the Bellingham International Airport in the historic Fairhaven shopping district, 87 miles north of Seattle. From the Interstate 5 Hwy, you depart west on Fairhaven Parkway (exit 250) for 1.1 miles and then turn right onto 12th St where signs will direct you to the terminus at the end of Harris Ave.

The ferries are extremely popular during the peak season from June to August. Reservations are needed for cabin or vehicle space and for walk-on passengers departing from Bellingham. Space for summer sailings from Bellingham is often filled by April, forcing walk-on passengers to wait stand-by for an available spot.

If you plan to depart from Bellingham in June or July, it is best to make reservations. The state ferry's reservation office will take written requests anytime and telephone requests from the first working day of January for summer sailings. As telephone lines are jammed most of the time after the first day of the year, it is wise to send in a written request as soon as you decide your itinerary.

The summer sailing schedule comes out in December and you can obtain one by contacting the Alaska Marine Highway (☎ (907) 465-3941), PO Box R, Juneau, AK 99811. There is now a toll-free telephone number (☎ (800) 642-0066 from the Lower 48) to handle schedule requests and reservations but you'll often find it nonstop busy, forcing you to pay for the call anyway.

The ferries to Alaska stop first at Prince Rupert in British Columbia, and then continue onto Ketchikan in Alaska. Most ferries then depart for Wrangell, Petersburg, Sitka, Juneau, Haines and Skagway before heading back south. A trip from Bellingham to Juneau takes 2½ to four days depending on the route. Most ferry terminals are a few miles out of town and the short in-port time doesn't allow passengers to view the area without making it a stopover.

If you intend to use the ferries to go trekking in the Southeast, obtain a current schedule and keep it handy at all times. State ferries stop almost every day at larger centers like Juneau, but the smaller villages may only have one ferry every three or four days and many places won't have a service at all.

There are six ships working Southeast Alaska; four of them are larger vessels that sail the entire route from Bellingham to Skagway. The *Columbia*, *Malaspina*, *Matanuska* and *Taku* all have cabins, lounges, eating facilities and public showers for both walk-on passengers and cabin renters.

The other two ships are smaller, do not have cabins, and serve out-of-the-way villages from Juneau or Ketchikan. In the summer, the *Aurora* sails between Ketchikan, Metlakatla, Hollis, Hyder and Prince Rupert. The *Le Conte* stops at Juneau, Hoonah, Angoon, Sitka, Kake, Tenakee Springs, Skagway, Haines and Petersburg, and makes a special run to Pelican once a month. The *Chilkat*, the original ship of the fleet, is no longer in service during the summer and only operates in the winter when another vessel is in dry dock.

It's important when you book a passage on the state ferry that you have an idea of what ports you want to visit along the route. Stopovers are free but you must arrange them, with exact dates, when you make the reservation or purchase the ticket. By doing so, a Billingham-to-Haines ticket would then allow you to leave the boat at a handful of cities, including Ketchikan, Petersburg and Juneau, at no additional cost. Once on the boat, you can still arrange a stopover but will be charged an additional fee.

If you plan to spend a good deal of time or the entire summer in the region, purchase a ticket to Juneau and then use that as your base, taking shorter trips to other towns on the *Le Conte*. The fare for walk-on passengers from Bellingham to Haines is $230, while the ticket from Bellingham to Juneau is $216.

One way to save money is to take a bus or hitchhike to Prince Rupert in British Columbia where the dramatic mountain scenery begins, and hop on the ferry from there. The fare from Prince Rupert to Haines is $112 and to Juneau $98. Fares for travel within the Southeast include Ketchikan to Juneau $72, Petersburg to Juneau $42, Juneau to Haines $18, Haines to Skagway $12 and Juneau to Angoon $22.

The *Alaska Marine Highway Schedule* is now a magazine with not only departure times and fares but also ads, blurbs on each port and a section titled 'What to Expect on Board'. Here are a few tips they don't tell you: when boarding in Bellingham, it is best to scramble to the solarium and either stake out a lounge chair or at least an area on the floor. The solarium and observation deck are the best places to sleep as the air is clean and the night-time peace is unbroken. The other place to crash out is the indoor lounges, which can be smoky, noisy or both.

Backpackers are still allowed to pitch free-standing tents outside the solarium and the ferry staff have even designated the correct area for this. Bring duck tape to attach the tent to the floor but remember that during the busy summer months tents tend to take up more space than two people really need in an already popular and crowded section of the ship.

Food on board is reasonable compared to what you will pay on shore, with breakfast and lunches costing around $6 and dinner $10. Still it's cheaper to bring your own grub and eat it in the solarium or the cafeteria. Some backpackers bring their own tea bags, coffee or Cup-a-Soup and then just purchase the cup of hot water. The pursers, however, do not allow any camp stoves to be used on board and are very strict about enforcing this. Bringing your own liquor is also prohibited as there is a bar aboard the larger ships, but I have yet to see a cruise where a happy traveler isn't handing out beers from an ice-chest in the solarium.

The only thing cheaper than the food on board are the showers. They're free on all ferries except the MV *Tustumena* and then it's only 25c for 10 minutes. It's the best bargain you'll find in Alaska.

There is a tariff for carrying on bicycles or kayaks, but compared to the cost of bringing a car or motorcycle it is very reasonable. It's only $37 to take what ferry officials call an 'alternative means of conveyance' from Bellingham to Haines. A bicycle can be a handy way to reach many of the trailheads that lie outside of town in the Southeast.

When using the Alaska Marine Ferry system, check and double-check the departures of ferries once you have arrived in the Southeast. It is worth a phone call to the terminus to find out the actual arrival and departure times; the state ferries are notorious for being late or breaking down and having their departures cancelled. It's something that happens every summer without fail.

Leaving Prince Rupert If the Alaska State ferries are full in Bellingham, one alternative is to begin your cruise in Seattle, utilizing two ferry systems before switching to the Alaska line in Prince Rupert.

From Pier 69 in the heart of Seattle off Alaskan Way, catch the *Victoria Clipper* to Victoria on Vancouver Island. During the summer, boats depart four times daily at 7.50 am, 8.40 am, 9.30 am and 2.30 pm for a trip that takes a 2½ to 3 hours. A one-way fare for walk-on passengers is $52. For pretrip planning or reservations call ☎ (800) 888-2535 if you are in the USA.

Once you land on Vancouver Island, head north to Port Hardy and catch the British Columbia ferry to Prince Rupert. From this Canadian city, there is a much better chance to board the Alaska Marine Ferry because there are five vessels that connect Prince Rupert to Southeast Alaska. Port Hardy can be reached by bus from Victoria on Island Coast Lines (☎ (604) 385-4411), which leaves once a day at 6.20 am, C$74 one way. The bus depot is at 700 Douglas St, behind the Empress Hotel in the center of Victoria.

At Port Hardy, the BC ferries dock at Bear Cove, about five miles from town but there is a shuttle van service from the Island Coach Line bus terminal on Main St. At Bear Cove the *Queen of the North* sails to Prince Rupert one day and returns to Vancouver Island the next, maintaining this every-other-day schedule from June to the end of September. The trip is scenic and the daylight voyage takes 15 hours; the one-way fare for walk-on passengers is C$93. The same ship also makes a stop once a week at the isolated town of Bella Bella in British Columbia.

More information and complete schedules for the BC ferries can be obtained by calling or writing to BC Ferries (☎ (604) 386-3431), 1112 Fort St, Victoria, BC, Canada V8V 4V2. In Vancouver call ☎ (604) 669-1211 and in Seattle call ☎ (206) 441-6865 for ferry information and reservations.

From Hyder, Alaska Finally, if for some strange reason you can't catch an Alaska State Ferry at Prince Rupert, there's one last alternative to waiting. Make your way east along the Yellowhead Hwy from Prince Rupert and then head north along the Cassiar Hwy. Hitching is about the only way to travel this route if you don't have a vehicle as there is no bus service. You travel 99 miles along the scenic Cassiar Hwy and then turn off at

Meziadin Lake for Stewart. Right across the border from the British Columbia town is Hyder, a Southeast Alaska hamlet of about 100 people with a few cafés, bars and gift shops.

During the summer, the Alaska State Ferry *Aurora* usually departs from here every Friday at 2 pm for Ketchikan, where you can continue north on one of several other boats. The one-way fare from Hyder to Ketchikan is $36.

Note It is important to double check the departure time for the Hyder ferry as it may leave on Pacific Time as opposed to Alaska Time.

ORGANIZED TOURS

The land of the midnight sun is also the land of the package tour. Every cruise-ship line and sightseeing company loves Alaska and the draw it has on travelers, especially older tourists with lots of disposable income and a low sense of adventure.

Many outfitters and companies organize wilderness trips, which include trekking, sea kayaking, rafting or canoeing. Most of them are based in Alaska (see Tours in the Getting Around chapter) but a few are located in other states.

National Outdoor Leadership School (NOLS) teaches low-impact camping, survival techniques and environmental awareness through a wide range of activities, including backpacking, sea kayaking and rafting. They sponsor trips that range from two weeks to a month in Chugach, Brooks and Alaska ranges as well as the Denali area and Prince William Sound. Their month-long backpacking and rafting trip in the Brooks Range costs $4400 (not including transport to Alaska). Contact NOLS (☎ (307) 332-6973) at PO Box AA-AK, Lander, WY 82520.

North Star offers a range of sea kayaking, canoeing, trekking and base camp/hiking trips as well as natural history tours where participants stay at remote lodges. Prices range from $1400 for a week of kayaking in

Kenai Fjords National Park to more than $1650 for 10 days of backpacking in the Gates of the Arctic National Park. Transportation is not included. Contact North Star (☎ (602) 773-9917) at PO Box 1724, Flagstaff, AZ 86002.

Natural Habitat Adventures specializes in wildlife watching tours around the world and has two 13-day trips that begin in Anchorage and include Katmai and Denali National Park as well as the Kenai Fjords in Prince William Sound. You get to spot and photograph whales, bald eagles, brown bears, moose and caribou. At $3895 the price does not include the airfare to Alaska. Contact Natural Habitat Adventures (☎ (800) 543-8917), 2945 Center Green Court South, Boulder, CO 80301.

LEAVING ALASKA

There is a $10 fee for international travelers passing through customs in Anchorage from any foreign destination except Canada and Mexico. This tax is included in the price of your ticket – when you leave Alaska, there are no additional state or airport departure taxes to worry about.

WARNING

This chapter is particularly vulnerable to change – prices for international travel are volatile, routes are introduced and canceled, schedules change, rules are amended, and special deals come and go. Airlines and governments seem to take perverse pleasure in making price structures and regulations as complicated as possible and you should check directly with the airline or travel agent to make sure you understand how a fare (and ticket you may buy) works.

In addition, the travel industry is highly competitive and there are many lurks and perks. You should get opinions, quotes and advice from as many airlines and travel agents as possible before you part with you hard-earned cash. The details given in this chapter should be regarded only as pointers and cannot be any substitute for your own careful up-to-date research.

Top: Moose (JD)
Bottom Left: Dead salmon from a late summer salmon run (JD)
Middle Right: Caribou (JD)
Bottom Right: Oystercatcher (JD)

Top Left: Bald eagle (DP)
Middle Left: Brown bear (JD)
Top Right: Mountain goat (CP)
Bottom: Moose (DP)

Top: Infant dall sheep (DP)
Middle Left: Kittiwake colony (JD)
Bottom Left: Merganser (JD)
Bottom Right: Immature eagle (AD)

Top: Moose (JD)
Middle Left: Dall sheep (JD)
Bottom Left: Puffin (JD)
Bottom Right: Black bear (JD)

Getting Around

Travel around Alaska is unlike travel in any other state in the country. The fledgling public transport system has stabilized and improved remarkably in the last five years but the overwhelming distances between regions make getting around Alaska almost as hard as getting there. Any long visit to Alaska usually combines transportation by car, bus, marine ferry, train and often a bush plane for access into the wilderness. Although the roads in Alaska and the State Marine Ferry system cover only about a quarter of the state, they provide affordable access to an endless number of trails, treks and parks.

AIR
Bush Planes

When you want to see more than the roadside attractions, you go to a dirt runway or small airfield outside of town and climb into a bush plane. With 75% of the state not accessible by road, these small, single-engine planes are the backbone of intrastate transportation. They carry residents and supplies to desolate areas of the Bush, take anglers to some of the best fishing spots in the country and drop off trekkers in the middle of prime, untouched wilderness.

The person at the controls is a bush pilot, someone who might be fresh out of the air force or somebody who arrived in Alaska 'way bee-fore statehood' and learned to fly by trial and error. A ride with such a person is not only transportation to isolated areas and a scenic overview of the state but it sometimes includes an earful of flying tales – some believable, some not.

Don't be alarmed when you hear that Alaska has the highest number of airplane crashes per capita in the country – it also has the greatest percentage of pilots. One in every 58 residents has a license, and one resident in almost 60 owns a plane. That's six times more pilots and 16 times more planes per capita than any other state in the USA.

Bush pilots are safe flyers who know their territory and its weather patterns; they don't want to go down any more than you do.

A ride in a bush plane is essential if you want to go beyond the common sights and see some of Alaska's most memorable scenery. In the larger cities of Anchorage, Fairbanks, Juneau and Ketchikan it pays to check around before chartering. In most small towns and villages, you'll be lucky if there is a choice.

Bush aircraft include float planes that land and take off on water and beach-landers with oversized tyres that can use rough gravel shorelines as airstrips. Other planes are equipped with skis to land on glaciers, with sophisticated radar instruments for stormy areas like the Aleutian Islands, or boat racks to carry canoes or hard-shell kayaks.

The fares differ with the type of plane, its size, the number of passengers and the amount of flying time. On average, a Cessna 185 that can carry three passengers and a limited amount of gear will cost up to $250 to charter for an hour of flying time. A Cessna 206, a slightly larger plane that will hold four passengers, costs around $400. Keep in mind that when chartering a plane to drop you off at an isolated USFS cabin or for a wilderness trek, you must pay for both the air time to your drop-off point and for the return time to the departure point.

As a general rule, if one of the domestic carriers, Alaska Airlines or the intrastate carrier MarkAir, has a flight to your destination, it will be the cheapest way of flying there. Alaska Airlines provides the most extensive service for travel within Alaska and there is a huge difference between a one-way fare and a round-trip fare that is purchased 14 days in advance and includes staying over on a Saturday. Alaska Airlines fares for intrastate flights from Anchorage to Fairbanks cost from $87 to $135 (one way), 14-day advance round trip $230; Juneau to Anchorage one way costs from $109 to

$140, a 21-day advance round trip $280; from Juneau to Fairbanks it costs $163 (one way).

Before chartering a plane, check out all the possibilities first. Most air-taxi companies have regularly scheduled flights to small towns and villages in six to nine-seater aircraft with single-seat fares that are a fraction of the cost of chartering an entire plane. Others offer a 'mail flight' to small villages. These run on a regular basis with one or two seats available to travelers.

Even when your destination is a USFS cabin or some wilderness spot, check with the local air-taxi companies. It is common practice to match up a party departing from the cabin with another that's arriving, so that the air-charter costs can be split by filling the plane on both runs.

Air travel in small bush planes is expensive, but the more passengers, the cheaper the charter; two people chartering an entire plane, no matter what the distance, is a costly exercise.

Booking a plane is easy and can often be done the day before or at the last minute if need be. Double-check all pick-up times and places when flying to a wilderness area. Bush pilots fly over the pick-up point and if you are not there, they usually return, call the Forest Service and still charge you for the flight.

When flying in and out of bays, fjords or coastal waterways, check the tides before determining your pick-up time. It is best to schedule pick-ups and drop-offs at high tide or else you may end up trekking half a mile through mud flats.

If a pilot doesn't want to fly, don't push the subject, just reschedule your charter. The pilot is the best judge of weather patterns and can see, or sometimes feel, bad flying conditions when others can't. Always schedule extra days around a charter flight. It's not uncommon to be 'socked in' by weather for a day or two until a plane can fly in. Don't panic, they know you are there. Think of the high school basketball team in the mid-1960s which flew to King Cove in the Aleutians for a weekend game – they were 'socked in' for a month before they could fly out again.

When traveling to small Bush towns, a scheduled flight or mail run is the cheapest way to go. Don't hesitate, however, to charter a flight to some desolate wilderness spot; the best that Alaska has to offer is usually just a short flight away.

BUS

Regular bus services within Alaska are limited, but they are available between the larger towns and cities for independent travelers (as opposed to package tours) at reasonable rates. The only problem is that as one bus company goes under another appears, so the phone numbers, schedules, rates and pick-up points change drastically from one summer to the next. It pays to call ahead after arriving in Alaska to make sure that buses are still running to where you want to go.

Alaskon Express

These buses are the Gray Line motorcoaches which mainly serve travelers needing transportation along the last leg of the Alcan from Whitehorse into Haines, Skagway, Anchorage or Fairbanks (see Overland in the Getting There & Away chapter for information on the Alcan). You can also use the bus line to travel from Anchorage to Glennallen ($55), from Anchorage to Seward ($35),

Float plane

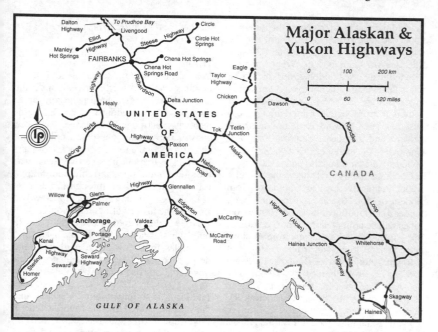

Major Alaskan & Yukon Highways

from Anchorage to Fairbanks ($109) or from Delta Junction to Fairbanks ($49).

From Haines, you can book a passage on Alaskon Express for the two-day run to Anchorage which leaves every Tuesday, Thursday and Sunday at 8.15 am, for $194. The service is offered from mid-May through mid-September and the fare does not include overnight lodging at Beaver Creek. The same is true for Skagway where there is an Alaskon Express bus departing at 7.30 am on the same days, overnighting at Beaver Creek and reaching Anchorage at 7.30 pm. The reverse routes are also possible.

Local passenger boarding points, departure times and phone numbers are given in later chapters. For information or reservations while planning your trip, contact Gray Line of Alaska toll free (☎ (800) 544-2206), 300 Elliott Ave West, Seattle, WA 98119.

Alaska Direct Bus Line

Alaska Direct offers affordable transporta-

tion from Anchorage to the rest of the state on a number of routes. On Monday, Wednesday and Saturday another bus departs Anchorage at 6 am and reaches Haines Junction at 10 pm that night. The next day the bus continues its journey at noon and reaches Haines at 4 pm. The one-way fare is $175.

A bus also departs from Fairbanks on Monday, Wednesday and Saturday at 9 am, linking up with the run to Haines. The one-way fare from Fairbanks to Tok is $40, to Haines $150.

Buses stop at the major hotels in Anchorage for passengers or you can pick them up at the company office at 125 Oklahoma at the north end of town. For more information call Alaska Direct Bus Line at ☎ (907) 277-6652 or (800) 770-6652.

Seward & Homer Bus Lines

This company provides services between Anchorage and Seward and in 1992 added a Homer bus line to its schedule. A bus leaves

Seward daily at 9 am, reaches Anchorage at noon and then departs at 2.30 pm for the return run, arriving in Seward at 5.30 pm. The one-way fare is $30. When there is demand there are additional runs, including a bus that departs Anchorage at 5 am, arriving at Seward at 7.30 am and another that departs from Seward at 7 pm. Pick up these buses at 1915 Seward Hwy just north of Seward and at Alaska Samovar Inn, 720 Gambell St in Anchorage. Call ☎ (907) 224-3608 for current schedules and rates.

Catching a bus to Homer, the popular Kenai Peninsula town and home of Tom Bodette of Motel 6 fame, used to change with the season. Hopefully Seward & Homer Bus Lines will be around until the next edition of this guidebook. A bus departs from Anchorage daily at 9.45 am and arrives in Homer at 3.40 pm. Another leaves Homer at 10.20 am and arrives in Anchorage at 4.10 pm. The one-way fare is $38, round-trip $68. In Homer, pick up the bus at Oceanview RV Park just outside of town at 455 Sterling Hwy. In Anchorage pick it up at the Alaska Samovar Inn, 720 Gambell St 720.

They'll also provide transportation to both Soldotna and Kenai for $30 one way, $54 for the round trip. This company should be around for a while but call to make sure (Anchorage ☎ (907) 278-0800; Homer ☎ (907) 235-8280).

Denali National Park Van Service

A number of small companies offer van transportation between Denali National Park and both Anchorage and Fairbanks. The companies come and go with great regularity but generally offer the cheapest transportation to the popular park and usually get you there well ahead of the train – important if you are hoping to arrange shuttle-bus rides, campground sites or trekking permits.

In Anchorage, try Moon Bay Express (☎ (907) 274-6454) which departs daily from the youth hostel at 8 am and reaches the park at 1 pm. A one-way fare is $35, round trip $60. In Fairbanks, there is Fireweed Express (☎ (907) 488-7928) which departs from the Fairbanks Visitor Center at 8 am,

reaches the park at 10.30 am and charges $25 one way.

TRAIN

In a state the size of Alaska, the logistics of building a railroad were overwhelming at the turn of the century; many private companies tried but failed, leading to federal government intervention in 1912. Three years later, construction began on a route from the tent city of Anchorage to the boom town of Fairbanks. The line cut its way over what was thought to be impenetrable mountains, across raging rivers and through a wilderness as challenging as any construction crew had faced in the history of US railroading.

No wonder it took them eight years to build the Alaska Railroad. Today, it stretches 470 miles from Seward to Fairbanks, and despite the state's heavy dependence on air travel, the railroad remains a vital artery in moving people and goods across Alaska's Interior. It is so important to Alaskans, that the state purchased the line from the federal government in 1985 for $23.3 million, making it the only state-owned commercial line in the country.

The Alaska Railroad provides a good, though rarely the cheapest, means of transportation for travelers, and the scenery on each route is spectacular. You'll save more hitching along the George Parks Hwy, but few travelers, even those counting their dimes, regret booking a seat on the line and viewing one of the world's most pristine wilderness areas from the train's comfortable and, if you're willing to pay a little extra, even gracious carriages.

Anchorage to Fairbanks

The Alaska Railroad operates a year-round service between Fairbanks and Anchorage, and summer services from late May to mid-September between Anchorage and Whittier on Prince William Sound, and from Anchorage to Seward. Although the 114-mile trip down to Seward is a spectacular ride, unquestionably the most popular run is the 336-mile trip from Anchorage to Fairbanks with a stop at Denali National Park. Heading north, the train passes within 46 miles of Mt McKinley at *Mile 279*, a stunning sight from the train's viewing domes on a clear day, and then slows down to cross the 918-foot bridge over Hurricane Gulch, one of the most spectacular views of the trip.

North of the Denali National Park, the train hugs the side of the Nenana River Canyon, passes numerous views of the Alaska Range and, 60 miles south of Fairbanks, crosses the 700-foot Mears Memorial Bridge over the Tanana River, one of the longest single-span bridges in the world. Before the bridge was completed, this was the end of the line in both directions as people and goods were then ferried across the river to waiting cars on the other bank.

From late May to mid-September, two express trains run daily between Anchorage and Fairbanks with stops at Wasilla, Talkeetna, Denali National Park and Nenana. The express trains are geared for out-of-state travelers as they offer vista-dome cars for all passengers to share, reclining seats and a full dining and beverage service. You can also take your own food and drink on board, which isn't a bad idea as dinner on the train can cost from $12 to $15.

The northbound train departs from Anchorage daily at 8.30 am, reaches Denali National Park at 3.50 pm and Fairbanks at 8 pm. The southbound train departs from Fairbanks at 8 am, reaches Denali National Park at 12.30 pm and Anchorage at 8.30 pm. The one-way fare from Anchorage to Denali National Park is $88, and $125 to Fairbanks; from Fairbanks to Denali it is $48. From late September to mid-May the schedule changes to one train per week, which departs from Anchorage at 8.30 am on Saturday and then leaves Fairbanks at 8 am on Sunday for the return trip.

The Alaska Railroad still makes a 'milk run' in which a train stops at every town and can even be flagged down by trekkers, anglers and mountain climbers emerging from their treks at the railroad tracks. The run used to extend all the way to Fairbanks but now stops at Hurricane Gulch, where it turns around and heads back to Anchorage the same day. Still, the trip takes you within view of Mt McKinley and into some remote areas of the state and allows you to mingle with more local residents than you would on the express train.

During the May to mid-September summer season, this diesel train departs from Anchorage at 6.30 am and returns by 4.30 pm on Wednesday and Saturday. On Sunday, it departs at noon and returns by 10.30 pm. The rest of the year it only makes the trip on the first Thursday of the month, departing from Anchorage at 8.30 am. A round-trip ticket is $88.

The Alaska Railroad receives considerable ink by travel writers so it pays to book early. In Anchorage call ☎ (907) 265-2623. If you're still planning your trip, call the toll-free number (☎ (800) 544-0552) or write to Alaska Railroad, PO Box 107500, Anchorage, AK 99510.

Anchorage to Seward

Some say the ride between Anchorage and Seward is one of the most spectacular train trips in the world, rivaling those in the Swiss Alps or the New Zealand train that climbs over Arthur's Pass in the Southern Alps. From Anchorage, the 114-mile trip begins by skirting the 60-mile long Turnagain Arm on Cook Inlet where travelers can study the bore tides. After leaving Portage, the train swings south and climbs over mountain passes, across deep river gorges and comes within half a mile of three glaciers: Spencer, Bartlett and Trail. The trip ends in Seward, a quaint town surrounded by mountains on one side and Resurrection Bay on the other.

The service is offered daily from late May to early September with a train departing from Anchorage at 7 am and reaching Seward at 11 am. It departs from Seward the same day at 6 pm and reaches Anchorage at 10 pm; the round-trip fare is $80. The Seward run does not include a baggage car, like northbound trains to Denali, and ticket agents will warn you of 'hand-carried luggage only'. But don't despair if you have a hefty backpack or even a Klepper kayak.

The train is rarely full and extra luggage can be placed in the empty seats.

White Pass & Yukon Route

The White Pass & Yukon Railroad (WP&YR), a historical narrow-gauge railroad, was built during the height of the Klondike Gold Rush in 1898 and connected Skagway to Whitehorse. It was the first railroad to be built in Alaska and at that time the northernmost line in North America.

The railroad was carved out of the rugged mountains by workers who, in places, had to be suspended by ropes from vertical cliffs in order to chip and blast the granite away. It followed the 40-mile White Pass Trail from Skagway to Lake Bennett where the miners would build rafts to float the rest of the way to Dawson City on the Yukon River. The line reached Whitehorse in 1900 and by then had made the Chilkoot Trail obsolete.

The railroad also played an important role in building the Alcan during WW II and was then used for transporting ore by mining companies in the Yukon Territory. In 1982, after world metal prices fell and the Canadian mines closed, operation of the White Pass & Yukon Railroad was suspended. But it has always been a popular tourist attraction, especially with big cruise ships, and in 1988, under the name of White Pass & Yukon Route, the railroad resumed limited service.

Today, it's still the incredible ride it must have been for the Klondike miners. The White Pass & Yukon Railroad has one of the steepest grades in North America as it climbs from sea level in Skagway to 2885 feet at White Pass in only 20 miles. The mountain scenery is fantastic, the old narrow-gauge cars are intriguing, and the trip is a must for anyone passing through Southeast Alaska.

The train runs from late May to September and offers a one-day summit excursion, a Chilkoot Trail service (see the Skagway section in the Southeast chapter for details) and a scheduled through-service for travelers who actually want to use it as a means of transportation to Whitehorse and the Alcan. Northbound trains depart Skagway daily at 12.40 pm and arrive in Fraser at 2.40 pm, where passengers transfer to buses which arrive in Whitehorse at 6 pm (Pacific Time). Southbound buses depart from Whitehorse at 8 am (Pacific Time), and the train leaves Fraser at 10.20 am arriving in Skagway at noon. The one-way fare from Skagway to Whitehorse is $92.

Knowing the history of this train, reservations wouldn't be a bad idea. Call toll free ☎ (800) 343-7373 or write to the White Pass & Yukon Route (☎ (907) 983-2217), PO Box 435, Skagway, AK 99840.

BOAT
State Marine Ferry

In the Southeast, the State Marine Ferry replaces bus services and operates from Juneau or Ketchikan to Skagway, Haines, Hoonah, Tenakee Springs, Angoon, Sitka, Kake, Petersburg, Hyder and Hollis, with an occasional special run to the tiny fishing village of Pelican (see the Inside Passage section in the Getting There & Away chapter for more details).

There are also marine ferry services in Southcentral and Southwest Alaska, where the MV *Bartlett* and the MV *Tustumena* connect towns along Prince William Sound and the Gulf of Alaska. The Southwest marine ferry does not connect with the Southeast line, but travelers can get around that by picking up an Alaska Airlines flight from Juneau to Cordova for $176 to continue their ferry trip around the Alaskan coast.

The MV *Bartlett* sails from Cordova and Valdez to Whittier across Prince William Sound, passing the Columbia Glacier along the way. The MV *Tustumena* provides a service between Seward, Homer and Seldovia on the Kenai Peninsula; Port Lions and Kodiak on Kodiak Island; and Valdez on the eastern shore of Prince William Sound.

In 1993, the Alaska State Ferry instituted a new direct service from Whittier to Cordova, on board the MV *Bartlett*. From May through September, the ship makes a round trip between the two sea ports on Monday and Tuesday, leaving Cordova at 6.30 am and arriving at Whittier at 1.30 pm and then turning around for the return trip at

2.45 pm. This makes the charming town of Cordova a delightful side trip from Anchorage as it would be possible to arrive on a Friday and return to Anchorage by Monday.

Also five times during the summer – in mid-May, June, July, August and September – the MV *Tustumena* also makes a special run to Sand Point, King Cove, Cold Bay and Dutch Harbor at the end of the Alaska Peninsula. The cruise takes three full days from Kodiak and is the cheapest way to see part of Alaska's stormy arm.

Sample fares for marine ferry travel along the Southcentral routes for walk-on passengers are:

Valdez to Cordova	$30
Valdez to Whittier	$58
Valdez to Seward	$58
Seward to Kodiak	$54
Homer to Kodiak	$48
Kodiak to Dutch Harbor	$202
Homer to Seldovia	$18

CAR & MOTORHOME
Car Rental
Having your own car in Alaska, as in any other place, provides freedom and flexibility that cannot be obtained from public transportation. Car rental, however, is a costly way to travel for one person but for two or more it can be an affordable way to travel out of Anchorage, which has the best car rental rates by far. In Alaska, it isn't the charge per day for the rental but the mileage rate and the distances covered that make it so expensive. Outside of Anchorage and Fairbanks, drivers will find gas 20 to 30c more expensive than in the rest of the USA.

The Alaska tourist boom of the 1980s has produced a network of cheap car rental companies that offer rates almost 50% lower than those of national firms such as Avis, Hertz and National Car Rental. The largest of these is Practical Car Rental (it used to be AllStar and in Alaska they still refer to themselves as such), which has offices in 10 Alaskan towns including Anchorage, Fairbanks, Kenai, Ketchikan, Petersburg, Wrangell and Sitka. Their rates change from city to city but

in Anchorage (940 West International Airport Rd; ☎ (907) 561-0350) they offer a daily rate of $29 a day for a Ford Fiesta with unlimited mileage.

Other companies include Rent-A-Wreck, which has an outlet in Anchorage (512 West International Airport Rd; ☎ (907) 562-5499). Rent-A-Wreck also has a $29 day rate and a weekly rate of $199. But you only get a 100 free miles a day, after that it's 25c a mile. In Fairbanks, there is also AllStar and Rent-A-Wreck outlets but their rates jump up to $40 a day for a subcompact and 30c a mile. Without question, Anchorage is by far the best place to pick up a long-term rental.

The used cars, though functional, are not pretty and are occasionally stubborn about starting up right away.

Used-car rental companies are listed in the regional chapters under the towns where they maintain offices. For those who want to reserve a car in advance, AllStar's toll-free number is ☎ (800) 426-5243. Call Rent-A-Wreck at ☎ (800) 666-9799 (toll free) or ☎ (907) 562-5499 and U-Save at (800) 272-8728 (toll free) or ☎ (907) 561-8728.

Motorhome Rental
Want to be a road hog? You can also rent a motorhome in Alaska if that's the way you like to travel. And many people do. RVers flock to the land of the midnight sun in numbers that are astounding. Some roads, like the George Parks Hwy, are often nothing but an endless stream of trailers, pop-ups and land cruisers.

More than a dozen companies, almost all of them based in Anchorage, will rent you a motorhome, ranging from 20 to 35 feet in length, that accommodates up to six people. The price can vary from $100 to $150 per day but again you have to consider all the extra charges. Many offer a 100 free miles per day and charge 15 to 25c per mile for any additional miles.

You also have to pay for insurance and possibly even a 'housekeeping kit' – the pots, pans and sheets you'll need to survive. It's best to anticipate a daily fee of between $150 and $200. Full-hook-up campground fees cost from $15 to $20 a night. Still, when divided between four to six people costs comes out to around $28 to $35 a day per person for both transportation and a soft bed at night. Not such a bad deal if you can round up several other people who want to share the same itinerary. Other costs include gasoline, food and camping sites.

You almost have to reserve a motorhome in advance to be insured of securing one when you arrive during the summer. A few of the larger Anchorage rental companies include Alaska Panorama Fleet (☎ (907) 561-8762), Clippership Motorhome Rentals (☎ (800) 421-3456 toll free) and ABC Motorhome Rentals (☎ (800) 421-7456 toll free).

BICYCLE

For those who want to bike it, Alaska offers a variety of cycling adventures on paved roads during long days with comfortably cool temperatures. Most cyclists hop on the State Marine Ferry, where they can carry their bike on for an additional fee ranging anywhere from $7 to $38 for the longest run from Billingham to Skagway. The individual Southeast communities are good places to gear up for the longer rides north.

From Haines, you can catch an Alaskon Express bus to Tok or Anchorage in the heart of Alaska. There is no charge for the bike but be prepared to have it stored in the luggage compartment under the bus. You can also take your bike on Alaska Airlines for a $30 excess-baggage fee each way – you don't have to put the bike in a crate, merely hand it over to the ticket officials at the counter.

Summer cyclists have to take some extra precautions in Alaska. There are few towns with comprehensively equipped bike shops so it is wise to carry not only metric tools but also a tube-patch repair kit, brake cables, spokes, brake pads and any other parts you may need during the trip.

Due to the high rainfall, especially in the Southeast, waterproof saddle bags are useful, as are tyre fenders. Rain gear is a must, and storing gear in zip-lock plastic bags within your side saddles is not being over-cautious. Warm clothing, mittens and a woollen hat should be carried, along with a tent and rain tarpaulin.

Some roads do not have much of a shoulder – the Seward Hwy between Anchorage and Girdwood being the classic example – so cyclists should utilize the long hours of sunlight to pedal when the traffic is light in such areas. It is not necessary to carry a lot of food, as you can easily restock every couple of days on all major roads.

Most cyclists avoid gravel, but biking the Alcan, an increasingly popular trip, does involve some short gravel breaks in the paved asphalt. When riding along gravel roads, figure on making 50% to 70% of your normal distance and take spare inner tubes – flat tyres will be a daily occurrence.

Mountain bikers, on the other hand, are in heaven with gravel roads like the Denali Hwy in the Interior; the logging roads in Prince of Wales Island in the Southeast and the park road in Denali National Park. Mountain bikers even pedal the Dalton Hwy to Prudhoe Bay.

The following cities and towns in Alaska have bike shops that offer a good selection of spare parts and information on riding in the local area. However, by the end of the summer many are low on, or completely out of, certain spare parts.

Anchorage
    The Bicycle Shop, 1035 West Northern Lights Blvd (☎ (907) 272-5219)
    Gary King Sporting Goods, 202 East Northern Lights Blvd (☎ (907) 279-7454)
    REI Co-op, 1200 West Northern Lights Blvd (☎ (907) 272-4565)
Fairbanks
    Beaver Sports, 2400 College Rd (☎ (907) 479-2494)
    Campbell Sports, 609 3rd St (☎ (907) 452-2757)
Juneau
    Adventure Sports, 2092 Jordan Ave (near Nugget Mall, ☎ (907) 789-5696)
Sitka
    Southeast Diving & Sport Shop, 203 Lincoln St (☎ (907) 747-8279)
Haines
    Sockeye Cycle, Portage St in Fort Seward (☎ (907) 766-2869)

Cycling Books

You might also consider the *Alaska Bicycle Touring Guide* by Pete Praetorius & Alys Culhane (The Denali Press, PO Box 021535, Juneau, AK 99802-1535; 1989, 328 pages, maps, photos, $17.50), which is the first guide put together for touring Alaska on two wheels. It's been called the 'bicycling equivalent of the *The Milepost*' for its thorough description of routes throughout the state, including two that go north of the Arctic Circle.

Mountain Bike Alaska by Richard Larson (Glacier House Publications, PO Box 201901, Anchorage, AK 99520; 1991, 120 pages, maps, $14) is a guide to 49 trails for mountain bikers. The trails range from the Denali Hwy and the Denali park road to many of the traditional hiking trails found in the Kenai Peninsula.

HITCHING

Hitching is never entirely safe in any country in the world. Travelers who decide to hitch should understand that they are taking a small but potentially serious risk. People who do choose to hitch will be safer if they travel in pairs and let someone know where they are planning to go.

TOURS

Guide Companies

As vast and endless as the Alaska wilderness appears on a map, the fact is there's probably an outfitter with guides to where ever you want to trek, paddle, climb or float. From climbing Mt McKinley and dog-sledding north of the Arctic Circle to photographing brown bears on Admiralty Island, Alaska-based guide companies offer a remarkable variety of adventures in almost every corner of the state.

Costs vary widely from one company to another but expect to pay from $150 to more than $200 per day, depending upon the amount of air travel involved. Expeditions usually have between five and 12 clients; guide companies are hesitant to take larger groups because of their environmental impact. The tour season is from late May to

September, while a select group of companies specialize in winter expeditions of Nordic skiing or dog-sledding.

Although most companies begin taking reservations in April, don't hesitate to call one after you've arrived in Alaska. Often you can score a hefty discount of 30% to 50% in the middle of the summer as guide companies are eager to fill any remaining places on a scheduled trip.

The following is a list of recreational guide companies in Alaska. You can also contact Alaska Wilderness Guides Association, a professional organization whose members must meet certain safety and ethical requirements to be AWGA certified. Contact Alaska Wilderness Guides, PO Box 141061, Anchorage, AK 99514-1061 or call ☎ (907) 276-6634.

Southeast Southeast Exposure (☎ (907) 225-8829), PO Box 9143, Ketchikan, AK 99901, is a Ketchikan guide company that rents kayaks and offers guided trips to Misty Fjords National Monument and Barrier Islands, a wilderness area on Prince of Wales Island. A four-day paddle to the heart of Rudyerd Bay, the most scenic part of Misty Fjords, along with Manzanita Bay and Behm Canal is $630 per person and includes boat transportation from Ketchikan. A six-day trip that also includes Walker Cove is $870 per person while an eight-day expedition to the Barrier Islands is $1210.

Alaska Discovery (☎ (907) 586-1911), 234 Gold St, Juneau, AK 99801, was organized in 1972 and today is one of the oldest and largest guide companies in Alaska. They used to operate mainly in the Southeast but have since expanded and offer raft trips down the Kongakat River in the Arctic National Wildlife Refuge and even hiking expeditions into the Russian Far East. Still, kayak trips in Glacier Bay and Russell Fjord, home of Hubbard Glacier, and raft trips down the Tatshenshini River are their specialty. Among their expeditions are a five-day paddle in Glacier Bay for $1500 per person and a spectacular nine-day Hubbard Glacier adventure for $1550 per person.

They also offer a seven-day canoe journey to Pack Creek on Admiralty Island to photograph brown bears for $1250 per person.

Chilkat Guides (☎ (907) 766-2491), PO Box 170, Haines, AK 99827, offers a handful of raft trips from its base in Haines, including a four-hour float down the Chilkat River to view bald eagles. The small guiding company is best known for its raft trips down the Tatshenshini and Alsek rivers. Both are spectacular trips and pass dozens of glaciers. The 'Tat' is a 10-day float for $1650 per person and the Alsek, which involves a helicopter ride to bypass Turnback Canyon, is a 13-day trip costing $2125.

Alaska Cross Country Guiding & Rafting (☎ (907) 767-5522), PO Box 124, Haines, AK 99827, is based in Haines and runs trips around the Chilkat Bald Eagle Preserve. Wildlife photography and hiking trips are supported by raft, canoe and at times air boats. The outfitter's best trip begins with a flight to remote mountainous cabins just outside Glacier Bay National Park for a night and then continues with a float down to the Chilkat River back to Haines. This two-day adventure is $452 per person.

Extreme Dreams (☎ (907) 766-2097), PO Box 449, Haines, AK 99827, is another small Haines-based guiding company specializing in mountain climbing and other alpine adventures in Southeast Alaska.

Anchorage Area & Southcentral Adventures & Delights (☎ (907) 276-8282 or (800) 288-3134), 414 K St, Anchorage, AK 99501, specializes in sea kayak adventures in Prince William Sound and Kenai Fjords National Park. A three-day paddle into Resurrection Bay from Seward is $575 per person, a three-day trip into Kenai Fjords and Fox Island is $795. The company also rents kayaks in Seward and can arrange drop-off and pick-up service.

Hugh Glass Backpacking Co (☎ (907) 344-1340), PO Box 110796, Anchorage, AK 99511, is a long-established guide company which offers a wide range of trips into Prince William Sound, Kenai Fjords National Park,

the Arctic National Wildlife Refuge, Katmai National Park, Brooks Range, and the Wrangell and St Elias mountains. Trips include trekking, canoeing, rafting or sea kayaking, and can be designed as photography or fishing adventures. Among its expeditions is a nine-day expedition into Lake Clark National Park that combines hiking with rafting for $1,695 per person.

Alaska Whitewater Wilderness Raft Trips (☎ (907) 337-7238), PO Box 142294, Anchorage, AK 99514, offers a wide range of adventures, including both white-water rafting and scenic floats. Trips range from day trips near Anchorage to more extended floats around the state. The company's five-day raft trip down the Talkeetna is $1000 per person.

Alaska River Adventures (☎ (907) 595-1733), Mile 48.2 Sterling Hwy, Cooper Landing, AK 99572, offers guided tours all year round. In summer, their boat trips include an overnight trip along the Kenai River for $149 per person, a five day/four night white-water paddling excursion through Talkeetna Canyon for $1600, and five days on Lake Creek, south of Mt McKinley, for $1695. There are also longer expeditions to the Alagnak River and the Kanektok River in the Bristol Bay region as well as sea kayaking on Prince William Sound and Kenai Fjords; six days $1795.

CampAlaska (☎ (907) 376-9438), PO Box 872247, Wasilla, AK 99687, is not quite a true wilderness guide company. They offer van tours that combine camping with day hikes, rafting, canoeing and, of course, sight-seeing, from the Alaskan highways. CampAlaska also runs a seven-day trip along the George Parks and Richardson highways that includes Denali National Park, Fairbanks and Valdez for $625 per person. A 10-day 'Alaska Range Bike & Hike' trip that includes biking Denali Hwy and hiking in Denali National Park is $1100 per person.

Alaska Wildtrek (☎ (907) 235-6463), PO Box 1741, Homer, AK 99603, offers guided tours throughout the state from the Brooks Range to the Alaska Peninsula. Directed by Chlaus Lotscher, a German transplant in

Alaska, the company caters almost entirely to Europeans, especially Germans.

Earth Tours Inc (☎ (907) 279-9907), 705 West 6th Ave, Suite 207, Anchorage, AK 99501, is more of a booking agency for wilderness trips than a guide company and will assist trekkers with a variety of adventures. Owner Margriet Ekvall speaks several languages, including Dutch, French and Italian, and offers trips like a three-day Talkeetna Mountain crossing for $595 per person, a 12-day glacier trekking trip in Wrangell-St Elias National Park for $1155 and eight days of hiking in Denali National Park for $1995.

Kenai Peninsula Guided Hikes (☎ (907) 288-3141), PO Box 468, Seward, AK 99664-9707, is a small company that offers day hikes in the Chugach National Forest and throughout the Kenai Peninsula.

Mt McKinley & the Interior St Elias Alpine Guides (☎ (907) 277-6867), PO Box 111241, Anchorage, AK 99511, specializes in mountaineering and glacier skiing adventures in Wrangell-St Elias National Park. Along with trips like an 11-day backpacking adventure around Chitistone Canyon they offer a 12-day trip down the Copper River to Cordova. Many of the trips begin and end in Anchorage and prices range from $1900 to $2200 per person.

Denali Raft Adventures (☎ (907) 683-2234), Drawer 190, Denali Park, AK 99755, offers a variety of day rafting trips down the Nenana River near Denali National Park; some are in calm waters while others involve two hours of white-water rafting. Prices range from $36 to $60 per person for two to five-hour trips. They also have a full-day trip.

Nova (☎ (907) 745-5753), PO Box 1129, Chickaloon, AK 99674, specializes in river rafting. Their trips range from a day run down the Matanuska River for $50 per person to a three-day journey along the Talkeetna River that involves flying to the heart of the Talkeetna Mountains and class IV white-water rafting for $700 per person. The company also has trips to the Kobuck

River in the Brooks Range (10 days, $2500 per person) and to the Cooper River in Wrangell-St Elias National Park (six days, $1200).

Alaska Back Country Guides Co-op (☎ (907) 479-8907), PO Box 81533, Fairbanks, AK 99708, is based in Fairbanks and offers a variety of backpacking, glacier trekking, rafting and canoeing trips. These include canoe trips in the Wrangell-St Elias National Park and throughout the Kenai Peninsula.

Llama Buddies Expeditions (☎ (907) 376-8472), PO Box 874995, Wasilla, AK 99687-4995, is for trekkers tired of carrying a backpack. Their wilderness adventures involve llamas carrying the load into the mountains and around glaciers.

Fairbanks & Brooks Range Alaska Fish & Trails Unlimited (☎ (907) 479-7630), 1177 Shypoke Drive, Fairbanks, AK 99709, runs backpacking, kayaking and canoeing trips in the Gates of the Arctic National Park. They also offer a late-fall photography trip, spring Nordic ski tours and fishing adventures that include rafting out of the Brooks Range to Bettles.

Arctic Treks (☎ (907) 455-6502), PO Box 73452, Fairbanks, AK 99707, is a family operation that specializes in treks and rafting in the Gates of the Arctic National Park and the Arctic National Wildlife Refuge. A 10-day trip circumnavigating the highest peak in the western Brooks Range combines backpacking and rafting in the Gates of the Arctic and costs $2375. They also float the Hulahula River through the Arctic North Slope for 10 days for $2530 and offer an eight-day fall base camp to witness the caribou migration for $2350.

Sourdough Outfitters (☎ (907) 692-5252), PO Box 90, Bettles, AK 99726, runs canoe, kayak and backpacking trips to the Gates of the Arctic National Park, Noatak and Kobuk rivers and other areas. They also provide unguided trips for individuals who have the experience to make an independent journey but want a guide company to handle the logistics of a major expedition, such as trip planning, transportation and canoe or raft rental. Unguided trips through the Brooks Range cost from $300 to $800 per person depending on the number of people in your party. Guided trips range from an eight-day backpacking trek in the Gates of the Arctic National Park for $1250 per person to a 10-day canoe trip along the Noatak River for $1900 per person and a five-day paddle of the Wild River in the Brooks Range for $1050 per person.

CanoeAlaska (☎ (907) 479-5183), PO Box 81750, Fairbanks, AK 99708, specializes in canoeing trips that teach boating skills and explore scenic rivers. Classes are limited to eight people and rafts are used to support and assist paddlers. Throughout the summer, the guide company runs two-day trips on the Chena River and three day outings on the Gulkana River. The cost is $125 per person and includes instruction, canoe and paddling equipment, meals and transportation.

Southeast Alaska

Some of the best trekking in Alaska, and maybe in the USA, is found in Southeast Alaska. There is hardly a town or village from where trails don't lead into the surrounding mountains and remote valleys or along glaciers. Easy and affordable ferry travel, stunning scenery, excellent wildlife and trails maintained by the USFS as part of the Tongass National Forest, explain why some trekkers spend their entire summer in Alaska's Panhandle.

The only drawbacks are the weather and the lack of long trails. Other than the famous Chilkoot Trail in Skagway, most of the trails in the Southeast are good for day hikes or at best, overnight treks. Many trekkers, however, are attracted to spending days in the mountains and nights back at town.

Travel around the Southeast is easy. The Alaska State Marine Ferry system connects this region to Bellingham in the US state of Washington and provides transportation around the area, making it the most extensive public ferry system in North America. The state ferry links 14 ports and services 64,000 residents, 75% of whom live in Juneau, Ketchikan, Sitka, Petersburg and Wrangell.

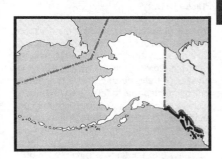

Ketchikan

The first port of call in the Southeast is Ketchikan (population 13,000) on the southwest side of Revillagigedo (ra-vee-ah-ga-GAY-doh) Island, only 90 miles north of Prince Rupert. Ketchikan is the departure point for a number of wilderness adventures and trails but most of the trailheads can only be reached by float plane or tour boat. The trails accessible by road (Ward Lake Nature Walk, Perseverance Trail and Talbot Lake Trail) are short treks under three miles long. The exception is the Deer Mountain Trail, which can be picked up from downtown and

offers an overnight adventure in the mountains surrounding the city.

Climate

The region doesn't have ideal trekking weather; more often than not it will be cloudy or drizzly rather than clear. The Southeast, affected greatly by warm ocean currents, offers warm summer temperatures averaging 69°F (you get the most sun in August). It also receives a good deal of rain, even in July and August – annual rainfall in Ketchikan averages 162 inches, but it has been known to exceed 200 inches in some years. The heavy precipitation is responsible for the dense, lush forests and numerous waterfalls that most trekkers come to cherish.

Information

For information about hiking trails, cabin reservations and other outdoor opportunities, contact the USFS information center (☎ 225-3101) in the Federal Building on the corner of Stedman and Mill Sts. It is open from 7.30 am to 4.30 pm weekdays and has information and hand-outs on activities in the Ketchikan area and a list of cabins still available during the summer. There is also an interesting slide presentation and other displays.

For general tourist information on accommodations, tours, transportation etc head to the Ketchikan Visitor Bureau (☎ 225-6166) on the City Dock. The bureau is open Monday to Friday from 8 am to 6 pm.

Places to Stay

Camping There are four public campgrounds in Ketchikan and all of them, except Settler's Cove, are $5 per night for a site and have a 14-day limit. Unfortunately, none of them are close to town. *Settler's Cove* (12 sites) is 16 miles north of the ferry terminal and has tables, pit toilets, firewood and a beach area but no hook-ups. It costs $6 per night and the seven-day limit is enforced.

The other three campgrounds are on Ward Lake Rd. Take North Tongass Hwy four miles north of the ferry terminal to the pulp mill on Ward Cove and then turn right onto Ward Lake Rd. The first campground is *Signal Creek* (25 sites), a mile up the road. It is followed by *CCC Campground* (four sites) a quarter of a mile further up and *Last Chance Campground* (25 sites), another 1.8 miles along Ward Lake Rd.

Hostels On the corner of Grant and Main Sts in the basement of the United Methodist Church in the center of the city is the *Ketchikan Youth Hostel* (☎ 225-3319). It's open from Memorial Day (25 May) to Labor Day (7 September) and provides kitchen facilities (50c extra per meal), showers and a space on the floor with a mat to sleep on. The fee is $5 per night for youth hostel members and $8 per night for nonmembers.

The *Rain Forest Inn* (☎ 225-7246) is at 2311 Hemlock St, 0.7 miles from the state ferry terminal and half a block from the bus stop on the corner of Tongass Ave and Jefferson St. The Inn offers dormitory bunks for $25 per night and provides showers, laundry facilities and a guest lounge.

B&Bs Check with Ketchikan Bed & Breakfast (☎ 225-8550) to arrange a stay in a private home. Rates begin at $50/60 a single/double and include breakfast and transportation (usually) from the ferry terminal or airport. Swing by the visitors' bureau for a list of the most current B&Bs.

Hotels There is a wide range of hotels in Ketchikan, from those catering to cruise-ship tourists to the more dilapidated ones. The *Gilmore Hotel* (☎ 225-9423) at 326 Front St used to be run-down before recent major renovations gave it an historical flavor. Rooms with private bath range from $49 to $64 per night. There's also *Super 8 Motel* (☎ 225-9088) half a mile south of the ferry terminal at 2151 Sea Level with rooms from $80. From here, prices at the rest of the hotels jump to $85 per night or more during the summer.

Maps

The USGS 1:63,360 series quad, *Ketchikan B-5*, shows the entire alpine route of the Deer Mountain Trail and much more in the best possible detail. Keep in mind that only the three-mile trail to the top of Deer Mountain is on the map. The rest of the route is not labeled. You can purchase quads at Tongass Trading Company (☎ 225-5101) downtown at 201 Dock Street.

Equipment

If you're lacking some equipment, need white gas or have a craving for freeze-dried dinners on your trek, *The Outfitter* (☎ 225-6888) at 3232 Tongass Ave has a limited stock of backpacking gear. The best supermarket to stock up on noodle dinners and instant oatmeal is *Super Valu* nearby at 3816 Tongass Ave. It's open 24 hours.

Cabins

There are 30 cabins in the Ketchikan area, including the Deer Mountain Cabin, which is reached on foot along the trail. The rest of the units are reached only by a float plane and all of them, especially the Deer Mountain Cabin, must be booked in advance. The cost is $25 per night.

The USFS office can provide a complete list and description of the cabins in the Ketchikan area. There are numerous bush-plane operators in Ketchikan who can fly you to them, including Taquan Air (☎ 225-9668), 1007 Water St, Ketchikan, AK 99901 and Ketchikan Air Service (☎ 225-6608),

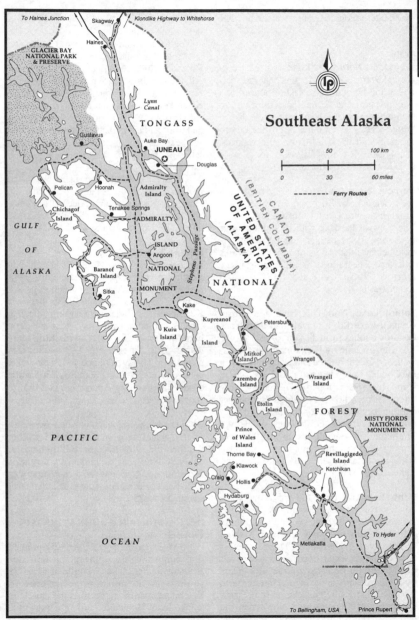

Southeast Alaska

To Haines Junction
Skagway
Klondike Highway to Whitehorse
Haines
GLACIER BAY
NATIONAL PARK
& PRESERVE
Lynn
Canal
TONGASS
Gustavus
Auke Bay
JUNEAU
Douglas
Pelican
Hoonah
Admiralty
Island
Chichagof
Island
Tenakee Springs
ADMIRALTY
GULF
ISLAND
Angoon
OF
Baranof
Island
NATIONAL
ALASKA
MONUMENT
Sitka
Kake
Kupreanof
Petersburg
Kuiu
Island
Island
Mitkof
Island
Wrangell
Zarembo
Island
Wrangell
Island
Etolin
Island
FOREST
MISTY FJORDS
NATIONAL
MONUMENT
Prince
of Wales
Island
PACIFIC
Thorne Bay
Revillagigedo
Island
Klawock
Ketchikan
Craig
Hollis
Hydaburg
OCEAN
Metlakatla
To Hyder

UNITED STATES
(BRITISH COLUMBIA)
CANADA
OF AMERICA
(ALASKA)
Stephens Passage
NATIONAL

0   50   100 km
0   30   60 miles
- - - - - - - Ferry Routes

To Bellingham, USA
Prince Rupert

1600 International Airport, Ketchikan, AK 99901.

Trails

Ward Lake Nature Walk This is an easy trail around Ward Lake that begins near the shelters at the far end of the lake. The trail is a 1.3 miles of flat terrain and information signs. To reach the lake, follow the North Tongass Hwy seven miles out of the city to the pulp mill on Ward Cove, turn right on Ward Lake Rd and follow it for a mile (USGS quad *Ketchikan B-5*).

Perseverance Trail This is a 2.2-mile walk from Ward Lake Rd to Perseverance Lake through mature coastal forest and muskeg. The view of the lake with its mountainous backdrop is spectacular and the hiking is easy because the trail is mainly boardwalks and steps. The trailhead is 1.5 miles from the start of Ward Lake Rd (USGS quad *Ketchikan B-5*).

Talbot Lake Trail This trail starts from Connell Lake Rd, a gravel road that heads east, three miles from the start of Ward Lake Rd. The 1.6-mile trail is a mixture of boardwalk and gravel surface and leads north from the Connell Lake Dam to Talbot Lake, where it ends on private property. The more adventurous trekker, however, can cross a beaver dam at the south end of the lake and hike eastward onto the north ridge of Brown Mountain to eventually reach its 2978-foot summit. Keep in mind this is steep country with no established trail (USGS quad *Ketchikan B-5*).

Naha River Trail From the end of the North Tongass Hwy, it's an eight-mile paddle to the trailhead for the Naha River Trail, a 6.5-mile path that follows the river and leads to three USFS cabins and two lakes. The trailhead is on Naha Bay which leads into Roosevelt Lagoon through a narrow outlet. Kayakers trying to paddle into the lagoon must enter it at high slack tide, as the narrow pass becomes a frothy, roaring chute when the tide is moving in or out. The current in the salt chuck actually changes directions depending on the tide.

The trail is a combination of boardwalk, swing bridges and an uphill walk to Naha River and Jordan and Heckman Lake cabins. All three cabins ($25 per night) must be reserved in advance at the USFS office in Ketchikan. This is an interesting and popular side trip. Locals fish the waters for salmon and trout and in August it's often possible to see bears catching salmon at a small waterfall two miles up the trail from the Roosevelt Lagoon.

Kayaks can be rented from *Southeast Exposure* (☎ 225-8829) at 507 Stedman St. Double kayaks cost $45 for one to three days, $40 for four days or more. Singles are available. (Use USGS quad *Ketchikan C-5*.)

Getting There & Away

Air Alaska Airlines (☎ 225-2141) flies to Ketchikan with stops at other major Southeast communities as well as Anchorage and Seattle. There are several flights between Ketchikan and Juneau, including one that locals call the 'milk run', as it stops at Petersburg, Wrangell and Sitka and is little more than a series of take-offs and landings. A round trip 21-day advance purchase ticket between Ketchikan and Seattle is $365 while a one-way ticket to Anchorage is $165, to Juneau $124.

Boat It's an exceptional day when there isn't a ferry departing from Ketchikan for other Southeast destinations or Bellingham. A one-way fare from Ketchikan to Juneau is $74, Sitka $54, Haines $88 and Skagway $92. For exact sailing times call the ferry terminal (☎ 225-6181).

DEER MOUNTAIN & JOHN MOUNTAIN TRAILS

Deer Mountain is the distinctively pointed peak dominating the alpine region above the downtown area. The 3.1-mile trail to its summit is the most popular hike in Ketchikan and the trailhead is the easiest to reach. John Mountain Trail is a four-mile trek from the Beaver Falls Power House at

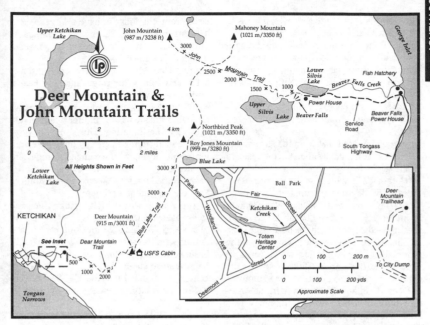

Deer Mountain & John Mountain Trails

Upper Ketchikan Lake

John Mountain (987 m/3238 ft)

Mahoney Mountain (1021 m/3350 ft)

Lower Silvis Lake

Fish Hatchery

Beaver Falls Creek

3000

John Mountain Trail

2500

2000

1500

1000

Power House

Beaver Falls

Upper Silvis Lake

Service Road

Beaver Falls Power House

0   2   4 km

0   1   2 miles

All Heights Shown in Feet

Northbird Peak (1021 m/3350 ft)

Roy Jones Mountain (999 m/3280 ft)

Blue Lake

South Tongass Highway

Lower Ketchikan Lake

3000

3000

Ball Park

Deer Mountain Trailhead

KETCHIKAN

Deer Mountain (915 m/3001 ft)

Blue Lake Trail

Fair

Park Ave

Woodland Ave

Ketchikan Creek

Street

See Inset

Dear Mountain Trail

USFS Cabin

500

1000   2000

Deermont Street

Totem Heritage Center

0   100   200 m

0   100   200 yds

To City Dump

Tongass Narrows

Approximate Scale

the south end of Tongass Hwy to the 3238-foot peak.

By combining the ridge walk known as the Blue Lake Trail you can turn the two trails into an 11.9-mile trek into the mountains that surround Ketchikan. You can spend a night at the USFS cabin (if you have booked it in advance) or camp along beautiful Blue Lake.

Heavy snow lingers well into June then the alpine region comes to life with flowers and blueberries in July and August, the preferred months to hike this route. The hike to Deer Mountain is rated moderate while the combined trek is challenging.

Access

Getting to the Deer Mountain trailhead is easy. You can walk to it or jump on a Ketchikan borough bus. The public service operates small buses that hold up to 30 passengers which follow a circular route from the ferry terminal to the area south of Thomas Basin, circling back by the Totem

Heritage Center and the trailhead to Deer Mountain. Buses return to each stop every hour; the fare is $1 and they operate from 6 am to 6 pm.

Getting back from Beaver Falls, 14 miles from town at the end of the South Tongass Hwy, is much more challenging, however. Your best bet is to arrange a pick-up in town with somebody like a B&B operator or a taxi company like Alaska Cab (☎ 225-2133) at 1504 Tongass Ave or Yellow Taxi (☎ 225-3900).

Stage 1: Deer Mountain Trailhead to Blue Lake

(5.3 miles, 4-5 hours)
(USFS cabin, backcountry camping)
The trailhead for the Deer Mountain Trail can be reached by following the gravel road from the corner of Deermont and Fair Sts (just across Ketchikan Creek), past a subdivision (to the south-east) towards the city dump. Just before reaching the dump, a trail

sign points left to a side road which leads to the trailhead and a small parking area.

The Deer Mountain Trail begins with boardwalks as your cross a muskeg area then begins to climb the mountain, skirting its western-southwestern slope with a series of switchbacks. The first view of Tongass Narrows pops up within a mile as you reach 1500 feet and it improves the higher you climb.

Several hundred feet from the summit, or 2.9 miles from the trailhead, you reach a junction. To the right (east) is the trail to the 3001-foot peak which on a clear day provides a 360-degree panorama of Ketchikan, Tongass Narrows and Prince of Wales Island. From there you descend to the USFS cabin just below the summit on the north side. The left-hand fork traverses the north slope of the mountain to the ridge line which leads to Blue Lake. It's a more direct route to the cabin as opposed to climbing the summit.

Deer Mountain Cabin is an A-frame structure built in 1962. At one time it was a free-use shelter until it was heavily vandalised. It has since been repaired and turned into a USFS rental unit. The cabin

Mountain goat

sleeps four but does not have a stove inside. The maximum stay during the summer is three consecutive nights and, as you can imagine, you must book in advance.

From Deer Mountain you descend past the cabin and follow the ridge line as it heads north-east towards another 3000-foot peak. Metal posts mark the route across the open ridge line and are needed in June when heavy snow is often lingering. This stretch is very steep and difficult in places and offers no protection during foul weather. During such periods of bad weather the steep drop-offs have claimed lives because of poor visibility. Stay on the trail at all times.

You ascend to the higher ridge line and follow it as it skirts high above Granite Basin to the west. Within 2.2 miles of Deer Mountain, the trail descends sharply to the small basin surrounding Blue Lake. There used to be a free-use shelter here too, but it was so heavily vandalised that the USFS removed it. Still, the spot is an ideal place to camp.

Stage 2: Blue Lake to Tongass Hwy
(6.6 miles, 4-6 hours)
The first half of this day is spent above the tree line in the alpine area. It is a stunning trek if the weather is clear, if it's not, be extremely careful to follow the route correctly, especially on the sharp descent of Northbird Peak.

From Blue Lake, the trail skirts the west end of the lake and continues north along the ridge. Within the first half-mile you gently climb 3280-foot Roy Jones Mountain, descend and then climb Northbird Peak (around 3350 feet), generally flanked by snowfields throughout the summer. Descend the peak in a north-west direction. The route climbs a 3100-foot knob and then descends almost 300 feet to where the ridge line dips near an alpine pond and a few dwarf hemlocks. Be careful on this stretch as it is very steep and rocky and marked only by an occasional steel post.

The trail eventually resumes climbing and joins the John Mountain Trail, two miles from Blue Lake at the south end of a basin overlooking another alpine lake. The ridge line and route to the north-west leads to the 3238-foot summit of John Mountain, a one-mile climb from the junction.

To the east the trail leads gently up a ridge to 3000 feet and arrives at a junction with the route to the top of 3350-foot Mahoney Mountain, a shorter and easier climb than John Mountain. The trail to the Silvis lakes and Tongass Hwy descends sharply off that ridge into a small bowl at the tree line. Staying well above Upper Silvis Lake at first, you continue down into the forest for the first time to eventually bottom out at the old dam outlet of the lake.

This is the old trailhead of the John Mountain Trail. Keep in mind the trail is not well marked as it approaches Upper Silvis Lake and once in the trees you'll be looking for blazes. The final mile from the tree line to the old dam outlet is a steep descent. Be careful here.

To continue on to Lower Silvis Lake you descend a steep hillside along an access road that was destroyed by a 1969 landslide. Some scrambling might be necessary on this stretch before reaching the upper power house on the lake. At the power house a dirt road leads around the south side of Lower Silvis Lake and two miles later reaches Beaver Falls Power House and Tongass Hwy.

WRANGELL & PETERSBURG

The hiking opportunities are more limited in these two Southeast towns as the better trails either lie away from the road or require a boat or float plane to reach them. Both towns, however, have a USFS office where you can get information on treks, camping, cabin rental and current trail conditions. In Wrangell, the USFS office (☎ 874-2323) is 0.75 miles north of town at 525 Bennett St. In Petersburg, the USFS office (☎ 722-3871) is upstairs in the post office on Nordic Drive.

Wrangell Trails
Petroglyphs An interesting afternoon can be spent looking for petroglyphs – primitive rock carvings believed to be 8000 years old. The best set lie 0.75 miles from the ferry

terminal and can be reached by heading north on Evergreen Rd or, as the locals call it, Old Airport Rd. Walk past Stough's Trailer Court and proceed to a marked wooden walkway. Follow the boardwalk to the beach and then turn right and start walking north toward the end of the island. With your back to the water, look for the carvings on the large rocks.

Many of the petroglyphs are spirals and faces, and there are about 20 in the area but most are submerged during high tide. Check a tide book before you leave and remember that the entire walk takes an hour or two – longer than the state ferry stopover.

Mt Dewey Trail This half-mile trail winds its way up a hill to an observation point overlooking Wrangell and the surrounding waterways. From Mission St, walk a block and turn left at the first corner, 3rd St. Follow the street past a brown and red A-frame house with a white balcony. The trail, marked by a white sign, begins 50 yards past the house on the right. Once you're at the trailhead, the hike is a short one, 15 minutes or so to the top, but it is often muddy. John Muir fanatics will appreciate the fact that the great naturalist himself climbed the mountain in 1879 and built a bonfire at the top, alarming the Tlingits living in the village below.

Rainbow Falls Trail This old trail was rebuilt and extended in 1985 by the USFS. The trailhead for the Rainbow Falls Trail is signposted 4.7 miles south of the ferry terminal on the Zimovia Hwy. The trail begins directly across from the Shoemaker Bay Recreation Area and just before the Wrangell Institute Complex.

From the trailhead it is a mile hike to the waterfalls and then another 2.5 miles to an observation point overlooking Shoemaker Bay on Institute Ridge, where the USFS has built a three-sided shelter. The lower section can be soggy at times so it is best hiked in rubber boots, while upper sections are steep. The views are worth the hike and a pleasant evening can be spent on the ridge. A return trip to the ridge takes four to six hours (USGS quads *Petersburg B-1* and *B-2*).

Thoms Lake Trail At the end of the paved Zimovia Hwy is a dirt road, known officially as Forest Rd 6290, that extends 30 miles south along Wrangell Island. On this road, 23 miles south of Wrangell, is the Thoms Lake Trail, which leads 1.2 miles to a state park recreation cabin and a skiff on the lake. Since there is no state park office in Wrangell, you have to reserve the cabin through the Division of Parks office in Juneau (☎ 465-4563). Keep in mind that this trail cuts through muskeg and during wet weather can get extremely muddy. It is a 1½-hour hike to the cabin (USGS quad *Petersburg A-1*).

Long Lake Trail The trailhead for the Long Lake Trail is 27 miles south-east of Wrangell on Forest Rd 6270. This pleasant hike is only 0.6 miles and planked the entire way. It leads to a shelter, skiff and outhouses on the shores of the lake. Plan a half-hour for the trek into the lake or out (USGS quad *Petersburg A-1*).

Highbush Lake Trail This very short 300-foot path leads to the lake where there's a skiff and oars. Fishing is fair and the surrounding views excellent. The parking lot for the trailhead is 29 miles from Wrangell on Forest Rd 6265 and Forest Rd 50040.

Petersburg Trails
Frederick Point Boardwalk Near the downtown area is this mile-long boardwalk that begins off Nordic Drive next to Sandy Beach Recreation Area. The trail winds through rainforest, across muskeg and then crosses a salmon stream that is quite a sight during the peak spawning runs in August (USGS quad *Petersburg D-3*).

Raven's Roost Trail This four-mile trail begins at the water tower on the south-east side of the airport, accessible from Haugen Drive. A boardwalk crosses muskeg areas at the start of the trail, while much of the route

is a climb to beautiful open alpine areas at 2013 feet; some of it is steep and requires a little scrambling. A two-story USFS cabin (reservations, $25 per night) is above the tree line in an area that provides good summer trekking and spectacular views of Petersburg, Frederick Sound and Wrangell Narrows (USGS quad *Petersburg D-3*).

Petersburg Mountain Trail On Kupreanof Island, this trail ascends 2.5 miles from Wrangell Narrows behind Sasby Island to the top of Petersburg Mountain. There are outstanding views from here (the best in the area) of Petersburg, the Coastal Mountains, glaciers and Wrangell Narrows. Plan on spending three hours to get to the top of the mountain and two hours for the return. To get across the channel, go to the skiff float at the North Boat Harbor (Old Boat Harbor) and hitch a ride with somebody who lives on Kupreanof Island. From the Kupreanof Public Dock, head right on the overgrown road towards Sasby Island (USGS quad *Petersburg D-3*).

Petersburg Creek Trail This 6.5-mile trail, part of the trail system in the Petersburg Creek-Duncan Salt Chuck Wilderness on Kupreanof Island, leads to a USFS cabin (reservations, $25 per night) on Petersburg Lake. Like with Petersburg Mountain Trail, you need to catch a ride across to Kupreanof Island from the skiff float at the North Boat Harbor. From here it's a five-mile trek up the tidewater arm to the trailhead at Petersburg Creek.

Petersburg Creek Trail is entirely planked and easy to follow. To go beyond the lake, however, to Portage Bay or the USFS cabins on Salt Chuck you definitely need rubber boots for the wet portions of these flagged routes. Getting to the cabins on Salt Chuck is a challenging but worthwhile trek (you must have good map and compass experience). The Salt Chuck East Cabin is in a beautiful spot surrounded by mountains and in August is a hot spot for salmon anglers (USGS quads *Petersburg D-3* and *D-4*).

Three Lakes Trails These four short trails, connecting three lakes and Ideal Cove, are off Three Lakes Rd, a Forest Service road that heads east off Mitkof Hwy at *Mile 13.6* and returns at *Mile 23.8*. Beginning at *Mile 14.2* of Three Lakes Rd is a three-mile loop with boardwalks leading to Sand, Crane and Hill lakes, known for their good trout fishing.

On each lake there is a skiff and a picnic platform. Tennis shoes are fine for the trail but to explore around the lakes you need rubber boots. There is a free-use shelter on Sand Lake. From the Sand Lake Trail there is a 1.5-mile trail to Ideal Cove on Frederick Sound (USGS quad *Petersburg C-3*).

Blind River Rapids Boardwalk Starting at *Mile 14.5* of the Mitkof Hwy this easy mile-long boardwalk winds through muskeg before arriving at the rapids, a popular fishing spot during the summer (USGS quad *Petersburg C-3*).

Sitka

Known best for its beautiful setting and its Russian heritage, Sitka also offers good trekking in the lush forest and high peaks that surround the city as well as on Baranof, Kruzof and Chichagof islands. Most trails are on Tongass National Forest land maintained by the USFS. Along with the usual hand-outs, the Forest Service office in town sells a useful booklet, *Sitka Trails* ($3), which has information and rough maps of 30 trails. The trails include beach walks, short hikes to hot springs, and access routes to sub-alpine and alpine areas. Unfortunately you require a boat, kayak or float plane to reach most of them – but not all.

Sitka has a number of trails that you can get to on foot – eight trails, totaling almost 20 miles, begin from its roads. Half of them are under a mile long but the Gavan Hill and Harbor Mountain trails can be combined to

---

Tongass National Forest

Tongass National Forest received its name from the Tongass clan of the Tlingit Indians who lived near its southern edge. This area's preservation dates back to 1902 when President Theodore Roosevelt created the Alexander Archipelago Forest Reserve. Five years later, Tongass Reserve was placed in the national forest system and the following year the two reserves were consolidated to form Tongass National Forest.

Today, at 16.9 million acres, Tongass is the largest national forest in the country. It stretches from the Pacific Ocean to the vast inland ice fields that border British Columbia, and from the southern tip of Prince of Wales Island to Malaspina Glacier, 500 miles to the north. More than 90% of Southeast Alaska lies in Tongass National Forest. Even more amazing is that Tongass, with its thousands of islands, bays and fjords, has 11,000 miles of coastline (about half that of North America).

As a result of the Alaska National Interest Lands Conservation Act that was legislated in 1980, more than five million acres were set aside in Tongass as 14 separate wilderness areas. The largest is Misty Fjords National Monument, a 2.1 million-acre wilderness area 22 miles east of Ketchikan. The smallest is Maurelle Islands, a 4937-acre wilderness area off the north-west coast of Prince of Wales Island.

To many people, however, the most intriguing area in Tongass National Forest is Admiralty Island, a 937,396-acre wilderness area, 15 miles south-west of Juneau. Admiralty Island is known for having one of the largest brown-bear populations in Southeast Alaska. Bear numbers are so great that the Tlingit Indians called the area 'Fortress of Bears'. To see the bears of Admiralty Island, visit the Pack Bear Refuge. In July and August you can watch the animals feed on the salmon runs, in much the same way as the bears do at the McNeil River on the Alaska Peninsula. If you're hiked-out and have a free day or two for bear-watching in the refuge, contact Alaska Discovery (☎ 586-1911) about their guided trips. ■

form a 5.5-mile mountain trek; camp in the alpine area.

There's also the Mt Edgecumbe Trail, a 13.4-mile climb to the summit crater of the distinct volcano on Kruzof Island. This hike requires boat transportation to the trailhead and you can stay overnight in a USFS cabin or in the free-use shelter halfway up the mountain.

Climate

Like the rest of Southeast Alaska, Sitka lies in the coastal rainforest of the Tongass National Forest. Average precipitation in this region ranges from 80 to a soaking 220 inches a year on Baranof, Kruzof and Chichagof islands, depending how close to the ocean you are. The city of Sitka itself receives around 100 inches a year, the vast majority falling in the form of rain.

Summer temperatures average between 55°F and 60°F but if the sun is out in July and August the mercury can easily reach 80°F or even higher. The one thing to keep in mind about the weather in Sitka is the sudden appearance of fog, even on the nicest days. It rolls in unexpectedly from the Pacific Ocean and can reduce visibility to a few feet in no time at all. This is not such a problem on the Gavan Hill or Harbor Mountain trails where the paths are well cut and marked, but it has caused trekkers to get lost above the tree line on the Mt Edgecumbe Trail.

Information

The USFS office (☎ 747-6671), the place to go for trail information, cabin reservations and to get hand-outs about enjoying the wilderness, is in a three-story red building on the corner of Siginaka and Katlian Sts, across from the Thomas Boat Harbor. The office is open on weekdays from 8 am to 5 pm.

Sitka also has three state recreation areas; information about their use or any Alaska state park can be obtained from the Division of Parks office (☎ 747-6249) at Old Airport Turnaround on Halibut Point Rd. The office is open from Tuesday through Friday and has irregular hours. For general travel information swing by the Sitka Visitor Bureau

(☎ 747-5940), in the Centennial Building off Harbor Drive next to the Crescent Boat Harbor (open weekdays from 8 am to 5 pm).

Places to Stay

Camping The nearest campground to the center of town is *Sealing Cove* (☎ 747-3439), a commercial campground for RVers at Sealing Cove Harbor on Japonski Island. Unfortunately there are no tent sites here. There are two USFS campgrounds in the Sitka area but neither is close to town.

Starrigavan Campground is a 0.7-mile walk north of the ferry terminal at *Mile 7.8* of Halibut Point Rd. The campground (30 sites, $5 per night) is in a scenic setting and adjacent to a saltwater beach and hiking trails. *Sawmill Creek Campground* (nine sites) is six miles east of Sitka on Blue Lake Rd off Sawmill Creek Rd and past the pulp mill. Although the area is no longer maintained by the USFS, it provides mountain scenery with an interesting trail to Blue Lake, a good fishing spot. Others find informal campsites half a mile along the Indian River Trail right on the river.

Hostels The *Sitka Youth Hostel* (☎ 747-8356) is in the basement of the Methodist Church at 303 Kimsham Rd. Follow Halibut Point Rd north-west out of town and then turn right onto Peterson Rd, a quarter of a mile past the Lakeside Grocery Store. Once on Peterson Rd you immediately veer left onto Kimsham Rd. Registration is from 6 to 11 pm and check-out time is 8 am. The hostel is openly from June through August and the cost is $5 for members and $8 for nonmembers. Shuttle buses from the ferry will often drop you right at the doorstep.

B&Bs There are a large number of B&Bs in the Sitka area that offer rooms with a good breakfast for around $45/55 a single/double. Stop at the visitors' bureau for an updated list of them or try *Creek's Edge Guest House* (☎ 747-6484) which overlooks Sitka Sound and Mt Edgecumbe and provides a shuttle service. *Helga's Bed & Breakfast* (☎ 747-5497), right on the beach at 2821 Halibut

Point Rd, has five rooms for $50/60 a single/double. The ferry bus will drop you off here on the way to town.

Hotels There are five hotel/motels in Sitka. The cheapest is *The Bunkhouse* (☎ 747-8796) at 3302 Halibut Point Rd with four rooms at $46 for a single or double. A step up is *Potlatch House* (☎ 747-8611) at the end of Katlian St, near the intersection with Halibut Point Rd; the motel has 30 rooms from $76. There's also *Super 8 Motel* (☎ 747-8804) at 404 Sawmill Creek with rooms from $93.

Maps

The maps in this book and those in the USFS booklet, *Sitka Trails*, are not adequate for hiking most of the trails in Sitka. USGS topos can be purchased at Old Harbor Books (☎ 747-8808) downtown at 201 Lincoln St. In series 1:63,360 you need quads *Sitka A-5* and *A-4* for the Gavan Hill Trail, and *Sitka A-5* and *A-6* for the Mt Edgecombe Trail.

Equipment

Mac's Sporting Goods (☎ 747-6970) at 213 Harbor Drive has a limited supply of camping and backpacking equipment, including freeze-dried dinners. For Mt Edgecombe it's important to have rubber boots as the first half of the trail can be very muddy and wet. You should also be equipped with a roll or two of bright plastic tape to flag a route above the tree line where there is no trail and very few many markers.

If you want to use a kayak to reach any of the trailheads away from the Sitka road system, contact *Baidarka Boats* (☎ 747-8996) at PO Box 6001, Sitka, AK 99835. Rigid single kayaks are $35/175 a day/week and require a $50 deposit. Rigid doubles are $45/245 a day/week, and folding doubles are $55/315 a day/week.

Cabins

There are no USFS cabins on the Gavan Hill Trail or the Harbor Mountain circuit but there is one at the start of the Mt Edgecombe Trail. Fred's Creek Cabin is $25 a night and

will allow you to hike to the summit in one day. For information on any cabins in the area contact or stop at the USFS office in Sitka.

Both Gavan Hill and Mt Edgecombe trails, however, feature a free-use shelter halfway along the routes. The cabins are used on a first-come-first-served basis and don't have bunks or heating. For Gavan Hill, it's best to pack a tent as this is Sitka's most popular trail and the shelter is often full during the summer.

Trails

Indian River Trail This easy trail is a 5.5-mile walk along a clear salmon stream to the Indian River Falls, an 80-foot waterfall at the base of the Three Sisters Mountains. The hike takes you through a typical Southeast rainforest and offers the opportunity to view black bears, deer and bald eagles. The trailhead, a short walk from the center of town, is off Sawmill Creek Rd just east of the National Cemetery. Pass the driveway leading to the Public Safety Academy parking lot and turn up the dirt road with a gate across it. This leads back to the city water plant where the trail begins left of the pump house. Plan on four to five hours for a round trip to the falls (USGS quad *Sitka A-4*).

Mt Verstovia Trail This 2.5-mile trail is a challenging climb of 2550 feet to the 'shoulder', a small summit that is the most common end of the trail, although it is possible to climb to 3349 feet, the actual peak of Mt Verstovia. The view from the 'shoulder' on clear days is spectacular, undoubtedly the best in the area.

The trailhead is two miles east of Sitka along Sawmill Creek Rd. Once you reach the Kiksadi Club on the left, look for the trailhead marked 'Mt Verstovia Trail'. The Russian charcoal pits (signposted) are within a quarter of a mile and shortly after them the trail begins as a series of switchbacks. Plan on a four-hour round trip to the shoulder. From the shoulder, the true peak of Mt Verstovia lies to the north along a ridge that connects the two. Allow an extra hour each

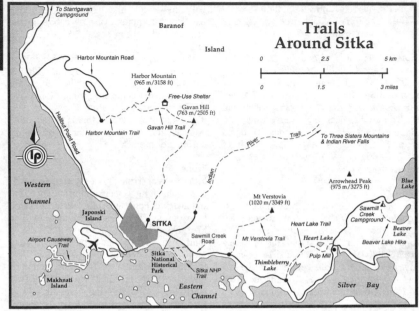

Trails Around Sitka

way to hike to the peak. Use USGS quad *Sitka A-4* for this hike.

Sitka National Historical Park Trail Beginning at the park visitors' center, this easy and well-maintained trail winds 1.5 miles along Sitka Sound and Indian River past an impressive collection of totems. Spur trails provide access to pebble and sandy beaches while a guidebook available at the visitors' center interprets the history of the area. The park is at the east end of Lincoln St.

Heart Lake Trail On Sawmill Creek Rd, four miles south-east of Sitka, this mile-long trail winds through hemlock-spruce forest to Thimbleberry Lake and Heart Lake. The trail begins just after you cross Thimbleberry Creek Bridge where there is a pull-out for parking. Conditions on the trail are often slippery and muddy and bears frequent the area (USGS quad *Sitka A-4*).

Beaver Lake Hike This short trail starts from Sawmill Creek Campground, which is reached from Sawmill Creek Rd, 5.5 miles east of Sitka. Across from the pulp mill on Sawmill Creek Rd, turn left onto Blue Lake Rd for the campground; the trailhead is on the south side of the campground.

Although steep at the beginning, the 0.8-mile trail levels out and ends up as a scenic walk through open forest and along muskeg and marsh areas to Beaver Lake which is surrounded by mountains. Vandals have made the skiff at the lake unsafe to use. Plan on an hour's hike for the round trip (USGS quad *Sitka A-4*).

Getting There & Away

Air Sitka is served by Alaska Airlines (☎ 966-2266) with flights to Juneau for $85 one way as well as to Ketchikan for $120 as part of the milk run that connects the city to Wrangell and Petersburg. The airport is on Japonski Island, 1.8 miles west of the town center. On a nice day, it can be a scenic 20-minute walk from the airport terminal over the O'Connell Bridge to the heart of Sitka. Otherwise, the white Airporter minibus of Sitka Tours meets all jet flights and charges $2.50 for a ride to the city hotels; it does not go to the hostel.

Regularly scheduled flights among the small air charter companies include Sitka to Pelican for $95 one way with Bellair (☎ 747-8636) at 475 Katlian St, and Sitka to Tenakee Springs with Mountain Aviation (☎ 966-2288), in the airport terminal, for $75 one way.

Boat The State Marine Ferry terminal is seven miles north of town on Halibut Point Rd, and there are northbound or southbound departures almost daily. Because of the unusual route the boats must follow to Sitka, it's a good idea to call the ferry terminal (☎ 747-8737) to double-check sailings and departure times.

Passage from Sitka to Juneau is $26, Sitka to Haines $40 and Sitka to Skagway $44. The Ferry Transit Bus (☎ 747-8443) meets all ferries for a trip into town. You can also catch the minibus out to the ferry terminal from the Westmark Shee Atika when it picks up hotel guests.

GAVAN HILL/HARBOR MOUNTAIN TRAILS

The only trail that actually begins downtown is Gavan Hill Trail, a three-mile climb to a 2505-foot point that is often referred to as Gavan Hill Summit. From the summit, you can continue along the Harbor Mountain Trail to reach a free-use shelter on an alpine saddle one mile later. The trail ends at Harbor Mountain Rd, the only road in Southeast Alaska that reaches sub-alpine terrain. Since Harbor Mountain Rd is a winding, gravel road, traffic is light and many backpackers end up walking the additional five miles to Halibut Point Rd. This makes the loop an 11-mile trek.

These trails are easy to access and provide well-marked routes to alpine areas where there are many spots to camp. Bring at least

a quart of water per person (two quarts if you're spending the night in the alpine area) as water is tough to find along most of the route. The hike is rated moderate and USGS 1:63,360 quads *Sitka A-4* and *A-5* are required.

Access

The Gavan Hill trailhead is within easy walking distance of the visitors' center in the Centennial Building. From Lincoln St, head north up Baranof St for six blocks to the house at 508 Baranof St past Merrill St. The trail begins just beyond this house and heads to the north-east.

Harbor Mountain Rd is four miles north-west from Sitka on Halibut Point Rd. Hitching back into town is easy as traffic is good due to the ferry terminal and camp-grounds at the end of Halibut Point Rd. If you want to arrange a ride back, check with Sitka Tours (☎ 747-8443) which runs the bus out to the ferry terminal.

Stage 1: Gavan Hill Trailhead to Free-Use Shelter

(3.5 miles, 4-5 hours)
(Free-use shelter, backcountry camping)
Departing from Baranof St, the trail follows an old pipeline path for the first half-mile through areas of muskeg. The walk is easy, however, as the wettest spots have been planked. Eventually you enter a forest of spruce and hemlock and begin climbing the south-east side of Gavan Hill and quickly pass what use to be the junction with Cross Trail. At one time this trail skirted Sitka and emerged near the high school but it is no longer maintained and is hard to follow.

Gavan Hill Trail continues to climb as a series of switchbacks to take you steeply from 500 feet until you reach the ridge line at 2000 feet, a two to three-hour hike from the trailhead. Along the way you pass a stream that provides the last reliable source of drinking water. Once on the ridge, you head north-east, first hiking through a stand of stunted trees then breaking out into the sub-alpine meadow within a quarter of a

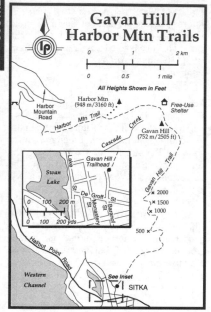

Gavan Hill/ Harbor Mtn Trails

All Heights Shown in Feet

Stage 2: Free-Use Shelter to Halibut Point Rd

(7.5 miles, 3-5 hours)

A recently cut and upgraded trail continues from the free-use shelter on the saddle towards Harbor Mountain where it curves almost due west and skirts the steep southern flank of the 3160-foot peak. Within 1.5 miles of the saddle, you climb several hundred feet to reach a south-west ridge of the mountain. This is the route most climbers follow when ascending the peaks of Harbor Mountain. Keep in mind that the craggy rock encountered during the ascent makes for poor footing and a challenging climb.

The trail heads south-west down the ridge. Within half a mile of the road end, you climb over a 2300-foot knob, where the views of Sitka and the surrounding area are stunning – you can see everything from the ferry terminal to Mt Edgecombe and the endless horizon of the Pacific Ocean.

Just before you reach Harbor Mountain Rd, the trail passes a junction. The short spur leads to the top of a 2370-foot knob where at one time the US Army built a lookout and other buildings here during WW II. The military remains are hard to find but the view is excellent. From the junction the main trail descends 300 feet off the ridge with a series of switchbacks to the end of Harbor Mountain Rd.

There is parking and an information board at the trailhead. Head half a mile down the road and you'll come to a covered picnic shelter and more tables in a sub-alpine meadow. From here Harbor Mountain Rd, a military project during WW II, heads steeply down to Halibut Point Rd, reaching it in 4.5 miles after a series of hairpin turns. It's so steep that people pulling trailers or driving recreational vehicles are strongly advised not to drive to the end of the road.

MT EDGECUMBE TRAIL

This 6.7-mile trail was originally constructed by the Civilian Conservation Corps in the 1930s; today it is a designated National Recreation Trail maintained by the USFS. It begins at Fred's Creek USFS cabin and

mile. That's followed by a short but rocky climb of 200 feet to a high point of 2100 feet.

From here the trail follows the Gavan Hill ridge past great views of the Indian River, the mountainous interior of Baranof Island and Sitka Sound. Within three miles of the trailhead the trail swings north-west and in a quarter of a mile you climb the 2505-foot summit of Gavan Hill. Needless to say, the views are spectacular on a clear day.

The trail descends the west side of the summit to the sub-alpine saddle that separates the drainage of Cascade Creek with an unnamed creek to the north. The USFS free-use shelter is in the saddle, half a mile from Gavan Hill summit. The four-sided, 10 by eight-foot shelter has no source of heat and no bunks and is used on a first-come-first-serve basis. Water is also scarce on the saddle. The alternative is to drop towards Cascade Creek and camp near a feeder stream but the view here is not nearly as good.

ascends to the summit crater of Sitka's extinct volcano. As you can imagine, the views from the summit are spectacular on a clear day. This is a moderate to challenging hike as it can be a steep climb at times – the final two miles to the summit are along a poorly marked route. From Fred's Creek Cabin to the summit crater you climb 3000 feet.

Beware of being fogged in and getting lost above the tree line (see the earlier Climate section). Carry a roll of bright plastic tape to mark the route once you're above the timber line. Begin the hike wearing rubber boots to cross the muskeg and muddy sections and then switch to sturdy hiking boots once you're higher.

The entire trek to the top and back is a 13.4-mile walk that takes most people six to eight hours. It's best to spend the first night at the shelter and turn the walk into an overnight hike or even a three-day adventure, seeing you have to spend $150 to be dropped off and picked up. The trail area is split between USGS 1:63,360 quads *Sitka A-5* and *A-6*.

Access

Mt Edgecumbe lies on Kruzof Island, 10 miles west of Sitka, and can only be reached by boat because large swells from the ocean prevent float planes from landing at Fred's Creek. Charter boat operators will drop off and pick up trekkers for around $75 one way per party. Stop at the visitors' bureau for a list of local operators or call Alaska Adven-

tures Unlimited (☎ 747-5576) and they will set up the boat charter for you.

Stage 1: Fred's Creek Cabin to Free-Use Shelter
(3 miles, 2 hours)
(USFS cabin, free-use shelter)

The trail begins behind Fred's Creek Cabin, which, if available, is a wonderful place to end the trek. The 16 by 16-foot A-frame cabin sits just inside the trees overlooking a scenic beach while its namesake creek runs along the north side of it. Inside you'll find two single bunks and a loft that sleeps four more people as well as the usual wood stove, table and cooking counter.

The trail departs west into a spruce and hemlock flat where the hiking is level at first. For the next two miles you gain little elevation, alternating between stretches of muskeg and stands of spruce. There is some planking but much of it is deteriorated and never where you really need it. Wear rubber boots and be ready to do a little 'slogging' through the mud.

The trail is not always clearly marked. Be aware of an occasional game trail; Sitka deer and black bears are common here, especially in spring. Generally, however, the main trail is easy to recognize.

At 2.5 miles you begin to parallel a stream briefly and at three miles from Fred's Creek Cabin you reach the free-use shelter at 700 feet. Built by a local conservation group, the shelter is a three-sided structure with no bunks or amenities and is often littered with

Mt Edgecumbe Trail

KRUZOF ISLAND

TONGASS NATIONAL FOREST

Fred's Creek Cabin

Mt Edgecumbe Trail

Free-Use Shelter

Sitka Sound

Mt Edgecumbe (975 m/3201 ft)

0   2   4 km

0   1   2 miles

the garbage of thoughtless hiking parties. It will keep you dry, however, if a rain storm rolls off the Pacific Ocean. Nearby is a stream for drinking water.

Stage 2: Free-Use Shelter to Summit Crater (Round Trip)
(7.4 miles, 4-6 hours)
(Free-use shelter)
The trail immediately crosses the stream in front of the shelter and continues its mild climb through the forest for another mile. When you reach 1000 feet, the climb steepens considerably as you begin to ascend the volcano's east flank.

Within another mile or so you reach 2000 feet and break out of the tree line. At this point the trail ends and the remaining 1.5 miles to the summit is for the most part a route of your own choosing. There is usually a flag to mark the trail at the tree line and a few rock cairns on the way up. But most of the cairns are destroyed each winter by the heavy snowfall.

It's important to mark the trail at the tree line with your own plastic tape and to take a second to visually memorize the ridge you are ascending in case a sudden bank of clouds or fog comes rolling in. Make sure you remove all your flagging on your way down.

Above the trees, the terrain is red volcanic ash. To reach the top, it's a stiff climb straight up but if the day is clear, you'll be stopping ever few feet to admire the views of Sitka and the mountains of Baranof Island. From the rim at the top you can peer into the crater which is several hundred feet deep. The true summit of Mt Edgecombe is a 3201-foot knob on the west side of the rim.

Once you are done playing at the peak, return along the route you climbed up, making sure you pick up the true trail at the tree line. It should take you only half the ascent time to descend to the shelter.

Juneau

Juneau is a mecca for trekkers. The city and the surrounding area offer almost everything you could want: more than 20 trails maintained by the USFS and the state of Alaska, spectacular scenery (mountains, glaciers and the Inside Passage) and a full range of commercial services and stores. It is the most developed city in the Southeast.

How good is the hiking in Alaska's state capital? The trailhead to one of the best alpine treks is only a few blocks away from the Capitol Building. The city's most popular trail system, the Perseverance, is not much further away and just as easy to reach. Several other trails can be reached on a city bus.

The only thing this area lacks is a long, multi-day hike like the Resurrection Pass Trail in the Kenai Peninsula. Although many trails can easily be turned into overnight hikes (including Dan Moller, Perseverance/ Mt Juneau circuit, Windfall Lake and Montana Creek trails) this area is for day hikers. With Juneau's excellent range of accommodations, you can enjoy scenic treks during the day and a soft bed at night – reach the alpine regions in the afternoon and sip a few with the locals in the Red Dog Saloon at night.

The highlight of Juneau's trail system is the glaciers. Thanks to the Juneau Ice Field, a number of glaciers spill out of the mountain and many of them can be viewed up close from a trail. The West Glacier Trail is one of the most spectacular hikes in the Southeast, and the Amalga Trail (Eagle Glacier) is also rewarding. Other trails providing icy views are East Glacier Trail (Mendenhall Glacier), Nugget Creek Trail (Nugget Glacier), Heintzleman Ridge Route (Mendenhall Glacier) and Herbert Glacier Trail.

While the city center clings to a mountainside, Juneau actually sprawls over 3100 sq miles to the Canadian border. There are five sections in Juneau and you'll find trailheads in all of them. Beginning in the downtown

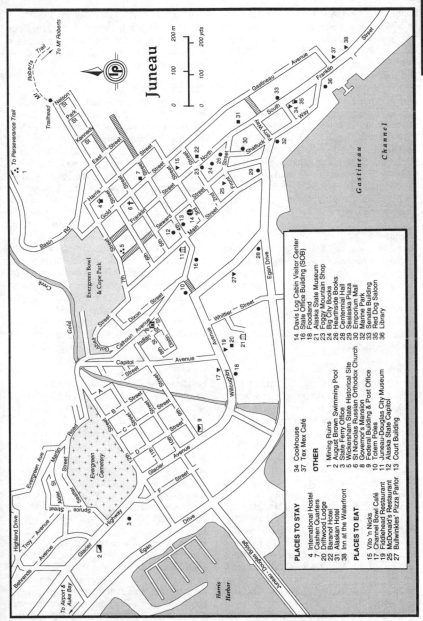

Juneau

0   100   200 m
0   100   200 yds

PLACES TO STAY
4   International Hostel
7   Cashen Quarters
20 Driftwood Lodge
22 Baranof Hotel
31 Alaskan Hotel
38 Inn at the Waterfront

PLACES TO EAT
15 Vito 'n Nicks
17 Channel Bowl Café
19 Fiddlehead Restaurant
25 McDonald's Restaurant
27 Bullwinkles' Pizza Parlor
34 Cookhouse
37 Tex Mex Café

OTHER
1   Mining Ruins
2   August Brown Swimming Pool
3   State Ferry Office
5   Wickersham State Historical Site
6   St Nicholas Russian Orthodox Church
8   Governor's Mansion
9   Federal Building & Post Office
10 Totem Poles
11 Juneau-Douglas City Museum
12 Alaska State Capitol
13 Court Building
14 Davis Log Cabin Visitor Center
16 State Office Building (SOB)
18 Foodland
21 Alaska State Museum
23 Foggy Mountain Shop
24 Big City Books
26 Hearthside Books
28 Centennial Hall
29 Sealaska Plaza
30 Emporium Mall
32 Marine Park
33 Senate Building
35 Red Dog Saloon
36 Library

area are Perseverance and Mt Roberts trails. In Mendenhall Valley and on the way to it are Salmon Creek, East Glacier, West Glacier, Nugget Creek, Heintzleman Ridge and Montana Creek trails. Beyond Mendenhall Valley, Egan Drive turns into Glacier Hwy, a two-lane road that takes you past Peterson Lake, Windfall Lake, Herbert Glacier, Amalga (Eagle Glacier) and Spaulding trails and the trails of Point Bridget State Park. Directly across the Gastineau Channel on Douglas Island is the Dan Moller Trail while from Douglas, a small town south-east of Juneau, you can access Mt Bradley and the Treadwell Ditch trails. In North Douglas you'll find Cropley Lake Trail in the Eaglecrest Ski Area.

Climate
Like Ketchikan and Sitka, Juneau is part of the coastal rainbelt of the Tongass National Forest but is somewhat drier. The average annual precipitation is 92 inches in the downtown area and only 52 inches in the Mendenhall Valley. The average temperature in Juneau from June through August is 55°F while in July it's 64°F (it often reaches the mid to high 70s).

Information
For information about cabin rental, hiking trails, Glacier Bay, Admiralty Island or any outdoor activity in the Tongass National Forest, stop at the information center (☎ 586-8751) in the Centennial Hall at 101 Egan Drive. The center is staffed by both USFS and NPS personnel and is open from 8 am to 5 pm daily in the summer. Among the items for sale is the USFS booklet *Juneau Trails* ($3).

For a map of Juneau's Point Bridget State Park or information on any state park in the Southeast, stop at the Alaska Division of State Parks office (☎ 465-4563) on the 3rd floor, 400 Willoughby Ave. It is open from 8 am to 4.30 pm Monday to Friday. Current fishing conditions can be obtained by calling the Alaska Fish & Game Department hot line on ☎ 465-4116.

The main visitors' center for travel infor-

mation is the Davis Log Cabin (☎ 586-2201) at 134 3rd St. It's open from 8.30 am to 5 pm Monday through Friday; during the summer it's also open on the weekend from 10 am until 5 pm.

Places to Stay
Camping There are some fine campgrounds beyond Mendenhall Valley and a dozen unofficial ones near the city center. *Mendenhall Lake Campground*, one of the most beautiful USFS campgrounds in Alaska, is 13 miles from downtown and five miles south of the Auke Bay Ferry Terminal. The campground (60 sites) has a separate seven-site backpacking unit and is on Montana Creek Rd, a dirt road that runs off Mendenhall Loop Rd. There is a 14-day limit and the nightly fee is $5 per site.

The other USFS campground, *Auke Village*, is two miles north of the ferry terminal on Glacier Hwy. The city of Juneau now allows RV parking at the Norway Point Parking Area near Aurora Basin off Egan Drive (downtown) and at Savikko Park in Douglas for $5 a night. There is also *Auke Bay RV Park* (☎ 789-9467), 1.5 miles east of the ferry terminal. It's a full-service campground and charges $16 per night.

Hostels The *Juneau International Hostel* (☎ 586-9559) is one of the best hostels in Alaska. The large yellow house is on the corner of Harris and 6th Sts, only four blocks from the Mt Roberts Trail and two blocks from Basin Rd which leads to the Perseverance Trail system. The hostel has cooking and laundry facilities, showers, and a common room with a fireplace. Fees are $10 for youth hostel members and $13 for non-members. For reservations contact the hostel at 614 Harris St, Juneau, AK 99801.

B&Bs Juneau has exploded with B&Bs. There are almost two dozen and most cost from $40 to $50 for a single and $60 and up for a double. The only problem is securing a room after stepping off the ferry late at night. For that reason, it's wise to book ahead, even a day or two, while traveling through the region. An easy way to do this is to contact the Alaska Bed & Breakfast Association (☎ 586-2959) which covers most of the Southeast, including Juneau.

The *Pearson's Pond* (☎ 789-3772) is in the Mendenhall Valley, within walking distance of most of the trails around the famous glacier. Prices start at $69 a night. Even further out is *Lost Cord Bed & Breakfast* (☎ 789-7296). It's 12 miles from downtown but features a private beach on Auke Bay. Rooms cost $50/55 a single/double and include a courtesy pick-up at the ferry terminal or airport.

Hotels Most hotels, especially the downtown ones, tend to be heavily booked during the summer tourist season. The cheapest hotel is the *Inn at the Waterfront* (☎ 586-2050), a small hotel across from the cold-storage plant on South Franklin St. The owners recently redecorated the rooms, but it would be wise to look before you rent. Rooms cost from $42 a single with shared bath (price includes the use of a steam bath). On South Franklin St is the *Alaskan Hotel* (☎ 586-1000) with charming historical décor in its lobby and rooms dating back to 1913 when it first opened. Singles without bath are $50 a night. There is also *Driftwood Lodge* (☎ 586-2280), downtown near the Alaska State Museum. Rooms cost from $66. The motel has a courtesy van that meets the ferry and you can't beat the location. Other motels in Juneau cost between $75 and $80 a single.

Maps
You can purchase USGS quads in the downtown area at the Forest Service Information Center in the Centennial Hall on Egan Drive, from Foggy Mountain Shop (☎ 586-6780) at 134 North Franklin St, and at Big City Books (☎ 586-1772) nearby at 100 North Franklin St. In the Valley area, try Heartside Books (☎ 789-2750) in the Nugget Mall. All trails are covered on USGS 1:63,360 quads *Juneau A-1, B-1, B-2, B-3* and *C-3*.

Equipment
An excellent selection of backpacking equipment, mountaineering tools and just about anything you need on a trek or to climb a glacier can be found at *Foggy Mountain Shop* (see Maps, above). You might want to invest in rubber boots or 'Southeast sneakers' as they are affectionately called by the locals. Many of the trails can be quite muddy so these brown rubber boots are more suitable than hiking boots. They can be purchased from several places around town.

Cabins
Numerous USFS cabins are accessible from Juneau but all are heavily used, requiring reservations as early as 180 days in advance. If you're just passing through, however, check with the USFS information center in the Centennial Building, where staff maintain a list showing which cabins are still available and when.

Four USFS cabins are accessible from the Juneau 'trail system. The Spaulding Trail leads to the John Muir Cabin in the alpine area above the tree line. There are also cabins at the end of Dan Moller, Peterson Lake and Amalga trails (the latter is a recently renovated unit overlooking Eagle Glacier). All cabins along the road system can be used by anybody from 10 am to 5 pm as warming shelters.

Cabins cost $25 a night and you can get a description of them from the USFS information center in Centennial Building. The only free-use shelter on the Juneau trail system is Vista Shelter near the end of the Nugget Creek Trail, a one-way hike of four miles from Mendenhall Glacier Visitor Center.

The state Division of Parks & Outdoor Recreation also maintains a cabin in Point Bridget State Park that is accessible by foot and costs $25 a night. Call the Juneau office (☎ 465-4563) to reserve it in advance.

Trails
For those who don't feel up to walking the trails on their own, Juneau Parks & Recreation (☎ 586-5226) leads adult hikes every Wednesday, and family hikes along easier

trails every Saturday. The hikes begin at the chosen trailhead at 10 am. On Wednesday there is often car-pooling to the trail, with hikers meeting at Cope Park, a short walk from the hostel. Call Juneau Parks & Recreation for more details. Alaska Rainforest Tours (☎ 463-3466) offers guided hikes into the surrounding area, supplying transportation, lunch and any equipment you might need such as rain gear or boots.

Mt Roberts Trail This is the one of two hikes accessible on foot from downtown. The trail is a 2.7-mile ascent to the mountain above the city. The trail begins at a marked wooden staircase at the north-eastern end of 6th St and consists of a series of switchbacks with good resting spots. When you break out of the trees at Gastineau Peak you come across a wooden cross and good views of Juneau, Douglas and the entire Gastineau Channel. The Mt Roberts summit is a steep climb through the alpine brush to the north of the city. Plan about three hours to hike up and half that time coming back down (USGS quad *Juneau B-2*).

Treadwell Ditch Trail This trail on Douglas Island can be picked up either a mile up the Dan Moller Trail or just above D St in Douglas. The trail stretches 12 miles north from Douglas to Eagle Crest, although most people only hike to the Dan Moller Trail and then return to the road, a five-mile trip. The path is rated easy and provides views of the Gastineau Channel while winding through scenic muskeg meadows (USGS quad *Juneau B-2*).

Mt Bradley Trail Also known as Mt Jumbo, this 2.6-mile trail begins in Douglas through a vacant lot behind section 300 of 5th St and is a much harder climb than the hikes up Mt Roberts or Mt Juneau. Both rubber boots and sturdy hiking boots are needed as the trail can be muddy in the lower sections before you reach the beautiful alpine areas above the tree line. The climb to the 3337-foot peak should only be attempted by experienced hikers as there are dangerous drop-offs near

the top. Plan on four hours to the top even if the weather is good (USGS quads *Juneau A-2* and *B-2*).

Cropley Lake Trail Also on Douglas Island is the 1.5-mile route to Cropley Lake. The trail was built primarily for cross-country skiing but in the summer it can be hiked to the alpine lake, which provides good scenery and camping. The trailhead is up Fish Creek Rd, a short way past the Eagle Crest Ski Lodge in a creek gully to the right (USGS quad *Juneau B-2*).

Sheep Creek Trail South-east of Juneau along Thane Rd is the very scenic Sheep Creek Trail, a three-mile walk into the valley south of Mt Roberts where there are many historical mining relics. The trailhead is four miles from Juneau at a staircase on the gravel spur to a Snettisham Power Plant substation. The trail is relatively flat in the valley, from where you scramble up forested hillsides to the alpine zone. Many hikers follow the power line once there you are above the tree line to reach the ridge to Sheep Mountain. From here it is possible to continue from Sheep Mountain over Mt Roberts and return to Juneau along the Mt Roberts Trail. This is a very long 10 to 12-hour day hike, if attempted (*USGS quad Juneau B-1*).

Point Bishop Trail At the end of Thane Rd, 7.5 miles south-east of Juneau, is this eight-mile trail to Point Bishop, a scenic spot that overlooks the junction between Stephens Passage and Taku Inlet. The trail is flat but can be wet in many spots, making waterproof boots the preferred footwear. The hike makes an ideal overnight trip as there is good camping at Point Bishop (USGS quads *Juneau A-1* and *B-1*).

Salmon Creek Trail Just off the northbound lane of Egan Drive there is access to this 3.5-mile trail to Salmon Creek Dam. The trail is reached by heading north 2.5 miles on the divided highway and turning right into Salmon Creek Power House grounds, just past the long retaining wall along Egan

Pinnell Mountain Trail (JD)

Top: August snowfall in Morino Campground, Denali National Park (JD)
Middle: Panning for gold, Perseverance Trail (JD)
Bottom: Cabin near Susitna Ranges (JW)

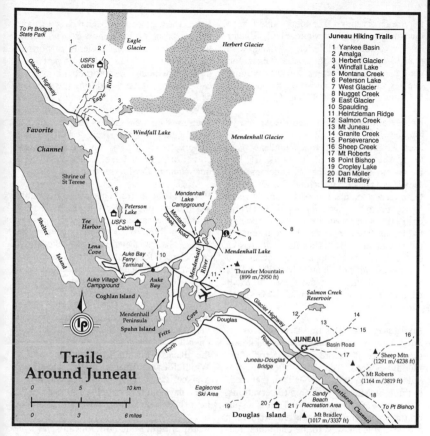

Juneau Hiking Trails

1 Yankee Basin
2 Amalga
3 Herbert Glacier
4 Windfall Lake
5 Montana Creek
6 Peterson Lake
7 West Glacier
8 Nugget Creek
9 East Glacier
10 Spaulding
11 Heintzleman Ridge
12 Salmon Creek
13 Mt Juneau
14 Granite Creek
15 Perseverance
16 Sheep Creek
17 Mt Roberts
18 Point Bishop
19 Cropley Lake
20 Dan Moller
21 Mt Bradley

Trails Around Juneau

Drive. The trail is posted. Hikers used to follow the old tramway and flume up to the reservoir but for safety reasons you now must walk along an access road for the first two miles. After crossing Salmon Creek a trail departs into the woods and leads you to the foot of the dam. Steep stairways take you up to the dam catwalk and to a view of the surrounding mountains. Use USGS quad *Juneau B-2* for this trail.

East Glacier Trail This trail, one of several near the Mendenhall Glacier, is a three-mile round trip that provides good views of the glacier from a scenic lookout at the halfway point. The trail begins off the half-mile nature walk near the Mendenhall Glacier Visitor Center and ends at a junction with the Nugget Creek Trail. Halfway along the trail you pass AJ Waterfalls. Like all the trails at the end of the Mendenhall Valley, you can get reasonably close to the trailheads on a city bus (USGS quad *Juneau B-2*).

Nugget Creek Trail Just beyond the East Glacier Trail's scenic lookout is the start of the 2.5-mile Nugget Creek Trail to the Vista Creek Shelter, a free-use shelter that doesn't require reservations. The total round trip to the shelter from the Mendenhall Glacier Visitor Center is eight miles. Hikers who plan to spend the night at the shelter can continue along the creek towards Nugget Glacier, though the route is bushy and hard to follow at times (USGS quad *Juneau B-2*).

Heintzleman Ridge Route A sparsely marked route, not a well-maintained trail, it leads 2.5 miles to 2950-foot Thunder Mountain, the southernmost peak of the Heintzleman Ridge. The route begins as a trail which you pick up behind Glacier Valley Elementary School in the Mendenhall Valley. From Mendenhall Loop Rd turn right onto Trinity Drive and then left at the school to pick up Jennifer Drive – the trail starts at the end of this road. After the trail crosses Jordan Creek, it begins a steep ascent of a south-west ridge of Thunder Mountain. This is a difficult hike but the views of Mendenhall Glacier are spectacular (USGS quad *Juneau B-2*).

Spaulding Trail This trail's primary use is cross-country skiing, but it can be trekked in the summer if you're prepared for some muddy sections. The three-mile trail provides access to the Auke Nu Trail that leads to the John Muir USFS Cabin (reservations, $25 per night). The Auke Nu Trail is a spur off the Spaulding Trail that is reached within a mile and leads west to the cabin, a three-mile hike from Glacier Hwy in Auke Bay. It is well planked. The Spaulding Trail continues for another 1.5 miles and ends in Spaulding Meadows, an alpine area that is a favorite with cross-country skiers in the winter.

The trailhead is at Glacier Hwy opposite the Auke Bay post office and 12.3 miles north-west of Juneau. Check at the information center in Centennial Building for information on the availability of the cabin (USGS quads *Juneau B-2* and *B-3*).

Peterson Lake Trail This four-mile trail provides access to good Dolly Varden fishing in both Peterson Creek and Peterson Lake. The trailhead has been moved to avoid private property and is now 20 feet before the *Mile 24* marker on Glacier Hwy, north of the Shrine of St Terese. Although part of the trail is now planked, wear rubber boots as it can still be very muddy during the summer. Most of the route is through heavy hemlock forest but occasionally you trek through open muskeg areas or pass anglers' spurs to fishing holes in the river. A USFS cabin (reservations, $25) is on the south-west corner of Peterson Lake. You'll need USGS quad *Juneau B-3* for this trail.

Herbert Glacier Trail This level trail extends 4.6 miles along Herbert River to Herbert Glacier. The trail is easy, though wet in some places, and the round trip takes four to five hours. The trail begins just past the bridge over Herbert River at *Mile 28* of Glacier Hwy in a small parking lot to the left and skirts the base of Goat Mountain. It ends just before the glacier's terminal moraine. By scrambling onto rock piles to the left of the glacier you can reach an excellent vantage point to view the ice and a spectacular waterfall. Plan on at least five hours for a round-trip hike to the glacier. This trail is in the same area as Windfall Lake, Amalga (Eagle Glacier) and Yankee Basin trails. You can spend two or three days out here hopping from one to the next (USGS quad *Juneau C-3*).

Point Bridget State Park Juneau's first state park (2850 acres) was created in 1988. Reached at *Mile 39* of Glacier Hwy, only two miles short of its end at Echo Cove, the park features more than 10 miles of trails. These include a stroll along a beach overlooking Lynn Canal where occasionally you'll spot sea lions or humpback whales. By combining the Point Bridget Trail with Cedar Lake and Trappers trails you form a nine-mile loop that passes the best scenery of the park, including Point Bridget, Cedar Lake and Camping Cove. This is one of the few trails in the Juneau area where the state park map is adequate for hikers.

The park also features one of the newest Division of Parks & Outdoor Recreation cabins. A 2.5-mile walk off Point Bridget Trail, the nine-bunk cabin costs $25. You can also backcountry camp throughout the park, and the beaches overlooking Berners Bay make a particularly pleasant place to set up a tent for a night or two. Call the Division of Parks & Outdoor Recreation in Juneau (☎ 465-4563) to book the cabin in advance (USGS quad *Juneau C-3*).

Getting There & Away
Air Alaska Airlines (☎ 789-0600) has scheduled services to Seattle, all major Southeast communities, Glacier Bay, Anchorage, and Cordova from Juneau daily during the summer. The one-way fare from Juneau to Anchorage ranges from $109 to $140. To fly from Juneau to Cordova (to pick up the state ferries to the Southcentral ports of Valdez, Seward, Homer and Kodiak) costs $176 one way. Delta Airlines (☎ 789-9771) has daily scheduled flights from Juneau to Anchorage, Fairbanks and Seattle. Both airlines have a ticket office in the Baranof Hotel on South Franklin St.

Boat The state ferry arrives and departs from the Auke Bay Ferry Terminal (☎ 789-7453), some 12 miles from the city center. There are daily state ferry departures during the summer from Juneau to Sitka for $26, Petersburg $44, Ketchikan $74, Haines $20 and Skagway $26. A smaller ferry, *Le Conte*, connects Juneau with Hoonah, Angoon and Tenakee Springs. The main ticket office for the ferry (☎ 465-3941) is at 1591 Glacier Ave. You can either call that office or the Auke Bay terminal for ferry information.

Getting Around
To/From the Airport & Ferry Terminal
Transport can be a problem when you arrive at Juneau Airport or the Auke Bay Ferry Terminal. Late-night arrivals heading for the downtown area are best off getting the Mendenhall Glacier Transport bus (☎ 789-5460) that meets all ferry arrivals or the Gray Line Shuttle Bus (☎ 586-3773) that provides a service from the airport. Fares to the city

center are $6 from the airport and $6 from the Auke Bay Ferry Terminal.

During the day, it is possible to walk to the nearest public bus stop to catch a $1 ride into town. From the ferry terminal, walk south along the Glacier Hwy for a little over a mile to Dehart's Grocery Store near the Auke Bay Terminal. From the airport, just stroll from the terminal to Airport Mall on Old Glacier Hwy.

Car Rental For the trails out on Glacier Hwy, the only available transportation (besides an expensive taxi ride) are rental cars. There are almost a dozen car rental places in Juneau and most offer either unlimited mileage or at least 100 free miles. For a $29 special, call Rent-A-Wreck (☎ 789-4111) at 8600 Airport Blvd or Mendenhall Auto Center (☎ 789-1386) in the Valley at 8725 Mallard St. The rest tend to charge $40 a day. Try All Star Rental (☎ 790-2414), Payless Rentals (☎ 780-4144) or Budget Rent-A-Car (☎ 789-5186).

Bus Capital Transit, Juneau's public bus system, runs hourly during the week with alternating local and express services from 7 am until 11.45 pm and from 9 am to 6.30 pm on Sunday. The main route circles the downtown area, stops at the City Dock Ferry Terminal, the Capitol Building and the Federal Building, and then heads out to Mendenhall Valley and Auke Bay Boat Harbor via the Mendenhall Loop Rd, where it travels close to the Mendenhall Lake Campground and the Montana Creek Trail. There is also a minibus that runs every hour from city stops to Douglas. Fares are $1 each way. Grab a route map at the city offices on Marine Way or from the visitors' center; call ☎ 789-6901 for more information.

PERSEVERANCE TRAIL
Tucked away behind a mountain is the upper valley of Gold Creek and the city's most popular place to walk and hike, the Perseverance Trail system. Named after a mine that operated from 1885 to 1895 in the Silverbow Basin, the 3.5-mile trail also provides access

to the 1.5-mile Granite Creek Trail and the two-mile climb to the top of 3576-foot Mt Juneau.

When you combine all three treks, plus the ridge walk between the Granite Creek Trail and the Mt Juneau peak you have a 10-mile trek that can be done in one long Alaska summer day or be turned into an overnight excursion with a camp in the upper basin of Granite Creek.

Access to this trail is easy and the scenery is excellent. Locals and visitors alike make their way up Basin Rd to the Perseverance trails so you'll undoubtedly meet a number of people on this trek. Perseverance Trail itself is rated easy. The entire loop is a moderately challenging hike and is covered on the USGS 1:63,360 quad *Juneau B-2*.

Access

From downtown, head up Gold St which leads to Basin Rd. This scenic dirt road will skirt along the steep ravine of Gold Creek and then finally cross the creek itself. After crossing the bridge over Gold Creek, take the left-hand fork and follow it to a posted trailhead.

Stage 1: Basin Rd to Granite Creek's Upper Basin

(3.5 miles, 2-3 hours)

(Backcountry campsite)

The loop begins with the Perseverance Trail. From its Basin Rd trailhead you begin with a gentle climb above Gold Creek and quickly reach a fenced-in lookout high above the stream. On the other side of the ravine, in full view, are buildings and other remains of the Alaska-Juneau Mine.

Within half a mile is the posted trailhead of the Mt Juneau Trail, reached just before the spur descends in the opposite direction to Ebner Falls. Named after a miner who operated a stamping mill here in 1896, the falls are a thundering sight and well worth the extra effort of following the short spur to them.

The main trail continues heading north along rushing Gold Creek while skirting the base of the ridge that you will be returning

on. It was here, in the streams draining this valley, where Joe Juneau and Richard Harris turned up flakes of gold in 1880 that resulted in the gold rush and tent city that today is the capital of Alaska. Much of the trail itself is an old wagon road back to the mines in Silverbow Basin. You cross Gold Creek twice in the next 1.5 miles and just after the second time arrive at a bridge over Granite Creek. Just up the trail is the junction to the Granite Creek Trail.

Perseverance heads right and gently climbs for another 1.5 miles until it ends at Silverbow Basin, site of the Perseverance Mine that operated until 1895. In the early 1890s the complex included a boarding house, a blacksmith shop and a compressor plant near the end of the trail but little remains today. Less than half a mile from the end of the trail you pass a well-beaten spur that leads to the Glory Hole, a hard-rock mine shaft almost 300 feet deep.

Granite Creek Trail heads left at the junction and skirts the valley slope along the east side of the creek. Mud and snow will persist late into June. The trail climbs into the first basin, the site of many waterfalls and wild flowers through much of July. From here you continue to follow the creek to reach the upper basin at the base of Olds Mountain, 1.5 miles from the junction with the Perseverance Trail. Good camping abounds in both basins.

Stage 2: Granite Creek to Basin Rd via Mt Juneau

(6.5 miles, 5-6 hours)

Those who detest backtracking more than being swatted by devil's club can return to Basin Rd via a ridge walk and the Mt Juneau Trail. Even without a backpack this can be a challenging all-day work-out. But if the weather is nice, the alpine area is great and well worth all the effort you spend climbing. The alternative, of course, is to leave the equipment at Granite Creek and spend a morning romping along the ridge and then return to hike out the way you came. Either way, make sure your water bottle is filled

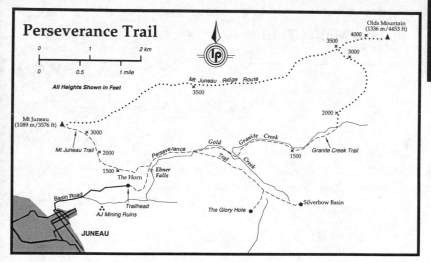

Perseverance Trail

0   1   2 km

0   0.5   1 mile

All Heights Shown in Feet

Olds Mountain
(1336 m/4453 ft)
4000
3500
3000

Mt Juneau Ridge Route
3500

Mt Juneau
(1089 m/3576 ft)
3000

2000

Mt Juneau Trail 2000

Granite Creek

Gold Creek

Granite Creek Trail
1500

1500

Perseverance Trail

Ebner Falls
The Horn

Basin Road

Trailhead
AJ Mining Ruins

The Glory Hole

Silverbow Basin

JUNEAU

because water will be difficult to find once you're on the ridges.

From the upper basin at 2200 feet, you access the ridge line to Mt Juneau by scrambling up the brushy and open grass slopes to the west (left) of Olds Mountain. Once on the saddle to the west side of the distinctively rocky mountain, you can drop the packs for a scramble up the 4453-foot peak. You continue the trek back by following the ridge line west. There is no official trail but the route is a natural one as it follows the ridge for 3.5 miles.

Eventually you reach Mt Juneau where from near its 3576-foot summit, you get a sweeping panorama that includes downtown Juneau, the Gastineau Channel, Douglas Island and, if the day is clear enough, the north end of Admiralty Island. On the open grassy slopes to the south, the two-mile long Mt Juneau Trail which leads to the Perseverance Trail is easy to pick up. It begins with an extremely steep descent of the mountain, dropping almost 2000 feet, and passes a small patch of trees.

Eventually the trail skirts the open slopes for almost a mile, crossing one cascading stream after another. In June, this area will often be a series of snow slides that should be avoided or crossed with extreme caution using an ice axe. If you're traveling in the opposite direction in July or August, gather water here because there is little to be found on top.

You resume descending, pass through a stand of hemlocks where at the edge there is a view of Gold Creek and then finish off the trail with a series of switchbacks through shoulder-high alder. Mt Juneau Trail joins the Perseverance Trail near the spur to Ebner Falls. Head west (right) on Perseverance to return to Basin Rd within half a mile.

DAN MOLLER TRAIL

This is another easy-to-access trail that climbs to a beautiful alpine area overlooking the capital city. The Dan Moller Trail also provides access to the peaks and ridges that make up the backbone of Douglas Island. While the trail to the USFS cabin is only a 3.3-mile easy trek, if you're experienced with a map and compass could spend an entire day walking the ridges and even return via Cropley Lake and the road to Eaglecrest Ski Area.

This trek can also be done as an overnight

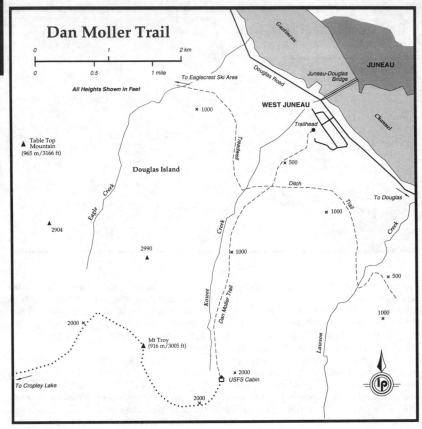

Dan Moller Trail

All Heights Shown in Feet

To Eaglecrest Ski Area

× 1000

Table Top Mountain (965 m/3166 ft)

Douglas Island

Eagle Creek

▲ 2904

▲ 2990

2000 ×

To Cropley Lake

Mt Troy (916 m/3005 ft) ▲

2000 ×

Kowee Creek

Dan Moller Trail

× 2000 USFS Cabin

Gastineau

Douglas Road

Juneau-Douglas Bridge

JUNEAU

WEST JUNEAU

Trailhead

× 500

Ditch

Treadwell

Trail

× 1000

To Douglas

Creek

× 500

1000 ×

Lawson

Channel

---

excursion. Either reserve the USFS cabin in advance ($25) or carry up a tent to make camp in Kowee Basin. In August, also carry up a small container – the blueberries will be hard to pass up.

The trail, Cropley Lake and the alpine route to Eaglecrest access road is covered on USGS 1:63,360 quad *Juneau B-2*.

Access

The trailhead is 1.5 miles from the Juneau International Hostel. You can easily walk to it or catch the minibus to Douglas ($1) that runs every hour. Depart at Cordova St, which

leads up into a growth of apartments and condominiums known as West Juneau. From Cordova St turn left onto Pioneer Ave and follow it to the end of the pavement. The trail begins past the fifth house on the right where there is a trailhead and a small parking area.

Stage 1: Pioneer Street to USFS Cabin
(3.3 miles, 1½-2 hours)
(USFS cabin, backcountry campsites)
From the trailhead parking area, the Dan Moller Trail begins as an old road and climbs steadily through the lush spruce forest. But within half a mile you break out at the first

of several muskeg meadows on the way to the cabin. Most of them have been planked, making the hiking considerably easier or allowing you to pause in mid-summer to enjoy the abundance of wild flowers. If it's August, look for blueberries and other wild berries.

Shortly after the first meadow, you reach the posted junction of the Treadwell Ditch Trail. By heading right here, you will quickly reach a bridge over Kowee Creek. The creek is named after the Native chief who lived at the base of it at one time and supposedly led Joe Juneau and Richard Harris up Gold Creek to the precious metal that quickly gave rise to the city of Juneau.

The Dan Moller Trail continues to climb to eventually break out of the tree line. In the final mile, it skirts Kowee Creek before reaching the USFS cabin in a beautiful alpine bowl, surrounded by the high ridges that form the crest of Douglas Island. Before there was Eaglecrest in 1976, this was the place to go downhill skiing. Known as the Douglas Ski Bowl, you would have to hike up here with your skis and then use tow ropes to ski.

Forester Dan Moller was responsible for building the trail in the early 1930s and by 1936 a warming cabin was constructed in the bowl. Once Eaglecrest opened, the cabin was vandalised periodically until a local Juneau group, mostly cross-country skiers, donated time and materials and rebuilt it in 1983. The cabin is rented out at night but serves as a warming hut from 10 am to 5 pm.

Even if you can't reserve the cabin in advance, the bowl is a wonderful place to camp. Arrive in the morning and then spend the afternoon bushwhacking brush and small trees up the ridge to the top of Douglas Island. The distinctive peak just west along the ridge from the bowl is Mt Troy, whose 3005-foot summit is an easy side trip.

Stage 2: The Return – USFS Cabin to Pioneer Rd

(3.3 miles, 1-2 hours)

For most people the only way up is the only way down along this point-to-point trail. But you can deviate near the end once you reach the junction with Treadwell Ditch Trail in the first meadow. If you head east (right) on the trail, in five miles you'll reach the Mt Jumbo trailhead on 5th St in Douglas. Keep in mind that sections of the trail at this end can be wet and boggy during the summer.

If you head west (left) the trail leads seven miles to Fish Creek and the access road to Eaglecrest in North Douglas.

WEST GLACIER TRAIL

This is one of the most spectacular trails in not only the Juneau area but in all of the Southeast. The 3.4-mile trail begins off Montana Creek Rd past Mendenhall Lake Campground and hugs the mountainside along Mendenhall Glacier, providing exceptional views of the ice falls and other glacial features. It ends at a rocky outcrop but a rough route continues from here to the summit of McGinnis Mountain, another two miles away.

Plan on four to five hours for the West Glacier Trail, a moderately easy hike that can be done in tennis shoes. If you want to tackle the difficult McGinnis Mountain Route, plan on a long day and wear sturdy hiking boots. Snow persists along this route well into June but later in the summer you can do an overnight trek and camp above the tree line. The round trip on the West Glacier Trail is 6.8 miles; the climb to McGinnis Mountain is 10.8 miles.

For those equipped with crampons, an ice axe and a climbing rope, the West Glacier Trail is the most common route to Mendenhall Glacier. Ice climbers generally hike 1.5 miles or so up the trail before cutting over to the glacier. The trail and route to McGinnis Mountain are covered on the USGS 1:63,360 quad *Juneau B-2*.

Access

From Mendenhall Hall Loop Rd, turn north onto Montana Creek Rd and then follow the signs to the campground. Go past the entrance of the campground to a parking area and you'll find the trailhead at the end of the dirt road. A Juneau city bus ($1) will drop you off at the corner of Mendenhall Loop and Montana Creek Rds and from there it's an extra mile to the beginning of the trail.

Stage 1: Mendenhall Lake Campground to Rocky Outcrop

(3.4 miles, 2-3 hours)

From the north side of the parking lot the trail departs into a stand of willow, cottonwood and alder as it begins to skirt Mendenhall Lake. Within half a mile you cross the first of two bridged streams but rarely see the lake or the glacier. After crossing the second

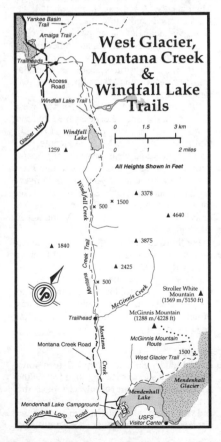

West Glacier, Montana Creek & Windfall Lake Trails

stream, roughly a mile from the parking lot, the trail begins climbing the eastern flank of McGinnis Mountain along a series of switchbacks. Just before the trail starts ascending, look for spurs that will lead you down to the lake and close views of the glacier's face.

The trail climbs up a bluff and in the next mile you begin enjoying spectacular views of Mendenhall Glacier from above. The trail then begins skirting the flank of McGinnis Mountain and becomes more challenging to follow. Look for rock cairns if in doubt. Eventually, after crossing many small streams and climbing some steep sections, the first ice fall, where the glacier makes a sharp descent towards the valley, appears and is easy to recognize even for those whose only experience with ice falls is the hotel ice machine.

The trail ends at the top of a rocky outcrop where there are spectacular 180-degree views of the glacier and ice pinnacles. Looming above this frozen river are sheer-sided mountains. If the day is nice and the sun is out, cancel the rest of your itinerary and spend an afternoon on this rock ledge. This is one of the most beautiful spots in Juneau. If it's drizzling out, consider yourself lucky. The deepest blues and other shades of glaciers are always better on a cloudy day in light rain.

Stage 2: The Return – McGinnis Mountain Route

(3.4 miles, 2 hours)

For most, the second stage of this trek is a return to the parking lot and the Mendenhall Lake Campground, a faster trek of two hours or less.

The alternative for very experienced hikers, who are in good physical shape, is to continue on the McGinnis Mountain Route. This route is not maintained and usually flagged only with plastic. From the rocky outcrop look for a trail that departs into thick brush and climbs steeply up a forested ridge on the east side of the mountain.

The trail breaks out of the trees at 2300 feet and ends at an alpine meadow, featuring a small tarn. From here you continue west ascending through alpine meadows to the 4228-foot summit, a two-mile trek from the end of the West Glacier Trail. The views on a clear day are almost infinite and include not only all of Mendenhall Glacier, Auke Bay and the Juneau Ice Field but the distant Fair-weather Mountains in Glacier Bay National Park to the north-west. If you haul up a tent and sleeping bags, there are many spots to camp above the tree line.

MONTANA CREEK & WINDFALL LAKE TRAILS

These two trails connect at Windfall Lake and can be combined for an interesting 13-mile overnight trip. Both trails are noted for being extremely wet and muddy at times. On the 9.5-mile Montana Creek Trail hikers used to contend with a rock-slide area, but in 1993 the USFS rebuilt the trail and improved the conditions considerably. So much so, that they held a foot race on it that year and the winner covered the 13 miles in an hour and 10 minutes.

Trekkers generally take a little longer, anywhere from seven to nine hours to walk from the end of Montana Creek Rd, over a low pass to Glacier Hwy via Windfall Lake Trail. There are no cabins or shelters but it's possible to camp around Windfall Lake. During July and early August Montana Creek supports sockeye, and silver salmon runs. The fishing for sockeye can be espe-cially good.

During this time watch out for bears and hang your food. Also watch out for an occa-sional mountain biker; cyclists take to this route now that it has been improved. Montana Creek Trail is covered on USGS 1:63,350 quads *Juneau B-2* and *B-3*, Wind-fall Lake Trail on quad *Juneau C-3*. The entire route is easy to moderate.

Access

The Montana Creek Trail begins near the end of Montana Creek Rd, three miles from its junction with Mendenhall Loop Rd, where a city bus will drop you off. The 3.5-mile Windfall Lake Trail begins off a gravel spur that leaves the Glacier Hwy just before it crosses Herbert River, 27 miles north-west of Juneau. There is no public transportation to this end.

Stage 1: Montana Creek Rd to Windfall Lake

(9.5 miles, 4-5 hours)
(Backcountry campsites)
The Montana Creek Trail, once part of a gold miners' trail that extended all the way to Echo Cove, begins as an easy walk in the forest. Within half a mile you cross a bridge to the east side of the creek and continue upstream into the slide area. There are about a dozen slides above the creek. In 1993 the USFS used the stone to build a trail bed and fill in many of the wet areas. Now the hike up to the pass is easy and for the most part, dry.

The river here draws the heaviest runs of salmon, attracting both fly fishers and bears. Beware. Beyond the slide area you continue a gentle climb along the river through the woods eventually to cross a bridge over Montana Creek and then a smaller feeder stream. Within three hours of the trailhead you gain over 200 feet to reach the pass. This low saddle is a series of large, boggy meadows that serves as the headwaters for Windfall and Montana creeks. From here, experienced trekkers will be able to reach the John Muir Cabin in Spaulding Meadows.

The trail continues north-west through the meadows and then begins descending into the Windfall Creek watershed via a series of switchbacks. At first you're above the creek but then after passing through a meadow you reach Windfall Creek and cross it nine miles from the trailhead.

You are now only two miles from the south end of Windfall Lake and the trail here is easy to follow. You cross two feeder streams and then emerge at the outflow of the lake into Windfall Creek where at one time there was a free-use shelter. The shelter is long gone but the meadow still makes it one of the best spots to camp. Near the south end a breeze comes off the lake. That's important – the bugs can be bad here at times.

Most of Windfall's shoreline is heavily forested and the only other spot to camp is at the north-west corner. Continue on the trail which skirts the east side of the lake to arrive at a junction with Windfall Lake Trail. Here a half-mile spur leads around a hill to an open area that can be wet and boggy at times.

Stage 2: Windfall Lake to Glacier Hwy
(3.5 miles, 2 hours)
The walk out to Glacier Hwy is along Windfall Lake Trail which begins at the junction with Montana Creek Trail and extends 3.5 miles north-west. This is an easy hike along a well-maintained trail. Plan on two hours to reach Glacier Hwy, less if you are intentionally hustling along.

From the junction, you skirt around a hill that overlooks the north end of Windfall Lake and then immediately come to a large beaver pond. This used to be a wet section of the trail but the USFS has since installed an elevated boardwalk across the pond to help you keep your boots dry. The trail continues north passing several other beaver ponds. At one time you could pick up a spur that lead to Herbert Glacier from here but the beavers and their dams have made maintenance of that route impossible.

Within a mile of the junction, you cross a bridge over a stream diverting off nearby Herbert River and then continue into the lush forest of spruce, western hemlock and devil's club. In another mile, you cross the same stream and on the other side of the bridge reach the glacial river.

The final 1.5 miles of the trail closely skirts the Herbert River and is a scenic trek. You'll have the rushing water at your feet and the peaks that surround Herbert Glacier, above you. The trail ends in a parking area and from here you follow a gravel road for a quarter of a mile out to Glacier Hwy.

AMALGA TRAIL
Practically next door to Windfall Lake Trail is Amalga Trail. Also known as the Eagle Glacier Trail, this level route winds 5.5 miles one way to the lake formed by Eagle Glacier, where there is now a USFS cabin (reservations, $25). The view from the Eagle Glacier cabin is one of the best from any of the USFS

cabins in the area. It's the cabin well worth reserving in advance.

Even if you can't secure the unit, don't pass up the trail. This is a very scenic hike and there are plenty of places to pitch a tent. As long as you've made your way this far out, you may as well stay for a day or two and soak up the scenery.

Camp in a pleasant open area half a mile south of the lake. You can then day hike to the glacier which has retreated two miles beyond the lake. The round trip for this moderate trek is 15 miles. Most people cover it in seven to eight hours. The trail is covered on USGS 1:63,360 quad *Juneau B-3*.

Access
The trailhead is at *Mile 28* of Glacier Hwy, just beyond the bridge across Eagle River and a quarter of a mile past the trailhead for Herbert Glacier Trail. There is no public transportation this far out.

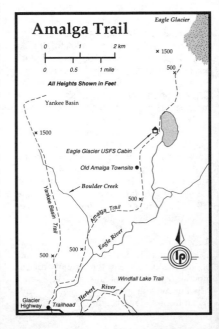

Stage 1: Glacier Hwy to Eagle Glacier
(7.5 miles, 4 hours)
(USFS cabin, backcountry campsites)
From the parking lot off Glacier Hwy, the trail departs from the highway and heads north-east along Eagle River. At 1.3 miles you come to a junction with the Yankee Basin Trail. This six-mile trail heads due north, following the route of an old tramway to the headwaters of the south fork of Kowee Creek. In the past, this trail has been in poor condition and nearly impossible to follow in places. There are plans to brush it out and upgrade it. Check with the USFS office in Juneau for the trail's current condition.

The Amalga Trail continues to head upstream with the Eagle River but within a quarter of a mile veers away to climb up the bordering slopes. Eventually you descend to cross Boulder Creek roughly three miles from the trailhead. The trail is now in an area of beaver pools and flooding. At one time the trail had to be re-routed into the hillsides to the north to avoid the water, and this made it a considerably harder hike. In recent years the USFS has used boardwalks and fill to return Amalga Trail to its original course in the lowlands of the glacial valley.

In the next two miles you swing away from the river again and do some climbing before arriving at an open area and stream near the old Amalga townsite. Amalga Mine was actually located four miles inland and the trail was originally a horse-tram route. The mine was productive enough to warrant a settlement from 1902 to 1927 and had its own post office. It's now almost impossible to find the mine, and little remains of the townsite.

This is a good spot to pitch a tent and you'll find evidence of other backpackers stopping in the open area for the night. From here it's half a mile to the USFS cabin and the lake. The log cabin was purchased by a local conservation group in 1991 and that fall, volunteers renovated it. Right on the lake facing the glacier, the cabin creates a dramatic setting. It's rented at night but is open to the public from 10 am to 5 pm daily as a warming hut.

From here the trail continues along the lake. The heavy shoreline thicket of alders and willow has been brushed back so you can continue another two miles to the face of the glacier. The glacier has retreated considerably in recent years but the view of the surrounding peaks and the lake is a hard one to match in the Southeast.

Stage 2: Eagle Glacier to Glacier Hwy
(7.5 miles, 4 hours)
Once at Eagle Glacier, you have little choice but to return the way you came. By camping at old Amalga townsite, you can walk out in less than three hours and get an early start on the next trail.

Haines

North along the Inside Passage (and the state ferry route) is Haines, a town of almost 1200 residents with a road that actually leads to the 'outside'. Haines may lack the touristy charm of Petersburg or Sitka but it is definitely not lacking hiking opportunities and superb scenery. From the center of town you're surrounded by mountains: to the west, looming over Fort Seward (Port Chilkoot), are the jagged peaks of the Chilkat Mountains, to the east is the Chilkoot Range, and standing guard over Haines is Mt Ripinsky.

From the heart of Haines, you can walk to two trails – the challenging Mt Ripinsky Trail to the north and the easier Mt Riley Trail to the south. Further south on the Chilkat Peninsula is the Seduction Point Trail in Chilkat State Park. Want more hiking opportunities? You can either jump on the next ferry to Skagway for the Chilkoot Trail or head north on the Haines Hwy,120 miles to Kluane National Park, one of Canada's most spectacular wilderness parks and home of the country's highest peak (Mt Logan, 19,636 feet). The park visitors' center (☎ (403) 634-2251) is at Haines Junction off the Alaska Hwy. It supplies information on hiking and wilderness trips in the 8649-sq-mile preserve.

Juneau has the most extensive trail system in the Southeast and Skagway has the longest trek in the Chilkoot Trail. But Haines has a friendly, small-town atmosphere where you can spend a few days trekking and then head north to continue your summer in Alaska.

Climate

Haines is drier than the rest of the Southeast, especially Ketchikan. Annual precipitation is 53 inches, most of which is winter snow. Still, cloudy conditions are the norm throughout the summer, the reason the average high in July is 65°F. If the sun is out and the wind is down, you can expect those summer temperatures to zoom into the 70s and even 80s at times, especially if you're in the surrounding alpine regions.

Information

The trails in Haines are either maintained by the Borough of Haines or the state Division of Parks & Outdoor Recreation. For this reason, the best place for hiking information and trail conditions in Haines is the state park district office (☎ 766-2292) on Main St above Helen's Shop. The office is open Monday to Friday from 8 am to 4.30 pm.

For travel information or a *Haines is for Hikers* brochure, head to the Haines Visitor Center (☎ 766-2202) at the corner of 2nd Ave and Willard St. During the summer the office is open daily from 8 am to 8 pm. There is also the Alaska Department of Fish & Game for angling advice. The office (☎ 766-2830) is at corner of the Haines Hwy and Main St and is open Monday through Friday from 9 am to 3 pm.

Places to Stay

Camping Haines has three state campgrounds with the closest to town being *Portage Cove* (nine sites, $6), half a mile south-east of Fort Seward at the start of the Battery Point Trail (see the later Mt Riley Trail section). The other two, *Chilkoot Lake State Park* (32 sites, $8) and *Chilkat State*

Park (33 sites, $6), are five miles north of the ferry terminal and seven miles south-east of town. On the edge of Haines are several commercial campgrounds catering predominantly to the RV trade. Try *Port Chilkoot Camper Park* (☎ 766-2755), where you can pitch your tent for $7 a night and get a shower for $1.50.

Hostels *Bear Creek Camp Hostel* (☎ 766-2259) is 2.5 miles from town on Small Tract Rd which veers left off Mud Bay Rd. The camp is affiliated with International Hostelling and has bunks in a dorm for $12 a night for members, $15 for nonmembers. There are also tent sites at $7.50 a night and a few cabins. The site is on the rustic side and for many travelers of late it has been a dismal experience.

Hotels There are six hotels in Haines and a number of B&Bs. *Fort Seward Lodge* (☎ 766-2009), the former post exchange, is the cheapest with rooms from $45 a single with shared bath, $55 a double. Also inside the old military complex are two B&Bs while near the entrance on Mud Bay Rd *Mountain View Motel* (☎ 766-2900) has rooms for $61/67 a single/double. The rooms have kitchenettes but you pay $7 a night to use them.

Maps

For USGS quads of the Haines area, stop at Chilkoot Gardens (☎ 766-2703), a gift shop on Main St and Union Ave across from Howsers (supermarket). If you're coming from Juneau, purchase your maps there to avoid missing out in Haines.

Equipment

Limited backpacking and camping equipment is available at *Alaska Sport Shop* (☎ 766-2441) at 4th Ave and Main St. Again, it's far better to purchase what you need in Juneau.

Trails

Mt Ripinsky Trail Maintained by the city of Haines, this trail system includes a 4.5-mile trek to the 3563-foot summit of Mt Ripinsky from where you can continue along a ridge to climb a second peak and emerge at the Haines Hwy. The ridge walk is a 10-mile, challenging trek that can be turned into an overnighter.

The round trip to Mt Ripinsky is a nine-mile hike that takes from six to eight hours but rewards you with sweeping views from Juneau to Skagway. Get to the trailhead by following 2nd Ave north to Lutak Rd (the road to the ferry terminal), past the fire station. Leave Lutak Rd when it curves right and head up the hill on Young St. Turn right along an old buried pipeline and follow it for a mile to the start of the trail, just as the pipeline heads downhill to the tank farm.

The trail crosses a pair of streams, passes by an old reservoir and then ascends steadily through spruce and hemlock, reaching open muskeg at 1300 feet. After a second climb you come to Johnson's Creek at 2500 feet where there is drinking water and impressive views of the Southeast's snow-capped

Snowshoe hare

mountains all the way to Admiralty Island. From here, the route goes from dwarfed hemlock to open slope where there is snow until late summer, to climb over Mt Ripinsky's first peak. The North Summit is another third of a mile along the ridge and here you'll find a USGS marker.

The longer ridge route is a strenuous 10-hour journey which includes Peak 3920 and a descent from Seven-Mile Saddle to the Haines Hwy. You can make it an overnight trip by camping in the alpine area between Mt Ripinsky's two peaks. The next day you can descend the North Summit and hike west along the ridge to Peak 3920. You emerge at the Haines Hwy, seven miles north-west of town. This trek is steep in places and the trail is easy to lose at times, but on a clear day it offers some of the best panoramas of any trek in the Southeast (USGS quads *Skagway A-2* and *B-2*).

Seduction Point Trail The trail begins at Chilkat State Park Campground and is a 6.5-mile, one-way hike to the point that separates Chilkoot and Chilkat inlets. The trail swings between inland forest and beaches and provides excellent views of Davidson Glacier.

It can also be turned into an overnight trek by setting up camp at the cove east of Seduction Point. Carry in water and check the tides before departing as the final stretch along the beach after David's Cove should be walked at low or mid-tide. The entire round trip takes most trekkers nine to 10 hours (USGS quads *Skagway A-1* and *A-2*).

Getting There & Away

Air There is no jet service to Haines, but several charter companies run regularly scheduled north and southbound flights. The cheapest service, Wings of Alaska (☎ 766-2030), has four daily flights to Juneau for $65 and four flights to Skagway for $40. Also check with Haines Airways (☎ 766-2646) or LAB Flying Service (☎ 766-2222).

Bus From Haines you can catch buses north to Whitehorse, Fairbanks and Anchorage.

Gray Line's Alaskon Express bus departs at 8.15 am on Tuesday, Wednesday, Friday and Sunday and overnights in Beaver Creek. The next day you can pick up a bus for any of the three cities. The one-way fare from Haines to Anchorage is $189, to Fairbanks $165 and to Whitehorse $76. Pick up the bus at the Wings of Alaska office (☎ 766-2030) on 2nd Ave.

Alaska Direct Busline (☎ (800) 770-6652) has a bus that departs Tuesday, Friday and Sunday at 6 am for Haines Junction from where you can pick up a bus to any of the three cities. The fare is slightly cheaper on this line; call to see if it's still operating.

Boat State ferries arrive and depart almost daily from the terminal (☎ 766-2111) in Lutak Inlet north of town. The one-way fare north to Skagway is $14 and south to Juneau, $18. Haines Taxi (☎ 766-3138) runs a shuttle bus that meets all ferries. Another way to reach Skagway is on Haines-Skagway Water Taxi (☎ 766-2295) which has a 40-passenger boat departing twice daily during the summer ($20 one way).

MT RILEY LOOP

South of town is the Mt Riley trail system in the Chilkat State Park. All the trails lead to the 1760-foot summit, the highest peak on the Chilkat Peninsula. This 10.7-mile loop is rated easy and is considerably easier than the Mt Ripinsky climb. It provides access to a peak with spectacular views, including Rainbow and Davidson glaciers, and even overnight camping. Getting back to town isn't the hassle it is from the Mt Ripinsky ridge walk.

The three trailheads are at Portage Cove Campground, the end of the FAA road from Fort Seward, and Mud Bay Rd (the steepest and most direct route to the peak). But the loop described here connects the scenic Battery Point Trail with a return on the FAA road to eliminate finding a three-mile ride back from Mud Bay Rd. The trails are covered on USGS 1:63,360 quads *Skagway A-1* and *A-2*.

Access
The trail can easily be reached on foot from the center of Haines. Follow Front St along the waterfront towards Fort Seward and then continue as it becomes Portage Cove Rd to its end. You'll return to the fort on the FAA road.

Stage 1: Portage Cove to Battery Point
(2.7 miles, 1-2 hours)
(Backcountry campsites)
For most, the hike actually beings on Portage Cove Rd, the beach road that heads southeast from Fort Seward to reach Portage Cove Campground in three quarters of a mile. The campground is for hikers and cyclists only and features nine tent sites as well as tables and a water supply. The road continues for another quarter of a mile beyond the campground to a trailhead at the end.

For the most part, Battery Point Trail is a level walk near the shoreline but first passes a handful of private homes overlooking Lynn Canal. In less than two miles, just before crossing a small stream, you arrive at a junction. The trail heading west goes to Mt Riley (3.5 miles), the other continues to Battery Point.

If you plan to camp at the point, first fill your water bottle from the stream and then cross it to quickly emerge on the pebbled beach on the west side of Kelgaya Point. In the final 0.7 miles, the trail follows the beach then cuts across Kelgaya Point to arrive at Battery Point. In the small cove the point forms, you'll find a pleasant beach, areas to set up camp and a panoramic view of Lynn Canal.

Stage 2: Battery Point to Haines via Mt Riley
(8 miles, 4-5 hours)
Backtrack to the junction to Mt Riley. Head south-west (left-hand fork). The trail to the peak begins with a steep climb through a spruce forest with heavy undergrowth of devil's club. The trekking becomes easier within two miles when the trail skirts a ridge to Half Dome, a muskeg meadow at about 1000 feet and loaded with blueberries in August.

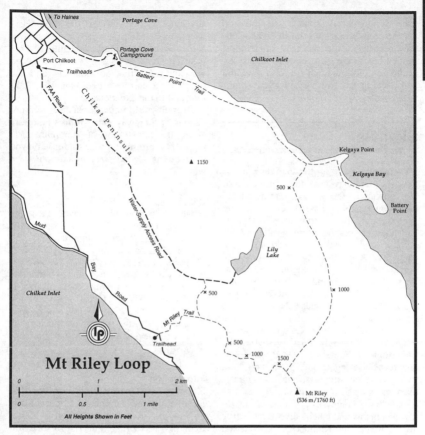

Portage Cove
To Haines
Portage Cove
Campground
Port Chilkoot
Trailheads
FAA Road
Battery Point Trail
Chilkat Peninsula
Chilkoot Inlet
Kelgaya Point
Kelgaya Bay
▲ 1150
500 ×
Battery Point
Water Supply Access Road
Mud
Bay
Road
Lily Lake
Chilkat Inlet
× 500
× 1000
Mt Riley Trail
Trailhead
× 500
× 1000
1500
Mt Riley Loop
0   1   2 km
0   0.5   1 mile
All Heights Shown in Feet
▲ Mt Riley
(536 m/1760 ft)

From here you make the final climb up Mt Riley through open muskeg meadows and emerge at the main trail from Mud Bay just before reaching the peak, 4.2 miles from Battery Point, or 5.5 miles from Portage Cove Campground. Follow a couple of hundred yards of planking along the Mud Bay Rd Trail to reach the summit.

Despite Mt Riley's low elevation (only 1760 feet) there are excellent views in every direction, including the entire Chilkat Peninsula, the city of Haines and Davidson Glacier across Lynn Canal.

To loop back to town, stay on the Mud Bay Rd Trail as it descends the west side of the mountain through muskeg meadows for the first half-mile before moving into a spruce forest. Within 1.5 miles after leaving the peak, you cross a small stream and then come to the junction with the trail from Port Chilkoot. By heading west (left-hand fork), you will remain on the trail as it descends to Mud Bay Rd in half a mile. The posted trailhead and small parking area are three miles south of town.

If you take the right-hand fork at the junction you'll reach Port Chilkoot. In less than a quarter of a mile, the trail arrives at the water-supply access road a few hundred yards from where it ends at Lily Lake. Continue north on the road for the next two miles. You emerge at the FAA road for the last leg of the trek. Follow this road for a mile and you'll end up at Officer's Row in the southwest corner of Port Chilkoot.

Skagway

The end of the line for the state ferry in the Southeast is Skagway, a quiet little town of 800 people in the winter, a reincarnated boom town in the summer. Every year, from June through August, thousands of tourists and hikers flood this narrow valley at the head of Lynn Canal in search of the gold-rush era. A century ago Skagway and neighboring Dyea, now a ghost town, was the starting point for more than 40,000 gold-rush stampeders who were determined to reach the Yukon and make their fortune in the Klondike fields.

The actual Klondike Gold Rush lasted only from 1896 to the early 1900s (see the introductory Facts for the Backpacker chapter), but its legacy and the Chilkoot Trail that stampeders immortalized has endured, even blossomed, and is now the basis for Skagway's economy. Today, most of downtown Skagway and much of the surrounding area is part of the Klondike Gold National Historical Park, which extends from Seattle to Dawson in the Yukon Territory. Not only is the NPS constantly restoring the historical buildings to return Skagway to its boom-town appearance, but many of the locals dress in turn-of-the-century costumes to welcome the modern-day stampeders from the state ferry and 'Love Boat'-type cruise ships.

A little touristy for backpackers who come to Alaska for wilderness solitude? Perhaps, but the 33-mile long Chilkoot Trail is not so much a trek in the mountains as a walk through history. The alpine scenery is great and you might see some wildlife, but the most fascinating aspect of this three-day adventure is the story of the stampeders which trekkers retrace step by step. As it was at the turn of the century, the Chilkoot Trail is still a grand adventure and the crowded wooden sidewalks of Skagway and the return on the narrow-gauge White Pass Railroad add to the experience.

Overall, you'll find affordable accommodations in Skagway, other trails to explore during the day and lots of entertainment at night. If the cruise-ship tourists don't run you over, this is a good place to stay put for a while.

Climate

In what up to now might have been a soggy Southeast for many, Skagway is one of the driest places. While Ketchikan gets 154 inches of rain a year and Sitka 100 inches, Skagway averages only 26 inches.

Skagway is also known for its moderate temperatures (the average high in July is 67°F) and high winds. Occasionally referred to as 'Home of the North Wind', strong gusts can blow down the mountains and into the valleys to steal your hat on the streets of Skagway.

Information

Skagway doesn't have a USFS office. For information and current conditions of any trail in the area, stop at the NPS Visitor Center (☎ 983-2921) in the refurbished railroad depot on the corner of 2nd Ave and Broadway St. From mid-May through September the center is open from 8 am to 6 pm daily. You can also receive a weather forecast or take in exhibits and films for a better understanding of the trail's history. For more information contact the NPS at PO Box 517, Skagway, AK 99840. At the trailhead of the Chilkoot Trail near Dyea, there is also a NPS ranger's station open daily from 1 June to 1 September.

For any other travel information, head to the Skagway Visitor Bureau (☎ 983-2854) in City Hall on the corner of Spring St and 7th Ave. It's open from 8.30 am to 5 pm Monday to Friday. During the summer, the bureau also operates a visitors' center (☎ 983-2855) in the Arctic Brotherhood Hall, the driftwood building on Broadway. The visitors' center is open daily.

Places to Stay

Camping The city manages a pair of campgrounds for either RVers or backpackers and both are within easy walking distance of everything else. On the corner of Broadway St and 14th Ave *Hanouske Park* has tent sites for $8. Near the ferry terminal is *Pullen Creek Park Campground* with 33 RV sites for $15. You can also get showers there for $1. Both campgrounds are operated by the City of Skagway and information or reservations can be obtained by calling ☎ (907) 983-2768.

Near the trailhead of the Chilkoot Trail, nine miles north of Skagway, is *Dyea Camping Area*, whose 22 free sites are used on a first-come-first-serve basis. The campground has vault toilets and tables but no source of drinking water.

Hostels The fine *Skagway Home Hostel* (☎ 983-2131) is only half a mile from the ferry terminal on 3rd Ave near Main St. The hostel has 15 beds ($13 a night) and a kitchen and baggage storage area.

B&Bs & Hotels There are a number of B&Bs and more are planned for the area. Try *Skagway Inn* (☎ 983-2289) on the corner of Broadway St and 7th Ave. Rooms are $60/68 for a single/double and they provide a free ride out to the Chilkoot Trail. Check the visitors' center for other B&Bs.

Irene's Inn (☎ 983-2520) is the most affordable place to stay with singles from $35. It's on the corner of Broadway St and 6th Ave. There is also *Golden North Hotel* (☎ 983-2294) with some triple rooms for $86 and quads for $92. Keep in mind that in Skagway the hotels and motels are often booked solid throughout the summer months well in advance.

Maps

Because the Chilkoot Trail is split between the USA and Canada, four topographical maps are required to cover the entire route. You begin with the USGS 1:63,360 quads *Skagway B-1* and *C-1* for the first half to Chilkoot Pass, then switch to Canada 1:50,000 quads, produced by the Department of Energy, Mines & Resources; *White Pass 104M/11 East* and *Homan Lake 104M/14 East* cover Chilkoot Pass to Bennett. To obtain Canadian maps in advance, write to Canada Map Office, 615 Booth St, Ottawa, Canada KIA OE9.

That's a steep investment in topos for a three-day hike so many trekkers just use the map from the NPS Visitor Center. It's adequate because the trail is popular and well marked. The best map, if you can find a copy, is *A Hiker's Guide to the Chilkoot Trail* produced by the Canada Parks Service.

The rest of the trails in Skagway are covered in the USGS quads *Skagway B-1* and *C-1*. All area maps are sold at Skagway Sports Emporium (☎ 983-2480) on 4th Ave between Broadway and State Sts.

Equipment

Black bears have become an increasing problem along the trail in recent years and now all the camps on the US side have been equipped with 18-foot-high bear poles (you'll need roughly 30 feet of rope to use the poles). Rope and other pieces of camping, backpacking and climbing gear can be purchased at *Skagway Sports Emporium* (see Maps, above).

Cabins

The Chilkoot Trail has warming cabins at many of the camps but they are not designed for sleeping and could not possibly handle all the people who pass through. There are a number of USFS cabins in the Skagway area, including one on the Laughton Glacier Trail (see Trails, below), but there is no USFS office in town. Cabins must be reserved through the Juneau USFS Information Center (☎ 586-8751). There is also a free-use shelter on the Dewey Lake trail system.

Trails

AB Mountain Trail Also known as the Skyline Trail, this route ascends 5.5 miles to the 5100-foot summit of AB Mountain, named for the AB that appears on its south side in the form of a snow-melt every spring. The trailhead (easy to reach) is on Dyea Rd about a mile from Skagway via the Skagway River foot bridge off the north-west end of 1st Ave. The trailhead, with parking for a couple of cars, is near *Mile 4* of Dyea Rd. The first two miles are easy to follow as the trail climbs steadily through a hemlock forest. After that things get more challenging and you have to keep a sharp eye out for cairns at times. It's 3.5 miles to a 3500-foot summit with stunning views of Skagway and the surrounding coastal mountains. From here you can follow the alpine ridge to AB Mountain, the 11-mile hike being a challenging trek that requires a full day (USGS quads *Skagway B-1* and *C-1*).

Denver Glacier Trail This is the first of two trails off the White Pass & Yukon Route. From *Mile 6*, the trail heads up the east fork of the Skagway River for two miles. Near the ruins of an old miner's cabin, the trail swings south and continues another 1.5 miles up a glacial outwash to Denver Glacier. This leg of the route is overgrown with brush and is tough hiking. The trailhead is a flag stop of the White Pass & Yukon Route (☎ 983-2217). Use USGS quads *Skagway B-1* and *C-1* for this trail.

Laughton Glacier Trail At *Mile 14* of the White Pass & Yukon Route is a short hike to a USFS cabin ($25 per night, reservations). The trailhead is at Glacier Station, an old rail depot, and from here it is a two-mile trek to Laughton Glacier, an impressive hanging glacier between 3000-foot walls of the Sawtooth Range. The alpine scenery from the windows of this cabin is worth all the hassle of reserving it in advance. On both this and the Denver Glacier Trail, book train drop-off and pick-up with the White Pass & Yukon

Route office in Skagway at the railroad depot (USGS quad *Skagway C-1*).

Getting There & Away

Air There is no jet service here but there are regularly scheduled flights to Skagway from Haines and Juneau with LAB Flying Service (☎ 983-2471), Wings of Alaska (☎ 983-2442), and Skagway Air (☎ 983-2218). The best rates are usually with Skagway Air but be prepared to pay $85 one way from Juneau and $60 from Haines.

Boat Unlike most communities in the Southeast, the ferry dock is right at the foot of Skagway's downtown area. State ferries (☎ 983-2229 ferry terminal) depart daily for Haines and then Juneau. There is also Haines-Skagway Water Taxi which sells tickets at the Pullen Creek RV Park Office (☎ 983-2083) on Congress Way. The 40-passenger ship departs from Skagway twice daily during the summer and charges $18 one way to Haines.

Bus Also unlike most Southeast communities, Skagway has a road that leads to the 'outside'. Gray Line's Alaskon Express has a bus that departs from Beaver Creek on Monday, Wednesday and Saturday at 9.30 am, reaching Skagway at 6.30 pm after stopping to pick up trekkers from the Chilkoot Trail. You can make connections from both Anchorage and Fairbanks on Alaskon Express to Beaver Creek, where you overnight and then reach Skagway the next day. There is also a daily bus that departs from Whitehorse at 4.30 pm. A one-way fare from Fairbanks is $194, Anchorage $199 and Whitehorse $52. In Skagway the Alaskon Express bus departs from the Westmark Hotel (☎ 983-2241) on 3rd Ave.

Train It is now possible to reach Whitehorse from Skagway on the White Pass & Yukon Route with a bus connection. For information, visit the White Pass & Yukon Route ticket office (☎ 983-2217) in the railroad depot next to the NPS Visitor Center (see Access & Customs, below).

CHILKOOT TRAIL

Even before the Klondike Gold Rush, the Chilkoot Trail was a vital route to the Interior of the North. As one of only three glacier-free corridors through the Coastal Range between Juneau and Yakutat, the Chilkoot was first used by Chilkat tribes trading fish oil, clam shells and dried fish with Interior tribes for animal skins and copper. Dyea was originally a small year-round Chilkat-Tlingit village, whose residents jealously guarded access to the pass.

All that changed when the gold rush brought a tide of people, supplies and progress at the turn of the century. Today, close to 3000 trekkers each summer follow the natural and historic route. Passing from the USA into Canada you cross the coastal rainforest of the Pacific Northwest into alpine areas, ending in the drier boreal forest of British Columbia.

It is important to remember this trek is not so much a wilderness adventure as a history lesson. The well-developed and well-marked trail is littered from one end to the other with artefacts of the era – everything from entire ghost towns and huge mining dredges to a rotting wagon wheel or a rusty coffee pot lying next to the trail. All the artefacts are protected by state, federal and provincial laws preventing people from stuffing them in their backpacks. Even so, trekkers still need to take great care to avoid inadvertently setting up camp on artefacts, stepping on them or using them as firewood.

The trip is from 33 to 35 miles long (depending on where you exit) and includes the Chilkoot Pass – a steep climb up loose rocks to 3550 feet, where most hikers end up scrambling on all fours to reach the top. The trail can be attempted by anyone in good physical condition with the right equipment and enough time. The hike normally takes from three to four days, though it can be done in two days by experienced trekkers. Despite being well marked and well traveled, the trail is rated moderate to challenging. Keep in mind the weather can often turn nasty in the middle of the summer, making the alpine stretch, especially the climb from the Scales to the summit, a wet, cold, even intimidating experience.

The Chilkoot Trail can be hiked from either direction (starting at Skagway or Bennett Lake) but it's easier and safer when you start from Dyea and climb up the loose scree of the Chilkoot Pass rather than down. Besides, there is something special about following the footsteps of the Klondike miners that makes this a special adventure.

Access & Customs

To reach the trailhead from Skagway, make your way to Dyea, eight miles to the northwest. *Mile 0* of the Chilkoot Trail is just before the Taiya River crossing. Near the trailhead is an NPS ranger station open daily during the summer. It's tough reaching Dyea by hitchhiking due to steep and narrow roads with blind curves. After the first two miles, there are few places for motorists to pull over. Many B&Bs and hotels in town include a trip to the trailhead in the price of a room, or contact any of the taxi companies. Pioneer Taxi (☎ 983-2623) charges $10 per person for a ride out to the trailhead, which seems to be the going rate. You can also check Sourdough Shuttle & Tours (☎ 983-2521) on the corner of 6th Ave and Broadway St.

At the northern end of the trail, hikers can follow the White Pass & Yukon Route from mid-June to mid-September. The historic narrow-gauge train departs from Bennett daily at 3.45 pm and arrives in Skagway at 6.15 pm. The fare from Bennett to Skagway is $59. From Skagway, the train departs at 12.45 pm for those who want to begin at the northern trailhead. You can also depart from Fraser on the Klondike Hwy for $20 to pick up a bus north to Whitehorse. Call WP&YR toll free at ☎ (800) 343-7373.

There is another way to leave the trail at the northern end – you can hike six miles south from Bare Loon Lake Campground to Log Cabin on the Klondike Hwy. An Alaskon Express bus stops daily at Log Cabin at 6.15 pm on its way south to

Skagway while a north-traveling bus reaches the warming hut at 9.15 am on its way to Whitehorse. The one-way fare from Log Cabin to Skagway is $18 and from Log Cabin to Whitehorse it's $53. The bus company can be contacted in Skagway during the summer at ☎ 983-2241; all departures from Log Cabin are given in Yukon Time.

The Chilkoot Trail involves crossing the international border into Canada so if you are beginning your trip in Dyea you must clear Canadian customs *before leaving Skagway*. You can do this by either calling Fraser Customs Office (☎ (403) 821-4111) or by signing the customs register at the National Park Visitor Center in the railroad depot in Skagway. Hikers beginning their trip in Canada must clear US customs. You can either do that ahead of time by calling US customs in Skagway (☎ (907) 983-2725) or stop at the office after the hike. The US customs office has moved recently to Dyea Rd, two miles from the trailhead.

Stage 1: Dyea to Canyon City
(7.8 miles, 3-4 hours)
(Finnegan's Point & Canyon City campgrounds)
The Alaska trailhead for the Chilkoot Trail begins at the old townsite of Dyea. On the banks of the Taiya River, Dyea grew from a trading post of Healy and Wilson to the largest town in Alaska, at one point rivaling Skagway, Dawson and Seattle in importance to the stampeders. From October 1897 to May 1898 the town held a miner's population of more than 10,000 before a devastating avalanche and the completion of the White Pass Railroad convinced miners to head north on other routes.

Dyea is nine miles from Skagway over a bridge across the Taiya River. You pass a campground and the ranger station eight miles from Skagway and just before crossing the bridge, arrive at the southern trailhead and *Mile 0* of the Chilkoot Trail. The route begins with an immediate climb of almost 300 feet and then descends to the Taiya River that flows through a flat lowland of willow and brush. Within a mile from the start, the trail merges into an old logging road that provides three miles of easy trekking.

The old road first passes an abandoned sawmill at *Mile 3* and then ends at Finnegan's Point, the site of the first trail-side campground, 4.9 miles from Dyea. The point is named after Pat Finnegan who, with his two sons, maintained a toll bridge over a creek here until he was overrun by stampeders in too much of a hurry to stop and pay the fee. The campground has vault toilets and a nice view of Irene Glacier across the river but no warming shelter.

The trail leaves the old road and dips to the river which it follows for a quarter of a mile. It

Climbing the Chilkoot Pass
Not only was Klondike 'the last great gold rush' in the minds of many people, it was also one of the most photographed, especially when it came to the ordeals of miners struggling up the Chilkoot Trail. Of all the pictures taken along the route, the most amazing one is of the long line of men carrying their heavy loads up the Chilkoot Pass in the winter of 1897-98.

'The final climb produced one of the most moving photographic images in American history', writes William Bronson in *The Last Grand Adventure*. 'No staged version of this event could ever match the incredible drama created by the thousands of men and women who struggled up the 30-degree incline to cross the Chilkoot Pass that winter.'

Unless they were rich enough to hire porters, most stampeders carried roughly 50 lbs on each trip up the pass which included 1500 steps carved out of the snow and ice. Most men could endure only one climb a day which meant they would make as many as 40 trips in 40 days before they could get their 'year's worth of supplies' and equipment to the top.

But as Bronson noted 'whether gold lay at the end of their trails or not, they had crossed the Chilkoot, an achievement that for many was the crowning event in their lives'. ■

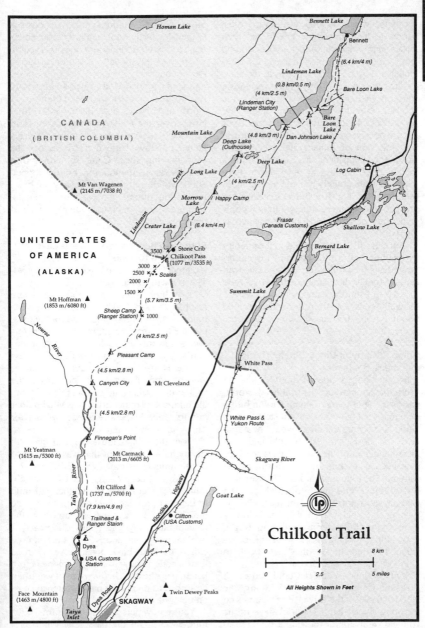

Homan Lake

Bennett Lake

Bennett

(6.4 km/4 m)

Lindeman Lake

(0.8 km/0.5 m)

Bare Loon Lake

(4 km/2.5 m)

Lindeman City
(Ranger Station)

Bare
Loon
Lake

CANADA

(BRITISH COLUMBIA)

Mountain Lake

(4.8 km/3 m)

Dan Johnson Lake

Deep Lake
(Outhouse)

Deep Lake

Log Cabin

Long Lake

Creek

(4 km/2.5 m)

Mt Van Wagenen
▲ (2145 m/7038 ft)

Morrow
Lake

Happy Camp

Fraser
(Canada Customs)

Shallow Lake

Lindeman

Crater Lake

(6.4 km/4 m)

UNITED STATES

OF AMERICA

(ALASKA)

3500 • Stone Crib
      •∴ Chilkoot Pass
        (1077 m/3535 ft)

Bernard Lake

3000 ✕
2500 ✕ ∴ Scales
2000 ✕
1500 ✕

Summit Lake

Mt Hoffman ▲
(1853 m/6080 ft)

(5.7 km/3.5 m)

Nourse River

Sheep Camp
(Ranger Station) ✕ 1000

(4 km/2.5 m)

Pleasant Camp

(4.5 km/2.8 m)

White Pass

Canyon City   ▲ Mt Cleveland

(4.5 km/2.8 m)

White Pass &
Yukon Route

Finnegan's Point

Mt Yeatman ▲
(1615 m/5300 ft)

Taiya River

Mt Carmack ▲
(2013 m/6605 ft)

Skagway River

Mt Clifford ▲
(1737 m/5700 ft)

(7.9 km/4.9 m)

Klondike Highway

Goat Lake

Trailhead &
Ranger Station

Clifton
(USA Customs)

Dyea

USA Customs
Station

Chilkoot Trail

0   4   8 km

0   2.5   5 miles

All Heights Shown in Feet

Face Mountain
(1463 m/4800 ft)
▲

Taiya
Inlet

Dyea Road

▲ Twin Dewey Peaks

SKAGWAY

leaves the water to climb over several hills, returns to the Taiya River briefly and then makes one final climb before descending into Canyon City, almost three miles from Finnegan's Point, or 7.8 miles from the start.

The Canyon City Campground includes a warming shelter with a wood-burning stove and some interesting literature about the Klondike Gold Rush. It's near the mouth of the Taiya River Canyon and was a natural camping spot of Indians and others long before the stampeders arrived. Most miners cached their supplies at old Canyon City which in 1898 quickly became a permanent settlement of log structures. It became a prosperous settlement after two freight companies built a tramway to transfer gear across the river.

You can still see the remains of the old city by heading half a mile north of the campground and then following a posted side trail across a foot bridge to the site. It's a two-mile round trip from the campground, however, the walk is easy and the ruins, which include a boiler from the tramway companies, are interesting.

Stage 2: Canyon City to Sheep Camp
(5.2 miles, 3-4 hours)
(Pleasant Camp & Sheep Camp)
From the campground the trail heads north, passes the spur to old Canyon City in half a mile and then begins to ascend steeply as it works its way around the canyon. The climb lasts for more than half a mile and is a knee-bender until the trail reaches the altitude needed to skirt the eastern rim of the canyon. The hiking is hard but the views of the glaciers and mountains above the canyon, most notably Mt Hoffman, and the rushing water below it are worth it. Within a mile from the campground you begin descending, passing the first of the occasional telegraph poles (they date back to 1898) on the way to Chilkoot Pass.

You continue to descend until you reach Pleasant Camp, at *Mile 10.5*, along the wooded banks of the Taiya River. There is no warming shelter here. The trail stays in the wooded valley for the remaining 2.5 miles to

Sheep Camp. Within a mile you cross a suspension bridge and then just before entering the campground pass a ranger cabin where park personnel are stationed during the summer.

Sheep Camp at *Mile 13* was an important spot for the miners who cached their year's worth of supplies here during that brutal climb over the Chilkoot Pass. Often from February to April fierce winter storms halted or slowed down traffic across the pass, making Sheep Camp something of a bottleneck. Its population briefly topped 8000 which supported a variety of businesses, including general stores, hotels, restaurants and, of course, saloons, three of them to be exact.

Stage 3: Sheep Camp to Deep Lake
(10 miles, 7-10 hours)
(Happy Camp & Deep Lake campgrounds)
The trek will take all day, so get an early start. You'll climb more than 2500 feet before reaching the saddle. The Chilkoot Pass is 3.5 miles north of Sheep Camp and for the most part the trail makes a gradual but continuous ascent towards it. In less than two miles you'll leave the tree line and quickly pass 'Stone House' a huge, squarish boulder whose overhanging shelf provides some shelter in an emergency. From this point on, the hiking gets more difficult as you boulder hop towards the pass. Keep an eye out for cairns and other trail markers.

From the Stone House the trail makes a steady half-mile ascent that was referred to by the miners as the 'Long Hill', and 2.5 miles from Sheep Camp arrives at an old tramway power house. It's another half-mile to the next prominent set of ruins along the trail known as the 'Scales', almost at the head of the valley. The Scales, the second of two tramway operations built here, are so called because hired packers re-weighed their goods here and charged more before heading up the pass. In the winter it was often described as one of the most wretched spots on the trail.

You're now poised to make the final half-mile ascent over the pass. The climb is a steep one – a 45-degree scramble over boulders, lose rock and scree from the Scales at 2600 feet, to the summit of the pass at 3535 feet. Make sure you choose the right route. When facing the pass from the bottom, the Chilkoot route is the left-hand pass and is posted by metal poles and marked by a old tramway cable. Take extra caution when the weather is bad, however, as the rocks can be slippery, the visibility poor due to fog or snow, and the high winds at the top almost unbearable.

The rocky slope you climb was known as the 'Golden Stairs' to the miners, who took up to six hours in bad weather to reach the pass. Once at the top you cross the international border between the USA and Canada and it was here that the royal mounted police established a customs station to ensure that each miner entered the country with enough supplies to last a year.

From the top of the pass you begin a rapid descent and cross a perpetual snowfield. Most likely boot prints will lead the way across the snowfield but it's important to remember to keep well to the right. The trail skirts Crater Lake from high above it and 300 feet below the pass summit you come to Stone Crib. This crib was an anchor for the aerial tramway and is now the site of two emergency shelters for those caught on the pass in bad weather.

The route, marked by cairns and poles, continues along the east side of Crater Lake through the open country and crosses a handful of streams. Near the northern end of the lake the trail should be quite visible as it follows sections of an old wagon road to Lindeman City. From here, the trail continues its gradual descent through the alpine tundra, passing a tarn known as Morrow Lake and a small waterfall near *Mile 20* as you approach Long Lake. Nearby is Happy Camp, a small sparsely wooded campground four miles north of the pass summit. Most hikers, however, prefer to push on and stay at Deep Lake.

Past Happy Camp the trail enters a small canyon, turns right and then climbs 350 feet to skirt Long Lake from above and avoid its rugged east shore. Once beyond the lake, the trail descends, crosses a bridge over a river to the west side of Deep Lake and then arrives at Deep Lake Campground at *Mile 23*. Although you've returned to the tree line here, the forest is still sparse and the views are excellent from this campground. There is no warming shelter here but for those who need to dry off, Lindeman City has two shelters and is an easy three-mile hike down the trail.

Stage 4: Deep Lake to Bennett
(10 miles, 6-8 hours)
(Lindeman City, Bare Loon Lake & Bennett Lake campgrounds)
The trail follows the west side of Deep Lake as it leaves the campground and continues north. You round the northern end of the lake and then gradually descend the 700 feet to Lindeman City by skirting the top of a canyon along the west side of the river. This is a pleasant stretch with an occasional view of the surrounding mountains through the fir and lodgepole pine forest. Just before arriving at the lake, you pass an old cemetery on top of a hill where 11 stampeders are buried. The view of the lake and the surrounding peaks is excellent from the hill.

At *Mile 26*, or three miles from Deep Lake, you reach Lindeman City at the south end of its namesake lake. In the spring of 1898, this was a tent city of 10,000 miners who stopped to build boats for their 600-mile journey to Dawson and the Klondike gold fields. Today it's a campground with two warming cabins and a Canadian ranger station.

From the cabins, the trail skirts beneath the hilltop cemetery and then crosses a foot bridge over Moose Creek for the remaining seven miles to Bennett. You begin with a gradual climb and then level off for a two-mile forested walk until you break out at a campground at Dan Johnson Lake. In another half a mile you reach Bare Loon Lake, another camping area at *Mile 29* of the trail. Both areas have vault toilets and often during July and August overheated trekkers can be seen swimming in Bare Loon Lake.

Just beyond the campground at Bare Loon Lake there is a junction in the trail. The right-hand fork leads to the White Pass & Yukon Railroad, a 20 to 30-minute hike. Once at the track you can head south and after a five-mile gradual climb reach the Log Cabin on the Klondike Hwy to pick up a bus in either direction or the train back to Skagway.

The left-hand fork heads to Bennett and follows the lake fairly close for good views of the water in the remaining four miles. Bennett, with its church on the hill and the old White Pass & Yukon depot, is a picturesque place to camp for a night if you're not in a hurry. At one time the town boasted a short-lived population of 20,000 as stampeders from both the Chilkoot Trail and the route over White Pass gathered here. In May of 1898, more than 7000 boats headed down the lake when the ice broke and the following year St Andrews Church was completed.

In Bennett, you can secure rail transportation along the White Pass & Yukon Railroad to Fraser on the Klondike Hwy or all the way back to Skagway (see Access & Customs, earlier).

UPPER DEWEY LAKE TRAIL

Just east of Skagway is a series of trails maintained by the city. They lead to a handful of alpine and sub-alpine lakes, waterfalls and historic sites. This popular hiking area has picnic areas, camping spots, even a free-use shelter enabling you to quickly escape bustling, touristy Skagway for a night in the mountains.

The trail to Lower Dewey Lake is a half-hour stroll, a good way to warm up the legs before hitting the Chilkoot Trail. From here you can continue onto Sturgill's Landing, a 3.5-mile hike from town. At the scenic point there are campsites and a picnic area. The other overnight possibility is the three-mile climb to Upper Dewey Lake, where there is a free-use shelter. From here you can hike the alpine area to Devil's Punch Bowl before returning along the same route. This is a nine-mile return trek from Skagway.

The hike to Lower Dewey Lake and

Sturgill's Landing is rated easy. The climb to the alpine regions of Upper Dewey Lake are challenging due to a very steep climb. The USGS 1:63,360 quad *Skagway B-1* covers all the trails.

Access
The trails are an easy walk from the heart of Skagway. From Broadway St follow 3rd Ave south-east to the railroad tracks. On the other side of the tracks is the posted trailhead.

Stage 1: Skagway to Upper Dewey Lake
(3 miles, 3 hours)
(Free-use shelter, backcountry campsites)
As a wide path, the trail heads uphill, immediately crosses a stream via a small foot bridge and then arrives at a junction, less than an eighth of a mile from town. The well-beaten right-hand fork is the direct route to Lower Dewey Lake. The left-hand fork leads to the trail to Icy Lake and Upper Reid Falls.

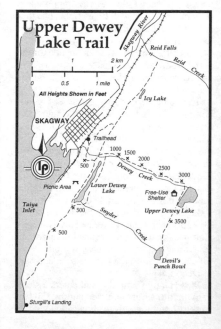

Upper Dewey Lake Trail

The trail to Lower Dewey Lake continues to climb, steeply at times, and half a mile from the trailhead, you come to the reservoir. Here you'll find another path that closely skirts the shoreline while the main trail swings around its south side to quickly meet another junction.

The right-hand fork heads south where it merges into the trail along the west shore of Lower Dewey Lake, enabling you to continue along the lake to reach a picnic area. At the south end is the junction with the trail to Sturgill's Landing. The Landing is a two-mile trek from Lower Dewey Lake, or a 3.5-mile walk from town, and features a beach campground, tables and vault toilets. This is the destination for those who want an overnight hike but don't want to endure the hard climb to Upper Dewey Lake. Also at the south end you can continue on a trail along the lake's east shore and eventually return to the junction at the reservoir for a 1.3-mile loop around the lake.

For those heading to the alpine region take the left-hand fork. The trail heads north, quickly crosses a bridge over a stream at the northern end of Lower Dewey Lake and passes the junction with the trail to the lake's east shore. Almost a quarter of a mile from the lake, or a mile from the trailhead, you cross a larger stream and arrive at the junction to Upper Dewey Lake.

The climb to the lake is a knee-bender, especially the first mile. It's easy to follow because basically it's a straight two-mile climb with few switchbacks. The ascent does ease briefly when the trail closely skirts Dewey Creek but then you resume the strenuous climb until finally emerging from the tree line in a muskeg opening. Here the trail crosses the meadow to reach the west side of Upper Dewey Lake, a beautiful sub-alpine lake at 3097 feet surrounded by mountains and peaks. The view of Taiya Inlet is equally impressive.

The free-use shelter is an old cabin that is now used by those spending the night in the alpine region. It has bunks for two people, holds maybe four at the most and is a little too run-down for many backpackers. If you hauled up a tent there are many places to set up camp around the lake. Upper Dewey Lake is planted with rainbow trout but they can be tough to catch most of the summer.

If overnighting at the lake, a 2.5-mile round trip to Devil's Punch Bowl is a scenic side trip. Pick up the trail as it heads south from the shelter and quickly emerges from the trees to an alpine bench with stunning views of Skagway and the Inside Passage. The small lake is reached in 1.2 miles, and at 3550 feet is often not free of ice until August.

Stage 2: Upper Dewey Lake to Skagway
(3.5 miles, 2 hours)

Descend the two miles from Upper Dewey Lake back to the junction with Lower Dewey Lake but be careful. You'll find the descent as hard on the knees as the climb the day before. To avoid completely retracing your steps head north at the junction towards Icy Lake. The trail gently ascends through the forest and half a mile from Lower Dewey Lake you come to a junction.

The right-hand fork continues north to Icy Lake (one mile) and then to the upper portion of Reid Falls (two miles). Reid Falls is a spectacular 300-foot cascade but the view from the trail is less than inspiring and hardly worth the hike. You'll get a better view of the falls from the short trail through Gold Rush Cemetery.

The left-hand fork leads back to town and after half a mile connects with the trail to Lower Dewey Lake (the first junction you met after leaving the trailhead).

Anchorage

From downtown Anchorage, the sight that commands your attention the most is the Chugach Mountains looming over the state's tallest buildings. Almost half the state's population looks up at these mountains, one of the most rugged ranges in the country. Anchorage is Alaska's largest metropolitan area. Complete with fast-food restaurants, traffic jams and shopping malls it lies at the foot of one of the largest state parks in the USA: Chugach State Park is 495,204 acres of sharp peaks, blue glaciers, pristine alpine lakes and board valleys.

The contrast certainly isn't lost on trekkers, who can be sipping a cafe latte in a coffee shop downtown, and within 20 minutes be at a trailhead to an alpine peak. Is this paradise or just another example of Alaska, the land of extremes?

Anchorage is the hub of Alaska's road system and an international air junction, so trekkers usually have to pass through the city at least once, if not several times, during an extended trip. You may as well stay for a few days to restock, rejuvenate, enjoy the city's nightlife and fine selection of restaurants, and take in a few of the local hikes.

Like Juneau in the Southeast, the Anchorage area offers a fine network of trails making it possible to hike all day and then return to the city at night. However, unlike Juneau, Anchorage has both good public transportation to most of the trailheads and longer multi-day treks in the valleys and passes of Chugach State Park.

Even though this wild area is close to the city, it should not be underestimated; more than one ill-prepared hiker has perished in Chugach State Park as well as in nearby Chugach National Forest.

Chugach is one of the most heavily used parks in Alaska, offering a wide variety of developed trails suitable for all levels of trekking. You can join others in climbing Flattop Mountain (the first Alaska peak for many) or spend a week traversing trail-less

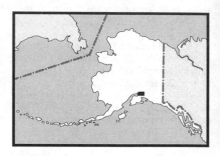

areas and exploring one valley and ridge line after another.

CLIMATE

Anchorage has the advantage of being north of the Kenai Mountains which shield the city from the excess moisture experienced by Southcentral Alaska. The Anchorage Bowl – the city and surrounding area – receives only 14 inches of rain annually. It also avoids the extreme temperatures of the Interior due to the moderating effect of Cook Inlet. The average temperature in January is 13°F, while at the height of the summer it's only 58°F.

Spring in Anchorage begins in mid-April when the longer daylight hours bring out buds on the trees and wild flowers in the mountains. At this time of year, most trekkers begin on the trails along the Turnagain Arm. Due to their southern exposure, trails like Indian Valley, Turnagain Arm, and especially Bird Ridge, are the first to be free of snow and painted by the colorful blossoms of wild flowers. Throughout most of June and July you can count on 19 hours of sunlight and temperatures around 65°F. Unfortunately, the area has more than its fair share of overcast days, especially in early and late summer.

INFORMATION

One of the first places to head to after you

ANCHORAGE

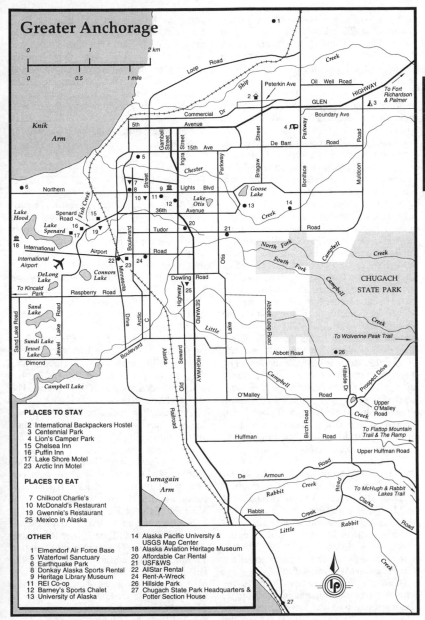

Greater Anchorage

0   1   2 km

0   0.5   1 mile

PLACES TO STAY

2 International Backpackers Hostel
3 Centennial Park
4 Lion's Camper Park
15 Chelsea Inn
16 Puffin Inn
17 Lake Shore Motel
23 Arctic Inn Motel

PLACES TO EAT

7 Chilkoot Charlie's
10 McDonald's Restaurant
19 Gwennie's Restaurant
25 Mexico in Alaska

OTHER

1 Elmendorf Air Force Base
5 Waterfowl Sanctuary
6 Earthquake Park
8 Donkay Alaska Sports Rental
9 Heritage Library Museum
11 REI Co-op
12 Barney's Sports Chalet
13 University of Alaska

14 Alaska Pacific University &
    USGS Map Center
18 Alaska Aviation Heritage Museum
20 Affordable Car Rental
21 USF&WS
22 AllStar Rental
24 Rent-A-Wreck
26 Hillside Park
27 Chugach State Park Headquarters &
    Potter Section House

arrive in Anchorage is the Alaska Public Lands Information Center (☎ 271-2737) in the Old Federal Building at the corner of 4th Ave and F St (diagonally opposite the Log Cabin Visitor Information Center). Along with interesting displays on the Alaska wilderness and wildlife, the center has information and hand-outs on any national park, federal refuge or state park in Alaska and sells a limited selection of topographic maps and books. The center also handles the reservations for USFS cabins and a limited number of campground sites, and hands out tokens for the shuttle bus that the NPS operates inside Denali National Park. It's open daily from 9 am to 7 pm.

In the city, information on Chugach and other state parks can also be obtained from the Alaska Department of Natural Resources Public Information Center (☎ 762-2261 or (800) 770-2257 in Alaska) at 3601 C St. The Chugach State Park headquarters (☎ 345-5014) at *Mile 115* of the Seward Hwy in the Potter Section House has historical displays as well as a wealth of information on the park. Hours are 8 am to 4.30 pm Monday through Friday. To the north is the Eagle River Visitor Center (☎ 694-2108) at *Mile 12* of Eagle River Rd off Glenn Hwy. The center is at the north end of the Historic Iditarod Trail and has displays, a phone and hand-outs. It's open Thursday through Monday from 10 am to 6 pm. If you plan to spend a great deal of time in the park, pick up a copy of *Ridgelines*, an information newspaper the park staff put out.

The Chugach National Forest office (☎ 271-2500) at Suite 206, 201 East 9th St, has details on any USFS national forest, trail or cabin. The Bureau of Land Management (☎ 271-5555) maintains an office at 222 West 7th Ave (see them for information on the Pinnell Mountain Trail). The office of the US Fish & Wildlife Service (☎ 786-3487) is at 1011 East Tudor Rd (see them about the Kenai National Wildlife Refuge).

There are several visitors' centers for general travel information in Anchorage. The main one is in the Log Cabin Visitor Information Center (☎ 274-3531) on the corner of 4th Ave and F St. It's open daily from 7.30 am to 7 pm June to August, 8.30 am to 6 pm May and September, and 9 am to 4 pm the rest of the year. Other smaller information centers are at the Anchorage International Airport on the baggage-claim level of the South (Domestic) Terminal, in the North (International) terminal (self-service information), in the railroad depot downtown, and in the Valley River Mall in Eagle River.

PLACES TO STAY
Camping

The Anchorage Parks & Recreation Department (☎ 343-4474) maintains two parks where there is overnight camping. The main one is *Centennial Park*, which has 83 sites, showers and rest rooms but is 4.6 miles from the downtown area on Glenn Hwy. Take the Muldoon Rd exit south of the highway and turn west onto Boundary Ave for half a block (to the entrance driveway). The cost is $12 per night for either campground and there is a limit of seven days. When Centennial is full, the city uses *Lion's Camper Park* (☎ 333-1495) in Russian Jack Springs Park as an overflow camping area. There is also *Ship Creek Landings* (☎ 277-0877) that offers 180 RV sites just off East 1st Ave. The rate is $12 per night.

Chugach State Park also has three public campgrounds but none are close and they always fill up fast. The nearest facilities are at *Bird Creek Campground* (28 sites, $8) at *Mile 101* of the Seward Hwy, about 20 miles south-east of the city. A site here puts you near most of the Turnagain Arm trails, including Bird Ridge, Indian Valley and McHugh & Rabbit Lakes trails.

North of the city is *Eagle River Campground* (56 sites, $12) on Hiland Rd at *Mile 12* of Glenn Hwy. The campground is within 12 miles of the northern trailhead of the Historic Iditarod Trail and the Eagle River Visitor Center, and is one of the most popular campgrounds in the state. Further north is *Eklutna Lake Campground* (50 sites, $10), reached from the Eklutna exit at *Mile 26* of

Glenn Hwy. Within this campground is the trailhead of the Eklutna Lakeside Trail.

Hostels

Anchorage International Hostel (☎ 276-3635), one of the main hostels in the Alaska Council, is downtown, one block south of the Transit Center at 700 H St. The cost is $12 per night for members and $15 for nonmembers. There is a four-night maximum stay unless special arrangements are made. From the airport, take bus No 6 for the 5.7-mile trip into the Transit Center.

The hostel now also has an overflow hostel on Spenard Rd in Anchorage and a list of the growing number of backpacker hostels in the city. Among them is *International Backpackers Hostel* (☎ 274-3870) on the north-east side of the city. The hostel is actually five homes in the same neighborhood that can accommodate up to 45 people a night (two to four people per room). Rates range from $12 to $15 a night. To reach the hostel from the Transit Center take Bus No 45 to the corner of Bragaw St and Peterkin Ave and head west on Peterkin Ave for four blocks.

There is also a small hostel in Girdwood, handy for anybody needing a cheap sleep before undertaking the Historic Iditarod (Crow Pass) Trail. The *Alyeska International Home Hostel* (☎ 277-7388) is a cabin with wood heating, kitchen, sauna and sleeping space for six people. Fees are $12 a night for nonmembers, $10 for members. Turn right on Timberline Drive off Alyeska Hwy and then right on Alpine Rd for 0.4 miles.

B&Bs

B&Bs have blossomed in Anchorage. There are now several hundred residents who have opened up their spare bedrooms to summer travelers. Most places are on the fringes or in the suburbs of the city and provide a clean bed, a good breakfast and local insight into both the city and the Alaska way of life. The going rate is a bit steeper in Anchorage than in the rest of the state as you generally pay from $65 to $75 a night. Stop at the Log Cabin Visitor Information Center for an entire rack of B&B brochures or call either Alaska Private Lodging (☎ 258-1717) or Stay with a Friend (☎ 278-8800) to arrange such accommodation.

Motels

If you arrive late at the airport you have a choice of motels that offer courtesy transportation and are located nearby along Spenard Rd, just north of International Airport Rd. Be prepared for Alaska-size rates at around $100 a night. *Puffin Inn* (☎ 243-4044) at 4400 Spenard Rd is exceptionally clean, has van service to the airport until 1 am and has complimentary muffins, coffee and newspapers in the morning. Nearby, *Lake Shore Motel* (☎ 248-3485 or (800) 770-3000) at 3009 Lake Shore Drive, has courtesy transportation and rooms cost just under $100.

Not far from the airport in the midtown area of Anchorage is *Arctic Inn Motel* (☎ 561-1328) at 842 West International Airport Rd. It has singles/doubles for $69/79. A big step up is *Chelsea Inn* (☎ 276-5002 or (800) 770-5002) nearby at 3836 Spenard Rd. Singles with shared bath are $75, doubles $85. The rooms are clean and comfortable and a continental breakfast is served.

The most affordable motel with the best location downtown is *Inlet Inn* (☎ 277-5541). It's across the street from the Transit Center at 539 H St and has singles/doubles for $60/70. The motel also shares a courtesy van service with several other motels to provide free transportation from the airport. To the west near the corner of Gambell St and 6th Ave is the *Alaskan Samovar Inn* (☎ 277-1511). The large rooms are situated around a courtyard; summer rates are $50/54 a single/double. *Alaska Budget Motel* (☎ 277-0088), at 545 East 4th St, is far enough away from the seedy section of 4th St for a quiet evening.

MAPS

The USGS map center, which sells topos for the entire state, is now in Grace Hall at Alaska Pacific University at the east end of Providence Drive. Hours are from 8.30 am to 4.30 pm weekdays and the center can be

ANCHORAGE

reached on bus No 11 or 45. Maps, Maps, Maps (☎ 562-6277) at the corner of Arctic Blvd and 34th Ave also sells USGS topos, as does the Public Lands Information Center downtown.

Most of Chugach State Park is covered on four USGS 1:63,360 quads – *Anchorage A-6, A-7, A-8* and *B-6*. Only trails that were originally roads are shown on the topos, so it is important to also pick up a park trail map.

EQUIPMENT

Whatever you need, from crampons to a spare tent stake, you'll find it in Anchorage, probably somewhere along Northern Lights Blvd. For backpacking, kayaking or camping gear, there's an impressive *REI* (☎ 272-4565) at 1200 West Northern Lights Blvd in the Northern Lights Shopping Center, while a block away is *Barney's Sports Chalet* (☎ 561-5242). At 202 East Northern Lights Blvd *Gary King Sporting Goods* (☎ 272-5401) carries hiking and backpacking equipment. You might also want to check out *Alaska Mountaineering & Hiking* (☎ 272-1811) at 2633 Spenard Rd near Northern Lights Blvd. It is open daily in the summer and has an excellent selection.

You can also rent gear in Anchorage – everything from a tent and sleeping bag to a fly rod. Try *Donkay Alaska Sports Rental* (☎ 561-3434) at 2428 East Tudor Rd or *Alaska Mineshaft* (☎ 277-3303) at 1343 G St. Keep in mind that campfires are prohibited along most trails in Chugach State Park which for some means purchasing or renting a stove or eating gorp and candy bars for three days in a row.

CABINS

There are two cabins available for rent along the trails described here. The USFS Crow Pass Cabin on the Historic Iditarod Trail and within Chugach State Park, the Eklutna Alex Cabin (at the east end of Eklutna Lake). Both cost $25 a night and can be rented in advance through the Alaska Public Lands Information Center (☎ (907) 271-2599), 605 West 4th Ave, Suite 105, Anchorage, AK 99501.

TRAILS

At $1 a ride, the People Mover bus is the cheapest way to get within walking distance of many of the Anchorage trails. But there is also Alaska Backpacker Shuttle (☎ 344-8775) which provides transportation right to the trailheads. The van service picks up hikers at the Anchorage International Hostel, at REI in the midtown area and from Centennial Park, and then continues on to a variety of trails, including Bird Creek and Crow Pass along the Seward Hwy, and Ship Creek and the Eagle River trails. The one-way fare ranges from $5 for transportation to trails like Flattop Mountain to $20 for Crow Pass.

Chugach Hiking Tours (☎ 278-4453) offers three guided hikes into the surrounding state park, including a sunset tour that begins at 6 pm and returns at 11 pm. The treks are from two to five-miles long and are lead by a naturalist (who describes and explains what you see along the way), trail snacks and photography. All trips depart from the Log Cabin Visitor Information Center downtown and cost $45 per person.

Anchorage Area

Wolverine Peak Trail Part of the Chugach State Park hillside trail system, this 5.2-mile trail ascends to the 4455-foot triangular peak that can be seen to the east of Anchorage. It is a strenuous but rewarding full-day trip resulting in good views of the city, Cook Inlet and the Alaska Range.

From the Prospect Heights trailhead (see the later Williwaw Lakes Trail for directions) the trail begins as an old homestead road. It crosses South Fork Campbell Creek and then passes junctions with Middle Fork and Near Point trails in the first 2.3 miles. Keep heading east, and the old road becomes a footpath that ascends above the bush line and eventually fades out. Make sure to mark its whereabouts in order to find it on the way back. From here it is three miles to the Wolverine Peak.

The return trip from the corner of O'Malley Rd and Hillside Drive, where the city bus drops you, is 13.8 miles – a nine-hour hike. Many people just trek to the good views above the bush line, shortening the trip to 7.8 miles (USGS quads *Anchorage A-7* and *A-8*).

The Ramp This is another of the many alpine summit hikes from the east side of the city that includes hiking through tranquil tundra valleys with good chances of seeing dall sheep during the summer. Catch bus No 92 to the corner of Hillside Drive and Upper Huffman Rd. Walk 0.7 miles east along Upper Huffman Rd and then turn right on Toilsome Hill Drive for two miles to the Glen Alps trailhead.

This switchback road ascends steeply to the Glen Alps park entrance, one of the most popular access points into the hillside trail system. Alaska Backpacker Shuttle drops trekkers here for $5 one way.

Most people will be heading up to Flattop Mountain, but to reach The Ramp, follow the lower trail in the parking lot for half a mile to the Powerline Trail. Turn right and follow the trail for two miles, past 13 power poles, to where an old jeep trail crosses over from the left and heads downhill to South Fork Campbell Creek.

The trail crosses the creek and continues up the hill beyond it to a valley on the other side. Hike up the alpine valley to Ship Pass, which lies between The Ramp at 5240 feet to the north and The Wedge at 4660 feet to the south. Either peak can be climbed, though The Wedge is easier. The round trip from the Glen Alps trailhead is 11 miles, an eight to 10-hour hike (USGS quads *Anchorage A-7* and *A-8*).

Powerline Trail This trail, an old road now closed to vehicles, is an easy hike through the heart of the Chugach foothills and over the 3550-foot Powerline Pass. You begin at the Glen Alps trailhead and end on the Indian Valley Trail near the Seward Hwy. The 11-mile one-way trip is more of a mountain bike route, though cyclists have problems with the steep and rocky descent from the pass to Indian Valley (USGS quads *Anchorage A-7* and *A-8*).

Far North Bicentennial Park A 4000-acre tract of forest and muskeg in east central Anchorage, this park features more than 20 miles of trails for hiking and mountain biking. In the center of the park is BLM's Campbell Tract, a 700-acre wildlife oasis where it's possible to see moose and bears in the spring. Come back in mid-September and the fall colors can be brilliant here. To reach the Hilltop Ski Area, take O'Malley Rd east to Hillside Drive and follow the road to the parking area. Buses Nos 91 and 92 go past it. Pick up a trail guide map in the chalet at the park's Hilltop Ski Area (☎ 346-1446).

Watching the Park

Chugach State Park is unusual in that it's a 500,000-acre wilderness area at the back door of Alaska's largest city. This makes it not only a quick getaway for trekkers, campers and rock climbers but also for vandals (the overwhelming majority of them teenagers). By 1992, park users were so fed up with vehicles being broken into and other acts of vandalism at the trailheads that they worked with park staff to form Park Watch.

Based on successful Neighborhood Watch programs, Park Watch recruits volunteers who patrol the trailheads and even camp at them throughout the summer. The volunteers 'are not vigilantes, just observers', said one park official. Just having somebody out there keeping an eye on the trailhead facilities has greatly reduced the number of incidents.

In 1994, 70 people signed up as volunteers for Park Watch and more than 20 of them did duty on a regular basis at the trailheads in the Hillside area of the park and along Turnagain Arm. The program has caught the eye of other state park systems in the US, where vandalism occurs in the remote areas. Interested? Contact Park Watch through the Chugach State Park, HC, Box 8999, Indian, AK 99540 (☎ (907) 345-5014). ∎

Ptarmigan

Tony Knowles Coastal Trail This 11-mile paved path is more of a trail for cyclists and in-line skaters than hikers but it is still a scenic trek. The Coastal Trail begins at the west end of 2nd Ave downtown and reaches Elderberry Park within a mile. From there it winds 10 miles west of Anchorage through Earthquake Park, around Point Woronzof and finally to Point Campbell in Kincaid Park. On clear days you can see the Alaska Range.

Rendezvous Peak Route The trek to the 4050-foot peak is an easy five-hour round trip, less from the trailhead, and rewards hikers with incredible views of Mt McKinley, Cook Inlet, Turnagain and Knik arms, and the city far below. Take bus No 75 for 6.5 miles north-east on Glenn Hwy to Arctic Valley Rd. Turn right (east) on Arctic Valley Rd (this section is also known as Ski Bowl Rd) and head seven miles to the Alpenglow Ski Area at the end. From the parking lot, a short trail leads along the right-hand side of the stream up the valley to the north-west. It ends at a pass where a short ascent to Rendezvous Peak is easily seen and climbed.

The round trip from the ski area parking lot is only 3.5 miles, but it is a much longer day if you can't thumb a ride up Arctic Valley Rd. Alaska Backpacker Shuttle will drop you at the trailhead for $5 one way (USGS quads *Anchorage A-7* and *B-7*).

Ship Creek Valley Also beginning from the Alpenglow Ski Area is the hike through Ship Creek Valley to Indian Valley. This is a challenging 22-mile overnight hike that involves steep, muddy sections and 10 miles of unmarked routes with unbridged stream crossings. You pick it up from a pullout on Ski Bowl Rd, across from a gated military road and 0.75 miles below the ski area. From here you begin on a trail that descends three miles into the valley. You end up on the Indian Valley Trail at Indian Pass that leads you six miles to the Seward Hwy (USGS quads *Anchorage A-7* and *Seward D-7*).

Turnagain Arm & Portage Glacier
Indian Valley Trail This six-mile path to Indian Pass is steep in some places, making it moderately hard, but the trail leads to good views of Turnagain Arm. The trail crosses bridges over Indian Creek and then climbs 2100 feet to reach the alpine setting of the pass. The trailhead is at *Mile 102* of the Seward Hwy, just west of Turnagain House Restaurant, where you turn into the mountain and follow a dirt road for 1.4 miles. Plan on five to seven hours for the 12-mile round trip (USGS quads *Anchorage A-7* and *Seward D-7*).

Bird Ridge Trail This moderately easy hike is the first snow-free trail in spring. The trail begins as an uphill climb to a power line access road, follows it for a third of a mile and then turns left and climbs Bird Ridge, which runs along the valley of Bird Creek. The hike is steep in many places but quickly leaves the bush behind for the alpine beauty above. You can hike over four miles on the ridge itself, reaching views of the headwaters of Ship Creek below. Viewing points of Turnagain Arm are plentiful. You pick up the trailhead near *Mile 102* of Seward Hwy by turning into a large marked parking area to the north. Don't confuse this trail with Bird

Top: Fording a river, Dixie Pass (JD)
Middle: Ski plane (JW)
Bottom: Tram over the Kennicott River (JD)

   Top: Polychrome Pass, Denali National Park (JW)
Middle: Icebergs from Grewingk Glacier (JD)
Bottom: Backcountry camping, Kachemak Bay State Park (DP)

Valley Trail which is open to off-road vehicles (USGS quads *Anchorage A-7* and *Seward D-7*).

Falls Creek Trail This path is only 1.5-miles long but follows a scenic stream through a narrow valley and ends above the tree line. From here you can easily spend a long afternoon exploring the open tundra area. The trail is rated moderate because it is steep in some places as it climbs to 1450 feet and is often confusing due to the many side trails. The main route stays right of the creek until it ends (it does not fork off to the east). The trailhead is half a mile east of *Mile 105* of the Seward Hwy and is posted along the highway. You'll find a small parking area near Falls Creek.

Alyeska Glacier View Trail You begin this trek by taking the chair lift to the Skyline Restaurant and then scrambling up the knob behind the sun deck. From here, you follow the ridge into an alpine area where there are views of the tiny Alyeska Glacier. The entire return hike is less than a mile. You can continue up the ridge to climb the so-called summit of Mt Alyeska, a high point of 3939 feet. The true summit lies further to the south but is not a suitable climb for casual hikers.

Winter Creek Gorge This is an easy and pleasant hike that winds 3.5 miles through a tall spruce and hemlock forest and ends in the gorge itself. The gorge is where Winter Creek flows through a small cleft in the rocks and becomes a series of small falls and cascades on its way to emptying into Glacier Creek. You pick up the trail at Alyeska Ski Resort by parking on Arlberg Rd and walking the bike path past the new hotel towards the bottom of the new tram. Follow the edge of a ski trail above the tram and look for the footpath heading into the forest.

Byron Glacier Trail This is an easy mile-long path in the Portage Glacier area to the base of Byron Glacier. Once you reach the permanent snow in front of the glacier, look for the thread-like ice worms that were immortalized in a Robert Service poem. You reach the trailhead from the road to the boat-tour dock on Portage Glacier Lake.

North of Anchorage & Palmer

Rodak Nature Trail The 0.7-mile loop begins at the Eagle River Visitor Center and passes a series of interpretive panels and an impressive observation deck straddling a salmon stream. The state park visitors' center is at *Mile 12* of Eagle River Rd off Glenn Hwy.

Albert Loop Trail Also beginning from the visitors' center is this three-mile trek through a boreal forest and along gravel bars of Eagle River. The hiking is easy and the views of the glacial river are pleasant. Part of the loop is the end of the Historic Iditarod Trail.

Thunderbird Falls Trail The mile-long trail is a quick uphill climb to the scenic falls formed by a small, rocky gorge. At the end is a deck with benches overlooking the cascade; a great place to enjoy lunch. At *Mile 25* of the Glenn Hwy, depart at Thunderbird Falls exit and follow the signs north along the Old Glenn Hwy to reach the trailhead parking lot in a mile.

Lazy Mountain The climb to the top of this 3720-foot peak is the best hike in the Palmer area. The 2.5-mile one-way trail is steep at times, but is a pleasant trek that ends in an alpine setting with good views of the Matanuska Valley and its farms below. From the Glenn Hwy in Palmer, head east on Arctic Ave, the third exit into town, which turns into Old Glenn Hwy. After crossing the Matanuska River, turn left onto Clark-Wolverine Rd and then left in half a mile at a T-junction. This puts you onto the unmarked Huntly Rd which you follow for a mile to the Equestrian Center parking lot at its end. The trailhead, marked 'Foot Trail', is on the north side of the parking lot. Plan on three to five hours for the return hike (USGS quad *Anchorage C-6*).

McRoberts Creek Trail This trail is in the same area as Lazy Mountain and the two trailheads are connected by a 1.5-mile spur. McRoberts Creek Trail is a backcountry hike up the creek's valley and provides the best approach to climbing Matanuska Peak (6119 feet). The trail reaches the tree line in 2.5 miles and 3880-foot Summit Ridge in nine miles. The trek to Matanuska Peak is a challenging 18-mile hike. To reach the trailhead, take Old Glenn Hwy from Palmer towards Butte and turn left onto Smith Rd at *Mile 15.5*. Follow Smith Rd for 1.4 miles until it curves into Harmony Ave. There is no parking at the South Fork trailhead so leave the car at the bend in the road (USGS quad *Anchorage C-6*).

Pioneer Ridge Trail This three-mile one-way trail provides access to the main ridge extending south-east of Pioneer Peak. It involves some steep grades until you're above the tree line and then ends at 5330 feet. From here it's another two miles along the ridge to the 6398-foot peak. This alpine section is a route, not a trail. To the south-east from the end of the trail, an experienced trekker can follow a ridge to a saddle below Bold Peak and then continue on to Eklutna Lake trail system in Chugach State Park.

Plan on six to seven hours to reach the 5330-foot level of Pioneer Ridge, where the views are stunning. To reach the trailhead from Knit River Bridge on Old Glenn Hwy, follow Knik River Rd for 3.6 miles. Trailhead parking will appear on the right (USGS quads *Anchorage B-5* and *B-6*).

Gold Mint Trail Hatcher Pass, a wonderful alpine setting that includes Independence Mine State Historical Park, offers several possibilities for a trek in the mountains. One of the easiest hikes is Gold Mint Trail. It begins from a parking lot across from Motherlode Lodge at *Mile 14* of the Fishhook-Willow Rd. The trail follows the Little Susitna River into a gently sloping mountain valley and within three miles you spot the ruins of Lonesome Mine. Keep trekking and you will eventually reach the head of the

river at Mint Glacier (USGS quad *Anchorage D-6*).

Reed Lakes Trail A mile past Motherlode Lodge, a road to Archangel Valley splits off from Fishhook-Willow Rd and takes you to the posted trailhead of Reed Lakes. The trail begins as a wide road to an old cabin reached in two miles. From here you follow a trail that climbs to the crest of the valley. Lower Reed Lake is found within a quarter of a mile of reaching the crest, or 3.5 miles from the trailhead. Upper Reed Lake, a scenic place to camp, is another mile beyond (USGS quad *Anchorage D-6*).

Craigie Creek Trail This trek starts off as a road occasionally used by 4WDs. It's posted along the Fishhook-Willow Rd, 1.5 miles west of Hatcher Pass. The trail follows a valley up to the head of the creek where it's possible to cross a pass into the Independence Mine Bowl. The road makes a gentle climb for four miles past several abandoned mining operations and then becomes a very steep trail for three miles to Dogsled Pass (USGS quad *Anchorage D-7*).

GETTING THERE & AWAY
Air
Anchorage International Airport, 6.5 miles west of the city center, is one of the busiest airports in the country, handling 130 flights daily from the 14 major airlines that serve it. From here you can catch a flight to anywhere in Alaska. Alaska Airlines (☎ (800) 426-0333) and its system of contract carriers provide the most intrastate routes to travelers, with flights departing daily. Samples of one-way fares from Anchorage are: $87 to $135 to Fairbanks, $109 to $140 to Juneau, $190 to Kodiak and $290 to Nome.

ERA provides flights to Valdez, Homer, Cordova and Kodiak (book them through Alaska Airlines); Delta Airline (☎ (800) 221-1212) has flights to Fairbanks but not to Juneau; and MarkAir (☎ (800) 627-5247) provides services to Katmai and Kodiak among other places.

Bus

Alaskon Express (☎ 277-5581) departs from its office on 745 West 4th Ave as well as a handful of major hotels on Sunday, Tuesday and Friday at 7 am for Palmer, Glennallen, Tok and Beaver Creek in the Yukon Territory where the bus stops overnight. From Beaver Creek you can make connections to Whitehorse, Haines or Skagway. The overnight stop is at your own expense and the one-way fare to Haines is $194, Skagway $199, Tok $99 and Glennallen $55.

Alaska Direct (☎ 277-6652 or (800) 770-6652) offers a similar run for a slightly smaller fare. The bus departs from Anchorage on Monday, Wednesday and Saturday for Glennallen, Tok and Haines Junction where you can pick up a second bus for Haines the next day at noon. The one-way fare is $125 to Haines Junction, $175 to Haines, $37 to Glennallen and $65 to Tok.

Moon Bay Express (☎ 274-6454) has daily van service to Denali National Park and anywhere in between, including trailheads. The van leaves daily from the youth hostel at 8 am, reaching the park at 1 pm. The one-way fare is $35, round trip $30.

Seward/Homer Bus Lines (☎ 278-0800) takes on passengers at the Samovar Inn on the corner of 7th Ave and Gambell St and departs daily at 5 am and 2.30 pm for Seward (arriving three hours later). The one-way fare is $30. Another bus departs from the motel at 9.45 am daily and reaches Homer at 3.40 am after passing through the town of Kenai, and Soldotna. The one-way fare to Homer costs $38.

Train

The Alaska Railroad (☎ 265-2494) maintains its office in the depot at 421 West 1st Ave and provides services both north and south of Anchorage. To the north, the Denali Express departs from Anchorage daily at 8.30 am, reaching Denali Park at 3.45 pm and Fairbanks at 8.30 pm. The one-way fare to Denali is $88 and to Fairbanks $125. On Wednesday and Saturday a local 'Flag Stop' train departs from Anchorage at 6.30 am and makes an all-stops trip to Hurricane Gulch,

arriving at 11.21 am. The return fare to Hurricane Gulch is $88. On Sunday the same train departs at noon.

From late May to the first week of September you can also catch a rail diesel car to Seward from Thursday to Monday. The train departs from Anchorage at 6.45 am and arrives in Seward at 11 am. The one-way fare is $50, and the round trip is $80.

GETTING AROUND
To/From the Airport

People arriving at the International Airport have a couple of ways to reach the city. Catch the People Mover bus No 6, which departs from outside the South Terminal for the Transit Center downtown on weekdays. Times of departure are 7.21 and 8.30 am and 3.50, 4.50 and 5.50 pm. The fare is $1. Many hotels and B&Bs have courtesy van service – most are listed in the baggage-claim area. There is also an endless line of taxis eager to take your bags and your money. Plan on a $12 fare to the downtown area.

Bus

Anchorage has an excellent public bus system; the People Mover buses are clean and the drivers are friendly. All buses, except No 93, begin at the People Mover's downtown terminal in the Transit Center at the Municipal Building near the corner of 6th Ave and G St. Most buses pass by every half-hour and there's a time schedule posted at every stop. The fare is $1 a ride or $2.50 for an all-day, unlimited ticket. If the trip requires more than one bus, ask the driver for a transfer, which allows you to ride on the connecting bus for only an additional 15c. For information on any route call the Ride Line on ☎ 343-6543.

Car Rental

Anchorage has a variety of car rental companies and the most affordable rates anywhere in Alaska. It's often possible to pick up a compact vehicle for 10 days, with mileage, for under $350. Between two or more people, renting a car is cheaper than hopping on a bus and a great way to reach trails in the

Anchorage Bowl, Kenai Peninsula and other areas accessible from the Interior highways.

The cheapest deal is from Affordable Car Rental (☎ 243-3370 or (800) 248-3765) at 4707 Spenard Rd (they also have a counter in the Anchorage Hilton, downtown). They advertise some cars for as low as $24 but never seem to have any available when you call.

Better to try Rent-A-Wreck (☎ 562-5499 or (800) 478-5499 in Alaska) at 512 West International Airport Rd or AllStar Rental (☎ 561-0350 or (800) 722-6484 in Alaska) just a block down the street at 940 West International Airport Rd. Both have subcompacts for $29 a day with 100 free miles. They will also provide courtesy transportation from your motel or to the airport before or after you rent the car.

FLATTOP MOUNTAIN TRAIL
Because of its easy access and great views on a clear day, this climb to the peak of Flattop Mountain is the most popular hike in the Anchorage area and probably all of Alaska. The trail to the 3550-foot peak is easy to follow, not too hard to climb and once

you're on top there are good views of Mt McKinley (to the north) and most of Cook Inlet.

On a Saturday afternoon, the trail is busy with hikers, families and even joggers looking for a more challenging run. Occasionally somebody will camp on the flat summit of the mountain, despite the lack of water, just to catch the sunset over the Alaska Range. Others just pack a flashlight and follow the trail back at dusk (possible even though the trek has some steep sections). The trail is rated easy and covered on the USGS 1:63,360 series quad *Anchorage A-8*.

Access
The trail begins at the Glen Alps entrance to the Chugach State Park. To get there, catch bus No 92 to the corner of Hillside Drive and Upper Huffman Rd. Walk 0.7 miles east along Upper Huffman Rd and then turn right on Toilsome Hill Drive for two miles. This switchback road ascends steeply to the Glen Alps park entrance, a parking lot where trailhead signs point the way to Flattop Mountain. Alaska Backpacker Shuttle (☎ 344-8775) will also drop you off at the trailhead for $5 one way.

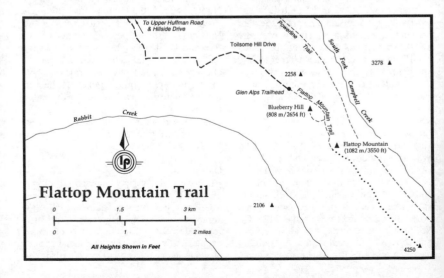

Flattop Mountain Trail

Stage 1: Glen Alps Trailhead to Flattop Mountain

(1.7 miles, 1-2 hours)

From the large parking area, you begin at a well-posted stairway and then climb through a stand of stunted mountain hemlock before breaking out in the alpine region of the ridge. The trail skirts the side of a 2654-foot point known as Blueberry Hill and in half a mile reaches a posted junction in the saddle between this hill and Flattop Mountain.

The right-hand fork is an easy trail to a high point of the ridge known as Blueberry Hill, an ideal alternative if you're not up to climbing the mountain. The trail to Flattop is the left-hand fork which skirts the ridge leading to the peak, following a series of switchbacks in some places to gain elevation. From the side of the ridge you look down at Powerline Trail or across the valley to the surrounding summits of False and O'Malley peaks.

The trail sidling the ridge is narrow and rocky and definitely not a casual stroll for most hikers. Yet it's amazing how many children you'll pass here on the weekends. Eventually the trail makes a sharp 90-degree turn to the right and you climb steeply to a second saddle. Be aware of those climbing above you and the possibility of falling rocks.

The second saddle provides views into the Rabbit Creek Valley on the south-west side of Flattop and is another good spot to take a break. There are plans for a trail from the south-west side of Flattop Mountain to Rabbit Creek Trail (presently closed because it crosses private land).

From the saddle, the 3550-foot summit of Flattop Mountain is still one more climb away along a boulder-strewn trail where falling rocks can again be a hazard. As its name indicates, this popular mountain has a table-top appearance. From its peak you are rewarded with a spectacular panorama that includes all of Anchorage, as well as Cook Inlet, the Kenai Peninsula and the interior of Chugach State Park. On a crystal-clear day it's even possible to see Mt McKinley (to the north-west) and Mt Redoubt (to the south-

west), the active volcano on the Alaska Peninsula.

Stage 2: Flattop Mountain to Glen Alps Trailhead

(1.7 miles, 1 hour)

From the Flattop summit, retrace your steps to the trailhead parking area. It takes much less time than the climb up, but be careful not kick rocks and stones down the slopes which could hit others below you.

If you're not satisfied with the climb to Flattop Mountain you can follow the ridge line for another three miles to the high point of 4250 feet. There is no maintained trail along this stretch but the crest of the ridge is a natural route that's easy to follow if you're an experienced alpine trekker.

WILLIWAW LAKES LOOP

A combination of trails and routes, the Williwaw Lakes Loop is a pleasant overnight hike. Many trekkers consider it the most scenic outing in the hillside area of Chugach State Park.

The trek follows Middle Fork Trail to a handful of alpine lakes at the base of Mt Williwaw. It crosses a pass into the drainage of North Fork Campbell Creek and then returns to the trailhead along Near Point Trail. Along the way, you might encounter some mountain bikers in the first three miles of both the Near Point and Middle Fork trails. You can also begin the loop from the Glen Alps trailhead, where you pick up the Flattop Mountain Trail, but it's easier to begin and end at Prospect Heights trailhead.

Rated moderate, it is a two-day 18-mile trek covered on USGS 1:63,360 series quads *Anchorage A-7* and *A-8*.

Access

Take bus No 92 to the intersection of Hillside Drive and O'Malley Rd. Head east on Upper O'Malley Rd for half a mile to a T-junction and then turn left (north) onto Prospect Drive. After 1.1 miles the road ends at the Prospect Heights entrance (and parking area) to the Chugach State Park.

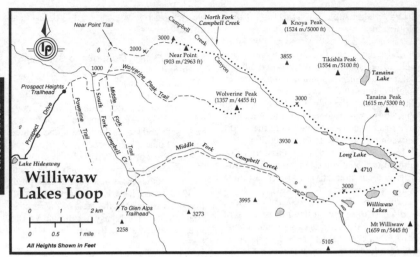

Williwaw Lakes Loop

Stage 1: Prospect Heights Trailhead to Williwaw Lakes

(8 miles, 5-7 hours)

(Backcountry camping)

The trail begins as an old homestead road from the parking area. It heads east under a power line before curving away from the towers and descending to cross a bridge over South Fork Campbell Creek. On the other side you climb to the top of a hill to reach the junction with Middle Fork Trail, 1.5 miles from the trailhead.

Take the right-hand fork to head south on Middle Fork Trail. It skirts the eastern flanks of Wolverine Peak to stay above South Fork Campbell Creek and within two miles descends to cross a bridge over Middle Fork Campbell Creek. On the other side is a posted junction with a trail that heads southwest and in two miles reaches the Glen Alps trailhead and parking area.

For Williwaw Lakes, take the left-hand fork and follow the trail that heads upstream along the south side of Campbell Creek's Middle Fork. The spruce eventually leads into mountain beech and finally, open tundra. The first lake is seven miles from the Prospect Heights trailhead and 3.5 miles

from the Middle Fork crossing. It is the first of seven jewel-like alpine lakes that lie at the foot of the sheer-face of 5445-foot-high Mt Williwaw.

The maintained trail ends at the first lake; beyond it you follow a route that climbs up the valley past several other lakes. The most scenic campsite is at the last lake before the pass. It's a two-mile trek from the first lake to the pass and a climb of 1100 feet.

Stage 2: Williwaw Lakes to Prospect Heights Trailhead via North Fork

(10 miles, 6-8 hours)

From the last Williwaw lake, head north-east towards the pass of the North Fork of Campbell Creek. From the 3700-foot saddle it's an easy descent of 600 feet to Long Lake. In this remote corner of Chugach State Park the lake is surrounded by several peaks, the most distinct being 5300-foot Tanaina Peak along its north shore.

You follow the lake along the north side (climbing on the hillside if necessary) and ford several streams before reaching the outlet of North Fork in 1.2 miles. Keep in mind that from the pass to Near Point you will have to pick and choose the best route down the valley.

After passing several small lakes, you skirt the North Fork for approximately three miles as the brush and alder increases. Ford to the south-west side of the stream before it enters the steep-sided Campbell Creek Canyon and ascend the north-west ridge of Wolverine Peak. Aim for a notch south-east of the 2963-foot knob known as Near Point (not labeled on the topos).

It's a steep climb, but once on the ridge you'll easily be able to head north-west to the top of Near Point. From this peak there are good views of Anchorage, Cook Inlet and even the Alaska Range on a clear day. The large boulders nearby were carried by a glacier from the Talkeetna Mountains (to the north). On the west side of the knob, look for Near Point Trail, a narrow path that begins with a steep descent off the ridge. Within a mile the trail arrives at an old homestead and the road here returns to the Prospect Heights trailhead.

It's roughly four miles from Near Point to the trailhead. When you're halfway you'll pass another old road that veers off to the left. This is the trail to Wolverine Peak. The 4455-foot summit is a 3.2-mile climb from this point. The next junction is the posted Middle Fork Trail and from there you retrace the start of the trek, crossing the bridge over South Fork Campbell Creek and ascending from the creek to the trailhead, 1.3 miles away.

McHUGH & RABBIT LAKES TRAIL

The newest trail in Chugach State Park is the seven-mile McHugh & Rabbit Lakes Trail. From the Seward Hwy it extends inland to a pair of beautiful alpine lakes, ideal for an overnight camp. When combined with portions of the Turnagain Arm and Powerline trails and a climb over Ptarmigan Pass, you form a near loop of roughly 16 miles that begins at the Potter Section House along the Seward Hwy and ends at the Glen Alps trailhead in the Hillside area of the state park.

Although the trek can be done in two days, you can just as easily spend several days climbing summits like McHugh Peak, Ptar-

migan Peak, The Wedge or The Ramp. You could also follow the Powerline Trail east over a low pass and emerge at the Indian Valley Trail and *Mile 102* of the Seward Hwy.

The first day can be shortened if you begin the trek at McHugh Creek Picnic Area at *Mile 112* of the Seward Hwy and skip the Turnagain Arm portion of the hike, though this is an easy stretch and the views from high above the highway make hiking the two extra miles well worth it.

USGS 1:63,360 series quads *Anchorage A-7* and *A-8* cover the complete trek which is rated moderate, mainly because the Ptarmigan Pass crossing is a route, not a trail. You'll find the Turnagain Arm and Powerline trails easy. Powerline Trail is also a popular mountain bike trip.

Access

The trail begins at the Chugach State Park headquarters in the Potter Section House on *Mile 115* of Seward Hwy and ends at the Glen Alps trailhead (see the earlier Flattop Mountain Trail for access information). Alaska Backpacker Shuttle (☎ 344-8775) will provide transportation to either end of the trail or to the McHugh Creek Picnic Area ($5 one way to any of the three trailheads).

Stage 1: Potter Section House to McHugh Lake

(9.4 miles, 5-6 hours)
(Backcountry camping)

From a parking lot across the highway from the Potter Section House, the trail heads uphill for almost half a mile and then levels out as it follows a bluff in a forest of birch, aspen and cottonwood. Originally cut in 1910 as a mail and telegraph route, the trail here is wide enough for a wagon. Within two miles you reach a viewpoint of Turnagain Arm and from here the trail begins a gentle descent off the bluff into McHugh Valley.

To the north you can view 4301-foot McHugh Peak and to the north-east, 5005-foot South Suicide Peak, just before arriving at a posted Y-junction 3.2 miles from the Potter trailhead. Here, the right-hand fork

McHugh & Rabbit Lakes Trail

All Heights Shown in Feet

0 ___ 1.5 ___ 3 km

0 ___ 1 ___ 2 miles

descends half a mile to the upper parking lot of the McHugh Creek Picnic Area, where there are toilets, tables, drinking water and a scenic view of Turnagain Arm. In the lower parking lot of the picnic area is a trailhead for the rest of the Turnagain Arm Trail to Windy Corner.

To reach McHugh Lake, take the left-hand fork at the Y-junction. It heads north along a series of switchbacks to climb 700 feet to Table Rock, an immense rocky outcrop rising above the trail. You can scramble to the top of the rock for excellent views of Turnagain Arm. From Table Rock the trail

enters the McHugh Creek drainage area, sidling the sides of the valley high above the creek. Two miles from the McHugh Creek Picnic Area you pass a trail that climbs steeply north out of the valley. This is a route to McHugh Peak.

The main trail continues to climb up the valley and four miles from the picnic area emerges from alder and other brush to reach the alpine tundra. In another two miles the trail ends at McHugh Lake. From here it's easy to hike over a low ridge to reach the much larger Rabbit Lake to the north. The lakes are in a spectacular alpine setting, with the Suicide peaks looming overhead and 4880-foot Ptarmigan Peak to the north. Good camping spots abound in this area and a spare day could be spent climbing either one of the Suicide peaks.

Stage 2: McHugh Lake to Glen Alps Trailhead
(7 miles, 4-6 hours)
From McHugh Lake, climb over the low ridge to Rabbit Lake and then follow the lakeshore west to its outlet into Rabbit Creek. An old trail can be picked up here and followed up Rabbit Creek Valley. At one time the trail extended 5.5 miles from the lake to Lower Canyon Rd but it has since been closed to the public because it crosses private property.

Follow the creek for 1.5 miles past Ptarmigan Creek to Ptarmigan Pass, a 3585-foot saddle on the west side of the peak. Leave Rabbit Creek and the old trail and ascend the ridge into the pass, a climb of more than 700 feet. Once on the saddle you'll see the east-west ridge that most people follow to reach the summit of 4880-foot-high Ptarmigan Peak.

When descending the north side of the pass, it's best to stay west of the stream flowing into South Fork Campbell Creek. This side is considerably steeper than the climb from Rabbit Creek but in less than half a mile, when you're well above the creek on the south side of the valley, you'll reach Powerline Trail, three miles from Rabbit Lake.

Powerline Trail is an old road closed to vehicles but open to mountain bikes. It's an easy hike out of the valley as you gradually descend towards the South Fork. A path under the power lines on the other side of the creek also leads through the valley. More mud is normally encountered on this trail.

Within a mile a trail merges into the road from the valley below. Follow it if you want to climb either The Wedge (4660 feet) or The Ramp (5240 feet). (See the earlier Trails section for details). The trail continues its gradual descent and in two miles reaches the half-mile spur that links the Powerline Trail to the parking area of the Glen Alps trailhead.

HISTORIC IDITAROD TRAIL
Also known as the Crow Pass Trail and the Old Iditarod Trail, this alpine crossing to Eagle River Valley is one of the most scenic routes in the Anchorage area. The 26-mile trail is part of the historic Iditarod route from Seward to Nome that was used by gold miners and dog-sled teams until 1918, when the Alaska Railroad was completed to Fairbanks.

Today, it is a popular overnight trek through excellent mountain scenery beginning with the climb to Crow Pass, from where you can view nearby Raven Glacier and Crystal Lake. You then hike down into Eagle River Valley and follow the river to the state park visitors' center at Eagle River.

The trail is maintained by both Alaska Division of Parks & Outdoor Recreation and the USFS because the first portion to Crow Pass lies in the Chugach National Forest while the rest is in Chugach State Park. Over the years, the trail has been improved and well posted, so much so, that a foot race is

Red fox

held on it annually. Most runners cover the entire 26 miles, including the deep ford at Eagle River, in less than five hours.

With a light day pack, and in good weather, you can cover the trail in one long Alaska summer day. But why rush? The scenery is remarkable, the mining ruins are interesting and the trek is reasonably challenging. And besides, this is why you came to Alaska – to wander in the mountains.

The trail is described here as a three-day trek which you can hike in either direction. However, by beginning at the Crow Pass trailhead you start 1000 feet higher, thus you have less to climb to reach the highest point of the trail (3883 feet). Plus, you'll get all the climbing done in the first few hours (adrenalin will help carry you into the alpine area).

You can find out the latest trail conditions from either the Chugach State Park headquarters at the Potter Section House (☎ 345-5014) at *Mile 115* of the Seward Hwy, or the Chugach National Forest ranger office (☎ 783-3242) just off the Seward Hwy on Alyeska Hwy. It's open daily during the summer. Check here to see if by some remote chance the Crow Pass Cabin is open. There are a number of backcountry campsites along the trail that feature metal rings for campfires. Still it's best to pack a stove because fires are prohibited elsewhere along the route.

The alpine crossing and fording Eagle River makes this trail a challenging one. USGS topos are essential – the route is covered on the 1:63,360 series quads *Anchorage A-7* and *A-6*.

Access

The Crow Pass trailhead is reached by turning onto the Alyeska Hwy at *Mile 90* of the Seward Hwy, 37 miles from Anchorage. Within two miles, veer left onto posted Crow Creek Rd and then in five miles veer right at the fork immediately following a bridge. Head up the hill and in a mile you'll reach the trailhead and parking area. The northern trailhead is at the Eagle River Visitor Center for the state park at *Mile 12* of Eagle River Rd, off the Glenn Hwy.

Alaska Backpacker Shuttle (☎ 344-8775) will provide transportation to both ends of the trail. It costs $20 per person to Crow Pass and $12 to the Eagle River Visitor Center. You can also save a few dollars by hitching from the visitors' center to the junction of Eagle River Rd and the Glenn Hwy where you can pick up People Mover buses Nos 74, 76 and 78 back to Anchorage.

Stage 1: Crow Creek Rd to Crow Pass
(4 miles, 3-4 hours)
(USFS cabin, backcountry campsites)
This leg of the trek is a steep climb of 2500 feet to Crow Pass and views of Raven Glacier. Keep in mind that snow will persist in the pass area until mid to late June, changing to a rainbow of color as tundra wild flowers begin to bloom.

From the trailhead parking area at the end of Crow Creek Rd the trail climbs into the alpine area along a series of switchbacks. The trail is an old miner's road and it gains more than 1000 feet within two miles before it reaches the ruins of Monarch Mine, also referred to as Girdwood Mine, on the flanks of Barnes and Jewel mountains. The hardrock gold mine operated from 1906 to 1948 and today the remains include a mill and miner's bunkhouse. Be very careful when exploring the ruins. A quarter of a mile beyond the ruins a spur leads west to Crow Creek Cascade.

The old miners' road ends at Monarch Mine and the trail climbs steeply towards the pass along switchbacks, skirting above scenic Crystal Lake. At *Mile 3* the trail reaches the USFS cabin ($25, reservations) at 3550 feet. The Crow Creek Cabin is an A-frame structure with bunks for six people and room for a few more in the loft. There is no stove. Being well above the timber line, the views from the cabin are spectacular. It sits right above Crystal Lake and mountain goats and dall sheep can be seen on the surrounding ridges.

From the cabin, follow rock cairns to Crow Pass. It's half a mile away at *Mile 4* and marked by a huge rock cairn. At 3883 feet, the pass offers a stunning panorama of the surrounding peaks and glaciers; Raven Glacier is at your feet. It is a scenic place to set up camp and there's water nearby. Be aware of strong winds that can whip through here; stake down free-standing dome tents.

Stage 2: Crow Pass to Thunder Gorge
(10 miles, 5-7 hours)
(Backcountry campsite)
From the pass, a trail well-marked by cairns descends to the moraine along the south-west side of Raven Glacier. Follow the moraine and enjoy the views of the glacier from it for half a mile and then skirt Raven Creek until Clear Creek merges into it at *Mile 6*. You ford Clear Creek and then in less than a mile cross Raven Creek on a bridge over its gorge.

This puts you on the east side of the creek and for the next three miles the trail skirts the hillsides above it. At *Mile 9.5* you cross Turbid Creek and then begin ascending towards the north end of Raven Ridge, ending near its crest with views of Eagle Glacier and the lake in front of it. It's a steep descent off the ridge at which point the trail swings east and heads upstream to the ford site on Eagle River.

The ford, the halfway point of the trek at *Mile 13*, is half a mile down from Glacier Lake and well marked and posted along Eagle River. Still, crossing this glacial river should not be taken lightly. Under normal conditions the water will be almost knee-deep. After a heavy rainfall it will be even higher so camp and wait for the water level to drop.

From the ford site the trail skirts the east bank of the river as it heads north-west towards the Eagle River Visitor Center. The hiking is considerably easier here and within a mile you reach Thunder Gorge at *Mile 14* where you'll find a backcountry campsite with a metal fire ring.

Stage 3: Thunder Gorge to Eagle River Visitor Center
(12 miles, 4-5 hours)
(Backcountry campsites)
The final leg of the trek is an easy walk

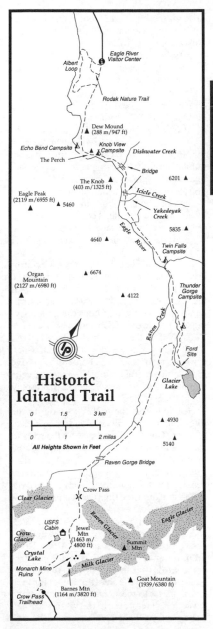

Historic Iterod Trail

ANCHORAGE

through the upper valley of Eagle River to the visitors' center, 12 miles away. From Crow Pass you will have descended more than 3000 feet to Thunder Gorge. To the northern trailhead you will descend only another 300 feet.

The trail continues north-west, staying above the river at first and then swinging close to it just before you arrive at Twin Falls at *Mile 16.5*. Near this stream is a backcountry campsite and fire ring. In the next 3.5 miles you'll cross three streams, all unnamed on the USGS quads. The second, reached at *Mile 20*, is Yakedeyak Creek and you'll come to the third, Icicle Creek, within a third of a mile. Cross the bridge to the backcountry campsite. Across the river from Icicle Creek is Heritage Falls but the best view of the mountainside cascade is further up the trail.

Skirting the river, the trail stays on a northerly course until you pass The Knob, a distinct 1325-foot bluff on the west side of the river. At this point Eagle River swings almost due west and so does the trail, arriving at a bridge over Dishwater Creek at *Mile 21.5*. Within the next half-mile you pass Knob View Camp and then The Perch which is posted at *Mile 22*. The Perch is a massive rocky outcrop. Take a break here to view the mountains and impressive peaks that box in Eagle River Valley.

Heading west, the trail stays close to the river and reaches Echo Bend campsite at *Mile 23*. This is a scenic spot by the river to camp and only three miles short of the visitors' center. At Echo Bend the trail swings away from Eagle River, passes beneath Dew Mound (947 feet) and arrives at Rapids Camp, the final backcountry campsite, at *Mile 24.5*.

In the final 1.5 miles, you stay in a birch and aspen forest away from the water and pass a posted junction to the Albert Loop Trail. If you're not in rush to reach civilization or a ride back to Anchorage, Albert Loop is an easy three-mile side trip. It goes through boreal forest to the gravel bars along Eagle River before returning to the visitors' center. Just before the center, you pass the two posted junctions of the Rodak Nature Trail (0.75-mile loop). If the salmon are spawning, take the time to hike to the viewing deck on this short trail.

EKLUTNA LAKESIDE TRAIL

At a length of more than seven miles, Eklutna Lake is the largest body of water in Chugach State Park. Surrounded by peaks and towering mountains, it's also one of the most scenic. The lake fills the glacially carved valley while just beyond its east end is Eklutna Glacier, the ice floe responsible for the sculpture. Chances to spot wildlife are good. Moose are often seen near the lakeshore, dall sheep frequent the ridges and slopes above the water, and mountain goats and brown bears are found in the more remote regions away from the lake. Backpackers are urged by the park staff to hang their food and bear-proof their backcountry camps.

At the west end of the lake is Eklutna Lake Campground (50 sites, $10), one of Chugach State Park's most popular campgrounds (there is an overflow area when it's full). A separate parking lot for the trailhead is nearby. It features a trail information kiosk and telescopes for viewing dall sheep; parking costs $2 a day. There is a ranger station (☎ 688-0908) near the campground that is open when volunteers are available.

At the east end of the lake there are two backcountry campgrounds and a rental cabin. In between the two campgrounds, skirting the north shore, is the Lakeside Trail. It used to be an old road until 1977 when numerous washouts turned it into a route for hikers, horses, mountain bikers and, unfortunately, those in all-terrain vehicles.

The saving grace of the trail, the only reason it's included in this book, is that off-road vehicles are only permitted on this road from Sunday to Wednesday. Hikers and mountain bikers can use it any day of the week. With three days free of vehicles, you can easily hike to the east end, spend a day exploring the glacier and then return, stopping to enjoy an afternoon in the alpine region.

Eklutna Lakeside Trail

All Heights Shown in Feet

The Lakeside Trail is actually the access route to an extensive trail system. At the beginning is Twin Peaks Trail, a 3.2-mile climb to above the tree line; just over halfway along the lake is Bold Ridge Trail, another route into the surrounding alpine region; and at the end are the East Fork and Eklutna Glacier trails.

Lakeside Trail, a 13-mile one-way hike out to the backcountry campsites and glacier, is rated easy. It even has mileposts to tell you how far you've walked. The climbs to the alpine area on Bold Ridge and Twin Peaks trails are challenging while the East Fork

Trail is a moderate hike. The entire area is covered on USGS 1:63,360 series quad *Anchorage B-6*.

Access

From Anchorage, head north on the Glenn Hwy and take the Eklutna exit at *Mile 26*. From the service drive, turn right onto the Old Glenn Hwy and then in half a mile turn left towards the mountains on Eklutna Lake Rd. Follow the road as it bumps and winds east for 10 miles to the west end of the lake. Park signs will keep you reassured that you're not lost. Alaska Backpacker Shuttle

ANCHORAGE

(☎ 344-8775) runs trekkers out to the lake; the drive from downtown Anchorage takes from 45 minutes to an hour and costs $15 per person.

Stage 1: Twin Peaks Creek to Eklutna Glacier
(13 miles, 6-8 hours)
(Backcountry campgrounds)
From the trailhead parking area, check out the information kiosk, take a peak at the surrounding mountains for dall sheep (through the telescope) and then cross the bridge over Twin Peaks Creek. On the other side is a posted junction; Twin Peaks Trail heads west (left).

The 3.2-mile Twin Peaks Trail is a popular and well-maintained route to the tundra areas surrounding East and West Twin Peaks and Goat Mountain. It's considered a challenging trek because you climb 1500 feet and some sections are steep. For most people, the trek is a three to four-hour round trip. You are rewarded with great views of Eklutna Lake and (possibly) dall sheep. The trail ends at an alpine bowl with a stream flowing through the middle. You can camp here. More adventurous souls can continue up the bowl to a pass at 4400 feet.

Lakeside Trail heads east (right). This wide, dirt road was originally built by the military and open to vehicle traffic (drive it if your dare!) until 1977 when it was closed due to continual rock and landslides that made maintenance a nightmare. If you are used to narrow mountain trails or no trails at all (like in Denali National Park) this route will be an easy walk. To the end of the lake the trail hugs the north shore for almost eight miles, providing constant views of turquoise water surrounded by snowy peaks.

You immediately pass an aqueduct in the mountain which supplies water from the lake to the city of Anchorage. Near *Mile 1* is a rock face that serves as a lambing area in the spring. It is a particularly good place to spot sheep anytime of the year.

The trail continues as a winding road for the next three miles, using culverts to cross four creeks that drain from the mountains

towering overhead. The fourth one is Yuditnu Creek and here the trail passes where the northern and southern shorelines 'pinch' the lake to its narrowest width.

At *Mile 5*, two miles past Yuditnu Creek, you cross Bold Creek and arrive at the posted trailhead for Bold Ridge Trail. This side trail is a one-way hike of 3.5 miles to the alpine tundra at the base of Bold Peak. It's a steep climb of switchbacks along an old road in the beginning until you break out of the brush in less than two miles at a 3400-foot knob. From there, a trail continues another mile or so up Bold Creek Valley to glacial moraines at the base of 7552-foot Bold Peak. You can camp here, but you'll have to search hard for water.

To the south, the valley is boxed in by Bold Ridge, an excellent ridge line to follow for views of Eklutna Lake and glacier, and the Knik Arm of Cook Inlet. To the north, the ridge can be followed to reach a 4800-foot pass into the remote Hunter Creek drainage area of Chugach State Park. For those who want to avoid the families and mountain bikers at the east end of the lake, this is an excellent alternative. Plan on two hours up, and an extra day if you want to hike the surrounding alpine ridges.

Lakeside Trail continues south-east along the shoreline for the next 1.5 miles until *Mile 7* when it swings away from the lake and into spruce and birch forest. Here it becomes a narrow winding road until it crosses Eight Mile Creek and begins curving around the east end of the lake. Just before *Mile 9* is Eklutna Alex Campground. The facility has four sites, vault toilets, fire rings and picnic tables. Nearby is Eklutna Alex Cabin, a two-bunk unit that comfortably sleeps three people.

At this point, Lakeside Trail heads towards the narrow, steep-walled canyon that the Eklutna River flows from. You reach the posted junction to the East Fork Trail in 1.5 miles and then cross East Fork Eklutna River on a wooden bridge where, from the middle, there are excellent views of the canyon. On the other side at *Mile 11* is Kanchee Campground. It has four sites and similar facilities as Eklutna Alex Campground.

Beyond the campground the trail reaches the Eklutna River which it skirts briefly before crossing it via another bridge. Once across the river you reach *Mile 12* and the spur that leads to a third campground. Cottonwood, a walk-in campground in a forested setting, was closed in 1994. Lakeside Trail continues another mile beyond the campground, quickly passing spectacular Serenity Falls and ending at *Mile 13*.

The final leg to the glacier is along Eklutna Glacier Trail, which is for foot traffic only. Motorized off-road vehicles and mountain bikes are prohibited. It leads 0.75 miles further up the steep canyon along the Eklutna River and across glacial debris. It ends at an interpretive display and viewing area of the Eklutna Glacier.

Stage 2: East Fork Trail
(11 miles, 6-7 hours)
This foot trail begins at a posted junction 10.5 miles along the Lakeshore Trail and winds east along the East Fork of the Eklutna River to a small knoll overlooking a glacial lake. It's a scenic side trip (12 miles if you're staying at Kanchee Campground) which can be done in one day. It's rated easy to moderate. A shorter trek is to Tulchina Falls, a little over two miles along the trail.

The junction to the trail is on the north side of East Fork from where you immediately parallel the river into another steep-sided canyon. The scenery here is dominated by Baleful, Bold and Bashful peaks to the northwest. At 8005 feet, Bashful is the tallest

mountain in Chugach State Park. Within a mile you'll pass the first waterfall tumbling out of the mountains.

A little more than two miles from the trailhead, the second cascade, Tulchina Falls, is visible from the trail. This one is much more impressive as it leaps more than 100 feet off the side of Bashful Peak before becoming a mountainside stream. The trail continues its mild climb along the East Fork until the final mile of the route. Here it swings away from the creek and begins a steep climb. You ascend more than 600 feet until the trail tops off on a 2190-foot-high knoll in open tundra, where the views, needless to say, are stunning. Just east of the knoll is a glacial lake where you can escape the campground crowds for the night.

Stage 3: The Return
(11 miles, 5-7 hours)
Return the way you came. If you're in a hurry to get back to the Eklutna Lake Campground you could probably make the trek from Kanchee Campground in four hours. For anything faster, you'd almost have to jog or be on a mountain bike.

It's possible to continue from the Lakeshore Trail and traverse Eklutna, Whiteout and Eagle glaciers, and eventually Raven Glacier, to emerge at the Crow Pass Trail near Girdwood. The Mountaineering Club of Alaska even maintains three huts along the 31-mile route for those adventurous souls traversing the glaciers. This is a highly technical trek requiring a lot of equipment and mountaineering expertise.

Kenai Peninsula

Just 50 road miles south-east of Anchorage, the Kenai Peninsula is a vast forested plateau, bounded to the east by the Kenai Mountains and the Harding Ice Field, to the west by Cook Inlet, and laced by hundreds of lakes, rivers and streams. This area is an outdoor paradise; it has an extensive trail system for trekkers, long glaciated fjords for kayakers, chains of lakes for canoeists, record king salmon for anglers and a campground around almost every bend in the road.

Most of the peninsula is set aside as Chugach National Forest, Kenai Fjords National Park, Kenai National Wildlife Refuge and Kachemak Bay State Park & Wilderness. Squeezed in between these wilderness preserves are a handful of small towns with supplies and services, paved roads and good public transportation, all within a few hour's drive of Anchorage International Airport.

Little wonder the Kenai Peninsula is Alaska's top recreational area. It is well serviced, well developed and, unfortunately, well used during the summer. There are times in the middle of the summer when people drive from one public campground to the next, looking for an open site anywhere. In the Kenai, kayakers will see tour boats full of whale watchers, hikers will see mountain bikers on many of the trails and backpackers will see, well, other backpackers.

Despite the crowds, this region of Alaska should not be skipped. The majestic blend of mountains and glaciers can be found along several trails covered here, and alpine lakes and meadows beckon you to strap on a backpack and spend a night among the peaks.

The campgrounds may be crowded and the highways an endless line of RVers, but trekkers can hike a little longer or climb a little higher to separate themselves from the three-month stampede to the peninsula known as the summer tourist season.

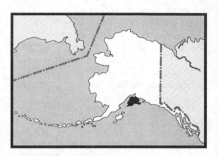

Chugach National Forest

Only a third as large as Tongass National Forest (its Alaskan counterpart in the South-east), Chugach is still the second-largest national forest in the USA and an impressive area of forests, rivers, lakes, mountains and glaciers. The 5,940,000-acre national forest spreads from its western boundary in the middle of the Kenai Peninsula to Cordova on the east side of Prince William Sound.

One-third of the national forest is rock (in the form of the Kenai Mountains and the Chugach Range) and glaciers (the most famous being Columbia and Portage). The rest of the land is a rich tapestry of forests, lakes and wildlife. Most trails begin in lush Sitka spruce forests or dense aspen. Almost impenetrable willow and alder take over at about 1000 feet, until you reach the alpine tundra.

Wildlife is plentiful for those who make the effort to hike away from the roads and highways. In the alpine region, mountain goats can be found throughout the national forest while you'll see dall sheep in the mountains of the Kenai Peninsula. Moose are abundant and both black bears and, to a lesser extent, brown bears may be encountered. River otters, marmots, porcupines,

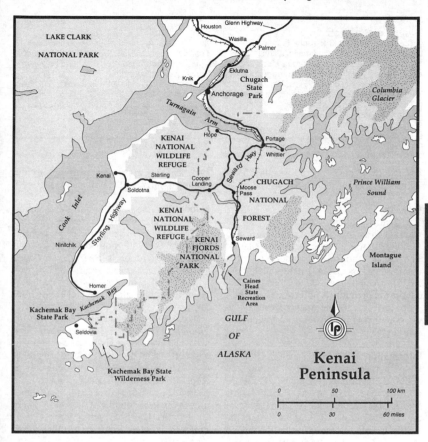

Kenai
Peninsula

KENAI PENINSULA

wolves and more than 200 species of birds also exist in the national forest.

The national forest offers a variety of fishing opportunities; anglers can cast for species like rainbow, lake and cutthroat trout as well as Dolly Varden, arctic grayling and salmon. However, because the area is easy to get to, roadside lakes and rivers are heavily fished and in most cases not productive if you have limited tackle and no boat. The best waters to concentrate on are the mountain lakes reached on foot which don't have USFS rental cabins. Chugach's most noted fishery, however, is the red-salmon run of the

Russian River. In July and August, anglers are often standing elbow-to-elbow along the river bank in hope of catching a 60-pound trophy.

The national forest has more than 200 miles of trails, most of which are on the Kenai Peninsula. Johnson Pass, Resurrection Pass, Russian Lakes and Resurrection River, and Primrose and Lost Lake trails are described here. These are the longest trails in the national forest and all of them are overnight treks. The Resurrection Pass, Russian Lakes and Resurrection River trails are often referred to as the Resurrection trail system

---

Inuits of Chugach

Chugach National Forest got its name from 'Chugatz' or 'Tchougatskoi' – names coined by the early Russians and what the local inhabitants were calling themselves. At the time, the Chugach Inuits – the southernmost tribes of the sea-oriented cultural group usually associated only with the Arctic – were found living throughout much of Prince William Sound.

Archaeological digs on Hawkins Island near Cordova, however, indicate that these Inuits had inhabited the area for thousands of years. Other indigenous Americans in Chugach National Forest included the Eyak Indians, who occupied the Copper River Delta, and the Athabascans, who lived along Turnagain Arm. ■

---

because they can be linked together for a 70-mile trek from Hope to Seward.

Climate

The Prince William Sound portion of the national forest has a maritime climate and weather patterns similar to Southeast Alaska. The Kenai Peninsula has cool and often overcast summers but not as much rain. Annual precipitation is 27 to 30 inches. The daytime high in July is 66°F while at night it drops to 40°F. Like the Anchorage area, you can count on 17 to 19 hours of daylight each summer day.

Information

In Anchorage, you can pick up information about the national forest and its campgrounds and trails at the Public Lands Information Center on 4th Ave and F St, from the USFS office on 201 East 9th St or at the USFS glacier district office in Girdwood (☎ 783-3242). The trails covered here, however, are under the jurisdiction of the Seward Ranger District, making the office in Seward the best source of information. The USFS district office (☎ 224-3374) is at the corner of 4th Ave and Jefferson St and open from 8 am to 5 pm Monday through Friday.

Places to Stay

Scattered along the highways and near the trailheads there's a variety of motels, lodges and in particular, campgrounds. There are 15 USFS campgrounds, many of them strategically located near the trails. But securing a site, especially those along the Kenai River which are overrun by salmon anglers during July, can be a problem throughout the summer – arrive at the trailhead early.

Hope Near the junction of Resurrection Creek Rd and Hope Hwy is *Henry's One Stop* (☎ 782-3222), where you can get a meal, beer, shower and room for $50 for two people. Next door is *Bear Creek Lodge* (☎ 782-3141), a scenic resort in the woods with a small restaurant. Its restored hand-hewn log cabins along the creek cost from $60 a night.

The USFS maintains *Porcupine Campground* (24 sites, $6), 1.3 miles beyond Hope at the end of the Hope Hwy. The campground has well spread out sites, a scenic overlook to watch the tide roll in and trailheads to Hope Point and Gull Rock. Beware, the place is often full on weekends (and sometimes even in the middle of the week). There is also the USFS *Coeur d'Alene Campground* (six sites, free) seven miles down Palmer Creek Rd.

Cooper Landing Stretched along several miles of the Sterling Hwy at *Mile 48.7* this service center is named after a miner who worked the area in the 1880s. Cooper Landing is the main commercial area near the southern trailhead of Resurrection Pass and the trailheads for the Russian Lakes Trail. Along with a five-building national historic district, which includes the colorful Old Cooper Landing Store, there is *Hamilton's Place* (☎ 595-1260). It has rooms for $35, cabins for $75, a restaurant, food store and, maybe most importantly, a laundromat and public showers. There is even a tent area with sites for $10 a night for those who want to skip the motel room. To the east at *Mile 45* is *Sunrise Inn* (☎ 595-1222) which has a restaurant, bar and RV sites. Motel rooms cost $79 a single/double.

To the west at *Mile 50.7* of the Sterling Hwy is the USFS *Cooper Creek Campground* (27 sites, $6) with campsites on both sides of the highway. The final national forest campground is *Russian River Campground* (84 sites, $8) at *Mile 52.8*. This is a beautiful spot where the Russian and Kenai rivers merge, and the most popular one by far. Both the Cooper Creek and Russian River campgrounds lie on prime red-salmon spawning areas and the campsites tend to fill up by noon in late summer. A mile along the campground road is the trailhead for the Russian Lakes Trail while practically across the highway is the southern trailhead for Resurrection Pass. Nearby at *Mile 52* is *Gwin's Lodge* (☎ 595-1266), an old roadhouse with a restaurant, bar and cabins for $85 for two people per night, $5 for each additional person.

Moose Pass This town of 145 residents is near the south end of the Johnson Pass Trail and is best known for its Moose Pass Summer Festival held on a weekend near summer solstice. The only motel in town is *Trail Lake Lodge* (☎ 288-3101 or 288-3103) which has a restaurant, laundromat, showers and a bar. Singles/doubles cost $65/75. The nearest campgrounds are *Trail River Campground* (64 sites, $6) and *Ptarmigan Creek* (16 sites, $6), five miles to the south on the Seward Hwy.

Snow River At *Mile 17.2* of the Seward Hwy there's a USFS campground and nearby, a unique hostel near the trailhead for the Primrose Trail. *Primrose Landing Campground* (10 sites, $6) is a scenic facility on the east end of the beautiful Kenai Lake.

Near the campground, 16 miles north of Seward, is *Snow River Hostel*. This home hostel has 14 beds, a kitchen, laundry facilities and a storage area but no phone. The rate is $10 a night.

Primrose Trail becomes Lost Lake Trail and ends at *Mile 5.3* of the Seward Hwy. For accommodations in Seward, see Places to Stay in the later Caines Head State Recreation Area section.

Maps

The national forest is covered on half a dozen USGS 1:63,360 quads (see the individual trails for details). Alternatively, purchase the Kenai Fjords National Park map by Trails Illustrated. This $7.95 map is printed on waterproof plastic coated paper and is revised regularly, showing all the trails and cabins. It only covers the southern half of the Chugach National Forest, however, and does not include Resurrection or Johnson Pass trails. At a scale of 1:105,600, it is not nearly as detailed as the USGS quads.

It's best to buy your maps in Anchorage. Some gift shops and stores along the highway sell maps but never the sections you want. In Seward, try the Kenai Fjords National Park Visitor Center (☎ 224-3175) in the Small Boat Harbor, or Seward Marine Adventures (☎ 224-3102) on the corner of 3rd Ave and D St.

Equipment

Purchase all your equipment in Anchorage, even your Lipton dinners and instant oatmeal. One-stop service stations/motels/stores along the highways will be able to supply food and white gas for the stove (at a very steep Alaskan price) but little else. In Seward you can purchase limited camping equipment at *Western Auto* on the corner of 5th Ave and Jefferson St.

Cabins

There are more than 40 cabins in Chugach National Forest. Seventeen of these cabins are in the Kenai Peninsula and many are on the trail system. Resurrection Pass Trail alone has nine rental cabins while there are three along Russian Lakes Trail, one on Resurrection River, two on the Crescent Creek/Carter Lake trails and one on the winter route of the Lost Lake Trail.

You can reach the cabins on foot so they

KENAI PENINSULA

are extremely popular. All cost $25 per night and should be reserved as much in advance as possible through the Public Lands Information Center (☎ (906) 271-2737), 605 West 4th Ave, Anchorage, AK 99501.

Trails

Crescent Creek Trail Half a mile beyond Crescent Creek Campground, this trail leads 6.5 miles to the outlet of Crescent Lake and a USFS cabin (reservations, $25 per night). The trail is an easy walk and the fall colors are beautiful in September. From the cabin there is access to the high country, and anglers can fish for arctic grayling in the lake during summer and fall (USGS quads *Seward B-7, C-7* and *C-8*).

Carter Lake Trail At the east end of Crescent Lake is Carter Lake Trail. Beginning at *Mile 33* of the Seward Hwy, this 3.5-mile trail provides quick but steep access into the subalpine area. It begins as an old jeep trail and from the parking area on the west side of the highway ascends almost 1000 feet to Carter Lake in 2.3 miles, where there are scenic camping spots.

From the lake, a trail continues another mile or so around the west side of the lake to Crescent Lake. Carter and Crescent Creek trails are connected by Crescent Lake Trail, a minimally maintained trail that follows the south shore for nine miles. The trail passes through alder thickets, grassy openings and small spruce forests and halfway along reaches the USFS Crescent Saddle Cabin, (reservations, $25 per night). You might encounter mountain bikes on the two trails but not usually on the route in between (USGS quads *Seward B-7* and *C-7*).

Ptarmigan Creek Trail Beginning in the USFS Ptarmigan Creek Campground (26 sites, $6) this 7.5-mile trail leads to Ptarmigan Lake, a beautiful body of water that reflects the mountains surrounding it. From the campground, the trail follows a creek and in 3.5 miles reaches the lake. A four-mile trail continues around the north side of the lake, which offers good fishing for Dolly Varden

at its outlet to the creek. Plan on five hours for a return hike to the lake as some parts of the trail are steep. The campground and trailhead are at Ptarmigan Creek Bridge, *Mile 23* of the Seward Hwy (USGS quads *Seward B-6* and *B-7*).

Victor Creek Trail Further south on the Seward Hwy at *Mile 19.7* is the trailhead for this fairly difficult path. In three miles (most of it in the first mile) Victor Creek gains 1100 feet to reach the alpine area and good views of the surrounding mountains, including Andy Simons Mountain and Sheep Mountain. Plan on at least two hours to reach the end of the trail from where often it's possible to see mountain goats on the slopes above (USGS quad *Seward B-7*).

Grayling Lake Trail This is an easy two-mile hike to Grayling Lake and the side trails to Meridian Lake and Leech Lake (a beautiful spot with good views of Snow River Valley). All three lakes can be fished for grayling and there are high-bush cranberries in the open meadows. The fisherman trail to Leech Lake is along the eastern shore of Grayling Lake, half a mile from where the main trail reaches the lake's north end. The trailhead is in a paved parking lot at *Mile 13.2* on the west side of the Seward Hwy. Use USGS quad *Seward B-7*.

Goldenfin Lake Trail This family hike is only 0.6 miles (one way) from the trailhead at *Mile 11.6* of Seward Hwy to the small lake. It's about a 30-minute hike and the trail can be wet and muddy at times. The lake can be fished for Dolly Varden while blueberry picking is excellent from mid to late August (USGS quad *Seward B-7*).

Gull Rock Trail There are two fine hikes for those spending an extra day or two in Hope. From Porcupine Campground this trail is an easy 5.1-mile one-way walk to Gull Rock, a rocky point 140 feet above the Turnagain shoreline. The trail follows an old wagon road built at the turn of the century, and along the way there are the remains of a cabin and

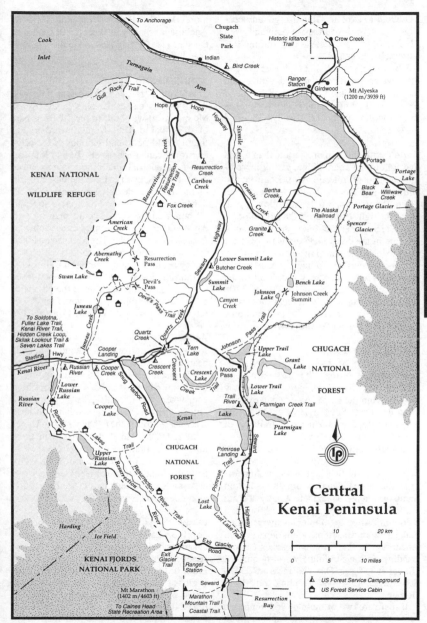

KENAI PENINSULA

Central
Kenai Peninsula

a sawmill to explore. You also get an occasional view of the Turnagain Arm and even Mt McKinley on a clear day during this extremely scenic trek.

It's possible to camp at Gull Rock if you pack water but it's better to day hike and return to Porcupine Campground to spend the night. The round trip to Gull Rock takes from four to six· hours. Use USGS quad *Seward D-8*.

Hope Point This is more a route than a trail that follows an alpine ridge, giving incredible views of Turnagain Arm. Begin at the entrance sign to Porcupine Campground, where the trail is posted, and follow a path along the right-hand side of the small Porcupine Creek. After 0.3 miles, the trail leaves the side of the creek and begins to ascend a bluff to the right, reaching an outcrop (offering good views of Turnagain Arm) in 45 minutes or so. From here, you can follow the ridge above the tree line to Hope Point (3708 feet). Other than an early summer snowfield, there is no water source after Porcupine Creek (USGS quad *Seward D-8*).

Getting There & Away
The Chugach National Forest trails are reached from either the 127-mile long Seward Hwy, the beginning of the Sterling Hwy or from the Hope Hwy, which extends 18 miles from Seward Hwy north to the hamlet of Hope and the northern trailhead of the Resurrection Pass Trail.

Seward/Homer Bus Lines (☎ 278-0800) provides transportation· along both the Seward and Sterling highways. In Anchorage, the buses depart from the Alaskan Samovar Inn at 70 Gambell St daily at 5 am and 2.30 pm, reaching Seward at 7.30 am and 5.30 pm. After a 90-minute layover they make a return run. Another bus departs from Anchorage at 9.45 am and reaches Cooper Landing on the Sterling Hwy at noon, and Homer at 3.40 pm. One-way fares are $30 to Seward, $25 to Cooper Landing and $38 to Homer.

If there are two or more of you, renting a car for a week is almost as cheap and much more flexible. Pick up the rental car in Anchorage where you'll get the best rates in the state (see Getting Around in the Anchorage chapter).

JOHNSON PASS TRAIL
This 23-mile trail is an overnight trek over its 1550-foot namesake pass in the Kenai Mountains. It was built in the 1890s as part of the Iditarod Trail from Seward to the Interior gold fields and sections of the original route can still be seen. Today, Johnson Pass is as much a trail for mountain bikers as it is for hikers; cyclists have increased traffic on the trail considerably in recent years.

Most bikers can cover the trail in seven to 10 hours but trekkers should plan on two days with an alpine camp at either Johnson Pass or Johnson Lake. The trail can be hiked in either direction but you endure less climbing by beginning at the northern trailhead.

Johnson Pass is rated moderate and for the most part is a gradual climb to the pass with a few steep sections. It is covered on USGS 1:63,360 series quads *Seward C-6* and *C-7*.

Access
Johnson Pass conveniently begins and ends near the Seward Hwy. Just past *Mile 64* heading south is the USFS sign pointing to the Granite Creek trailhead at the northern end, where a dirt road leads almost half a mile to a parking area. The southern trailhead is at *Mile 32.5* near the fish hatchery at Upper Trail Lake. Moose Pass is less than three miles to the south.

Transportation to the trailhead is by Seward/Homer Bus Lines (see Getting There & Away, above) a rental car or hitching (good along Seward Hwy).

Stage 1: Granite Creek Trailhead to Johnson Lake
(11 miles, 6-8 hours)
(Backcountry campsites)
From the northern end, Johnson Pass Trail begins as a somewhat level hike through the forest and a few open meadows. Within 2.2 miles, or an hour or so of hiking, you cross Center Creek on a bridge and then begin

climbing. The trail rises steadily, reaches Bench Creek and crosses a bridge over it at 3.8 miles and then makes a steep ascent up a rocky hill to pass a waterfall four miles from the Granite Creek trailhead.

You now enter a steep V-shaped valley where the trail follows Bench Creek on its west side and gains 200 feet before crossing Groundhog Creek at 5.2 miles. Eventually the trail recrosses Bench Creek to its east side and continues to steadily climb, reaching Gleason Creek at 8.2 miles and Ohio Creek less than a mile beyond that. At Ohio Creek you'll pass a stone monument dedicated to Paul Anderson, a forester who died in an accidental explosion while trying to divert a glacial stream from Bench Lake in an effort to improve its fishery.

In the next half-mile you gain 100 feet as you climb to the 1500-foot high point of the trail and then emerge at the north end of Bench Lake. The lake is above the tree line and in a mountainous alpine setting where it's easy to scramble the open slopes in almost any direction. You can fish here for grayling but the better campsites are found in the pass itself or at Johnson Lake.

The trail continues along the east shore of the lake and remains above the timber line to enter Johnson Pass and from there descends gently to Johnson Lake at 1300 feet. At the south end of the lake, 11 miles from the Granite Creek trailhead, there is a back-country campsite where the trail returns to the tree line. The lake supports rainbow trout and makes a good base camp from where you can spend a day climbing the surrounding ridges and peaks.

Stage 2: Johnson Lake to Upper Trail Lake Trailhead
(12 miles, 5-7 hours)
From Johnson Lake, the trail heads south in a forest setting and steadily loses elevation. You remain close to Johnson Creek along its east side but rarely see the water through the foliage.

After descending more than 400 feet, you arrive and cross the creek at mile 15.7 and then leave it for good. Within an hour of

steady hiking you cross King Creek and at 19.4 miles from the northern trailhead (almost nine miles from Johnson Lake), you break out of the woods at the shores of Upper Trail Lake near its northern end.

The remaining 3.5 miles is an easy and pleasant walk along a wide path that skirts the western shoreline of the large lake. Depending on your mood (energetic hiker or gatherer of sunrays) it's 1½ to two hours along the shoreline to the Upper Trail Lake trailhead near the southern end on Seward Hwy.

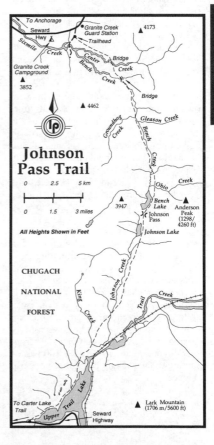

KENAI PENINSULA

RESURRECTION PASS TRAIL

What was cut in the 1890s by gold miners trying to find a way from Resurrection Bay to their riches in the Hope gold fields, is today the most popular multi-day trail in the Kenai Peninsula. The Resurrection Pass Trail is a 38.6-mile trek from the northern trailhead near Hope, across the 3400-foot pass and then a descent along Juneau Creek Valley to the Sterling Hwy near Cooper Landing. The southern trailhead is practically across the highway from the start of the Russian Lakes Trail which intersects the Resurrection River Trail which ends at Exit Glacier near Seward (see Russians Lakes Trail, below). Together, the three trails provide the hardy trekker with a seven to 10-day journey on foot from Hope to Seward.

Designated a National Recreation Trail, the Resurrection Pass Trail is a well maintained and well posted path that is also well used. Along with backpackers, you might encounter day hikers, cabin renters who were flown in, mountain bikers and, after 30 June, possibly horse riders. The popularity of the trail is also evident in how difficult it is to reserve one of the nine cabins along the trail. The cabins can be booked 179 days in advance (see Cabins, earlier) and special drawings are held for the five lakeside units along the southern half of the trail (for the moose hunting season in late August to early September).

Although there are some switchback sections, overall the trail gradually climbs and descends the alpine areas surrounding Resurrection Pass and is rated easy. Strong hikers can cover the distance in three days, the average walker in four days (the trail is described here as a four-day walk). Even families have few problems going from end to end in five days if the children are properly prepared and equipped. You can start from either direction though you save 100 feet of climbing to the pass by beginning your trip at Hope.

Staying in the cabins is a pleasant treat during the trek and well worth the effort of reserving them in advance. But there is no lack of camping spots along trail and the USFS even maintains a series of 13 backcountry campsites that each feature a tent pad and fire ring. Each site lies off the trail and away from the cabins for a bit of privacy but is marked along the route by a four-by-four post. Despite the fire ring, you should still pack a stove, especially if you plan to spend a night above the alpine area. Also bring a rod and reel, most of the lakes have several species of fish.

For those wishing to skip the trip to Hope, you can access the Resurrection Pass Trail via Devil's Pass Trail. This 10-mile spur begins along Seward Hwy, solving some of your transportation problems, and climbs over a 2400-foot gap to reach Resurrection Pass Trail just south of its pass. Devil's Pass is rated moderately difficult.

Most of the trail is covered on USGS 1:63,360 series quads *Seward C-8* and *D-8*, with the exception of the first two miles from the southern trailhead which is on *Seward B-8*. If you plan to enter or depart along Devil's Pass Trail, you'll also need *Seward C-7*. The trail and even most of the cabins are marked on the topos.

Access

To reach the northern trailhead, leave the Seward Hwy at *Mile 56.7* and head north on the Hope Hwy. At *Mile 16* of the Hope Hwy turn left on Resurrection Creek Rd. Four miles down Resurrection Creek Rd, at Resurrection Creek, is the trailhead and parking area. The southern trailhead is at *Mile 52* of the Sterling Hwy. The trailhead for Devil's Pass Trail is at *Mile 39.4* of the Seward Hwy.

Seward/Homer Bus Lines (see Getting There & Away, earlier) provides a drop-off and pick-up service at the southern trailhead and Devil's Pass. There's no public transportation to Hope other than car rental. Hitching to the town, however, is usually not a problem.

Stage 1: Northern Trailhead to Caribou Creek

(7.1 miles, 4-5 hours)
(USFS cabin, backcountry campsites)
From the parking area and trail sign, a bridge

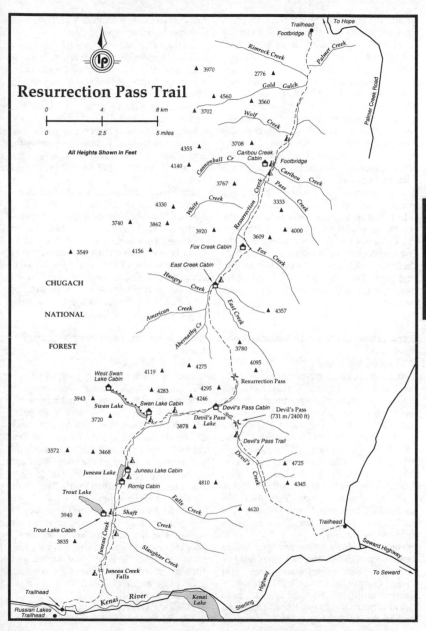

KENAI PENINSULA

crosses Resurrection Creek. The trail skirts the west side of the stream along a mining claim road. The first leg is an easy stroll through lush spruce forest and tracts of aspen until the mining road ends in two miles when it comes to where Rimrock Creek and Gold Gulch flow into Resurrection Creek. At this point the trail becomes a true foot path.

The trail remains on the west side of Resurrection Creek and begins to climb gently through the forest. At 5.5 miles from the trailhead, you cross Wolf Creek and reach the first backcountry campsite. Within half a mile the trail tops 1000 feet, levels out and finally crosses Resurrection Creek on a bridge, seven miles from the trailhead.

In less than a quarter of a mile from the bridge, you reach Caribou Creek and the first of two campsites. Across the bridge is the first USFS cabin on the trail. At 1000 feet, Caribou Creek Cabin is a 12 by 14-foot cabin with bunks for six people and a wood stove. Just beyond it is the second Caribou Creek campsite.

Stage 2: Caribou Creek to Resurrection Pass

(12.1 miles, 6-8 hours)
(USFS cabins, backcountry campsites)
You remain on the east side of the creek and resume gradually climbing up the valley again. Pass Creek is crossed at eight miles and within three miles the climb gets steeper as the trail reaches 1500 feet. At this point, 1.5 miles from the next USFS cabin, you swing away from the stream and head up Fox Creek. Eventually the trail crosses Fox Creek; on the south side is Fox Creek Cabin at 12.5 miles. Like Caribou Creek, the cabin has bunks for six people and a wood stove but it sits 700 feet higher. There is also a campsite posted nearby.

The gentle climb up Resurrection Valley continues and in less than two miles reaches the third USFS cabin, East Creek, and another campsite at 14.4 miles. The cabin is identical to the first two and is in a scenic spot near the confluence of Resurrection and East creeks. At 2200 feet, the surrounding

trees are sparse and stunted. You'll often see dall sheep on the ridges above.

At the cabin, the trail crosses East Creek and in 1.5 miles climbs 300 feet to arrive at the headwaters of Resurrection Creek, where American Creek, Abernathy Creek and an unnamed creek merge. You cross the unnamed stream and quickly leave the tree line to make the final climb to the pass. On a good day, the next three miles to the pass is a spectacular stretch. In the beginning the trail climbs between two streams, and the surrounding tundra will be alive with wild flowers.

Hiking between a pair of 4000-foot peaks, the pass is reached 2½ hours from the East Creek Cabin, 19.3 miles from the northern trailhead. Good camping spots abound in the 2600-foot pass and an extra day could be spent here climbing the surrounding ridges or hiking across a saddle to the south-east to reach the East Creek drainage area.

If you prefer staying at a campsite, the next one is four miles away, or two miles south of Devil's Pass Cabin.

Stage 3: Resurrection Pass to Swan Lake

(6.5 miles, 3-4 hours)
(USFS cabins, backcountry campsites)
This is a short day of hiking. Either enjoy the morning in the alpine area or make a side trip up Devil's Pass Trail without your pack. From Resurrection Pass, you quickly reach the headwaters of Juneau Creek and then skirt the ridge on its west side. Eventually the trail begins to swing to the south-west and within two miles you cross Juneau Creek to reach the junction with Devil's Pass Trail. Nearby is a USFS cabin.

Above the tree line at 2400 feet, Devil's Pass Cabin is in a spectacular mountain setting. The A-frame unit has bunks for six people but can sleep a few more in the loft. Unlike the other cabins it is not stocked with firewood so there is no wood stove. This is a good place to search for dall sheep on the surrounding ridges.

Devil's Pass Trail heads east from the cabin and leads 10 miles to *Mile 39* of the

Seward Hwy. It can be used to access or depart Resurrection Pass Trail or to explore the surrounding alpine valleys. The trail is well maintained but can be muddy and wet at times due to the creeks and run-off that cross it.

The trail is rated moderate in difficulty and the first eight miles from the Seward Hwy trailhead is a steady climb to 2400-foot Devil's Pass. You reach a backcountry campsite at Beaver Pond within two miles and then you'll come across the tree line a mile beyond that.

Even if you're just sticking to Resurrection Pass Trail, the first two miles of Devil's Pass Trail from its west end is an easy and interesting side trip. From the cabin, it's roughly a mile to Devil's Pass Lake, where you can fish for Dolly Varden. Continuing east from the lake it's a gradual climb to the pass.

From the junction, Resurrection Pass Trail continues its gradual descent for the next two miles, crossing Juneau Creek several times. After crossing Juneau Creek for the third time, the trail ascends more than 200 feet to skirt a 2600-foot knob and then begins its steep descent into the timber line and to Swan Creek. Just before the descent, you pass two backcountry campsites, and being above the tree line they are perhaps the two most scenic sites.

For two miles you endure switchbacks and steep sections as you drop from almost 2500 feet to 1400 feet to where the trail bottoms out at the junction to Swan Creek. A half-mile spur heads to Swan Lake Cabin, reached 4.4 miles beyond Devil's Pass. Along the way you pass a backcountry campsite.

Swan Lake is a six-bunk cabin overlooking the east end of its namesake lake. A boat is provided and the lake is considered fair for rainbow trout, Dolly Varden and, if you can troll deep enough, lake trout.

At the other end of the lake is West Swan Lake Cabin, which also has six bunks, a wood stove and its own boat. It's possible to follow a primitive route from one cabin to the other.

Brown bear

Stage 4: Swan Lake to Sterling Hwy
(12.8 miles, 6-7 hours)
(USFS cabins, backcountry campsites)

From the junction to Swan Lake, the trail briefly skirts Juneau Creek and stays above it as it makes a very gradual descent down the valley. Within two miles, the descent becomes rapid until you bottom out to cross Juneau Creek and pass another backcountry campsite. With a quarter of a mile from there you reach the northern end of Juneau Lake.

The trail skirts the eastern shore of the lake and 3.3 miles from Swan Lake junction, you arrive at the first of two USFS cabins. Juneau Lake Cabin is the standard 12 by 14-foot unit with six bunks, a wood stove and a boat. A mile down the shore is Romig Cabin, identical to Juneau Lake Cabin. Overlooking the water and surrounding mountains, both cabins are popular and difficult to reserve. The lake has rainbow trout, grayling and lake trout. Between the two cabins is a posted backcountry campsite.

From Juneau Lake the trail stays on the east side of Juneau Creek and continues down the valley in a spruce and aspen forest, passing a backcountry campsite at Falls Creek. In less than two miles from Romig Cabin you come to the junction of a spur to Trout Lake. The half-mile side trail first crosses Juneau Creek, passes a backcountry campsite and then ends at the last USFS cabin. Trout Lake Cabin is an A-frame structure with a loft and wood stove. It overlooks a small cove at the eastern end of the lake and has a boat. The fishing is fair for rainbow trout.

In the next stretch, the trail is level and an easy two-mile trek through the woods. It remains on the east side of Juneau Creek and passes a backcountry campsite half a mile past the junction to Trout Lake. When you close in on Juneau Creek Falls, the trail descends to cross a bridge over the creek. You reach the cascade from the west bank.

The falls, a five to six-hour walk of 8.3 miles from Swan Creek, is a roaring drop of water at the head of a steep gorge. It's a scenic spot for a long break. There's a backcountry campsite nearby so you could camp here and extend the 38-mile hike to five days.

You are now only 4.5 miles or 1½ hours from the southern trailhead and the Sterling Hwy. The trail continues south and skirts the gorge for 1.5 miles and then swings west. It stays on the edge of the bluff above the Kenai River before descending sharply in the final mile via a series of switchbacks. Just before reaching the trailhead, you are rewarded with views of this large river.

RUSSIAN LAKES TRAIL

Practically across the Sterling Hwy from the southern end of Resurrection Pass Trail is the access road to the USFS Russian River Campground and the trailhead to Russian Lakes Trail. This is the second stage of the seven to 10-day journey from Hope to Seward. You leave the trail 16 miles from the western trailhead for the final leg of the journey – the 16-mile trek to Exit Glacier (outside Seward) along the Resurrection River Trail.

For many trekkers, however, the Russian Lakes Trail is an easy and pleasant overnight trek, either following it from Russian River to Cooper Lake or using it to reach a USFS cabin or campsite then backtracking to their vehicles.

The 21.6-mile trail is a well-maintained foot path that receives moderate to heavy use during the summer. You gain 1000 feet but the climb is very gradual and overall this trail is rated easy – an ideal one for families.

Much of the time you're hiking in forest but views of the surrounding mountains, streams and the two Russian Lakes are common along the route.

There are three USFS cabins (see Cabins, earlier) and some backcountry campsites at Lower and Upper Russian lakes. Keep in mind that Russian River provides the largest sport fishery in Alaska for sockeye salmon during two runs, and come mid-June and again in mid-July the river is lined with anglers, many of whom you'll see on the first leg of the trail. Mountain bikers are also common. Along with the salmon, other wildlife that you might see include moose and bears. With a keen eye, or a set of binoculars, you'll also possibly see mountain goats and dall sheep on the ridges above.

The hiking is actually easier if you begin from the Cooper Lake trailhead at the east end of the trail, and you won't have to pay $2 a day to park. The trail, however, will be described in the other direction – by far the most popular route.

With the exception of a half-mile section that spills over onto *Kenai B-1*, the entire trail is covered on the USGS 1:63,360 series quad *Seward B-8*. The area featuring Resurrection River Trail is on quads *Seward B-8*, *A-7* and *A-8* but the trail itself is not on the topos. The entire trail system (but not Resurrection Pass Trail) is covered on Trails Illustrated map 231 of the Kenai Fjords National Park.

Access

The western trailhead is in the Russian River Campground at *Mile 52.8* of the Sterling Hwy, where the Russian and Kenai rivers merge. A mile down Russian River Campground Rd is the trailhead and parking area for the Russian Lakes Trail, while a quarter of a mile west of the campground on Sterling Hwy is the well-marked entrance to the Resurrection Pass Trail.

The eastern trailhead is considerably harder to reach. After crossing the Kenai River bridge, immediately turn south on Snug Harbor Rd at *Mile 48* of the Sterling Hwy. Follow this road for nine miles and

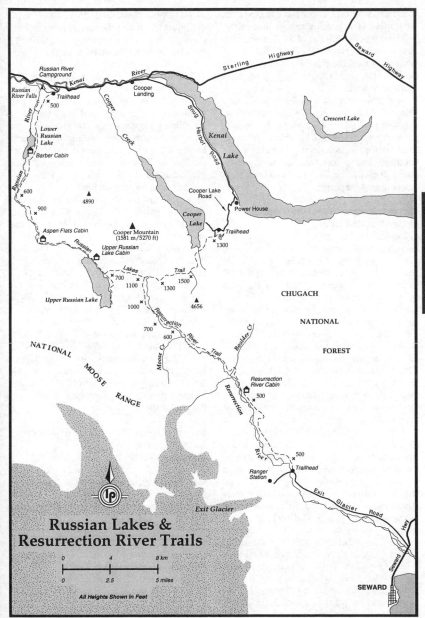

KENAI PENINSULA

Russian River Campground

Russian River Falls

Trailhead
500

Kenai River

River

Cooper Landing

Sterling Highway

Seward Highway

Crescent Lake

Lower Russian Lake

Barber Cabin

Cooper Creek

Snug Harbor Road

Kenai Lake

Russian River

600

900

4890

Aspen Flats Cabin

Cooper Mountain (1581 m/5270 ft)

Upper Russian Lake Cabin

Cooper Lake Road

Cooper Lake

Power House

Trailhead
1300

Russian Lakes Trail

700

1100

1300

1500

Upper Russian Lake

1000

4656

CHUGACH

NATIONAL

FOREST

Resurrection River

700

600

Moose Cr.

Trail

Boulder Cr.

NATIONAL

MOOSE

RANGE

Resurrection

Resurrection River Cabin
500

Resurrection

River

500

Trailhead

Ranger Station

Exit Glacier Road

Exit Glacier

Russian Lakes & Resurrection River Trails

Seward Hwy

SEWARD

0   4   8 km

0   2.5   5 miles

All Heights Shown in Feet

then head west on Cooper Lake Rd to reach the trailhead and parking area in three miles.

The southern trailhead of the Resurrection River Trail is posted on Exit Glacier Rd where it crosses the river, 7.4 miles from the Seward Hwy. Exit Glacier Rd is four miles north of Seward.

Seward/Homer Bus Lines (see Getting There & Away, earlier) provides transportation to Russian River Campground and to the start of Snug Harbor Rd, where you have little choice but to hitch the 12 miles to the trailhead. For access to/from Resurrection River Trail see the later Caines Head State Recreation Area section.

Stage 1: Russian River Trailhead to Upper Russian Lake
(12 miles, 7-8 hours)
(USFS cabins, backcountry campsites)
Pay a parking fee at the ranger's station in the Russian River Campground, and continue on the campground road for almost a mile to the well-marked trailhead. The first two miles of the trail follows the well-forested Russian River but not always directly along the water. It does pass several scenic viewing points of the river, and angler's paths to popular fishing holes are numerous. The main trail, however, is well marked and easy to identify. During the salmon runs from mid-June to mid-July this stretch can be a traffic jam of anglers trying to cash in on the spawning sockeyes

At 1.7 miles from the trailhead you come to a bridge over Rendezvous Creek and a junction. Here, Falls Trail swings down to the river and then heads a quarter of a mile upstream to Russian River Falls. The Russian Lakes Trail crosses the bridge over Rendezvous Creek and continues south where it comes to a second junction at 2.6 miles.

The right-hand fork skirts the shores of Lower Russian Lake at one point and four miles from the trailhead reaches Barber Cabin (also referred to as Lower Russian Lake Cabin). Situated on the shores of Lower Russian Lake (fair to good for rainbow trout), the five-bunk cabin has a wood stove,

wood supply, boat and dock. The cabin, including the vault toilet outside, has wheelchair facilities and there are plans to modify the first leg of the Russian Lakes Trail in this way.

The main trail continues along the left-hand fork and heads almost due south, passing the southern end of the lake and paralleling Upper Russian River. In the next six miles, you gently gain 200 feet and move more into a sub-alpine setting of birch and hemlock forest. Eventually 8.7 miles from the Russian River trailhead you reach Aspen Flats, the site of the second USFS cabin. Slightly smaller, Aspen Flats is a 12 by 14-foot cabin that has six bunks inside. Anglers fish this portion of the Upper Russian River for rainbow trout, Dolly Varden and even salmon.

At Aspen Flats the trail swings to the east with the valley and continues its mild climb around Cooper Mountain (5270 feet). It closely follows the Upper Russian River for a couple of miles until you break out at Upper Russian Lake and wind along its shoreline briefly until reaching the third USFS cabin, 12 miles from the trailhead. Upper Russian Lake Cabin is a rustic log cabin overlooking the water with four bunks and a boat. Upper Russian Lake has excellent fishing; rainbow trout often range in size from 12 to 18 inches. There is also a backcountry campsite just off the trail at the lake.

Stage 2: Upper Russian Lake to Cooper Lake Trailhead
(9.6 miles, 5-6 hours)
From the USFS cabin the trail continues to skirt the shoreline of Upper Russian Lake for more than a mile until it reaches a three-way junction. One trail continues south along the lake shore but the main trail heads east over a rolling forested terrain. Within two miles of leaving the lake, or four miles from the USFS cabin, you come to a posted junction of the Resurrection River Trail.

At the junction, Russian Lakes Trail continues east, winding through the wooded valley at the base of Cooper Mountain as it gradually climbs to the 1300-foot Cooper

Lake trailhead. Within two miles you cross an unnamed stream and half a mile beyond it the trail swings north-east. In another three miles you cross a second stream at the southern end of the lake.

The final 1.5 miles is a well-beaten path to the trailhead, reached 5.6 miles from the junction with the Resurrection River Trail, or 10.6 miles from the Upper Russian Lake Cabin. This trailhead is far more isolated than the other the two trailheads, something to consider when planning your route.

To return to the public bus that runs along Sterling Hwy, head three miles east on Cooper Lake Rd and then nine miles north on Snug Harbor Rd. It can be challenging to thumb a ride on these roads, so you may end up hiking most of this stretch.

RESURRECTION RIVER TRAIL

The 16-mile Resurrection River Trail is for the most part a level path with only a gradual descent in the first few miles from its junction with Russian Lakes Trail. The southern half, however, can be quite boggy and the hiking is sloppy when it's raining, despite the numerous drainage ditches.

It's easier hiking the trail from north to south. You begin by gently descending to the river to cross it near its headwaters and then follow the river valley the rest of the way, climbing only when the trail skirts the bordering ridges. Along the way, the trail passes several viewing points of the surrounding mountains before reaching the river near the confluence of Moose Creek.

You reach the bridge over Boulder Creek 8.5 miles south of the junction with Russian Lakes Trail and in less than a mile, pass Resurrection River Cabin. The 12 by 14-foot USFS cabin is one of the newer ones in the Kenai Peninsula and features six bunks inside and a wood stove. It's an excellent place to spend the night if you can reserve it; good camping spots are limited along the entire length of the trail.

From Boulder Creek, the trail continues to parallel the Resurrection River though dense forest limits your views. The path is level but extremely boggy in most places, making the

hike a slow and laborious process. Within two miles you reach the bridge over Martin Creek and 6.5 miles from the USFS cabin, you emerge at the trailhead right where Exit Glacier Rd crosses Resurrection River.

The ranger station is another mile west along the road and nearby is a free, walk-in campground managed by the NPS. Head east on the road and you'll reach the Seward Hwy in eight miles. During the summer it is fairly easy to hitch a ride into Seward because of the heavy volume of day visitors at Exit Glacier.

PRIMROSE & LOST LAKE TRAILS

Two trails, Primrose and Lost Lake, depart from the Seward Hwy and join at Lost Lake to form one of the best overnight treks in Chugach National Forest. A good slice of this 15-mile trek is spent above the tree line, where you can admire the stunning mountain scenery of the surrounding peaks. Camping is excellent at Lost Lake and a spare day can be spent scrambling the ridges towards Mt Ascension, a 5710-foot peak that forms the lake's west border.

You can hike the route in either direction but the trip is described here beginning with the Primrose Trail, which saves you about 300 feet of climbing. Snow lingers in the alpine areas into June, sometimes as late as early July if the winter has been especially brutal.

The USFS rates the use of these trails as light. Horses are prohibited from April through June and the Primrose leg is not recommended for mountain bikes. The trails are closed to motorized activity, except to miners with permits; there are still some active mines along the Primrose Trail.

There is public transportation to both trailheads and excellent lodging nearby. At the northern end, there is Primrose Landing Campground and Snow River Hostel (see Places to Stay, earlier); at the southern end, Seward is only five miles away (see Caines Head State Recreation Area, later). There is also a USFS cabin on a winter route off Lost Lake Trail.

This route is rated moderate and is

KENAI PENINSULA

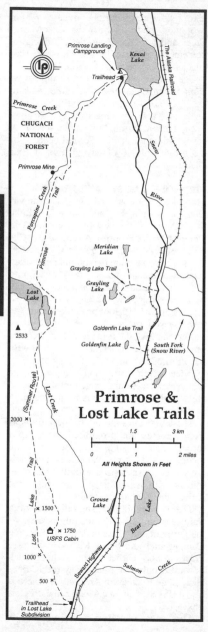

KENAI PENINSULA

Primrose Landing
Campground

Kenai
Lake

Trailhead

The Alaska Railroad

Primrose   Creek

CHUGACH
NATIONAL
FOREST

Primrose Mine

Snow

River

Meridian
Lake

Grayling Lake Trail

Grayling
Lake

Lost
Lake

▲
2533

Goldenfin Lake Trail

Goldenfin Lake

South Fork
(Snow River)

**Primrose &
Lost Lake Trails**

0   1.5   3 km

0   1   2 miles

All Heights Shown in Feet

Lost Creek

(Summer Route)

2000 ×

Lost   Lake   Trail

× 1500

🏠 × 1750
USFS Cabin

1000 ×

500 ×

Grouse
Lake

Bear   Lake

Seward Highway

Salmon   Creek

Trailhead
in Lost Lake
Subdivision

covered by the USGS 1:63,360 series quads
Seward B-7 and *A-7* and the Trails Illustrated
map of Kenai Fjords National Park.

Access
To reach the northern trailhead, turn off the
Seward Hwy at *Mile 17* and follow the signs
for 1.5 miles to Primrose Landing Campground. The well-posted trailhead is at the
end of the campground access road, away
from Kenai Lake.

To reach the southern trailhead, turn west
into Lost Lake Subdivision at *Mile 5.3* of
Seward Hwy and drive a quarter of a mile
uphill to a T-intersection. Turn left for a
quarter of a mile and then right – the trailhead
is 100 yards from the end of the road. The
trailhead and parking area are on private
property but the USFS is negotiating a land
swap to preserve access to the trail. Everything is well posted at both ends but you can
call the Seward Ranger District (☎ 224-
3374) for the latest information.

Seward/Homer Bus Lines passes both
trailheads twice daily during the summer on
its Anchorage-to-Seward runs (see Getting
There & Away, earlier).

**Stage 1: Primrose Landing
Campground to Lost Lake**
(8 miles, 4-5 hours)
(Backcountry camping)
The Primrose Trail follows an old mining
road for the first half, making it, for the most
part, a wide, easy-to-follow route to the tree
line. From the campground it heads south-
west, climbing gradually through a thick
spruce forest, which limits any views of the
mountains that loom overhead. You also stay
away from Porcupine Creek in the first
couple of miles but eventually the trail
swings near it and less than three miles from
the trailhead, a spur heads right for a short
distance to Porcupine Creek Falls, an ideal
destination for a day hike.

In the next mile, the trail passes the
remains of past mineral exploration and at
3.7 miles from the campground you reach the
historic Primrose Mine, still active. At this
point, the trail heads almost due south and

Worthington Glacier Trail (JD)

Top: Mining ruins at Kennicott, Wrangell-St Elias National Park (JD)
Bottom Left: Pinnell Mountain Trail (DP)
Bottom Right: Ebner Falls, Perseverance Trail (JD)

climbs steadily on a ridge above the creek until it reaches the tree line at about 2000 feet, or less than a mile from the mine site.

To break out of the trees along the Primrose Trail is an unexpected joy. Due west is a 4732-foot peak, to the south-west is 5710-foot Mt Ascension with its distinctively sheer-sided north face. The trail continues heading south and in less than two miles you reach Lost Lake. This stretch above the tree line is a beautiful alpine trek unless foul weather or fog create white-out conditions in which case you'll have to follow a series of four-by-four-inch posts across the open tundra to the lake.

Once at the lake, Primrose Trail skirts the east shoreline for more than a mile until it crosses a bridge over Lost Creek. At this point it swings west and ends at Lost Lake Trail at the south end of the lake.

Spots to pitch a tent abound in the tundra. The opportunity to sit in the door of your tent, gazing at this pretty little lake and the peaks towering above it, is priceless, and it's well worth spending an extra day here. Anglers can fish Lost Lake for rainbow trout while others can explore the alpine area in almost any direction.

Mt Ascension is a technical climb, requiring mountaineering skills, crampons and an ice axe. However, the ridges reached from the south-west corner of the lake are fun to scramble up and provide wonderful views. You can also hike north along the lake and continue up the valley. It leads west to an impressive view of the mountain's steep north face, and from here it's possible to see mountain goats or even a black bear (if it's early in the summer).

Stage 2: Lost Lake to Seward Hwy
(7 miles, 3-4 hours)

To continue south, head to the southern end of the lake, cross Lost Creek and end at the junction with Lost Lake Trail. This seven-mile trail back to Seward Hwy is actually a pair of trails – a summer-only one for hikers and a winter trail used primarily by snowmobilers. On the Primrose portion you will have gained 1500 feet climbing to Lost Lake;

on this leg you'll descend more than 1800 feet, quite easily.

From the lake, the trail heads almost due south but within a mile climbs a low ridge and skirts the top of it. All of this is above the tree line and, needless to say, the views are excellent on a clear day. Sometimes you can even see Resurrection Bay off in the distance.

Within two miles from the lake, the trail begins its steady decent and from here until you reach the tree line there are extensive thickets of salmon berries, the semi-sour berry that looks like an overgrown raspberry and ripens in August.

Three miles into the hike you descend into the spruce forest and in another mile or so, you arrive at a posted junction to the USFS Clemens Memorial Cabin. This trail veers off to the left and returns to the alpine area where white posts lead you to the new cabin in 1.5 miles. This USFS unit (reservations, $25) was finished only in 1993 and is designed primarily for winter use. The 14 by 18-foot cabin has bunks for four people, and a table, cooking counter and even a propane heater for snowmobilers who arrive in the winter. Located at the tree line at 1750 feet, the cabin provides spectacular views of Resurrection Peaks, Mt Ascension and also Resurrection Bay.

Within a mile of the junction, the summer trail begins a more rapid descent as it skirts above a stream on the east side of a forested ravine. Eventually the trail swings out of the ravine and 5.5 miles from Lost Lake arrives at the south end of the winter trail, though it's hard to pick up during the summer. Hikers are urged not to follow this route to the cabin as it is steep and wet in areas. The final leg of the trail is an old road that follows a steady descent to the trailhead in Lost Lake Subdivision.

KENAI PENINSULA

Caines Head State Recreation Area

Seward is surrounded by wilderness and rugged land. This town of 3000 people is flanked one side by Resurrection Bay, on the other by Marathon Mountain while towering overhead is the Harding Ice Field. Just to the north is Chugach National Forest, on its doorstep to the south is Caines Head State Recreation Area and all around is Kenai Fjords National Park. Stay awhile and play.

Within 25 miles north of Seward there are seven national forest trails: Resurrection River, Lost Lake, Primrose Creek, Goldenfin Lake, Grayling Lake, Victor Creek and Ptarmigan Creek (see the earlier Chugach National Forest section). There is also a limited trail system in Kenai Fjords National Park. The 587,000-acre park consists mainly of the Harding Ice Field (the rugged coastline of fjords where tidewater glaciers calve into the sea) and the offshore islands. But you don't need a kayak or tour-boat ticket to reach its trails at Exit Glacier.

This drive-to glacier attracts more than 100,000 visitors each summer. Most are 10-minute tourists who rush up to the ice, snap a picture then leave. Trekkers who have time, however, can view and even experience the Harding Ice Field. One of the largest ice fields in North America, it remained undiscovered until the early 1900s when a map-making team realized several coastal glaciers belonged to the same massive system. The ice field is 50-miles long and 30-miles wide and in some places 200-inches deep. Eight glaciers reach the sea from it, while Exit Glacier is a remnant of a larger one that once extended into Resurrection Bay. You can reach the edge of the ice field via the Harding Ice Field Trail. Experienced mountaineers, equipped with skis, ice axes and crampons, often venture onto the icy plateau.

This section, however, focuses on Caines Head State Recreation Area. This 6000-acre preserve lies along the shore of Resurrection Bay, 5.5 miles south of Seward. It's the scenic site of an abandoned WW II fort and includes military ruins and 650-foot headlands that rise above the water for sweeping views of the bay and the mountains around it.

It also features almost 10 miles of trails, old military roads and beach and alpine routes that can be combined for a two or three-day trek out of Seward. Because it is a favorite with local boaters and kayakers, facilities on the trails around the North Beach include shelters, toilets, campsites and a ranger station that is staffed throughout most of the summer. A spare day can be spent exploring the crumbling gun turrets and

---

Ghost Forests

The Good Friday Earthquake, the most powerful ever recorded in North America, that shook Alaska on 27 March 1964, not only killed more than 100 people and destroyed entire towns, it devastated much of Chugach National Forest and the surrounding areas.

The epicenter of the quake, which registered 9.2 on the Richter scale, was in the national forest near Miner's Lake, west of Columbia Glacier. Land to the east rose six feet and on Montague Island 35 feet, resulting in the death of millions of clams and other intertidal life. It also caused the destruction of a waterfowl habitat on the Copper River Delta and ruined salmon access to spawning streams.

To the west, land sunk as low as eight feet and literally drowned shoreline forests. The trees quickly died in the saltwater but their trunks remained standing and eventually were bleached by the sun to form 'ghost forests'. Many stands of these stark, lifeless trees can still be seen along Turnagain Arm between Girdwood and Portage. You also hike through a ghost forest on the Coastal Trail in Caines Head State Recreation Area when you leave the campground at Tonsina Point and begin following the shoreline of Resurrection Bay at low tide. ■

other army artefacts or following a route into the alpine area above Resurrection Bay.

The trailhead into the park is a three-mile walk south of Seward on Lowell Point Rd. Even if you're not up for an overnight trip, the hike to Tonsina Point is a round trip of only three miles, and fairly easy. At the point you can view the salmon spawning up Tonsina Creek (July or early August) or hike through a ghost forest along the bay (the stark trunks are the result of the Good Friday Earthquake).

Climate
Unlike Chugach National Park, protected to the north by the Kenai Mountains, Caines Head and Resurrection Bay have a wetter, maritime climate. Annual rainfall in Seward usually exceeds 60 inches while the average high in July is 63°F. July and August are the driest months by far but you should still bring warm clothes and rain gear for cool, wet weather.

Information
Information on Caines Head State Recreation Area can be obtained at the Alaska Division of Parks & Outdoor Recreation office (☎ 224-3434) on the 2nd floor of the City/State Building at the corner of 5th Ave and Adams St. Hours are from 8 am to 5 pm Monday through Friday.

There is also a USFS office in town (see Information in the earlier Chugach National Forest section) while the Kenai Fjords National Park Visitor Center (☎ 224-3175) in the Small Boat Harbor has displays, information and maps for sale on both its park and the surrounding area. The center is open daily during the summer from 8 am to 7 pm.

For travel information or a complete list of accommodations, head over to the Seward Railroad Car on the corner of 3rd Ave and Jefferson St. The Chamber of Commerce maintains the car as an Information Cache (☎ 224-3094) during the summer. Hours are from 11 am to 5 pm daily.

Places to Stay
Camping Seward is one of the few towns in Alaska that has an excellent and affordable campground right in the heart of its downtown area. The *Waterfront Campground*, managed by the city's Parks & Recreation Department (☎ 224-3331), is along Ballaine Blvd, overlooking the bay. Most of it is open-gravel parking for RVers, but you'll also find a grassy tent area and a day-use area with grills, picnic tables and small shelters. It costs $5 a night for tents, $6 for RVers.

Forest Acres Campground is two miles north of town on the west side of the Seward Hwy and has a $4.25 fee and a 14-day limit. Further out of town still, but free, is the 12-site *Exit Glacier Campground*, an NPS facility for tents only, nine miles out at the end of Exit Glacier Rd.

There is also *Miller's Landing* (☎ 224-5739), a commercial campground at Lowell Point, conveniently near the trailhead for the Coastal Trail in Caines Head State Recreation Area. Tent sites, which include the use of a shower building, cost $10.20 per night. There is also a small store within the campground. If you are coming here on the weekend, you might want to call ahead and make reservations.

B&Bs The dining car information center has a wire rack full of B&B brochures. Grab a few and try your luck but expect rates to run from $55 to $65 a night. If you're coming off the Resurrection River Trail, keep in mind that at the beginning of Exit Glacier Rd there are several inns and B&Bs, including *Creekside Bed & Breakfast* (☎ 224-3834). It has cabins, tent sites and a sauna, all overlooking Clear Creek.

Hotels None of the hotels in town are cheap. The best motel in the Small Boat Harbor area is *Breeze Inn* (☎ 224-5237) with singles/doubles at $81/92. *Murphy's Motel* (☎ 224-8090) nearby has singles/doubles for $75/85, and the *Marina Motel* (☎ 224-5518) just up the highway offers rooms in the same range but neither are as nice as Breeze Inn. Downtown there is *Taroka Inn* (☎ 224-8687), on the corner of 3rd Ave and Adams St, where rooms begin at $75 but include kitchenettes.

One of the nicest places to stay in Seward is the *Van Guilder Hotel* (☎ 224-3079) at 307 Adams St. Listed on the National Register of Historical Places, the renovated hotel has a few 'pension rooms' for $50 a night.

Maps

Caines Head State Recreation Area is covered on the USGS 1:63,360 series quad *Seward A-7*. The Trails Illustrated Kenai Fjords National Park map covers the entire area in smaller detail. If all you're going to do is hike to Fort McGilvray or the South Beach, this is one of the few times in Alaska you can get away with the park brochure which has a good map on one side. In Seward, maps can be purchased at the Kenai Fjords National Park Visitor Center (☎ 224-3175) in the Small Boat Harbor or at Seward Marine Adventures (☎ 224-3102) on the corner of 3rd Ave and D St.

Equipment

Pick up the equipment you need in Anchorage. Limited camping supplies can be purchased at *Western Auto* on the corner of 5th Ave and Jefferson St near the USFS ranger office.

Cabins

There are no cabins in the Caines Head State Recreation Area. Kenai Fjord National Park, however, has four cabins for rent during the summer and one at Exit Glacier during the winter only. All four summer cabins are on the fjords south of Resurrection Bay and are reached by bush plane, kayak or boat. The closest and perhaps most popular is Aialik Bay Cabin. Built in the late 1980s, this cabin is near one of the few beaches where you can reach the Aialik Bay shoreline on foot. The cabins cost $20 a night. Check with the Kenai Fjords National Park Visitor Center (☎ 224-3175) about cabin availability and reservations.

Trails

Race Point Trail The most popular trail near Seward is the trek towards the top of Mt Marathon, the mountain that sits behind the city. The route is well known throughout Alaska. In 1909, two sourdough miners wagered how long it would take to run to the top and back and then dashed off for the peak. After that, it became an official event at the Seward Fourth of July celebrations and today the race attracts hundreds of runners and an equal number of spectators. The fastest time is 43 minutes and 23 seconds, set in 1981. Most runners come down the mountain in less than 10 minutes, usually by sliding halfway on their behinds.

Hikers, on the other hand, can take their time and enjoy the spectacular views of Seward and Resurrection Bay. The hiker's trail begins at the end of Monroe St where a yellow gate blocks vehicle access on an old road. Follow the road and head left at the first fork. At one point a spur departs for the runner's route but the hiker's trail is the main one and after skirting a creek it arrives at Race Point.

The runner's trail begins at the west end of Jefferson St (also known as Lowell St) and heads up Lowell Canyon Rd to a picnic area where the trailhead is posted just past a pair of water tanks. Scramble up the ridge to the right of the gully; for fun return through the gully's scree. You never really reach Mt Marathon's 4603-foot summit – that's left to climbers with mountaineering equipment. Race Point, a high point of 3022 feet on the broad east shoulder, is still a good afternoon hike though. Plan on from three to four hours for the three-mile round trip (USGS quad *Seward A-7*).

Two Lakes Trail This easy one-mile loop goes through a wooded area and passes two small lakes at the base of Mt Marathon. Begin the hike near the first lake behind the Alaska Vocational & Training Center on the corner of 2nd Ave and B St. Near the start of the trail is a scenic waterfall.

Exit Glacier Nature Trail The NPS maintains a series of trails at Exit Glacier, reached from Exit Glacier Rd at *Mile 3.7* of Seward Hwy. The first is a half-mile nature trail that departs from the ranger station and winds through cottonwood forest, alder thickets and along old glacial moraines before emerging at the information shelter. It's a great way to return from the glacier if you're not up to facing the mass of humanity on the paved trail.

Exit Glacier Trails A network of loops provides close access to the ice itself from the information center. The Lower Loop Trail is an easy half-mile walk to the outwash plain in front of the ice. All around there are warning signs advising you to stay away from the face due to the danger of falling ice.

The Upper Loop Trail departs off the first loop and climbs steeply to an overlook at the side of the glacier before returning. Combined, the trails are not much more than a mile long; sections may be closed at times because of falling ice. Don't skip the short spur to Falls Overlook, a scenic cascade off the upper trail.

Harding Ice Field Trail Besides the trails from the ranger station to Exit Glacier, the only other developed hike in the glacier area is the trek to Harding Ice Field. The hike to the ice field is a challenging ascent which follows a steep, roughly cut and sometimes slippery route on the north side of Exit Glacier, beginning at its base. It's a five-mile, one-way hike to the ice field at 3500 feet and for reasonably fit trekkers, a good four-hour hike/climb.

The all-day trek is well worth it for those with the stamina, as it provides spectacular views of not only the ice field but of Exit Glacier and the valley below. The upper section of the route is snow covered for much of the year.

You pick up the trailhead at the start of the Lower Loop Trail and within 30 minutes you'll see the glacier. Above the tree line the trail is not the well-cut path it is in the beginning and at times you will have to look twice to see it. Near the ice field, the NPS maintains an emergency shelter. If you want some company on this challenging trek, a ranger leads an all-day hike to the ice field every Saturday at 8 am (USGS quad *Seward A-7*).

Getting There & Away
Bus Seward Bus Lines (☎ 224-3608) provides a daily service to Anchorage during the summer, with a bus departing from a small depot at 1915 Seward Hwy at 9 am and 7 pm. The one-way fare is $30. The bus company also has connecting vans to Soldotna, Kenai and Homer. Alaskon Express (☎ 277-5581 in Anchorage) also makes a run to Seward. A bus departs from Anchorage at 8 am daily, reaching Seward at 11 am where it lays over until 7 pm for the return trip. The one-way fare is $35.

Train The Alaska Railroad makes a daily run to Seward with trains leaving Anchorage daily at 7 am and then departing from Seward at 6 pm for the return trip. The route is spectacular and includes views of glaciers, steep gorges and rugged mountains. The one-way fare is $50 and the service is offered from late May to early September. There's no depot in Seward so you need to call the Anchorage terminal (☎ 265-2494) for more information.

Boat The state ferry terminal (☎ 224-5485) is on the waterfront near the corner of 5th and Railroad Aves. Ferries arrive in Seward twice a week, on Thursday and Friday, from Kodiak or Valdez and depart for the same communities before continuing onto other Southcentral ports. The fare to Valdez is $58, to Kodiak $54 and to Homer $96.

COASTAL TRAIL
Spanning from Lowell Point to the military ruins at North Beach the Coastal Trail is a 4.5-mile one-way trek into the heart of Caines Head State Recreation Area. The most dominant feature here is Caines Head itself, a massive headland that rises 650 feet above the water against a backdrop of peaks and mountains. It juts out into Resurrection Bay, forming a giant breakwater for Seward and from its edge, you can view the Pacific Ocean on a clear day.

As the southern terminus of The Alaska Railroad, Seward was the only transportation center available before the construction of the tunnel at Whittier and the Alaska Hwy, and it played a crucial role during WW II. Even before Japan bombed Pearl Harbor, the US Army was busy building a Harbor Defense System to protect Seward and Caines Head, the key point. At the top of the bluff they spent $8 million building Fort McGilvray, which boasted two piers, 6.5 miles of road, magazine bunkers, a submarine loop station and also an elaborate underground fortress with two massive six-inch guns, each with a range of 16 miles. On the South Beach a self-contained community for 500 men was constructed.

Although the Japanese eventually bombed Dutch Harbor and occupied the Aleutian Islands of Attu and Kiska, Seward was never threatened during the war. Amazingly, two years after breaking ground, the army ordered the cliff-ringed command post to be abandoned.

Today, Caines Head is a popular destination for boaters from Seward who pull in to picnic or explore the remains of Fort McGilvray. But the state park also draws the interest of trekkers as the Coastal Trail and old military roads make an ideal overnight hike. Although the Coastal Trail is only 4.5 miles one way to the campsites on North Beach, if you add the walk to the trailhead

from Seward, plus the treks to the fort and South Beach and allow for some backtracking, the trek becomes close to 22 miles long.

The trek is best done as an overnight trip (or longer) because part of the Coastal Trail is a beach route that must be walked at low tide. Tides are mild around Caines Head with an average high of 8.3 feet. A tide book is posted at the start of the beach section in Tonsina Campground.

This area has a great deal of natural beauty as well as historical significance. But the highlight of the park for most people is exploring the military ruins. Be aware that most of the buildings are rotting, especially those in South Beach, which you should never enter. Also remember that taking any historical artefact is strictly prohibited. Part of the unique aspect of these remnants is the lack of vandalism due to the remote location of the fort. This hike is rated easy.

Access
The trailhead for the Coastal Trail is three miles down Lowell Point Rd from the ferry terminal in Seward. There is no public transportation (unless you flag a taxi) but Lowell Point Rd, which runs right along the bay, is a scenic walk.

Stage 1: Lowell Point to North Beach
(4.5 miles, 2½-3 hours)
(Tonsina Point & North Beach walk-in campgrounds)
From the trailhead gate and parking area, the first half-mile is along a level gravel road until you reach a posted junction, which points the way to Tonsina Point, a mile away. The trail then indeed becomes a trail and begins a steady climb up a wooded ridge for the next half-mile. You eventually top off and break out to a view of Tonsina Point far below and Resurrection Bay all around. From this viewing point to Tonsina Creek it is a rapid descent of more than 200 feet.

Tonsina Creek is a river large enough to hold a strong run of silver salmon in July and early August, and occasionally by hiking upstream you can see eagles and other wildlife feeding on the spawned-out fish. If the

Bald eagle

run is on, the mouth of the creek will often be crowded with locals who boat down from Seward.

You cross Tonsina Creek on an impressive foot bridge, enter the woods and then cross two more bridges. The third one leads to the walk-in campground on Tonsina Point. The facility includes a handful of sites, some with picnic tables (well shaded in the woods), vault toilets, a fire grade and shelter. Use of the campground is on a first-come-first-serve basis but camping spots abound in this area.

The next leg of the journey, the 2.5-mile stretch from Tonsina Point to Derby Cove, is a beach walk and can only be hiked during low tide. A signpost marks where the trail accesses the beach and usually the current pages from the Seward tide book are taped to the sign. Even so, it's best to have that information before you leave Seward.

From the campground, the trail cuts through a ghost forest – trees killed by the 1964 Good Friday Earthquake – and then at an orange marker you emerge on the beach with Resurrection Bay lapping at the shore only a few yards away. The black-sand beach gently curves south-east towards North Beach and on a clear day you can see the headland that separates it from Derby Cove. Occasionally you have to clamber over beach boulders, especially if the tide is coming back in, but for the most part this stretch is an easy and very scenic walk.

In Derby Cove the trail cuts inland at a well-posted spot. The final half-mile is the climb and descent of the headland that separates the cove from the spot where the US Army arrived in 1941 to build Fort McGilvray. The most visible remains at North Beach are the army dock and pier that somehow survived the 1964 earthquake and tsunami that followed, even though the surrounding land sank five feet. Over time, however, weather and waves have taken their toll on the pier's decking so you're best to stay away from it.

North Beach is a popular spot for recreational boaters to anchor and come ashore for a picnic. There is another campground here

KENAI PENINSULA

with vault toilets, a fire ring and a picnic shelter while the surrounding beach area provides additional campsites. There is also a ranger station near the north end of the beach, staffed during the summer.

Stage 2: North Beach to Fort McGilvray & South Beach
(7 miles, 3-4 hours)
You can spend an afternoon or a whole day exploring the military ruins of this area and enjoying the view from Caines Head. Fort McGilvray boasted more than six miles of roads and two of them provide easy access to the ruins. It's a two-mile walk to the fort and 2.5 miles to South Beach, or seven miles to visit both and return to the campground.

From North Beach you head south on the posted roadbed as it heads inland and climbs gently. Within a mile you come to a junction. Head east (left fork) and follow the road as it continues to climb to the top of Caines Head. Along the way you pass the remains of four ammunition magazines and then emerge at Fort McGilvray at the edge of Caines Head.

Basically you are on top of a 650-foot rocky cliff that offers panoramic views of Resurrection Bay and the surrounding mountains. The excellent shape of the fort is amazing and there's no doubt its isolated location has kept vandalism to a minimum over the years. You can explore the elaborate underground fortress but it's best to have a flashlight to find your way around the maze of passages and other rooms. Above ground take time to examine the two firing platforms. In its effort to defend Seward, the army placed two six-inch guns here that had a firing range of 16 miles.

Backtrack up the roadbed and at the junction head west on the opposite fork to reach South Beach. It's a 1.5-mile walk to the beach from the junction along another roadbed that descends to the shoreline of Resurrection Bay. South Beach was where the 500 servicemen who lived here from July 1941 to May 1943 were stationed. Today the state park officials describe the utility buildings and barracks as a 'garrison ghost town'.

They're intriguing to look at from the outside but you should think twice before entering any of the wooden structures, many of which have already collapsed.

Stage 3: The Return – North Beach to Lowell Point
(4.5 miles, 2½-3 hours)
Unless you can hitch a ride with a boater heading back to town, the only way to return is the way you came in. Double check the tides at the ranger station and then wait for low tide in order to cover the 2.5 miles from Derby Cove to Tonsina Point without getting your boots too wet.

Kachemak Bay State Park & Wilderness

Kachemak Bay State Park is a wilderness area of 355,000 acres, ranging from 4000-foot peaks with glaciers spilling out between them from the Harding Ice Field to lush forests of spruce, moss and shoulder-high devil's club. The shoreline is a ragged series of protective coves, bays and lagoons with intertidal zones teeming with starfish, crabs and other marine life. The gravel beaches have long been favorites among Homer clam diggers.

Wildlife is plentiful here. The rich lagoons and waters just off shore attract whales, sea otters, seals, dolphins and impressive salmon runs. They also attract a wide variety of sea birds and other species, including puffins, bald eagles, and gyrfalcons. Moose are found in the lowlands; brown bears, black bears and mountain goats, in the alpine region.

Stretching into Kachemak Bay is Homer Spit – a long needle of land which is actually a five-mile-long sand bar. During the summer it is the center of activity in Homer and the heart of the fishing industry, drawing thousands of tourists and backpackers every year.

The wilderness of Kachemak Bay State

Park is only a short hop away from Homer. No wonder Alaskans were eager to preserve this rugged corner of the Kenai Peninsula. In 1970, having only been a state for less than 15 years, Alaska set aside 250,000 acres as Kachemak Bay State Park. But the Alaska Native Claims Settlement Act allowed the Seldovia Native Association to select 69,000 acres from 1971 to 1974, including 30,000 acres in the state park.

The Alaska Native Claims Settlement Act was a bill that was passed allowing oil companies to cross 'Native lands' to build the pipeline to the Prudhoe Bay oil fields. The 1971 Act created the Alaska Native Fund and formed 12 regional corporations, controlled and administered by the local tribes, that invested $900 million and developed 44 million acres received for their historical lands. The Seldovia Native Association was one of them and it selected land in the Kachemak Bay area that was designated as part of the state park and wilderness area. Thus within this state park, logging and mining could take place if the state didn't purchase the land.

Faced with the possibility of logging, residents formed Kachemak Bay Citizens Coalition to lobby the state to regain the lost parkland. Ironically the solution, and money, came from the worst oil spill in US history. The Seldovia Native Association sold the land to the state for $22 million in 1993 – the money came from the *Exxon Valdez* oil spill criminal penalty fund that had been set up the year before (for more details, see History in the introductory Facts about Alaska chapter).

In the past few years, the park has been developed with a variety of visitors' facilities, including almost 30 miles of trails, walk-in campgrounds, launch docks and a rental cabin at Halibut Cove Lagoon. Just outside the park boundaries are a number of small resorts and the community of Halibut Cove. Once a thriving fishing community from 1911 to 1928, today it is a quaint boardwalk town of art galleries, eateries and a lodge.

The park is only accessible by bush plane or boat from Homer. Most trekkers hop on a tour boat – the $50 round trip includes a swing past Gull Island, the site of hundreds of puffins and other sea-bird rookeries. Plan on spending at least two nights/three days here to camp near Grewingk Glacier and hike the Alpine Ridge Trail, the two most popular areas of the park. Plan on several more days if you want to escape and explore Wosnesenski River or other trail-less valleys.

Climate

Protected from the severe northern cold by the Kenai Mountains, Kachemak Bay has a mild maritime climate with cool, overcast summers typical of the Southeast. Average temperatures in July are in the low 60s and a day above 80°F is rare. Annual precipitation is less than 30 inches, much of it snow, but the area is subject to the severe and unpredictable weather that rolls in from the North Pacific Ocean. You'll often find the seas calm until mid-morning when three to six-foot waves and south-west winds from 15 to 20 knots take over.

Information

For information on the park in Homer, contact the Alaska Division of Parks & Outdoor Recreation office (☎ 235-7024) at *Mile 168.5* of Sterling Hwy, four miles north of town. If you're passing through Sterling, you can also stop at the Kenai Parks Area Office (☎ 262-5581) and see if the Halibut Cove Cabin is open. The office is reached by heading south on Scott Lake Loop Rd from *Mile 85* of the Sterling Hwy. Within 1.5 miles veer right on Lou Morgan Rd; the office is at the end of the road.

More information on hiking and kayaking in the area can be obtained at the Alaska Maritime National Wildlife Refuge Visitor Center (☎ 235-6961), on Sterling Hwy just before entering town. The center also has natural history exhibits, a video theater, a book and map counter and hosts guided bird walks throughout the summer. Hours in the summer are from 10 am to 5 pm daily.

For information on lodging, charter trips

into Kachemak Bay or other activities, head to the Homer Visitor Center (☎ 235-5300) near the end of the Spit. Hours are from 8 am to 8 pm from Memorial Day to Labor Day.

Most of the trails on the western half of the Kenai Peninsula are in the Kenai National Wildlife Refuge and administered by the US Fish & Wildlife Service. Stop at the refuge visitors' center (☎ 262-7021) for information on trekking or the booklet *Kenai National Wildlife Refuge Hiking Trails*. The center is reached from the Sterling Hwy just south of Soldotna by turning east on Funny River Rd and then turning immediately south onto Ski Hill Rd for a mile. Along with a good series of wildlife displays, daily slide shows and wildlife films in its theater, the center has naturalist-led outdoor programs on the weekends. Hours are from 8 am to 4.30 pm weekdays and from 10 am to 6 pm on weekends.

Places to Stay

Camping Beach camping is allowed in designated areas of the west side of Homer Spit, a beautiful spot to pitch a tent. The nightly fee is $3 if you camp in the city-controlled sections near the end of the spit; there are toilets next to the Harbormaster's office. Keep in mind the spit can get rowdy at times.

The *City Campground* is on a hill overlooking the town and can be reached by following the signs north up Bartlett St. There is a $4 nightly fee at the City Campground, and a 14-day limit applies at both campgrounds. You can take a shower ($3) and wash your clothes at Washboard Laundromat (☎ 235-6781) at 1204 Ocean Drive, passed on your way to the Spit.

Hostels There's no official youth hostel in Homer but there is *Seaside Farm* (☎ 235-7850 or 235-2670), five miles from Homer out on East End Rd. The working farm has a variety of accommodations, including a backpacker hostel with bunks for $15, cabins that sleep three to four people for $50 and even the 'hay barn' for $8. You can also pitch your tent for $6 in a grassy pasture overlooking Kachemak Bay. The farm has an outdoor

kitchen area for campers, and showers and laundry facilities.

B&Bs Like everywhere else in Alaska, Homer has an ever growing number of B&Bs; at last count there were more than 30. Check with the tourist office for a list of all of them. *Lily Pad* (☎ 235-6630) at 3954 Bartlett St in the heart of town has seven rooms. Doubles cost $65. *Beach House Bed & Breakfast* (☎ 235-5945) near the airport has four rooms from $50 with good views of the Spit and a jacuzzi. There's also *Jailhouse Bed & Breakfast*, a no-host lodge that was indeed Homer's first jail and then home of Tom Bodett's 'The End of the Road' radio show. A double is $100 a night but a triple is only $120.

Hotels There are almost a dozen hotels/motels in the area with mostly single rooms costing from $60 to $70. All of them are heavily booked during the summer. A delightful, small hotel is the *Driftwood Inn* (☎ 235-8019 or (800) 478-8019) on the corner of Main St and Bunnell Ave near Bishop Beach. Single rooms without bath begin at $66, doubles at $72. Also in town are *Homer Cabins* (☎ 235-6768) at 3601 Main St. The individual log cabins contain kitchens and even microwaves and rent for $55 a night.

Outside of town is *Road Runner Retreat* (☎ 235-3678), three miles out on East End Rd. Double rooms range from $45 to $55 and include a full breakfast. The *Heritage Hotel* (☎ 235-7787 or (800) 478-7789), an historical log lodge right on Pioneer Ave in the downtown area, has singles with shared bath for $45.

Halibut Cove If you become enchanted with the south shore of Kachemak Bay, you might want to extend your stay with a night in Halibut Cove. This small village of 50 people began as a fishing port and in the early 1920s supported 42 herring salteries and a population of more than 1000. Today, this boardwalk community is best known as a side trip out of Homer where you can view

Ferry dropping backpackers off, Kachemak Bay State Park

art galleries, dine at the noted Saltry Restaurant or spend a night in a cabin.

The *Quiet Place Lodge* (☎ 296-2212) has cabins for $150 per couple which includes breakfast. There is also *Halibut Cove Cabins* (☎ 296-2214) which offers a pair of cosy cabins that sleep four people (bring your own sleeping bags). You can book lodging as well as boat transportation at Central Charter Booking Agency (☎ 235-7847 or (800) 478-7847) which has an office on the Spit.

Danny J is the ferry that will run you across to the cove from the Spit. It departs at noon, swings pass Gull Island and then at 1.30 pm arrives at Halibut Cove where you have 2½ hours to explore the 12 blocks of boardwalks and galleries or have lunch on the outdoor deck of *Saltry Restaurant*. It returns to the Spit by 5 pm and then makes an evening run to the cove for dinner at the Saltry, returning to Homer at 10 pm. The noon tour costs $35 per person, the evening trip is $17.50. Dinner at the Saltry ranges from $8 to $15 and is well worth it.

Maps

The trail system in Kachemak Bay State Park is split between two USGS 1:63,360 series quads: *Seldovia C-4* and *C-3*. Neither one shows the trails because much of the system is relatively new. An alternative, especially if you plan to stick to the established paths, is the *Kachemak Bay Road & Recreation Map* published by Alaska Road & Recreation Maps. The scale is smaller (one inch to a mile) but the $3.95 map is updated regularly and shows the entire trail system.

You can purchase maps at Alaska Maritime National Wildlife Refuge Visitor Center (see Information, above) or at Quiet Sports (☎ 235-8620) on Pioneer Ave across from the library, downtown.

Equipment

For a spare part to your MSR stove or any other piece of equipment, stop at *Quiet Sports* on Pioneer Ave, the best backpacking shop in the Kenai Peninsula. From here you can also rent mountain bikes ($20 a day, $12 a half-day) and the staff will know where you can rent kayaks.

Cabins

In 1992 the Division of Parks converted a bunkhouse that used to house trail crews into a public-use cabin. The three-room cabin has a pair of bunk-bed sleeping platforms as well as electricity and water. It's at the southern end of Halibut Cove and can be reached by boat, water taxi or by hiking along the Lagoon Trail. The nightly rate is $35 for the first four people and $10 for each additional adult.

As with USFS cabins, this one is popular and advance reservations are strongly recommended. Make them through the Department of Natural Resources Public Information Center (☎ 762-2261 or (800) 770-2257) at 3601 C St in the Frontier Building in Anchorage. Otherwise stop at the Homer Ranger Station (☎ 235-5581) at *Mile 168.5* of the Sterling Hwy (if it happens to be open).

Trails

Fuller Lake Trail This three-mile trail begins at *Mile 57.2* of the Sterling Hwy and ends at Fuller Lake just above the tree line. The trail, an old road blocked by logs, climbs rapidly in the first half until you reach Lower Fuller Lake. Here you cross a stream and move into dwarf willow and birch to continue over a low pass to Fuller Lake.

There are several backcountry campsites along the trail between the two lakes but the best place to spend the night is at Fuller Lake where you'll enjoy spectacular views of the surrounding mountains.

A spare day can be spent scrambling up the nearby ridges or fishing for grayling in Lower Fuller Lake or Dolly Varden in the upper lake. The trail is rated moderate; plan on two to three hours to reach Fuller Lake (USGS quads *Kenai B-1* and *C-1*).

Skyline Trail Near Fuller Lake Trail, this 1.2-mile climb begins on the north side of the Sterling Hwy at *Mile 61*. It is a challenging climb of 1800 feet that provides quick access

to Mystery Hills. From the forest, the trail emerges above the tree line in 0.75 miles and ends in the alpine area where there are views of the Kenai Mountains in one direction and Cook Inlet in the other.

It's also possible to form a loop from the Skyline and Fuller Lake trails. Just beyond Fuller Lake is a junction; the left-hand fork leads up a ridge to the Skyline Trail. It is an alpine route that should only be attempted by experienced trekkers. The entire loop is 12 miles, and reaches the high point of 3520 feet (USGS quad *Kenai C-1*).

Kenai River Trail This 5.5-mile trail provides access to the lower Kenai River. The upper portion of the trail is a three-mile hike from Skilak Lake Rd past good views of Kenai River Canyon. It ends at a fork with either branch continuing to the lower section of the trail. Continue on the left-hand fork and you'll reach the river in half a mile. Follow it closely until the trail reaches a dead end after 1.5 miles.

There are two trailheads; the first is less than a mile west on Skilak Lake Rd from its junction with the Sterling Hwy at *Mile 58*. The second is 2.4 miles from the junction, at a USF&WS Visitor Center (USGS quad *Kenai B-1*).

Hidden Creek Loop This easy walk along level terrain begins a mile west of Hidden Lake Campground. In less than a mile, the trail divides: the right-hand fork heads directly to the shores of Skilak Lake while the other fork first swings past Hidden Creek. Along this branch it's possible to pick a spur that crosses the creek and joins the Kenai River Trail. Hidden Creek Trail is a three-mile round trip involving little climbing. It's possible to camp along the shores of Skilak Lake (USGS quad *Kenai B-1*).

Skilak Lookout Trail Beginning at *Mile 5.5* of Skilak Lake Rd, Skilak Lookout Trail ascends 2.6 miles to a knob at 1450 feet with excellent views of the surrounding mountains and lakes. Plan on four to five hours for the round trip and bring water as there is none on the trail. Campgrounds nearby include Upper Skilak Lake, three miles to the west on Skilak Lake Rd and Hidden Lake Campground, two miles to the east (USGS quad *Kenai B-1*).

Seven Lakes Trail This point-to-point trail is a five-mile hike to the Sterling Hwy from Skilak Lake Rd. The southern trailhead is at the end of a spur to Engineer Lake at *Mile 9.7* of Skilak Lake Rd. The trail is an easy walk over level terrain and passes Hidden and Hikers lakes before ending at Kelly Lake Campground on a side road off the Sterling Hwy. Be prepared for wet and muddy sections in the middle, especially between Hidden and Engineer lakes (USGS quads *Kenai B-1* and *C-1*).

Bishop Beach Hike For all the natural beauty that surrounds it, the city of Homer lacks good public trails. The best hiking is along the beaches, while most trails off the road system are private paths that usually lead to somebody's homestead or cabin. This hike begins at Bishop Park and makes either an excellent afternoon stroll or a 10-mile trek north of Homer. The views of Kachemak Bay and the Kenai Mountains are superb, while the marine life you'll see scurrying along the sand at low tide is fascinating.

Check a tide book, available from most gasoline stations or sports stores, and leave before low tide and return before high tide. High tides cover most of the sand, forcing you to scramble onto the base of the nearby cliffs. Within three miles of the park you'll pass a sea-otter rookery a few hundred yards offshore and in seven miles you'll reach Diamond Creek. Head south on Main St, then left on Bunnell Ave and right on Beluga Ave to reach Bishop Park (USGS quad *Seldovia C-5*).

Homestead Trail Also in Homer is this new trail, developed by Kachemak Heritage Land Trust. Homestead Trail links Rogers Loop Trail with Crossman Ridge Rd. It's best picked up at the trailhead on Diamond Ridge Rd, reached from the Sterling Hwy by turning north on West Hill Rd just west of town. From the Diamond Ridge Rd, it's 2.5 miles to the south to Rogers Loop Trail trailhead on Sterling Hwy. To the north it's 1.6 miles to Crossman Ridge (USGS quad *Seldovia C-5*).

Getting There & Away
Homer is the jump-off spot for Kachemak Bay State Park and can be reached from Anchorage by air, ferry, bus or rental car (see Car Rental in the Anchorage chapter).

Air ERA Aviation (☎ (800) 426-0333), the contract carrier for Alaska Airlines, provides seven daily flights between Homer and Anchorage from the Homer Airport, 1.7 miles east of town on Kachemak Drive. The one-way fare is $90; a round-trip, advance-purchase ticket $150.

Bus Seward/Homer Bus Lines (☎ 235-8280) departs from a small hut at 455 Sterling Hwy, on the edge of town, daily at 10.20 am for Kenai/Soldotna and Anchorage, which it reaches at 4.10 pm. A southbound bus departs from Anchorage at 9.45 am, reaching Homer at 3.40 am. The one-way fare is $38 ($40 if they drop you off at Homer Spit).

Boat The state ferry MV *Tustumena* provides a twice-weekly service from Homer to Seldovia and Homer to Kodiak, from where once a week it continues onto Seward and the rest of the Southcentral ports. The ferry terminal (☎ 235-8449) is at the end of Homer Spit.

The one-way fare from Homer to Seldovia costs $18 and from Homer to Kodiak it is $48.

GREWINGK GLACIER & LAGOON TRAILS
These two trails stretch from a tour boat drop-off at the Grewingk Glacier trailhead to

a dock at the head of Halibut Cove Lagoon, a walk of only 10.5 miles. But because many tour boats do not want to negotiate the strong tides flowing in and out of the cove, most trekkers end up backtracking a portion of the Lagoon Trail to add another six miles to the hike. Throw in a side trip to Alpine Ridge, Poot Peak or the Wosnesenski River and you could easily put together a three or four-day hike of 20 to 30 miles.

An extra day can be spent camped in front of Grewingk Glacier to hike the Alpine Ridge Trail but you'll find this a popular place during the summer and flight-seeing planes abound on any clear day. More than a thousand hikers visit the park every summer and most spend a night or two at the glacier. Some never go any further.

You can also set up camp for a spare day at the head of Halibut Cove Lagoon to hike to Poot Peak or Wosnesenski River. If you truly want to escape, consider hiking and camping in Halibut Creek from where you can explore the upper portions of this stream and valley.

The hike to Grewingk is rated easy while the Lagoon Trail is moderate. You'll find Alpine Ridge and Goat Pass generally challenging above the tree line.

Access

A number of tour boats drop-off and pick-up at Halibut Cove, charging $50 for a round-trip ticket. St Augustine's Charters will drop you off at Rusty Lagoon and pick you up at Saddle Trail to avoid some backtracking.

Make sure the tour boat swings past Gull Island on the way to the cove. This group of bare rock islets, halfway between the Spit and Halibut Cove, is the site of thousands of nesting sea birds: tufted puffins, black-legged kittiwakes, cormorants, common murres and many more species. So many that you can usually photograph the birds up close without a telephoto lens.

Book St Augustine's Charters or other tour companies through Inlet Charters (☎ 235-6126) on the Spit.

Stage 1: Rusty Lagoon to Grewingk Glacier
(3.5 miles, 1½-2 hours)
(Backcountry campground)

Most water taxis prefer to drop you off a quarter of a mile or so down the stony spit that forms Rusty Lagoon. From the landing site, you head north on the sloping gravel beach, passing a fair amount of driftwood and sea life washed up by the high tides, until a large orange triangular sign marks the start of the Grewingk Glacier Trail.

From a posted trailhead, the route heads east into a lush forest and after a quarter of a mile arrives at a well-posted junction to the Rusty Lagoon Campground, a rustic camping area that is a 10-minute hike down the spur. The campground features picnic tables, fire grades and vault toilets. The main trail continues in the lush forest for a spell and then breaks out to the glacial outwash which is rocky and dotted with young stands of cottonwood. At this point you reach a nature trail, a quarter-mile loop that was built as an Eagle Scout project and features numbered posts and a brochure that explains the natural history of the area.

Eventually the main trail swings southeast and skirts the edge between the forested ridge and the bushy growth of the level outwash. Hiking is easy and in three miles you reach the posted junction with the Saddle Trail. Ascend the Saddle Trail a hundred yards or so to refill your water bottles from a clear-running stream. This water is much better than the silt-filled lake in front of the glacier.

The final leg of the trail is a hike across rocky terrain to the lake; it's marked by a series of cairns, though they are hardly needed. You might have spotted the glacier earlier from a distance but emerging from the bush and seeing it properly for the first time is like Dorothy and the scarecrow seeing the emerald city of Oz – it takes your breath away.

This giant river of ice spills gracefully out of the mountains into the lake, sending wave after wave of icebergs to litter the shoreline where you pitch your tent. This is a gorgeous spot to camp for a day or two. There are lots of fire pits around. Remember to destroy yours before you move on, this scenic spot surely doesn't need another one.

Stage 2: Grewingk Glacier to Halibut Cove Lagoon

(7 miles, 6-7 hours)
(Backcountry campgrounds, rental cabin)
The easy trekking is over. On the leg to Halibut Cove Lagoon there is much more climbing as you skirt the side of the shoreline mountains. You begin by backtracking to the Saddle Trail junction and then follow the trail for almost a mile as it climbs the saddle between Halibut Cove and Grewingk Glacier. It then levels out and you'll pass a small creek along the way.

Just before it makes its steep descent to Halibut Cove, you pass a posted junction with the Lagoon Trail. This trail continues the steep climb until it reaches the posted junction with the Alpine Ridge Trail.

The Alpine Ridge Trail is a great side trip but it's a steep climb of two miles to the alpine area. The first half is a series of switchbacks through the lush spruce forest. The second half is above the tree line but the alder here is often at eye level. The alpine region is reached at 2000 feet and once you're on top the views of the surrounding area, including Grewingk Glacier, are stunning. From here you can climb along the ridge to get better views of the glacier. You'll reach the 3647-foot peak 1.5 miles after emerging in the tundra. It's an 11 to 12-mile round trip if you spend a spare day at the glacier.

If you're just dropping your packs at the junction, plan on at least an additional three hours for the side trip up to the alpine region and back. By hauling your packs up, however, you can spend a memorable night in the mountains as there are places to camp. Pack water in case the snow patches have melted.

Lagoon Trail levels out somewhat after the junction with the Alpine Ridge Trail and hugs the steep side of the coastal ridge for more than a mile. You descend sharply to

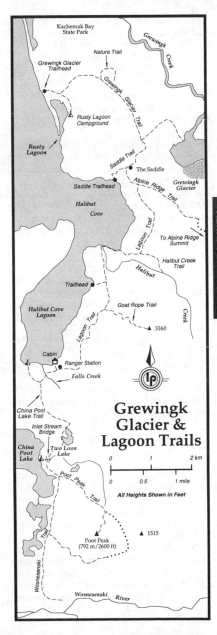

Grewingk Glacier & Lagoon Trails

All Heights Shown in Feet

KENAI PENINSULA

cross a creek, regain some of the elevation and then cross a bog before emerging at the junction with Halibut Creek Trail.

Halibut Creek Trail is a half-mile trail that briefly follows the ridge line above the creek and then descends sharply into the valley. It's not hiked nearly as much as the other trails and it has great spots to pitch a tent and escape the crowds at Grewingk Glacier.

From the junction with Halibut Creek Trail, Lagoon Trail descends sharply to bottom out at the mouth of the creek and the delta it formed in Halibut Cove. More orange triangles lead you across the gravel delta to the creek which has to be forded. It's considerably easier at low tide when you can go to the braided section at the mouth and practically hop across. Otherwise, be prepared to get your boots wet.

On the other side, orange trail markers lead you up the creek 100 yards or so to where the trail resumes in the spruce forest. You quickly pass a junction to a trailhead spur on the cove and then begin a steep climb via a series of switchbacks. The climb is steep until it reaches almost 1200 feet, the highest point of Lagoon Trail. Here you arrive at the posted junction of the Goat Rope Trail.

Goat Rope Trail is a one-way spur that continues the steep ascent for another half-mile through a notch to the alpine area at 2700 feet. The climb is challenging but the views are great. Plan on an additional two hours if you add this trail to your itinerary.

From the junction, Lagoon Trail quickly descends 400 feet and then levels out for half a mile before making a final and steep descent to the bottom where it passes Halibut Cove Ranger Station (staffed two or three days a week) and a public-use cabin within 100 yards.

The cabin, which at one time housed trail crews, overlooks the lagoon and has a stairway that leads to interesting floating dock and small raft. It features two bedrooms with bunk-bed sleeping platforms and a main room with a cooking counter, table and chairs. The unit is equipped with electricity,

water and a purifying filter. Attached to the cabin is an environmentaly correct composting outhouse.

A stairway takes you down to Falls Creek and the end of the trail at its junction with China Poot Lake Trail. Just to the north is a pair of campsites at the end of Halibut Cove Lagoon with picnic tables, fire rings and vault toilets. Hemmed in by mountains, you'll find the scenery at the end of the lagoon spectacular, making this area another excellent choice for a spare day. Day hiking opportunities here are numerous and Falls Creek has good fishing when the king and pink salmon runs are on.

Heading south is China Poot Lake Trail which extends 2.5 miles past three lakes to a campsite on its namesake lake. The trail is an easy hike but the first half-mile is an uphill walk of almost 500 feet to the first lake. It then levels out through a spruce forest and muskeg area and in a mile reaches Two Loon Lake. It remains level for the final mile to China Poot Lake and you pass the campsite just before crossing a bridge over Inlet Stream.

China Poot Lake Trail ends at a posted junction with Poot Peak Trail and Wosnesenski Trail. Poot Peak Trail is a two-mile climb to the 2600-foot summit that is challenging and generally takes three to fours hours from China Poot Lake. It's an unmaintained route that involves scrambling up scree and loose rock. Think twice before undertaking it in threatening weather.

Wosnesenski Trail is a two-mile trek south along the shoreline of three lakes formed by a geological fault. For the most part the trail is an easy walk along level terrain but near the end you climb over a low saddle and descend to Wosnesenski River, draining from its namesake glacier five miles to the east.

You can explore the valley but heading east towards the glacier you soon run into cliffs on the north side. It far easier to reach the glacier on the south shore but that means fording Wosnesenski River. This glacial river is very difficult to ford and should be attempted only at low levels.

Stage 3: Halibut Cove Lagoon to Saddle Trail Trailhead

(6 miles, 3-4 hours)

Few of the Halibut Cove ferry services will pick up trekkers at the head of the lagoon, meaning you're going to have to backtrack along Lagoon Trail. It's 5.5 miles of moderate hiking (see description above) from the ranger station to the posted junction with the Saddle Trail. From here you head south for a very steep descent to the Saddle Trail trailhead on the upper portion of Halibut Cove.

The trailhead is flanked to the north by private property and a dwelling, while on the south side is a small beach area with the piled remains of an old cannery. This is usually the preferred pick-up point, especially in bad weather as it offers considerable protection from the wicked surf off Kachemak Bay.

Wrangell-St Elias National Park

The road to McCarthy, the main access to Wrangell-St Elias National Park, begins with a highway sign informing you that the bridge at the end is washed out. Then it warns you to watch out for loose spikes. And finally it sends you off with this blessing: *Drive At Your Own Risk.*

To the historical mining town from the end of the Edgerton Hwy, it's 62 miles of dust and flying stones; a 25-mile-an-hour drive over a surface that resembles grandma's washboard with potholes that would be legendary if this was any other state than Alaska.

Built on the abandoned bed of the Copper River & Northwest Railroad, the road is littered with railroad artefacts. Iron rails line the shoulders, railroad ties are still half buried in the road and then there are those spikes: six inches long, sharp at one end, blunt at the other. They used to hold the rails in place but now the spikes chew tyres like a three-year-old eats candy on Easter morning – with reckless abandonment.

At *Mile 17* of the McCarthy Rd, you come to the Kuskulana River Bridge. Erected in 1910, the narrow three-span railroad bridge is 600-feet long and crosses a sheer-sided canyon 283 feet above a rushing river. It's a heart-pounding sight and until a few years ago, there were no guardrails on this bridge and the only planking was, hopefully, underneath your tyres. Locals called the crossing 'the biggest thrill on the road to McCarthy'.

But today, everybody agrees, the biggest thrill is at the end. At *Mile 60*, the road abruptly stops. Where there used to be a bridge over the Kennicott River, there is now an open tram – a platform with two seats that you pull across the river by hand. Sitting across from each other, backpacks squeezed in between your legs, pull the rope once and the tram goes flying across the river. A rushing mass of white water and standing waves are only 15 feet below. Carnival rides aren't half the thrill of this.

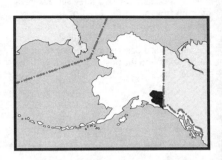

Welcome to McCarthy, a beautiful mountainous hamlet with a year-round population of eight to 12 people, depending on who's staying for the winter. What's amazing isn't that this century-old town can only be reached by a hand-pulled tram. Or that on Friday evenings, when there is often a 90-minute wait at the tram, five people at a time use it, two hanging onto the outside. What's truly amazing is that the McCarthy Rd, without guardrails, pavement or a single gasoline station, is the main access route to the largest national park in the USA. Created in 1980 as part of the Alaska Lands Bill, Wrangell-St Elias National Park & Preserve sprawls across 13.2 million acres in the south-central region of the state. It abuts against Canada's Kluane National Park and together their 20 million acres represent one of the largest wilderness areas left in the world.

The park's trademarks are high peaks and massive glaciers. Three great ranges, Chugach, Wrangell and St Elias, converge in an area the size of six Yellowstones to form a crossroads of the mountains. Within its borders are nine of the 16 highest peaks in the country, including the second highest, Mt St Elias (18,008 feet), Mt Bona (16,421 feet), Mt Blackburn (16,390 feet) and Mt Sanford (16,237 feet). And there's the Bagley Ice Field, the largest subpolar ice field in North America, and such giant glaciers as the

178

Malaspina, an ice floe bigger than the state of Rhode Island.

The highest peak, Mt McKinley (20,320 feet) is in Denali National Park, the reason (many will tell you) that the park is world renowned, and crowded, while Wrangell-St Elias is virtually unknown outside of Alaska.

From its glaciated roof of mountains and peaks, the terrain in the park descends to the north as treeless tundra and then boreal-forested uplands. To the south the glaciers extend from the mountains almost to the tidewaters of the Gulf of Alaska. Wildlife includes dall sheep and mountain goats in the alpine region, caribou around the Wrangell Mountains to the north and moose in the bogs and brushy areas of the lowlands. Bison were released in Copper River Valley in 1950 and along the Chitina River in 1962 and remnants of those herds remain today. Black and brown bears roam throughout the park.

There are few, if any, maintained foot trails in this park that are of the same standard as those in Chugach National Forest. But Wrangell-St Elias is laced with old mining roads, historical horse-packing trails and other avenues to its interior. Many trails require bush-plane travel to reach their remote locations, but the three routes described in this section – Dixie Pass, Nugget Creek and Bonanza Mine – can be reached from the McCarthy Rd thus eliminating the expensive air-taxi charter cost.

Even with public transport to McCarthy, the Wrangell-St Elias area is still not a quick side trip or a spur-of-the-moment outing. This is not Denali by any stretch of the imagination. There is no park bus, elaborate visitors' center or easy access to the campgrounds in the interior. In fact, there are no campgrounds in this park. Although the number of visitors to McCarthy and Kennicott is increasing by leaps and bounds every year (30,000 made their way to the historic towns in 1994) the logistics of putting a trek together here are far more difficult than almost any other area covered in this book.

Climate

The park has a rainy maritime climate in the south along the coast while further north you can enjoy the dry summers of Interior Alaska. Kennicott and the areas off the McCarthy Rd, for the most part, are shielded by the Wrangell Mountains to the north and by the Chugachs to the south. During much of the summer this creates a pattern of warm, dry weather. Even so, the range of temperatures between day and night is remarkable. In July it's not so unusual to experience a string of 80°F afternoons, while the temperatures drop to the 40s or even the 30s at night.

Like high, mountainous topography elsewhere, the Wrangells and Chugachs create weather that can change suddenly and often. Enjoy the sun but keep your rain gear handy. By mid to late August expect cool and cloudy days as well as rain. Annual precipitation is 17 inches, much of it falling as rain in late August and September.

Information

The park's main headquarters (☎ 822-5235)

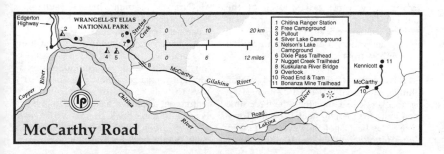

are at *Mile 105.5* of the Old Richardson Hwy, the highway bypass through Copper Center, reached from the Richardson Hwy 10 miles south of Glennallen. The office is open from 8 am to 6 pm daily during the summer and rangers can answer questions about the park as well as supply various hand-outs. This is also the best place to leave your trip itinerary. During the summer, rangers are stationed in a log cabin in Chitina (☎ 823-2205) at the end of the Edgerton Hwy. From here you can obtain information on hiking and backpacking in the area. Hours are from 8 am to 5 pm daily during the summer but because of its limited staff it occasionally closes in the middle of the afternoon.

Places to Stay

Copper Center Bypassed by the Richardson Hwy near *Mile 101*, Copper Center is not only home for the park headquarters but it is also an interesting village with a touch of Alaskan character that is so lacking in Glennallen to the north. At the turn of the century Copper Center was an important mining camp and today it's still a logical place to gather information and supplies for a journey into the park. Historic and affordable lodging is available at *Copper Center Lodge* (☎ 822-3245) which began in 1897 as the Blix Roadhouse and was the first lodge built north of Valdez. Don't pass up its breakfast of sourdough pancakes, reputedly made from century-old starter. Rooms range from $60 for a single to $75 for a triple.

The nearest campground to Edgerton Hwy is *Squirrel Creek State Campground* (14 sites, $6 per night) at *Mile 79.4* of Richardson Hwy, three miles south of the junction. The scenic little camping area is on the banks of the creek and is often filled with anglers and others trying to catch grayling and rainbow trout.

Edgerton Hwy & McCarthy Rd Within Chitina, at the end of the Edgerton Hwy, backpackers can camp along the three-mile road south to O'Brien Creek or beside Town Lake. The best spot, however, is *Liberty Falls State Recreation Site*, 10 miles before

you reach Chitina. The free campground has only three, maybe four sites for RVers but there are another half a dozen spots for tents, including four tent platforms right along rushing Liberty Creek. There is no piped-in water here but there is thundering Liberty Falls within the campground.

There is also a small campground with eight free sites next to the Copper River bridge. It is maintained by the Alaska Department of Transportation and used primarily by dipnetters who descend on Chitina in July and August to scoop up red and king salmon.

Along McCarthy Rd there are two commercial campgrounds with very limited services, gas not being one of them: at *Mile 11* is *Silver Lake Campground* and a mile further down the road is *Nelson's Lake Campground*. At Nelson's there is a small trading post that sells a limited amount of food.

At *Mile 13.5* you come to the access road to the trailheads for Dixie Pass and Nugget Creek Trail. By heading up the access road a couple of miles, you'll reach *Strelna Zephyr Bunkhouse*. Sandy Casteler and her family run the quaint log-cabin accommodations and inside you'll find four bunks, a wood-burning stove but no running water or electricity. Bunks are $25 a night. Don't worry about advance reservations, the family has no phone.

McCarthy & Kennicott Once you reach 'the end of the road', the cheapest accommodations is camping along the west side of the Kennicott River before crossing over to McCarthy on the tram. There are vault toilets but no piped-in water and on the weekends it can get crowded and dusty.

It's hard to camp around either McCarthy or Kennicott due to private ownership of most of the land. Accommodations in McCarthy change almost seasonally so it pays to walk around to see if anybody is renting out a cabin or has started up a B&B. For an affordable bunk, stop at the *McCarthy Country Store* which has four bunks in a cabin out the back for $20 a night.

Just down the street is the *McCarthy Lodge* (☎ 333-5402), full of mining relics and photographs of the era, and the place to get a cold beer in a frosty mug. Across the street, the lodge runs *Ma Johnson's Hotel*. Built in 1916 as a boarding house, it's now totally renovated and has singles/doubles for $95/105.

In Kennicott, *Kennicott Glacier Lodge* (advance reservation ☎ (800) 582-5128 outside Alaska; (800) 478-2350 within the state) offers beds, running water and electricity. Doubles cost $139 for the room only with no meals. They also have a dining room with a spectacular view of the surrounding peaks and glaciers.

Maps

It is unthinkable to enter this park without the proper USGS 1:63,360 series quads. Unfortunately none of the treks discussed in this section are conveniently covered by just one sheet. Dixie Pass and Nugget Creek Trail are covered on two maps, Bonanza Mine on three (see the individual trail descriptions for details). The best place to purchase the maps is at the park headquarters (see Information, above) in Copper Center, then get a ranger to outline the trek on your map. If you're already on your way to McCarthy, Willow Herb Mountain Depot, reached 2.5 miles before the tram on the McCarthy Rd, sells USGS maps and hopefully they will have the ones you need. They even take Visa and MasterCard.

Equipment

The one piece of equipment crucial for any trek into the Wrangell-St Elias area is head netting. More so than in the Southeast or Kenai Peninsula, insects can be horribly thick and nasty in this park. Count on mosquitos throughout the summer whenever you're in the lowlands. Relief from them is often only after you climb close to the tree line.

It is best to pick up food, white gas or other supplies in Valdez, Glennallen or Copper Center, which has a gas station, a store for food and general supplies, and a post office.

In Chitina, there is also a grocery store, post office and two restaurants; the *Chitina Cafe* is a good place to stop for your 'last supper' before the trek. You can also pick up food and even limited camping supplies from a small store near the McCarthy Lodge in McCarthy.

Cabins

At the end of Nugget Creek Trail there is an old miner's cabin owned by the NPS and available as a shelter to anybody: trekkers, mountain bikers or others who arrive on an off-road vehicle. There is no fee and reservations are not required but the cabin is not maintained. Mining ruins are scattered through the park, including old bunkhouses, but you should think twice before entering them much less before spending a night in the dilapidated structures.

Trails

If you want to do more than just view the glaciers, check in with St Elias Alpine Guides (☎ (907) 277-6867 in Anchorage) at the historic Mother Lode Powerhouse in McCarthy. The long-time Alaska guiding company offers a variety of day hikes on glaciers, including a half-day trek on Root Glacier for $55. There is also a half-day ice-climbing adventure for $75 and a fly-in trek on Kennicott Glacier at the base of Mt Blackburn for $95 for the full day. All outings include the proper mountaineering equipment and guides.

Root Glacier Trail From Kennicott Glacier Lodge, Root Glacier Trail is a 2.5-mile round trip past the mine ruins to the sparkling white-and-blue floe of ice. Hike west of the town and continue past an unmarked junction to Bonanza Mine, reached in less than a quarter of a mile. Along the way you cross Jumbo Creek; a plank upstream makes fording this creek easy in normal water conditions. You can climb the glacier but extreme caution should be used if you are inexperienced and lacking the proper equipment for walking on ice (crampons, ice axe etc). For this trail you'll need USGS quads *McCarthy B-6* and *C-6*.

Worthington Glacier Trail Worthington Glacier lies not within Wrangell-St Elias National Park but south-west of the park along the Richardson Hwy. For most people, it's a drive-in glacier, like Portage Glacier near Anchorage and Mendenhall Glacier outside Juneau – you drive-in, look at it and take off, hurrying to get somewhere else.

That's a shame because this two-mile round trip is well worth the one or two hours you spend on the trail as it provides the best vantage points to view this beautiful floe of ice. The trek is short and rated easy. It begins with a stiff climb and then involves following a narrow trail along a moraine that skirts steep drop-offs to the glacier itself. You could spend an entire day in this area, however, beginning with this trek and continuing with a romp in the tundra at Thompson Pass, less than three miles south along the Richardson Hwy.

Reached at *Mile 26*, Thompson Pass is an alpine area at 2771 feet where it is easy to pull off the highway and hike through the heather into meadows filled with wild flowers in early summer. Another two miles south along the highway is Blueberry Lake State Recreation Site, an alpine campground that borders two small lakes. This is a great place to spend a day almost entirely in the mountains above the tree line (USGS quad *Valdez A-5*).

Mineral Creek Trail Valdez is another town that has great potential for hikers but few trails. The most popular trek in this Prince William Sound oil port is the old road along Mineral Creek which becomes a mile-long trail to the ruins of Smith Stamping Mill. If you have a vehicle, you can usually follow the road but be prepared to bottom out a few times.

To reach the trailhead, follow Hazelet Ave north 10 blocks from Egan Drive to Hanagita St and turn left (west), then turn right (north) onto Mineral Creek Rd. The road winds for another 5.5 miles into the valley and then

becomes a mile-long trail to the old stamping mill. Beyond the mill at Brevier Creek, the route requires considerable brush hacking. If you are hiking the entire road, the trip up the canyon is an easy 13-mile adventure that requires from five to six hours (USGS quad *Valdez A-7*).

Solomon Gulch Trail A newer trail is across from the Solomon Gulch Fish Hatchery on Dayville Rd, off the Richardson Hwy. This 1.3-mile trail begins with a series of steps but is still a steep uphill climb that quickly leads to views of the Trans-Alaska Pipeline, the city of Valdez and the towering Chugach Mountains behind it. It ends at the top of the dams of Solomon Lake, the source of 80% of Valdez's power. Plan on two or three hours for this trek (USGS quad *Valdez A-7*).

Getting There & Away

The Richardson Hwy and Tok Cutoff Hwy border the north-west corner of the park and from each one a rough dirt road leads into the park's interior. At *Mile 59.8* of the Tok Cutoff is Nabesna Rd, which winds 45 miles into the north end of the park before ending at Nabesna, a small mining community of 25 people or so. The first 30 miles of this road is manageable gravel but the rest of it is extremely rough and has streams flowing over it. The only facility is a lodge with gas at *Mile 28.6*.

Most visitors to the park enter via Edgerton Hwy and McCarthy Rd, arriving from either Glennallen or Valdez. These two roads provide a 92-mile route into the heart of the park, ending at the tram which crosses the Kennicott River to McCarthy. The 32-mile Edgerton Hwy, fully paved, begins at *Mile 82.6* of Richardson Hwy and ends at Chitina. The town, which has 40 or so permanent residents, is the last place you can purchase gas and get a reasonably priced meal.

From Chitina, McCarthy Rd – a rough dirt road that is not regularly maintained – leads 60 miles to the Kennicott River. Your $29-a-day Rent-A-Wreck can usually travel this stretch during the summer, but plan on three

Mining ruins, Kennicott

to four hours for the trip. If it has been raining hard, don't attempt it at all.

To/From Valdez Gray Line's Alaskon Express buses will take you to Valdez. A bus departs from the Anchorage office (☎ 277-5581) daily at 8 am, passes the junction to Edgerton Hwy and reaches Valdez at 6 pm. The one-way fare is $59. In Valdez, Alaskon Express (☎ 835-2357) operates out of the Westmark Hotel and departs from Valdez at 8 am daily for the return trip.

If you're in Seward, Whittier or Cordova, you can reach Valdez on the Alaska Marine Ferry. Both the MV *Bartlett* and MV *Tustumena* call at Valdez, and between the two ships there are runs from Whittier four times a week, three weekly sailings from Cordova and a weekly run from Seward. If you're heading east from Whittier or Seward, you'll sail past the Columbia Glacier. The one-way fare to Valdez from Whittier is $58, Cordova $30 and Seward $58. In Valdez, the ferry terminal (☎ 835-4436) is at the southern end of Hazelet Ave.

Alaska Airlines, through its contract carrier ERA Aviation (☎ 835-2636), provides three flights during the week and two on the weekend between Valdez and Anchorage. Flights leave from the Valdez Airport, five miles from town on Airport Rd. MarkAir (☎ 835-5147) also services Valdez.

To/From Glennallen Any Alaskon Express bus making a run to Valdez from Anchorage can drop you off in Glennallen. The one-way fare is $55. Alaska Direct Busline (☎ (800) 770-6652 or 277-6652 in Anchorage) also has a bus that leaves Anchorage at 6 am on Monday, Wednesday and Saturday, reaching Glennallen at 11 am. The one-way fare will cost you $37.

If you're already in Glennallen, at least one Alaskon Express bus passes through daily in the early afternoon heading south to Valdez, skirting the park and passing the start of the Edgerton Hwy. Gray Line picks up passengers and sells tickets at the Caribou Cafe (☎ 822-3656) on the Glenn Hwy.

To/From McCarthy Backcountry Connection (☎ 822-5292 or (800) 478-5292, Alaska only) provides transport out of Glennallen to the McCarthy tram. The small tour company departs from Caribou Motel on Glenn Hwy at 7.15 pm Monday through Saturday for the four-hour trip to McCarthy, arriving at 11.30 am. It departs from McCarthy at 4.30 pm for the return trip. The one-way fare is $49, round trip $88.

Several small air companies fly daily between McCarthy and Glennallen. Ellis Air (☎ 822-3368) departs from the Gulkana airstrip at 9.45 am, arriving in McCarthy at 11 am and then turns around and heads back. The one-way fare is $56. Wrangell Mountain Air (☎ 345-1160 or (800) 478-1160) also has a daily service. The one-way fare between McCarthy and Chitina is $60, between McCarthy and Glennallen it costs $100 per person (minimum three people per flight).

DIXIE PASS

Easily accessed by the McCarthy Rd, Dixie Pass is probably the most popular trek for backpackers looking for a multi-day adventure in Wrangell-St Elias National Park. The fact that no bush-plane travel is required is what attracts most trekkers to this route. But once they're hiking, it doesn't take long for the mountain scenery, remoteness of the wilderness and the wildlife to replace the savings on airfares as the highlight of the trip.

Initially the trail is easy to identify but for much of the 11-mile trek to the pass you'll follow stream beds or use game trails to make your way up the valley. The trip is rated challenging, but it is certainly within the ability of most trekkers who have experienced the trail-less areas of Denali National Park and, of course, can use a map and compass. For treks like these, being able to look at mountains, streams and ridges and relate them to your topo is the key to successful trekking.

In July and August don't be surprised if you encounter another hiking party in the area. Most people take two days to climb to Dixie Pass where they spend a spare day and then backtrack to the trailhead. This makes a

four to five-day, 22-mile trek. The more adventurous trekker can continue on the Kotsina Trail, a 45-mile journey back to the trailhead along an old mining road that requires six days or more.

The route to Dixie Pass requires numerous bridgeless stream crossings. Either bring a spare pair of shoes, or accept that you'll be hiking in soggy boots for most of the second half of the trail. Also carry head nets and some potent bug repellent. The mosquitos can be murderous in the beginning when you are hiking through spruce and willow lowlands. And finally, be aware that bears can be encountered anywhere along the route. Keep your camp clean.

The area is covered on USGS 1:63,360 series quads *Valdez C-1* and *McCarthy C-8*. If you purchase them at the park headquarters in Copper Center, ask a ranger how the trailhead on Nugget Creek/Kotsina Rd is marked.

Access

From Chitina, follow the McCarthy Rd for roughly 13.5 miles to the grass Strelna airstrip on the south side. On the north side is Nugget Creek/Kotsina Rd, marked by a rail wheel painted white with 'Nugget Creek' written in red letters (it can be tough to spot in the tall brush at times). Follow this road north-west and in 2.5 miles you reach the intersection of Nugget Creek Rd which crosses the creek (see Nugget Creek Trail, later) and Kotsina Rd. If your car has low clearance, high mileage or a loose bumper, park here and walk the rest of the way. Continue on Kotsina Rd and in 1.3 miles you come to the trailhead on the right. Generally, a stick or pile of rocks marks the trail but don't bet on it.

If you're without a vehicle, make arrangements with Backcountry Connection (☎ 822-5292) to be dropped off and picked up at McCarthy Rd and then just add four miles to your trek on the first and last day. Backcountry Connection charges $23 one way from Glennallen to Strelna or $26 if you're coming from McCarthy.

Stage 1: Kotsina Rd to Strelna Creek Confluence

(6 miles, 4-6 hours)

(Backcountry camping)

From the Dixie Pass trailhead, if you can call it that, the initial two miles is on a well-defined trail along a level bench area forested in paper birch, spruce and willow. The hiking is easy and within a mile you break out to your first glimpse of the mountains.

Eventually you sharply descend a river bank to arrive at Strelna Creek, a fast-flowing stream at this point where the current is rippling around a series of boulders. The trail swings north-east and follows the west bank of the stream but first makes a very steep climb and an equally steep descent to bypass a narrow gorge-like area.

For the next three miles you stay along the west bank of the stream, the trail is fairly easy to recognize. You reach the first confluence of Strelna Creek approximately six miles from the trailhead when you enter an extremely wet muskeg area. Be forewarned – in an attempt to avoid getting their boots wet, some trekkers swing wide of the wet area and miss seeing the confluence altogether. If you do this, you'll mistakenly continue up Strelna Creek.

Instead, ford the Strelna and continue heading north-east along the stream that drains the Dixie Pass area. If the water is running high, you might have to continue hiking west along the Strelna to find a suitable crossing. Once along the new drainage creek, you'll immediately begin passing gravel bars where you can camp. You'll find more gravel bars half a mile upstream. Keep in mind that the further you hike upstream, the higher you'll climb and the more the bugs will diminish.

Stage 2: Strelna Confluence to Dixie Pass

(5 miles, 5-7 hours)

(Backcountry camping)

Remain on the north-west side of the drainage creek where there are easy-to-follow animal trails along the banks. Eventually, a sheer cliff forces you to ford the river back and forth, following game trails, dry stream beds or gravel bars.

Within one to two hours, approximately two miles from Strelna Creek, you reach the second confluence. Ford to the westerly channel and choose a side to travel on. I found the west side had a well-developed animal trail almost halfway to the gorge but that can change from season to season. At this point the brush begins to thin out and bashing the waist-high willow is no longer a painful experience.

Within a mile upstream, you can spot Dixie Pass briefly if the day is clear. You also pass numerous gravel bars that make excellent campsites if you get an early start the first day. After several fords, you round a huge and distinctive rock bluff and then enter the gorge. The short gorge features impressive walls on both sides and if the water is low you can practically skip through it. When the stream is at its normal level, you can slosh your way through it to reach the west end. But if the stream is high, it's best to climb the easterly ridge and avoid the gorge completely.

The valley broadens out on the other side and good camping spots abound on wide gravel bars. Many people set up camp here and continue on to Dixie Pass with only a day pack.

After reaching the third confluence at the end of the gravel bars, you begin the final leg to the pass. This two-mile trek climbs a ridge line between the two streams. Within a mile you emerge in the alpine tundra and then begin the final climb to the pass, along an apparent route. This climb is steep but is often done with heavy backpacks.

Needless to say, the views from the 5100-foot pass are spectacular if the weather is clear. You can see the Strelna Creek area and also Rock Creek Valley on the north side. On top you'll find camping spots for two or three small tents and ridge lines to follow for more adventure. For the best views, climb to the high point of 5770 feet on the ridge to the north-east. Water is available from a nearby snowfield run-off, making it possible to spend a comfortable night or two at the pass.

WRANGELL-ST ELIAS

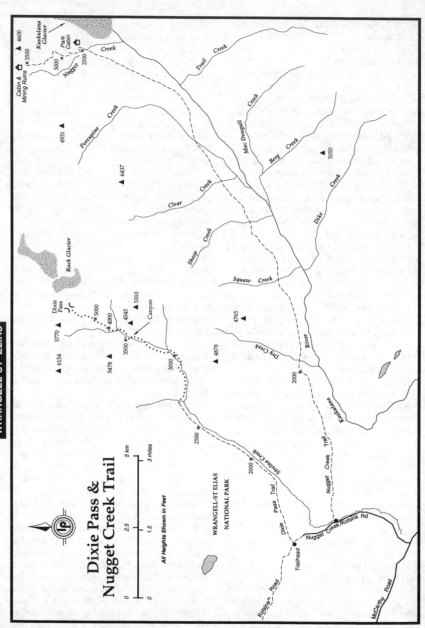

Dixie Pass & Nugget Creek Trail

Stage 3: The Return – Dixie Pass to Kotsina Rd

(11 miles, 9-14 hours)

Most trekkers who walk to Dixie Pass simply turn around and return along the side route they hiked in on. This makes a 22-mile, three to five-day trek into the heart of Wrangell-St Elias National Park.

The alternative is to turn this adventure into a 45-mile, five to seven-day trek by returning along Kotsina Trail, the miner's road that swings around Hubbard Peak before returning to McCarthy Rd. Unlike the route to Dixie Pass, Kotsina Trail is developed enough to be used by mountain bikers and occasionally even off-road vehicles.

The route begins by descending Dixie Pass to the north to the Rock Creek drainage area. You follow the west side of the creek for approximately four miles until you reach its confluence with Lime Creek. Here you must ford Rock Creek to its east side and then climb into the high country to avoid a canyon. You stay on the east side until you descend to the creek's confluence with the Kotsina River, where you're forced to continue along the south bank as the Kotsina River is usually too deep and running too fast to ford safely.

You generally have to follow the river west for two miles before picking up the miners' road at a washed-out bridge. Continue west on the road which for the first 10 miles parallels the river and passes an old camp near Cooper Creek before it begins to skirt around 5800-foot Hubbard Peak. In the final 20 miles, the road heads south-east back to McCarthy Rd, passing the trailheads to Dixie Pass and Nugget Creek near the end. Keep in mind that on the Kotsina Trail you must ford almost a dozen creeks of which Elliott Creek is the most challenging, often more than three-feet deep.

NUGGET CREEK TRAIL

Nugget Creek is a considerably easier trek than Dixie Pass as it follows an old mining road most of the way in gradually climbing 1000 feet to a park cabin and views of Kuskulana Glacier. For those not comfort-

able with the trail-less, backcountry travel to Dixie Pass, Nugget Creek Trail is a suitable alternative as it is hard to get lost following what is basically an old miners' road.

As much a mountain bike route as a hiking trail, Nugget Creek Trail is a round trip of 30 miles that most hikers cover in three to four days by returning on the same trail. The trip can be lengthened by spending another day or two at the end exploring mining ruins or ridge walking in the alpine areas above Nugget Creek.

Unlike Dixie Pass, you spend the entire hike in the forested lowlands where bugs can persist throughout much of the summer. There are eight major streams to ford and stretches in the beginning can be muddy. As always, bears can be encountered almost anywhere along this route. Also keep in mind that off-road vehicles can be driven here – all a driver needs is a permit from the park headquarters, which is relatively easy to get. Fortunately the road is much too rugged and rutted for anything but a four-wheel all-terrain vehicle (ATV). Chances are you'll only encounter miners heading off to their private claim.

By bringing in some extra supplies and caching them near the start of the Nugget Creek Trail, it would be easy to do both Dixie Pass and Nugget Creek Trail back-to-back before heading on to a cold beer and well deserved rest in McCarthy. The trailheads are only 1.3 miles apart on Nugget Creek/ Kotsina Rd and both treks are on the same USGS 1:63,360 series quads, *Valdez C-1* and *McCarthy C-8*. This trip is rated moderate.

Access

The trailhead to Nugget Creek Trail is considerably easier to spot along Nugget Creek/ Kotsina Rd than the Dixie Pass trailhead. From McCarthy Rd (see Access in the earlier Dixie Pass section) follow the rough dirt road north-west past the log cabins which belong to a handful of homesteaders. Within 2.5 miles the road arrives at a small clearing overlooking Strelna Creek where Kotsina Rd continues north and Nugget Creek Trail crosses the stream, the start of the trek. There is parking here for up to six cars. Transport to the junction of McCarthy and Nugget Creek/Kotsina Rds can be arranged through Backcountry Connection (see Access in the earlier Dixie Pass section).

Stage 1: Kotsina Rd to Sheep Creek

(8 miles, 5-6 hours)
(Backcountry camping)
From the parking area, you immediately cross Strelna Creek, the first of seven named creeks you have to cross to reach the NPS cabin. Strelna is manageable most of the time but high water can mean a quick end to this adventure. On the other side you climb up the bank and enter the forest along an old miner's pack trail that today also accommodates mountain bikers and even off-road vehicles occasionally. You will have little difficulty following the trail.

The beginning of the trail can be wet and quite boggy in places, be prepared to get your boots muddy negotiating a route through the ooze. The worst section is reached half a mile into the hike and you really don't escape it for good until the trail starts climbing gently, 3.5 miles from the trailhead. Eventually you reach 2000 feet and cross Dry Creek.

At this point the trail becomes a rolling wooded miners' road through the forest as it heads north-east along a low bench above the Kuskulana River. You don't actually see the river, in fact you don't see much of anything because you never leave the forest even when you cross Nugget Creek towards the end of the trail. You reach Squaw Creek two miles from Dry Creek, or six miles from the trailhead, and will find camping spots on the banks of this small but clear stream.

It's less than two miles to Sheep Creek, where just after fording it you will find the best spots on the banks of the stream to set up camp for the first night. Sheep Creek is also a clear-running stream.

Stage 2: Sheep Creek to NPS Cabin

(6.5 miles, 4-5 hours)
(Free-use shelter, backcountry camping)
The second day is a considerably drier, easier trek. Within 1.5 miles of Sheep Creek you

cross the appropriately named Clear Creek, descend slightly and then three miles into the trek cross Porcupine Creek. In another mile, the trail swings to its closest point with the Kuskulana River, though you still remain in a forested setting, and then begins a wide swing to the north-east.

The final leg is a three-mile march along a trail that gently climbs a couple of hundred feet and ends when you break out at the banks of Nugget Creek. The creek itself is a silty, braided glacial run-off that can usually be easily forded but may give you problems immediately after a heavy rainstorm or in early summer.

On the other side of the creek is an old miners' cabin that is owned by the NPS. The rustic log structure is not maintained, however, but is bear-proof, will keep you dry during a storm and has three bunks and a wood-burning stove. If there are too many mice running around the cabin for your taste, campsites abound in this area. It's even possible to set up the tent within view of Kuskulana Glacier, a gravel-covered ice floe. As inviting as it may seem, it's best to stay off the glacier unless you have the knowledge, expertise and equipment to hike on ice.

A better adventure is to continue along the trail as it leaves the cabin and steeply climbs almost 1000 feet in its final two miles, terminating at 4000 feet, well above the tree line. Along the way you pass a few historical miners' building and even an old horse stable. The trail ends near a private mining claim. From here it's easy to access the surrounding alpine area for day hikes along the ridge lines.

Stage 3: The Return – Nugget Creek to Kotsina Rd

(14.5 miles, 8-10 hours)
Being a one-way trail you must backtrack to where you started. If you are fit and have a light load you can probably cover the entire 14.5 miles in under seven hours, cutting a day off the return and using it for day hiking in the alpine areas at the end of the route. On

a mountain bike you'd cover the route in under three hours.

BONANZA MINE TRAIL

Out of all the hiking possibilities in the McCarthy/Kennicott area, Bonanza Mine offers the most developed route to the alpine region and spectacular views of the surrounding mountains and glaciers. Even more intriguing for many are the mining artefacts that litter this trail from beginning to end. It's a delightful hike when the weather is pleasant; haul up a tent and you can camp among the peaks above the tree line. Beware – even when the skies are blue and the sun is shining, it's a hard climb to the historic mine at the top.

You gain 4500 feet in the four-mile one-way trek and a good portion of it is a heart-pounding climb on a moderately steep slope. The trail is actually a rough dirt road to the tree line, picked up just west of the Kennicott ruins. Once above the brush (a three to four-hour climb for most trekkers), the views are stunning.

Like the Chilkoot Trail, this is a hike into history. The best way to begin is to stop at the McCarthy & Kennicott Museum – an old railroad depot that features faded photographs and dusty artefacts dating back to the days when Kennicott was the world's greatest producer of copper. The museum's brochure, *Walking Tour of Kennicott Alaska* ($1), describes the buildings in Kennicott that you'll pass through.

Pack extra water because there is none until you are near the end of the trail. And pack extra time if at all possible. The hike requires at least a full afternoon and, after working so hard to reach the area, it's a shame to have to rush back down. You could easily spend a whole day examining what the miners left behind or enjoying the mountaintop panoramas.

The hike is rated moderate because, though it is a steep climb, it is easy to follow. Arrange a ride to the tree line (see Access) and it becomes an easy trek. The area is covered on USGS 1:63,360 quads *McCarthy B-5*, *B-6* and *C-5*, though this is one of the

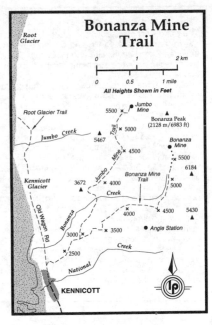

few hikes that the quads are not really necessary – just follow the road.

Access

If you don't have a vehicle or are not up to hitching, you can reach the Kennicott River with Backcountry Connection (☎ 822-5292), which will drop you off at the foot of the tram. Once you're across the glaciated river on the hand-pulled cart, follow the road to the McCarthy River that can now be crossed on a foot bridge. On the other side of the river the road leads half a mile to the former railroad depot and a fork in the road. To reach the town of McCarthy take the right-hand fork. To continue on to Kennicott and the Bonanza Mine trailhead, take the left-hand fork.

Kennicott is reached by either walking the railroad grade, now the main road, or by hiking the Old Wagon Rd. The Old Wagon Rd is more of a trail for hiking and mountain bikes and is picked up from the main road at

The Green Grass of Copper

The world's richest deposit of copper began as a patch of grass in 1900, when a pair of sourdough miners named Jack Smith and Clarence Warner spotted a large green spot on the mountain between Kennicott Glacier and McCarthy Creek. But after climbing the east side of the glacier, the prospectors were dumbfounded to discover that the grass was huge chunks of almost pure copper. The entire mountainside, in fact, held some of the richest copper ever uncovered. In the Lower 48, mines were operating on ore that contained only 2% copper. Here, the veins that miners eventually uncovered contained a copper average of almost 13%, some as high as 70%.

Eventually, a group of East Coast investors bought the existing stakes and formed the Kennecott Copper Corporation, named after a clerical worked misspelled 'Kennicott'. The first major hurdle was transporting the copper ore from the mines to the coastal town of Cordova, where it would be shipped to Tacoma, Washington for smelting.

For this task the syndicate called on Michael J Heney, the legendary railroad builder who was responsible for laying down the tracks of the White Pass & Yukon Railroad during the height of the Klondike Gold Rush. In the spring of 1908, construction began on the Copper River & Northwestern Railroad and most observers doubted that the 196-mile line through the wilderness could ever be built. To many, CR&NW stood for 'can't run and never will'. The amazing Heney proved them wrong by building a $23-million railroad that included Cordova's famous Million Dollar Bridge around Childs Glacier, and cutting the bed for what is now the McCarthy Rd.

Next, the syndicate built the company town of Kennicott, a sprawling red-painted complex that included offices, the crushing mills, bunkhouses for the workers, company stores, a theater, wooden tennis courts and a school, all perched on the side of a mountain above Kennicott Glacier. From 1911 until 1938, the mines operated 24 hours a day, produced 591,000 tons of copper and reported a net profit of more than $100 million.

But in November 1938, faced with falling world prices for copper, an uncertainty of how long the veins would pay out and, most of all, a possible labor strike, the company managers decided

a junction marked with a 'To Glacier' sign. Either way it's a five-mile trek.

It's always possible to hitch a ride up during the summer as there is a trickle of traffic between the two towns. There is also van transport; both Wrangell Mountain Air and McCarthy Air run between the two towns, charging $5 one way. Pick up the van at their log-cabin offices in McCarthy or at the Kennicott Glacier Lodge at Kennicott. You can also pedal to Kennicott as mountain bikes are the choice of transport for most of the locals. You'll be amazed how many zip past you in the morning as riders hurry off to work. If you didn't haul your own bike over on the tram, you can rent a Diamond Back mountain bike from St Elias Alpine Guides (☎ (907) 277-6867 in Anchorage) for $25 per day.

Once in Kennicott, if you want to skip the long haul up but still enjoy the alpine portion of the hike, check at the Kennicott Glacier Lodge to see if anybody is driving hikers up. Normally a local will run you to the tree line

for $15 one way or $20 round trip. From there it's still a good 90-minute trek to the mine.

Stage 1: Kennicott to Bonanza Mine
(4 miles, 5-7 hours)
(Backcountry camping)
From the Kennicott Glacier Lodge, walk past the huge red concentration mill and out of town, heading west on the Old Wagon Rd towards Root Glacier. The first junction is Silk Stocking Rd, where you turn right and follow it briefly as it curves back towards town. The next junction is with the Bonanza Mine Trail. Hang a left and start climbing.

In a quarter of a mile the road passes underneath the Jumbo Tramway and in another mile or so passes the junction to Jumbo Mine itself, though it's not marked or even well defined and most hikers frequently miss it. If you can find the start of the over-grown road to Jumbo Mine, it can be followed for roughly three miles to the ruins of Jumbo Mine situated on a rock glacier to close the operation. They made the decision one night and then the next morning told the workers that the mine was shut down and they could stay or leave but in two hours the last train out of Kennicott was leaving. The disgruntled miners left in what was one of the greatest exoduses of a US town.

What was left behind was a perfectly preserved slice of US mining history. Despite the pillage by thoughtless tourists in the 1970s after the McCarthy Rd opened up, Kennicott is still an amazing sight. The mill where the ore was crushed and where the copper was concentrated, towers above the surrounding buildings. Tram cables still lead up the mountain to the Bonanza and Jumbo mines. The rest of the buildings, including the bunkhouses, train depot, workers' cottages and power plant, sit perched above the Kennicott Glacier with peaks all around.

Keep in mind that most, if not all, the buildings are privately owned and it is illegal to enter them. Eventually several of the larger ones, the mill and power plant among others, will probably be acquired and renovated by the NPS as part of Wrangell-St Elias National Park but that will take years. Until then, you have to be content with strolling down the center of town and admiring the mining history through the windows.

Kennicott was a company town, self contained and serious. McCarthy, on the other hand, was created in the early 1900s for the miners as a place of 'wine, women and song'. In its heyday it featured several saloons, restaurants and a red-light district as well as several hundred residents, its own newspaper and a school. Today both O'Neill's Hardware Store and Mother Lode Power House, the site of St Elias Alpine Guides, has been listed on the National Register of Historical Places.

For a guided walk through Kennicott, search out Chris Richards, the town's only legally registered voter. The year-round resident lives across the street from the Kennicott Glacier Lodge and has a call box on the street – Kennicott-McCarthy Wilderness Guides. He provides a colorful 1½-hour tour of the mines for $12.50 per person, and explains what it is like to live in a one-person town in the winter (he reads a lot!). ∎

below Bonanza Peak (6983 feet). The trail crosses Bonanza Creek within a mile and then reaches the alpine tundra at 3700 feet.

There's no losing Bonanza Mine Trail, however. It continues to climb steeply along a series of switchbacks and soon spruce gives way to alder which gives way to lower brush and finally your first views of the surrounding mountains. Once above the tree line you are generally greeted with a 180-degree panorama of Mt Blackburn, Kennicott and Root glaciers and the Kennicott River.

From the start of the mining road, it takes most hikers three hours or more to reach a short spur where 4WD pick-ups drop off their passengers and park for the day. At this point you're still a good 90 minutes to two hours from the mine but it's by far the most enjoyable stretch of the hike.

The road becomes a narrow foot path that first follows a ridge line and then skirts the slope of a small rock knob. As you circle the knob into the final valley, the glory of the Kennicott mining era becomes apparent. At

one point you can look down and see the tram station, where miners switched trams, and then follow the cables up the mountain until they cross the trail right in front of your boots.

The final leg of the trek enters the valley. Here the trail clings to the valley's steep edge as it heads straight for the mine at the head of it. Halfway up, you come to the only source of water on the hike, a small mountain creek. Where you cross the creek is an area littered by mining artefacts: engines, wheels, parts of a building, the chassis of an old truck etc. There is also a wooden platform here that appears to be the floor of an old building. Use it as a convenient campsite for a free-standing dome tent.

From the stream the trail continues to climb, ending in an amphitheater with the mine perched up on one side. At the mine there are old bunkhouses, a tram station and other old buildings. The final climb to the site is a hard one across a steep slope of loose rock and scree. You should avoid entering the buildings or structures as they have long passed the stage of being safe to enter.

Stage 2: The Return – Bonanza Mine to Kennicott
(4 miles, 2-3 hours)

It's possible to camp in the high alpine area of the Bonanza Mine and if the weather is clear such an evening would be far more enjoyable than battling the hoards of RVers at the end of McCarthy Rd. Keep in mind that the surrounding ridges are not the best for day hiking as they are composed of loose scree, commonly referred to as 'rotten rock'.

The only way to return is the way you came up. If it took you five hours to climb to the mine site, you can make it down in half the time but should avoid the urge to run down the trail, even though gravity is pulling at you. Rest often on the way down or else you'll pay a heavy price the next morning with aching knees and ankles.

Rock formations, Pinnell Mountain Trail (JD)

Top: Taking a break during a midnight softball competition at Talkeetna (JW)
Middle: Competitors from the annual Iditarod foot race (JW)
Bottom: Preparing dinner in the backcountry (AD)

Denali

Once you give a mountain a name it's hard to take it back. In 1896, gold miner William Dickey named what he was sure was the tallest mountain in Alaska, Mt McKinley, in honor of the Ohio governor. A year later William McKinley became the 27th US president and the name stuck even though he never saw the peak that honors him or even set foot in the land it crowns.

This irked many Alaskans who protested angrily in 1980. As part of the battle over the Alaska National Interest Lands Conservation Act, Alaskans wanted to change the name back to Denali, the original Athabascan name that meant 'the high one'. But Ohio has a lot more political muscle in the nation's capital than Alaska does and the highest peak in North America remained named in honor of McKinley.

As a result of the 1980 Alaska Lands Bill, however, what was then called Mt McKinley National Park was enlarged to six million acres (larger than the state of Massachusetts) and redesignated as Denali National Park & Preserve. Ironically, today it's 'Denali' that conjures up the most vivid images among trekkers in the USA and around the world. For them it is the ultimate wilderness destination where they can throw on a backpack and follow treeless valleys and experience the wonders of wildlife. Say Denali, not McKinley, to a backpacker and they'll begin dreaming about a week in the wilderness.

Since the passage of the Alaska Lands Bill, this huge slice of Interior Alaska has been managed as three distinct units by the NPS. Denali Wilderness is the original national park and it is administered as a wilderness area, prohibiting fires and pets, and enforcing strict regulations for backcountry use and travel. The additions to Denali National Park in 1980 practically surround the original park and allow traditional subsistence use by local rural residents. Denali National Preserve – large tracts in the north-west and south-west corners of the

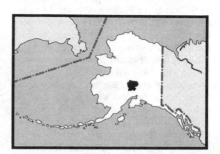

park – allows sport hunting, trapping and fishing.

Denali National Park

Denali Wilderness, with its park road, campgrounds, visitors' center at Eielson, and easy access to the backcountry draws the attention of both tourists and trekkers. Few backpackers enter the new park land with the exception of a trickle through Cantwell. Virtually no visitors explore the preserve areas.

Despite the size of the park tripling, trekkers are still concentrated in what is a relatively small section. In a modern day paradox, we're so eager to 'get away from it all' that we're overrunning Denali. In 1993, the park attracted more than 800,000 visitors for the first time, and topping a million is probably just a few seasons away.

Combine the park's easy viewing of wildlife and the grandeur of Mt McKinley with its wilderness reputation throughout the world, and suddenly the crowds are easy to understand. From late June to early September, Denali National Park is a busy and popular place. Riley Creek Campground overflows with campervans, nearby Morino Campground is crowded with backpackers, and the park's hotel is bustling with large tour groups. Pursuing shuttle-bus seats, backcountry permits and campground reservations at the Visitor Access Center (VAC) often creates long, Disneyland-type lines.

Although the crowds disappear once you are hiking in the backcountry (thanks to the backpackers' permit system), many people think they can avoid the long lines by visiting the park in early June or late September. Mid-September can be particularly pleasant as the bugs are gone and fall colors are sweeping through the area with valleys going from a dull green to a fiery red, while willow turns shades of yellow and gold. The problem is that the popularity of the park has been so great that in recent years the shuttle buses have stopped running before the crowds have thinned out. The park shuttle bus is your ticket into the backcountry. The service discontinues in the second week of September and a four-day vehicle lottery follows when 300 private cars a day are allowed into the park. The road is then closed to all traffic until the following May.

By late September, however, the snow has usually arrived and another backpacking season is over in the park. The crowds do begin to diminish somewhat in late August and early September but getting coupons for the shuttle bus, a campground site or a backcountry permit will still be an agonizing challenge.

Your best bet is to pack extra days. If all you want to do is camp at the entrance and take the shuttle bus out the road one day, a minimum of four days is needed at the park, possibly five if you arrive at the height of the season. If you want to put together a two or three-day trek into the backcountry, you'll need at least seven days. There's no getting around this because at the height of the tourist season you'll waste one day outside the park waiting to get into the Riley Creek area. You'll use another day or two waiting for a campground or backcountry area to become available unless you've managed to reserve a shuttle-bus seat or campground site in advance at either of the Public Lands Information Center offices in Anchorage or Fairbanks (see Shuttle Bus or Park Campgrounds, below).

In the end, however, if you are patient and follow the system, you will get into the backcountry and then, thanks to the rules and permit limits you were cussing just a day before, you will enjoy a quality wilderness experience.

Natural History

Situated on the northern and southern flanks of the Alaska Range, 237 miles from Anchorage and about half that distance from Fairbanks, Denali is the nation's first subarctic national park. Within it roam 37 species of mammals, ranging from lynx, marmots and dall sheep to foxes and snowshoe hares, while 130 different bird species have been spotted, including the impressive golden eagle. Most visitors, however, want to see four animals in particular: moose, caribou, wolf and the brown bear. If you see all four from the shuttle bus, it's a rare 'grand slam' according to the drivers.

There are an estimated 200 to 300 brown bears in the park and another 200 black bears, most of them west of Wonder Lake. It's everybody's favorite, the brown or grizzly bear, that is almost always seen while you're on the shuttle bus. Since Denali's streams are mostly glacially fed, the fishing is poor so subsequently the diet of the bears is 85% vegetable materials. This accounts for their small size. Most males range from only 300 to 600 pounds while their cousins on the salmon-rich coasts can easily top 1000 pounds. In the backcountry during the summer, grizzlies are usually seen traveling along river bars or on the open tundra. Their color can range from cream to dark brown while a distinct light brown is called the Toklat color phase, after the park's Toklat River.

All the caribou in the park belong to the Denali herd, one of 13 herds in Alaska, which fluctuates between 2500 and 3000 animals. Since the park has been enlarged, the entire range of the herd, from its calving grounds to where it winters, is now in Denali. The best time to spot caribou is often late in the summer when the animals begin to band into groups of six to a dozen in anticipation

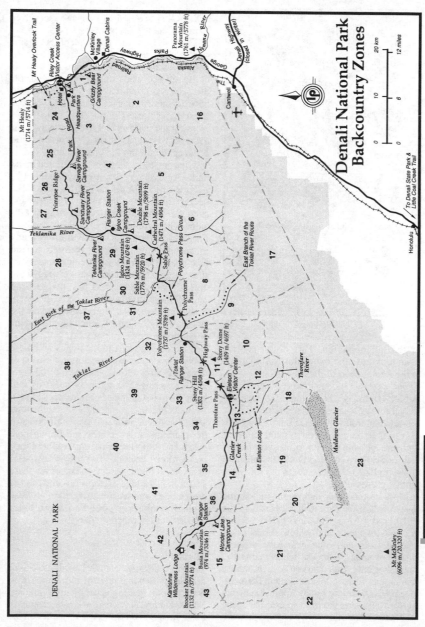

Denali National Park Backcountry Zones

Mt Healy Overlook Trail

Riley Creek
Visitor Access Center

Mt Healy
(1714 m/5574 ft)

McKinley
Village

Denali Cabins

Parks Highway

Railroad

Panorama
Mountain
(1761 m/5778 ft)

Nenana River

Denali Highway (closed in winter)

Hotel

Park
Road

Grizzly Bear
Campground

Park Headquarters

The George
Alaska

Cantwell

To Denali State Park &
Little Coal Creek Trail

Savage River
Campground

Primrose Ridge

Sanctuary River
Campground

Ranger Station

Igloo Creek
Campground

Double Mountain
(1798 m/5899 ft)

Cathedral Mountain
(1471 m/4904 ft)

Igloo Mountain
(1424 m/4749 ft)

Sable Mountain
(1776 m/5920 ft)

Sable Pass

Polychrome Pass Circuit

Teklanika River

Teklanika River
Campground

East Fork of the Toklat River

Polychrome Mountain
(1732 m/5789 ft)

Polychrome Pass

East Branch of the
Toklat River Route

Toklat River

Toklat
Ranger Station

Highway Pass

Stony Dome
(1409 m/4697 ft)

Stony Hill
(1362 m/4508 ft)

Eielson
Visitor Center

Thorofare Pass

Glacier Creek

Mt Eielson Loop

Thorofare River

Muldrow Glacier

Honolulu

DENALI NATIONAL PARK

Kantishna
Wilderness Lodge

Brooker Mountain
(1132 m/3774 ft)

Busia Mountain
(974 m/3246 ft)

Ranger Station

Wonder Lake
Campground

Mt McKinley
(6096 m/20,320 ft)

20 km

12 miles

DENALI

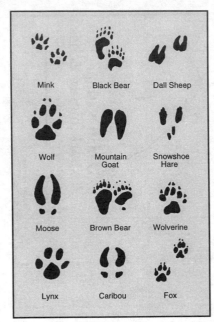

Wildlife tracks

of the fall migration. This often requires them to recross the mountains as they head to the western end of the park.

The best places to observe caribou are Sable, Highway, Thorofare, Grassy and Polychrome passes. In September, you may see caribou around Wonder Lake. They are easy to spot; their racks often stand four-feet high and look out of proportion to the rest of their body. Keep in mind that both bulls and cows, unlike other members of the deer family, grow antlers.

Most visitors will sight a moose on the eastern half of the park road, especially in the first 15 miles. Moose are almost always found in stands of spruce and willow shrubs (their favorite food) and often you have a better chance of seeing a moose while hiking the Horseshoe Lake Trail than you do in the tundra area around Eielson Visitor Center. There are roughly 2000 moose on the north side of the Alaska Range and the most spectacular scene in Denali comes in early September when the

bulls begin to clash their immense racks over breeding rights to a cow.

The wolf is the most difficult of the 'grand slam' four to see in the park. There is a stable population of 160 wolves and during much of the summer when small game is plentiful, the packs often break down and wolves become more solitary hunters. The best bet for most visitors is witnessing a lone wolf crossing the park road. Trekkers away from the road will occasionaly see wolves in the distance hunting in the open tundra.

There are more than 1000 dall sheep in the park. An average ram weighs around 160 pounds, the ewe around 110 pounds. Dall sheep forge predominantly on grasses, stunted willow and sedges on rugged hillsides. They winter in the foothills north of the park road and then in early summer many move south, often crossing the road, to feed near the headwaters of streams and rivers that drain the Alaska Range. Trekking around Polychrome Pass has always been one of the best places to spot dall sheep. Bands of sheep are often seen grazing the slopes of Igloo and Cathedral mountains near Igloo Creek Campground.

Trekkers who take to the ridges will inevitably encounter a hoary marmot, a cousin of the groundhog. Often when you're taking a break on a ridge the marmots' curiosity will bring them out of their holes for peek at you. At times like these, marmots are interesting, almost comical animals. In Denali, most of the marmots sport a grey-and-brown coat that blends into the talus slopes where they make their home. Marmots are social animals, so if you see one, chances are there are more in the area. Being a favorite food of brown bears and wolves, they often produce a shrill whistling sound to alert other marmots of approaching danger.

Climate

The Alaska Range causes Denali's weather to change often and rapidly, sometimes from hour to hour, making it very hard to predict. Mt McKinley is such a massive mountain that it literally creates its own weather on the north side where most of the trekking takes place. Annual precipitation is 15 inches, with rain in June, July and August accounting for more than half. On average, it will rain half of the days during the summer, much of it light showers or drizzle. In other words, be prepared for cool and cloudy conditions.

High temperatures in July average 66°F, in August only 63°F and in September 52°F. It's important to remember that it can, and has, snowed or dropped below freezing any day of the summer. Wild flowers, always a beautiful sight in the park, generally peak from mid-June to the end of July when the area enjoys from 18 to 19 hours of sunlight each day. Snow almost always closes the park road for good in September, usually by the third week.

Information

The new VAC (☎ 683-1266) near the entrance of the park is the place to organize your trip into the park and pick up permits and coupons as well as purchase topographic maps and books. The center is open daily during the summer from 7 am to 6 pm and queues begin forming outside the door at 6 am. At the height of the summer, there will often be more than 100 people in line and it's something of a stampede when the door is opened. This is necessary because shuttle-bus coupons and campsite reservations are handed out only two days in advance, backcountry permits one day in advance. It's almost imperative that you be at the VAC before 7 am to be able to book anything at all.

Within the VAC there is a bookstore, staff counters for backcountry permits, shuttle-bus coupons and campsite reservations as well as a video theater with shows every 10 and 40 minutes after the hour, and rest rooms. There is also an information area on other parks in Alaska and outside there is an information board listing all the park activities, a monitor that gives you a basic rundown on park procedures and storage lockers that are big enough for a backpack.

Eielson Visitor Center is a smaller center at *Mile 65* of the park road and features limited displays, a small bookstore and a great observation deck overlooking Mt McKinley. The ranger staff run their own hikes and naturalist programs. The center is open daily during the summer from 9 am to 6.30 pm.

If you're spending some time in Alaska you might be able to pick up campground reservations or shuttle-bus coupons in advance at the Public Lands Information Center offices in Anchorage and Fairbanks, and seek out the answers to most of your questions about visiting Denali (see those chapters for information on location and hours).

Fees Denali is one of the few national parks that charges an admission fee. It costs $3 per person to travel beyond the checkpoint at Savage River Campground or $5 per family. The fee is good for seven days in the park and is collected when you obtain a shuttle-bus coupon at the Riley Creek VAC. There is also a $4 shuttle-bus reservation fee. So when you

DENALI

Mt McKinley

In Denali National Park, the main attraction is Mt McKinley, an overwhelming sight on a clear day. At 20,320 feet, the peak of this massif is almost four miles high, but what makes it stunning is that it rises from an elevation of 2000 feet. From the park road or the backcountry you can see 18,000 feet (almost three miles) of rock, snow and glaciers reaching for the sky. In contrast, Mt Everest, the highest mountain in the world at 29,028 feet, only rises 11,000 feet from the Tibetan Plateau. Mt McKinley is such a massive mountain that when it's out, people in Fairbanks, Willow, Anchorage and even as far south as Hope and the Kenai Peninsula can see the peak. Unfortunately, the mountain isn't out all that often. The rule of thumb that park rangers use is that the mountain is hidden two out of every three days. Mt McKinley is so big, that it creates its own weather. Despite its Interior location, weather around it during the summer is typically cool, overcast and drizzly. ■

pick up the coupons you have to hand over $4. After that, the buses are free. Keep in mind this is only an entrance fee; you will still have to pay to stay in the park's campgrounds.

Permits For many people, the reason to come to Denali and endure the long lines at the VAC, is to escape into the backcountry for a true wilderness experience. Unlike many parks in the Lower 48, Denali's rigid restrictions ensure that you can trek and camp in a piece of wilderness that you can call your own, even if it's just for a few days.

The park is divided into 43 zones and in 37 of them only a regulated number of backpackers are allowed into each section at a time. You have to obtain a permit for the zone you want to stay overnight in, and that usually means waiting two days or more at Riley Creek until something opens up.

All of this is done at the VAC where at the Backcountry Desk you'll find two wall maps

DENALI

Packing a bear-resistant food container

with the zone outlines and a quota board indicating the number of vacancies in each unit. Permits are issued only a day in advance and at first glance most backpackers are horrified to find most units full for two or three days in a row.

Like getting into the campgrounds, the key to obtaining a permit is to first get into the backcountry. Once you're in, you can book a string of other units throughout the park for the next 14 days. Units that are easier to obtain include Nos 1, 2, 3 and 24 because they surround the park entrance and are heavily wooded. Spend a night or two here and then jump on a shuttle bus for a more favorable one deeper in the park. At the opposite end of the park are most of the zones with unlimited access. These tend to be areas of extensive tussock where the trekking is extremely difficult or involves a major fording of the McKinley River, a difficult feat even when the river is low. Again by camping here, you can enter the backcountry immediately and then book other units as they become available, bypassing the one-day-in-advance restriction.

Although any regulated zone can be filled, you'll generally find the more popular ones to be Nos 12, 13 and 18 in the tundra area south of Eielson Visitor Center; Nos 8, 9, 10 and 11 which include both branches of the Toklat River and tundra area south of Polychrome Pass; No 27 north of Sanctuary River Campground; and No 15, the unit just west of Wonder Lake.

The first step in the permit process is to watch the Backcountry Simulator Program in a video booth in the VAC. It's an interactive video that covers such topics as dealing with bears and backcountry travel. Then check which units might be closed due to bear activity or recent wolf kills. Check the quota board for an area that you can access within a day and finally, approach the ranger behind the desk to outline your entire backcountry itinerary.

Along with your permit, you'll receive a bear-resistant food container, free of charge, for food storage in the backcountry. They're bulky but they work. Since first using the

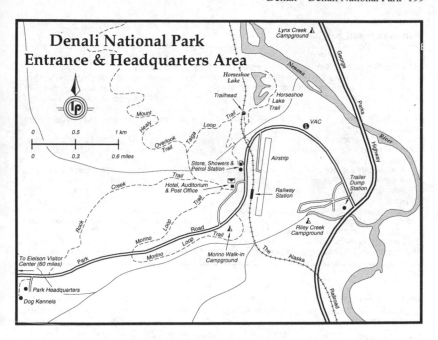

Denali National Park Entrance & Headquarters Area

containers in 1986, bear encounters in the park have dropped by 90%. Next, shuffle over to the shuttle-bus counter and sign up for a camper bus and then head over to the bookstore to purchase whatever topographical maps you will need; $2.50 each for the 1:63,000 scale topos.

It's important to realize that Denali is a trail-less park and the key to successful backcountry travel is being able to read a topographical map. You must be able to interpret the contours (elevation lines) on the map into the land formations in front of you. River beds are easy to follow and make the best avenues for the backpacker, and wildlife for that matter, as they provide mild grades, unobstructed views and solid footing. But they almost always involve fording a river. Pack a pair of tennis shoes or sport sandals for this.

Ridges are also good routes to hike if the weather is not foul. The tree line in Denali is at 2500 feet and above that you usually will find tussock or moist tundra – humps of grass and willow hummocks with water between to make for sloppy hiking. In extensive stretches of tussock, the hiking has been best described as 'walking on basketballs'. Above 3400 feet you'll encounter alpine or dry tundra which generally makes for excellent trekking. Avoid scree-covered slopes if you can, however, as footing here will inevitably be loose.

Regardless of where you are headed, five miles of backcountry trekking in Denali is a full day for the average backpacker. The NPS suggests that if there are three or four people in your party, try to stick to river beds, spread out, and avoid following each other as you will heavily damage the frail ground vegetation. Everybody in the backcountry should avoid camping in the same spot for more than two nights.

Three of the four hikes described here are in Denali's backcountry and three of them are routes, not trails by any means. They

On the Doorstep of Denali

Ultimately, there will be two entry points for Denali National Park. The congestion at the present entrance area around Riley Creek is so bad that in 1993, the NPS developed four plans aimed at siphoning some of the traffic to the south side of the park near Cantwell and Talkeetna.

The park staff favor the South Slope Denali plan, which proposes little development in the park itself, focusing on tourist facilities along the George Parks Hwy. The facilities would include six roadside exhibits and a visitors' center in both Denali State Park and Talkeetna. The only development in the park would be 42 miles of maintained trails that would allow trekkers to hike through the dense forest and across glacial rivers that presently prevent most people from backpacking on this side.

One of the proposed trails is a 27-mile trek from Cantwell along Windy Creek through a pass in the Alaska Range to Riley Creek on the north side. It ends at the VAC and passes two public-use cabins along the way.

The other plans propose building more trails and cabins. One calls for constructing eight cabins and cutting 183 miles of trails on the south side, including a 26-mile high-country loop off Petersville Rd, and a 22-mile trail along Alder Creek into the alpine areas at the snout of Ruth Glacier.

The exception to the development is the final plan, which proposes no action. This is the plan favored by officials in Denali State Park who fear that the fragile nature of their area will quickly be overrun by tourists and trekkers attracted to the national park's south side. Although something will eventually have to be done to reduce the crowds on the doorstep of Denali Wilderness, it will be years before there are any public facilities or trails on the south side of Mt McKinley. ■

involve following rivers or passes and are only described here to assist you to envision what the trek will involve. Mileage given is only a rough estimate; your exact distance will depend on the line you travel, where you choose to ford the river, etc. The routes – Polychrome Pass Circuit, East Branch of the Toklat River Route, and Mt Eielson Loop – also follow some of the best areas for trekking in the park thus there will be a heavy demand for the limited number of permits in their zones. You most likely will have to explore a different zone in the backcountry before being able to obtain a permit to explore an area like the East Branch of the Toklat River Route. The fourth hike, Mt Healy Overlook Trail, is a maintained trail but by far the most challenging trek in the Denali entrance area.

For the best overview of the different zones in the park, purchase the book *Backcountry Companion for Denali National Park* by Jon Nierenberg (Alaska National History Association, 605 West 4th Ave, Anchorage, AK 99501; 94 pages, $8.95). It's available at both the VAC and park hotel gift shop.

Places to Stay

Park Campgrounds The only way you can reserve a campsite before arriving at the park is through the Public Lands Information Center offices in Anchorage and Fairbanks. Like the bus coupons, the centers have a very limited number of sites available 21 days in advance and they tend to be snapped up quickly. Otherwise the campgrounds are filled on a first-come first-serve basis at the Riley Creek VAC two days in advance.

The key to getting into the campground of your choice, like Wonder Lake, is to just get into a campground, any campground (including either Morino or Riley Creek). Once in, you can secure a guaranteed site for the next 14 days in another campground when there is an opening. With this system, you can still get to Wonder Lake even during the busiest time of the year if you are willing to camp elsewhere in the park for four or five days. This is especially easy for walk-in travelers who can immediately pitch a tent in Morino Campground then return to the VAC that afternoon to book other campgrounds as soon as there are openings. The limit on staying in one campground or in a combination of them is 14 days.

The campground at the main entrance of the park is *Riley Creek*, the largest and nicest facility in Denali as well as the only one open year-round. A quarter of a mile west of Parks Hwy, Riley Creek has 102 sites, piped-in water, flush toilets and evening interpretive programs. The nightly fee is $12. Popular with RVers, in fact overrun by RVers, this is the only campground where sites are assigned at the visitors' center.

Near the railroad depot, *Morino* is a walk-in campground for backpackers without vehicles, providing only two metal caches to keep your food away from the bears, piped-in water and vault toilets. Though its capacity is listed as 60 persons, it's rare for anybody to be turned away. During much of the summer, however, this place can be packed and rangers are very strict about not allowing people to pitch a tent beyond the campground. The nightly fee is $3 per person (note that's per person not per site) and you self-register after pitching your tent.

Despite its name, *Savage River* at *Mile 13*, is a mile short of the actual river. It is one of only two campgrounds with a view of Mt McKinley. It has 34 sites that can accommodate both RVers and those with tents. It has water, flush toilets and evening interpretive programs. Those with a vehicle can drive to this campground. The nightly fee is $12.

Sanctuary River is the next campground down the road, at *Mile 23* on the banks of a large glacial river. There are seven sites for tents only and no piped-in water. It's a free facility, however, in a great area for day hiking. You can either head south along Sanctuary River or make a day out of climbing Mt Wright or Primrose Ridge to the north for an opportunity to see and photograph dall sheep.

At *Mile 29*, *Teklanika River* has 50 sites for either RVs or tents, piped-in water, evening programs, and costs $12 a night. You must book this one for a minimum of three days due to the fact that you are allowed to drive to the campground. Registered campers are issued a road pass for a single trip to the facility and then must leave their vehicles parked until they are ready to return to Riley Creek.

Igloo Creek is another free and waterless facility. Located at *Mile 34* it has seven sites

limited to tents. The day hiking in this area is excellent, especially on the numerous ridges around Igloo Mountain, Cathedral Mountain and Sable Pass that provide good routes into the alpine region.

The jewel of the Denali campgrounds is *Wonder Lake* at *Mile 85* of the park road. It has immense views of Mt McKinley, 28 sites for tents only, flush toilets and piped-in water. The nightly fee is $12. Pack plenty of insect repellent and maybe even a head net. In midsummer the bugs are vicious.

Other Park Accommodations Those opposed to sleeping in a tent have few alternatives at the main entrance of the park. The *Denali National Park Hotel* (☎ 683-2215 in the summer) only offers rooms that begin at $125 for two people per night. At the end of August, the hotel switches to its fall rates and rooms drop as low as $79 for a double.

Outside the Park On the edge of the wilderness area, there is a wide range of private campgrounds, cabins, hostels and other accommodations. Included among these are several private campgrounds where you can expect to pay from $10 to $15 for a campsite. The closest is the *Lynx Creek Campground* (☎ 683-2548), a mile north of the park entrance on George Parks Hwy. Campsites are $15 a night for tents, $20 for a full hook-up. The price includes showers. There is a store and pub on site.

Six miles south of the park entrance is the *Denali Grizzly Bear Campground* (☎ 683-2696) which offers campsites for $15 a night, tents for rent, cabins with cooking facilities and coin-operated showers. Near Healy, a small town 11 miles north of the park entrance, there is the *McKinley KOA* (☎ 683-2379), which has tent sites, a store and provides bus rides to the Riley Creek VAC.

If there are three or four people in your party, consider booking a cabin in advance. *Denali Cabins* (☎ 683-2643 during the summer) have large cedar cabins for one to four people with outdoor hot tub for $118 per night for two people. The cabins are a mile north of the park entrance at *Mile 238* of

DENALI

George Parks Hwy and there is a free shuttle-bus service to the entrance. Nearby at *Mile 238.5* of George Parks Hwy is *Denali Crow's Nest Log Cabins* (☎ 683-2723), looking like a Swiss Alpine village on the edge of Horseshoe Lake. Rates are the same as those for Denali Cabins.

There is also a pair of backpackers' hostels near the park. *Denali Hostel* (☎ 683-1295) is in Healy and has bunks for $22 a night along with kitchen facilities, showers and transportation back to the park. If you arrive on the train, there will be a Denali Hostel van at the depot. *The Happy Wanderer Hostel* (☎ 683-2690 or 683-2360) is closer to the park entrance at *Mile 238.6* of George Parks Hwy. It has eight beds; $15 a night.

For those with an RV, van or even a car, who arrive late, there are large gravel pull-outs north of the park entrance on both sides of George Parks Hwy where you can stop and spend the night in a pinch. There are almost a dozen of them between Healy and the park entrance and throughout the summer you'll see eight to 10 vehicles at each one every night.

Maps

Although trail-less, for the most part Denali is also treeless, allowing for far easier orientation than if you were hiking down a wooded trail in the Kenai Peninsula. The tree line at Denali is at 2500 feet; if you get lost, simply climb the nearest ridge for an overview of the area you are in.

Without trails or markers of any kind, a set of USGS 1:63,360 series quads is crucial. The USGS has a park map with a scale of 1:250,000, and Trails Illustrated sells *Denali National Park & Preserve* with a scale of 1:200,000 for $7.95. With detail at this scale, the maps are good for an overview of the park but should not be used for an extended trek in the backcountry.

The best place to purchase your maps is at the VAC after consulting rangers about your itinerary and obtaining a backcountry permit.

Equipment

A ban on fires in the Denali backcountry is strictly enforced so you'll need a camp stove. Purchase most of your supplies at the last major town you depart from, whether it is Anchorage, Wasilla or Talkeetna. Within the park *McKinley Mercantile*, a block from the hotel, sells a variety of food including dried items, some canned goods and other supplies. But the fact that it has a larger selection of wine than it does freeze-dried dinners should tell you something. It's open from 8 am to 11 pm during the summer and showers ($2) are available. Outside there is a larger store at Lynx Creek Campground.

Cabins

There are no cabins or any other kind of free-use shelters or structures within Denali Wilderness.

Trails

Even for those who have neither the desire nor the equipment for an overnight trek, hiking is still the best way to enjoy the park and to obtain a personal closeness with the land and its wildlife. The best way to undertake a day hike is to ride the shuttle bus and get off at any valley, river bed or ridge that takes your fancy. No backcountry permit is needed. There are few trails in the park as most hiking is done across open terrain. When you've had enough for one day, return to the road and flag down the first bus going in your direction.

You can hike virtually anywhere in the park that hasn't been closed because of the impact on wildlife. Popular areas include the Teklanika River south of the park road, the Toklat River, the ridges near Polychrome Pass and the tundra areas near the Eielson Visitor Center.

The VAC also offers daily activities, including numerous guided walks in the park. Naturalist's walks are easy two-hour hikes in the entrance area of the park. They begin at either the park hotel or the VAC, and a list of them and their times is posted at both places. Taiga hikes are moderately hard walks in the entrance area trails that last from three to four hours. They are held at 12.30 pm daily; meet at the park hotel auditorium.

In the backcountry, there are discovery hikes where a naturalist leads groups of up to 16 people for a three to five-hour trek that can cover anywhere from three to six miles. These range from moderate walks to strenuous climbs up ridges. You have to sign up for discovery hikes at the VAC one or two days in advance and then obtain the necessary shuttle-bus coupon for a ride out to where it begins on the park road. Examples of these adventurous treks are hiking Hogan Creek up to Primrose Ridge, following the West Branch of the Toklat River Route, and exploring the tundra around Eielson Visitor Center for an old miner's cabin. At Eielson there is also a tundra walk offered daily at 1.30 pm which last from 30 minutes to an hour.

The only maintained trails in the park are found around the main entrance area. See the following descriptions.

Horseshoe Lake Trail This trail is a leisurely 1.5-mile walk through the woods to an overlook of the oxbow lake and then down a steep trail to the water. The trailhead is 0.9 miles on the park road where the railroad tracks cross. Follow the tracks north a short way to the wide gravel path.

Morino Loop Trail This leisurely walk of 1.3 miles can be picked up at the back of Morino Campground as well as from the park hotel parking lot. It offers good views of Hines and Riley creeks.

Taiga Loop Trail This is another easy hike that begins off the parking lot of the park hotel and loops 1.3 miles through the taiga forest.

Rock Creek Trail This moderate 2.3-mile walk connects the hotel area with the park headquarters and dog kennels area. The trail begins just before the park road crosses Rock Creek but doesn't stay with the stream. Instead it climbs a gentle slope of mixed aspen and spruce forest, breaks out along a ridge with scenic views of Mt Healy and the Parks Hwy and then begins a rapid downhill

descent to the service road behind the hotel and ends on the Taiga Loop Trail. It's far easier hiking the trail to the hotel as all the elevation is gained with the drive up the park road.

Getting There & Away

The entrance to Denali National Park & Preserve is at *Mile 237.3* of George Parks Hwy and close to the highway is the VAC and Riley Creek Campground. Thanks to the popularity of Denali, the highway before and after the park entrance has become a tourist strip of private campgrounds, lodges, restaurants and other businesses, all feeding off Alaska's most famous drawing card. Hitching to the park is considerably easier than hitching out of it; near the entrance there are often a dozen other hitchhikers trying to thumb a ride.

Bus Both north and southbound bus services are available to and from Denali National Park. From Anchorage, there is Moon Bay Express (☎ 274-6454) which runs a daily service to the park, leaving the Anchorage International Hostel at 8 am and arriving at the park at 1 pm. Also running the same route with the same departure point and times is Alaska Backpacker Shuttle (☎ 344-8775). Both depart from the VAC at 3 pm for the return trip south and charge $35 one way or $60 round trip.

From Fairbanks, Fireweed Express (☎ 488-7928) departs from the Fairbanks Visitor Center at 8 am and arrives at Denali at 10.30 am. It departs from the VAC at 4 pm, arriving in Fairbanks at 6.30 am. The one-way fare is $25.

Other bus companies that make the Denali run (everybody does) include Alaska Direct (☎ (800) 770-6652) and Denali Express (☎ 274-8539 or (800) 327-7651). Surprisingly, Gray Line's Alaskon Express does not run this route.

Train The most enjoyable way to arrive at the park is aboard The Alaska Railroad (see Train in the introductory Getting Around chapter) with its viewing-dome cars that

DENALI

provide sweeping views of Mt McKinley and the Susitna and Nenana river valleys along the way. All trains arrive at the railroad depot between the Riley Creek Campground and the park hotel, and only stay long enough for passengers to board.

You can only arrive at Denali on the express train; the northbound train leaves Anchorage at 8.30 am daily from late May to mid-September arriving in Denali at 3.45 pm. The southbound train leaves Fairbanks at 8.30 am, arriving in Denali at 12.15 pm. The one-way fare from Denali National Park to Anchorage is $88; to Fairbanks it's $48. If you're heading south, consider getting off at Talkeetna for a day.

Getting Around

Courtesy Bus There is free transportation to the park entrance and to just about anywhere you want to go. The park has blue courtesy buses that run every half-hour from 6.30 am to 9 pm. They begin at the VAC and their loop includes the park hotel, the railroad depot, Riley Creek Campground and points in between. The park also runs free buses to the sled-dog demonstrations, departing from the VAC a half-hour before each show.

To head to the campgrounds and cabins outside the park entrance, look for the cream-color buses at the park hotel. They are up and running by 5 am and don't quit until 11 pm. A schedule is posted in the hotel. If you want to go to Lynx Pizza Parlor, the Salmon Bake or anywhere north of the entrance, grab the bus for the McKinley Chalets; to go south, jump on the bus for McKinley Village.

Shuttle Bus What makes the park and its wildlife so accessible is the 91.6-mile park road that runs the length of the preserve and the free shuttle buses that use it. It was put into service in 1972 after the George Parks Hwy was opened and attendance in the park doubled in a single season. Park officials then put a ban on private vehicles to prevent the park road from becoming a highway of cars and RVers and today the wildlife is so accustomed to the rambling yellow school

buses that they rarely stop their activities when one passes by.

The buses provide access for day hikers for which backcountry permits are not needed. Once in the backcountry, you can stop a bus in either direction on the park road by flagging it down for a ride back or to go further into the park. Some photographers ride the bus only until wildlife is spotted. Changing buses several times each day is a practice commonly referred to as 'shuttle-bus surfing'. By all means get off the buses, only then will you truly see and experience the park, but remember you can only get back on if there is an available seat. No one is ever left out in the backcountry against their will but it's not too uncommon at the height of the season to have to wait two or three hours because the first four buses that pass by are full.

If you're planning to just spend the day riding the bus, carry a park map so you know where you are and what ridges or river beds appeal to you for day hiking later. Also pack plenty of food and drinks. It can be a long, dusty ride and there are no services in the park, not even a vending machine at Eielson Visitor Center. The best seats to grab are generally those at the front of the bus but if you end up in the back, don't be shy about leaning over somebody to get a view out of a window.

Buses leave the VAC for Eielson Visitor Center every half-hour from 6.30 am until 1.30 pm when the last bus departs. There are also five buses that go all the way to Wonder Lake. They depart from Riley Creek every hour from 6 to 10 am and return that day. It's an 11-hour trip to ride out to the end of the road and back, a long day on a school bus. The ride to Eielson is an eight-hour journey and passes the most spectacular mountain scenery by far. The only exception to this is when Mt McKinley is out, then the ride to Wonder Lake provides 11 of the most scenic hours you'll ever spend on a bus of any kind.

On the flip side, the last bus from Wonder Lake leaves at 4 pm, the last one from Eielson Visitor Center at around 5.25 am. Unless you're prepared to go backpacking, don't miss them!

Technically the buses are free but there is a $4 reservation fee that is paid when you obtain a coupon. The demand for the 40 seats on each bus is so heavy that park officials must hand out bus coupons for every available seat. The coupon guarantees you a seat on a particular bus, and in theory it should work.

The problem is the overwhelming demand for the coupons throughout much of the summer. Boarding coupons are available up to two days in advance of when the bus leaves. Throughout much of the summer, the coupons are gone by mid-morning for all the buses the next day. At the peak of the tourist season in July and early August, people are lining up at the VAC at 6 am, an hour before it opens, to be ensured of getting a coupon for a bus two days later. If you don't have a coupon, don't bother showing up for a bus, hoping somebody oversleeps. Generally no-shows account for 15% of the tickets but drivers leave the seats empty in order to pick up backpackers returning from a trek. All this is a bit of a shame as many visitors now don't dare leave the bus, even for a few hours for a hike in the backcountry, for fear of not getting a seat on the way back.

Try picking up your coupons at the Public Lands Information Center offices in Anchorage or Fairbanks. The two centers receive 10% of the bus coupons and you can pick them up 21 days in advance of the date they are issued for. In fact you almost have to pick them up this early because they tend to be snapped up by both locals and knowledgeable travelers the morning they become available.

Camper Bus Due to the popularity of the shuttle buses, the park has set up a camper-bus system. They're the same yellow school buses but a third of the seats have been removed to make room for backpacks and mountain bikes. Four camper buses leave the VAC daily at 7 and 10.30 am and 1.30 and 3.30 pm and they are free. If you get a campsite or backcountry permit, there is no hassle or wait to getting a coupon on the camper bus.

Boarding the shuttle bus,
Denali National Park

Tour Bus The park concessionaire operates a wildlife bus tour along the park road. The bus departs from the Denali National Park Hotel daily as often as there is demand for the seats. The six-hour tour, designed primarily for package-tour groups, costs $45 per person and goes to Stony Hill when the mountain is out, the Toklat River when it isn't. Reserve a seat the night before at the Denali National Park Hotel reservation desk (☎ 276-7234).

Mountain Bike An increasingly popular way to explore the park road is on a mountain bike. No special permit is needed to ride your bike on the road but you are not allowed to leave the road at anytime. Most bikers book a campground site at the VAC and then carry the bike on the camper bus, using it to explore the road from there. You can even book a string of campgrounds and ride with your equipment from one to the next. The nearest place to rent a mountain bike is *Mountain Bike Rentals* (☎ 683-1295), next door to the Denali Hostel on Otto Lake Rd. Rental rates are $25 for a day and $17 for a half-day. You can also rent mountain bikes in Talkeetna at *Bikes,*

DENALI

Flights, Etc (☎ 733-2692) and take them on the train.

MT HEALY OVERLOOK TRAIL

The only maintained trails in Denali National Park are in the entrance area. Of the handful of trails there, only the climb to Mt Healy Overlook truly lets you escape the crowds and the bustle of this area. It's a five-mile round trip from the park hotel that climbs 1700 feet.

The uphill effort will reward you with excellent views of the Nenana River valley, Healy Ridge and other ridge lines. The entire hike takes most people from three to four hours, so after spending a frustrating morning at the VAC, you have ample time to get this hike in before dinner.

The Mt Healy Overlook Trail is well maintained and rated moderate due to the steep climb. It's covered on USGS 1:63,360 series quad *Healy C-4*. No camping is

allowed anywhere along the trail because the route is within the day-use area of the park entrance.

Access

The trail begins near the Denali Park Hotel at the start of the park road, a five-minute walk from Morino Campground.

Stage 1: Park Hotel to Mt Healy Overlook

(2.5 miles, 2-3 hours)

The hike begins near the guest parking lot west of Denali Park Hotel at the Taiga Loop Trail trailhead. This trail loops behind the hotel, passes a junction to Rock Creek Trail and then comes to a service road, immediately followed by another one. At the second service road turn left and follow the road for about 50 yards to the trailhead of the Mt Healy Overlook Trail.

Once on the trail you'll quickly cross a bridge over Horseshoe Creek and then continue a moderately steep climb through a forest of spruce mixed with aspen and alder. A mile from the hotel, you reach the scenic viewpoint where you can gaze upon Mt Fellows to the east and the Alaska Range to the south. At this point the trail moves from stunted spruce into thickets of alder and at the base of a ridge begins to follow a series of switchbacks as it heads for Mt Healy Overlook. You reach 'Halfway Rock', a 12-foot boulder at 1.2 miles, which provides an opportunity for you to catch your breath.

The steep climb continues with the switchbacks becoming shorter and at 1.6 miles you move from a taiga zone of alder to the alpine tundra: a world of moss, lichen, wild flowers and incredible views. Keep an eye out for the large hoary marmot, a northern cousin of the groundhog, and the pika, a small relative of the rabbit. Pikas will often sit motionless on the large stones of a rock slide.

In the final 0.4 miles the trail emerges below Mt Healy Overlook. You then curve steeply around the ridge to emerge at the rocky bench that is the overlook. The trail actually ends at a rock pile, two miles from the hotel.

The view from the overlook is excellent.

Mt Healy
Overlook Trail

0   1   2 km

0   0.5   1 mile

All Heights Shown in Feet

Overlook
(1238 m / 4127 ft)

5000

4500

4000

3500

3000   2500

2000

Horseshoe Creek

Nenana River

The Alaska Railroad

Park Hotel &
Trailhead

Park Road

Sugar Loaf Mountain at 4450 feet dominates the horizon to the east while above the overlook to the north-west is the actual summit of Mt Healy. If you have a pair of binoculars, search the slopes to the north for dall sheep. If the weather is clear, look to the south-west for the Mt McKinley massif, some 80 miles away.

Stage 2: The Return
(2.5 miles, 1-2 hours)
The overlook is a rocky shoulder of the Healy Ridge (3500 feet), a climb of more than 1700 feet from the hotel. You can continue up the ridge on a more gentle climb for another mile to reach the high point of 4300 feet. The 5700-foot summit of Mt Healy is still another two miles to the north-west.

To return, you have little choice but to retrace the route that you just climbed. Take heart, however, in the knowledge that it will take far less time, perhaps half the hiking time, to go downhill than it did to go up.

POLYCHROME PASS CIRCUIT
This can be a long day hike for experienced backcountry travelers, or an overnight trek for everybody else, into one of the most scenic sections of the park. The brilliantly colored rocks of Polychrome Pass are the result of volcanic action some 60 million years ago. Today, the multicolored hills and mountains here, including 5790-foot-high Polychrome Mountain and 4961-foot-high Cain Peak, are a stunning sight in the low-angle light of a clear Alaska summer day.

The first leg of this trek, following the East Fork of the Toklat River north from the park road, is a challenging hike over rough tundra that may include climbing around cliffs. There is also a narrow canyon to bushwhack through at one point, giving this eight-mile loop off the park road a rating of moderate to challenging.

You have a good opportunity to spot wildlife in the Polychrome Pass area, especially dall sheep in early summer. Bears are also found here in good numbers. The entire route is covered on USGS 1:63,360 series quad *Healy C-6* and lies in backcountry zone No 31.

Access
Depart the camper bus at *Mile 42.7* of the park road, just after it crosses the bridge over the East Fork of the Toklat River. Normally there is a bus stop at the west side of the river.

Stage 1: East Fork River Bridge to 3300-Foot Pass
(3.5 miles, 4-5 hours)
(Backcountry camping)
The loop begins on the west side of the park road bridge across the East Fork. Downstream, or north from the bridge, the East Fork flows as a braided river across a wide gravel bar for almost eight miles until it enters a seven-mile long canyon. During periods of low to medium water levels there are enough braids in the river for a safe crossing. At other times its volume is too high to cross and that's when you might run into problems. While following the river along its west bank it's possible that deep channels may force you to climb up and around the bordering cliffs to bypass a stretch of steep banks.

It's 1.5 miles from the park road to the first major tributary flowing out of the hills south of Polychrome Mountain. Head upstream along the unnamed tributary for another 1.5 miles, fording to its west side at the best possible crossing. Just before the stream enters a mile-long canyon, a low pass will appear to the west. It's a 200-foot ascent to the pass that forms a saddle between a 3608-foot peak to the north and a 4222-foot peak to the south.

From the top of the pass, it's an easy stroll into the next valley where two streams converge. For those wanting to spend a night in the backcountry the pass or the bench on its west side are the best places to set up camp. The confluence of the two streams to the west is also a possibility but keep in mind that the valley forms a natural route for wildlife, that includes, of course, brown bears.

If you arrive in the morning and have an afternoon to kill, it's possible to climb the 4222-foot peak. The easiest route is from the pass along the ridge line that heads almost due south. Be cautious near the top, however,

DENALI

as the rock and scree slopes here can be loose and hazardous. If the day is clear the views of Mt McKinley are stunning from near the peak.

Stage 2: 3300-Foot Pass to Polychrome Pass Rest Area

(4.5 miles, 4-5 hours)
Descend to the confluence and hike down the valley along either side of the creek. The scenery will be dominated by the northern slopes of Polychrome Mountain, whose colors, especially in late August and early September, justify its name. In early summer, search the slopes for dall sheep.

Within half a mile upstream from the confluence, the stream enters a narrow canyon that will be filled with willow, dwarf birch and alder. Search for animal trails to follow for easier hiking through the narrow area. Most likely, however, you'll have to ford the stream a few times. Be wary as you travel

through the canyon. Your visibility will be limited by the brush, and bears often pass through here. Clap your hands, sing songs, argue loudly about politics. Do anything to make noise.

It takes a mile of bushwhacking through the canyon before the stream breaks out into a wide area of the valley. Travel is far easier now, though at times it can be boggy and wet. Within another mile you arrive at the source of the stream, a small lake often frequented by waterfowl. The lake is less than a quarter of a mile north of the park road.

The easiest way to return to Polychrome Pass Rest Area is to hike the road, enjoying the views to the south of Toklat River, other valleys and, if you're lucky, Mt McKinley. At the rest area you'll find vault toilets and covered benches but no source of water.

For those who want one last climb, skip the road and climb the 4000-foot ridge due east of the lake. It's manageable at first, steep

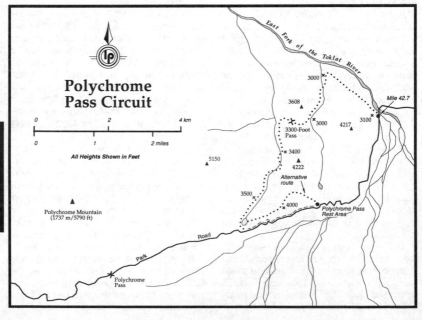

and loose at the end. Eventually you reach the 4200-foot high point and from there follow the ridge line to a low saddle at its north end. Head east from this pass, cross the bushy ravine and then climb a final hill where on the other side is Polychrome Pass Rest Area. You'll most likely see people on top of the hill, viewing Polychrome Mountain during their short bus stop.

EAST BRANCH OF THE TOKLAT RIVER ROUTE

Flowing north from glaciers in the Alaska Range are the West and East branches of the Toklat River that merge at *Mile 52.5* of the park road. Both are classic U-shaped glacially carved valleys where the rivers become braided channels across wide rocky bars. The East Branch is a particularly good area if you are new to Denali because you don't have to ford the Toklat River or any other major glacial streams to travel up the valley. There is also good visibility in all directions thanks to the surrounding vegetation of dry tundra and sparse willow while the rocky river bed provides sure footing.

The trek can be either a day hike or an overnight trek where you could hike six miles or so up the valley and then spend a morning or a day exploring the area before returning along the same route. This would make a round trip of 12 to 18 miles and provide you with a reasonably good chance of seeing wildlife. Small bands of caribou are often viewed on the river beds throughout the summer while dall sheep can be spotted on the ridges and slopes above. Grizzlies travel the route as well, to feed on the soapberry crop.

The required USGS 1:63,360 series topos are *Healy C-6*, *B-6* and *Mt McKinley C-1*, although all but the first mile falls on *Healy B-6*. This trip is rated moderate in difficulty and falls into backcountry zone 9, a tough one to secure a permit in.

Access

Depart the camper bus at the bridge over the Toklat River, *Mile 52.4* of the park road.

Stage 1: Toklat River Bridge to Upper Toklat Valley

(6 miles, 5-7 hours)
(Backcountry camping)

The Toklat River Bridge marks where the East Branch and the main branch of the Toklat River merge. After departing the bus at the bridge, you'll soon realize the East Branch here is too deep and cuts too close to the road to enter the valley. Head east along the park road, for half a mile to a mile, and look for a suitable place to descend the steep bank through the willows to where the Toklat River opens up into the board valley.

The East Branch of the Toklat River is highly braided which has resulted in an open terrain of board gravel bars and channels, the reason for its popularity among trekkers. It is also a popular place to see brown bears so keep an eye on the surrounding landscape. Two miles from the bridge the East Branch completes its wide curve south into the valley that is walled in on the west side by

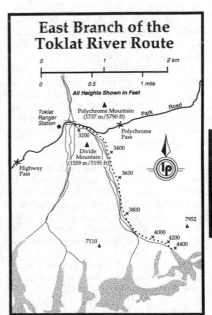

East Branch of the Toklat River Route

5195-foot-high Divide Mountain and on the east by an unnamed 5000-foot peak.

From this point on, the valley becomes narrower with every step you take towards the glaciers. Travel, however, is easy along the gravel bars. Search the mountain slopes to the east in the beginning for the best chances to spot dall sheep. The East Branch is a glacial river with mud-grey water but five miles after leaving the bridge you reach the first clear-water stream that flows out of the mountains to the east.

In another mile, or six miles from the bridge, you should reach a second stream flowing out of the steep mountain walls of the valley. This general area makes a particularly good campsite, providing a source of clear water, a scenic backdrop of the surrounding peaks of the Alaska Range and a good dose of backcountry solitude.

Stage 2: The Return
(6-10 miles, 8-9 hours)
You return the way you came. It's the same route but the view is different as you hike out of the widening valley with the colorful slopes of the Polychrome Pass area rising above the park road to your north.

Before heading back, adventurous hikers can take a side trip to one of the glaciers at the head of the valley. From the second stream, the steep walls of the valley close in on the east side, forcing the river to hug a cliff. This forces you to scramble up the slope and traverse the river from above for a mile or so.

You'll bypass where the East Branch splits into two main channels before being able to descend back to the valley floor. Each channel heads in the opposite direction to a glacier of its own. It's the stream and small valley to the left as you face south that is the easiest to explore. It's another good place to search for dall sheep.

You can follow the rocky terrain on either bank of the stream and the south side might even be a bit easier. Be especially cautious whenever you're fording glacially fed streams.

MT EIELSON LOOP
This is perhaps the most natural loop off the park road. It conveniently begins and ends at the Eielson Visitor Center, offers stunning views of Mt McKinley and Muldrow Glacier, and gets you far enough into the backcountry for a good sense of being in the wilderness area.

Needless to say, it's a popular area and the greatest demand for permits in the park is probably for backcountry zones 12 and 13 (where the loop falls). It's debatable which is harder: winning the New York lottery or getting these permits without first spending a week somewhere else in the backcountry.

A strong, experienced backcountry traveler can cover this 14-mile loop in a day, others can easily walk it in two days. But if you do obtain the permits, by all means spend three days or even longer in this special area of the park. Sighting wildlife, especially grizzly bears, is good and if Mt McKinley appears the sight of it will overwhelm you for a day. The trip is rated moderate because it involves fording the Thorofare River, twice – always a challenging crossing.

The entire route is covered on the USGS 1:63,360 series quad *Mt McKinley B-1*.

Access
Take the camper bus to Eielson Visitor Center at *Mile 65* of the park road. The center has bathrooms, drinking water, a picnic area, and an exhibit area and observation window equipped with a spotting scope. Other than interpretive material and books, the center sells no supplies or food.

Stage 1: Eielson Visitor Center to Pass Summit
(5.2 miles, 4-6 hours)
(Backcountry camping)
From Eielson Visitor Center, there is a trail that drops down a steep ridge to Gorge Creek. The creek is reached within a mile and is generally an easy ford; sometimes you can even leap across it. Once across, climb the bluff on the south side to an obvious bench of rolling tundra. This is open terrain so

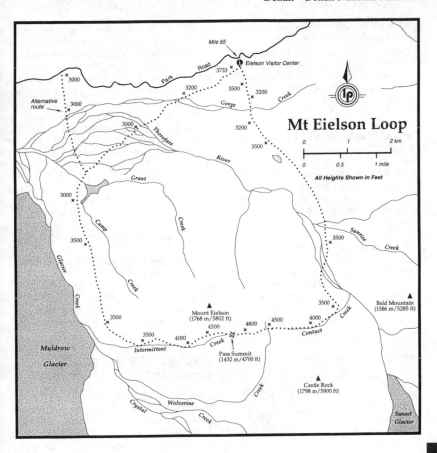

Mt Eielson Loop

All Heights Shown in Feet

visibility will be good. Head south for two miles, passing a small lake within a mile (if you are not too far off course).

Once past the lake, you'll mostly likely be able to pick up an animal trail that will lead you to the edge of the bench. Follow it until you come to where Sunrise Creek flows into Thorofare River. Ford Sunrise Creek and then cross Thorofare River. Be cautious at the river, however. Take time to scout the river for its most braided section and then unhook your hip straps and cross diagonally, heading downstream.

Once on the west side of the river, head downstream until you are directly west of a 5285-foot peak known as Bald Mountain and look for Contact Creek, a clear-water stream that flows into the Thorofare River. This is your route to Pass Summit. Follow the creek as it climbs more than 1000 feet in the next mile. It's hard work with a backpack on but a manageable climb for most trekkers. Eventually, 5.2 miles or so from Eielson Visitor Center, you should reach the pass.

At 4700 feet, Pass Summit is a scenic place to spend the night if the weather permits. Views of Mt McKinley to the southwest are possible on a clear day while to the north is Mt Eielson, a 5802-foot peak. It's a spectacular spot if it's calm. The pass funnels storms and strong winds, so you may have to continue through it and drop to a more sheltered location at a lower elevation. Water is usually available near the pass from Wolverine Creek to the south.

Stage 2: Pass Summit to Eielson Visitor Center
(8.8 miles, 6-8 hours)
Those with an extra day in their itinerary might want to spend it at the pass to scale Mt Eielson. The most obvious route is a talus and rocky slope due north of Wolverine Creek that provides easy access to the ridge line. From here it is a pleasant trek to the 5600-foot summit where views of Mt McKinley, Muldrow Glacier and the Alaska Range are stunning on a clear day. To reach the true summit at 5802 feet requires more scrambling and rock climbing. The mountain is also very accessible from its west side, in which case you might want to camp on a bench above Glacier Creek.

From the pass, hike west towards Intermittent Creek. This route is so popular that there will most likely be a few rock cairns pointing the way to the creek which you then follow down the slope to its confluence with Glacier Creek. It's approximately 3.5 miles from the pass to Glacier Creek; on the other side is the rubble-covered ice of Muldrow Glacier.

Head north along Glacier Creek and in the beginning you can follow the gravel bars. Eventually you're forced to climb the bench along its east side. Follow the rolling flanks of the mountain for almost two miles until you descend to the flood plains of Thorofare River. Heading north-east away from Glacier Creek, you first ford Camp Creek and then Thorofare River, taking time to choose the best spot possible along the braided river.

At this point you can head due north to reach the park road and bus transportation in a little over a mile, or continue north-east to Eielson Visitor Center, reached in another three miles. Keep in mind that Thorofare River is a natural route for brown bears.

Denali State Park

They share the same name and border but there could hardly be two more different parks than Denali National Park and Denali State Park. The national park is world renowned, heavily developed at its entrance, a 'must see' on everybody's Alaskan itinerary, and a wilderness area with a crowded doorstep.

Denali State Park, on the other hand, has no VAC or any kind of information area except for a few bulletin boards at the trailheads and pull-offs. There's no hotel, no shuttle-bus service and no park road (unless you count George Parks Hwy which divides the park in half from north to south). There are also no stunning peaks.

The 324,420-acre state park, the second-largest state park in Alaska, is 160 miles north of Anchorage and situated between the Talkeetna Mountains to the east and the

Caribou

Alaska Range to the west. This makes the park the transition zone from low, coastal environment to the spine of the Alaska Range. Its terrain ranges from heavily forested steams and river valleys to the alpine tundra of the Curry and Kesugi ridges, making up the 35-mile-long backbone of the park.

The tallest peak in North America doesn't lie in this park but the best views of it do. Denali State Park has superb vantage points to view both Mt McKinley and the mountains that surround it in the Alaska Range. Many say the best roadside view of 'The High One' anywhere in the state is from *Mile 135.2* of the Parks Hwy, just inside the state park's southern boundary. Here, motorists pull off at South Denali Viewpoint to gaze upon Ruth Glacier less than five miles to the north-west as well as Mt McKinley, Mt Hunter and Moose Tooth. Trekkers who climb Kesugi Ridge are stunned by the view of the Denali massif on a clear day. Earlier in the century the best views were from Peters Hills in the south-west corner of the park where Alaskan painter Sydney Laurence managed to capture the beauty of McKinley on his large canvases.

But the main difference between the two parks are the number of people visiting them. There is no comparison. Most travelers rushing up the Parks Hwy to get to the national park don't even know when they're passing through the state park. There are no crowds in the state park, no lines of people waiting for a permit and no need for backcountry zone quotas. That could change some day as more and more people, especially trekkers, discover this gem of a state park. But it's hard to imagine this wilderness area ever getting as overrun as its counterpart to the north.

Wildlife in the state park is similar to that found in the national park. The park, roughly half the size of Rhode Island, is home to both brown and black bears, moose and marmots – found above the tree lines of the Curry and Kesugi ridges. In the lower areas you'll encounter muskrats, beavers, possibly red foxes, and porcupines. On the west side of the park, the rivers are of glacial origin and are often clouded with pulverized rock known as 'glacial flour'. This makes them a poor habitat for fish. But on the east side the streams are clear and support populations of arctic grayling, Dolly Varden, rainbow trout and all five species of Pacific salmon. In Byers Lake, anglers concentrate on both lake trout and whitefish.

The timber line within the park is at 2500 feet and alpine areas, featuring moss campion and many wild flowers, are found on both the Curry and Kesugi ridges. Below the tree line, the park is dominated by spruce-paper birch forests and then patches of dense birch-alder-willow thickets that crowd the trails and make off-trail hiking nearly impossible in these transitional zones. You'll find black spruce around the many bogs and beaver ponds and abundant crops of wild berries above the tree line where you can eat blueberries to your heart's content.

Climate
Thanks to the Alaska Range, Denali State Park is much more tempered and doesn't suffer from the temperature extremes than often occur in the national park and the rest of Interior Alaska. In the summer, the temperatures are usually around 60°F; highs exceeding 80°F are rare. The park receives 30 inches of precipitation annually. Much of it falls as snow which begins accumulating in October, or as showers from late August through September.

Information
A Denali Ranger District Office (☎ 733-2675) is at Byers Lake State Campground, the most developed portion of the park at *Mile 147* of the George Parks Hwy. It is the best place to call for trail conditions. You can also contact the Mat-Su area office of the Division of Parks & Outdoor Recreation (☎ 745-3975) in Wasilla.

Places to Stay
Other than backcountry camping, accommodations within the park consist of two public campgrounds and a lodge. *Lower*

DENALI

Troublesome Creek State Recreation Site (10 sites, $6) is at *Mile 137.3. Byers Lake State Campground* (66 sites, $6) at *Mile 147* provides tables, an outhouse and access to its namesake lake. Also on the lake are walk-in campsites accessed from the Byers Lake Loop.

At *Mile 156* of Parks Hwy, is *Chulitna River Lodge* (☎ 733-2521), the only facility within the state park. The lodge has a small café, gas and log cabins for $50 to $80 a night. It's near the trailhead of the Ermine Hill Trail, an emergency trail that accesses the Kesugi Ridge Route.

Maps

The park's main trail system, including Troublesome Creek Trail, Byers Lake Loop, Little Coal Creek Trail and the Kesugi Ridge Route are covered on USGS 1:63,360 series quads *Talkeetna C-1*, and *Talkeetna Mountains C-6* and *D-6*.

Equipment

At *Mile 115* of the George Parks Hwy is Trappers Creek, at the junction with Petersville Rd. In this highway hamlet, you'll find a handful of businesses, including *Trapper Creek Trading Post* (☎ 733-2315), which sells groceries and gas, and also has showers and a café, cabins for rent and a laundromat. Keep in mind that no fires are allowed in the backcountry, other than on the gravel bars of Chulitna, Susitna and Tokositna rivers, so you must pack a stove.

Cabins

There are no cabins or any other kind of free-use shelters within Denali State Park.

Trails

Troublesome Creek Trail The trailhead is posted and in a parking area at *Mile 137.6* of the George Parks Hwy. The trail ascends along the creek until it reaches the tree line where you move into an open area dotted with alpine lakes and surrounded by mountainous views. From here, it becomes a route marked only by rock cairns as it heads north to Byers Lake.

The trek to Byers Lake State Campground is a 15-mile backpacking trip of moderate difficulty. Keep in mind that numerous black bears feeding on salmon are the reason for the creek's name and that often in July and August the trail is closed to hikers. Call the ranger office in advance (see Information, above) about possible closures due to bears otherwise you risk arriving at a trailhead that will clearly be posted 'No Hiking'. You'll need USGS quad *Talkeetna C-2*.

Byers Lake Loop This is an easy 4.8-mile trek around the lake. It begins at the Byers Lake State Campground and passes six hike-in campsites on the other side of the lake that are 1.8 miles from the posted trailhead. Although there is boat access onto the lake at the campground, Byers is closed to gasoline motors, ensuring you a quiet evening at the walk-in sites. You'll need USGS quad *Talkeetna C-2*.

Peters Hills Trail Petersville Rd leads from *Mile 115* of the George Parks Hwy 40 miles north-west, passing some homes and the historic Forks Roadhouse, and finally crosses over Peters Hills. The trail never enters the state park but it provides access close to the remote western section. The foothills of the Alaska Range are known for their magnificent views of Mt McKinley only 40 miles to the north.

The road to Forks Roadhouse can be handled by most cars but it quickly deteriorates after that. Continue 13 miles west of the roadhouse, past the Petersville Placer Mine, to an all-terrain vehicle track on the north side of the road. This hike begins on the ATV track but within a mile departs as a narrow foot path. Viewpoints of Mt McKinley are reached within another mile or you can hike seven miles to Long Point, the place where painter Sydney Laurence used to set up his canvases. The views of the mountain from here are breathtaking while the surrounding tundra makes an ideal spot to camp for a day or two (USGS quad *Talkeetna C-2*).

Getting There & Away

You enter Denali State Park when you cross the southern boundary at *Mile 132.2* of the George Parks Hwy. It extends north to *Mile 169.2*, just south of Hurricane.

Bus Any bus company that makes a run to Denali National Park (see Getting There & Away in the earlier Denali National Park section) will drop you off along the highway in the state park. Many of them, in fact, make a regular rest stop at Chulitna River Lodge, which is in the heart of the park at *Mile 156*. Moon Bay Express (☎ 274-6454), in particular, is used to dropping off trekkers at the various trailheads and then picking them up a few days later. It departs from the Anchorage International Hostel daily at 8 am, passing through the state park between 11 am and noon.

Train The Alaska Railroad (☎ 265-2492 in Anchorage) forms the eastern border of the state park and on Wednesday and Saturday runs a 'flag stop' train to Hurricane Gulch, just north of the park. This train departs from Anchorage at 6.30 am and will stop anywhere along the tracks – sounds ideal for trekkers but the problem is that the trailheads are all along the highway. Even those interested in off-trail travel in the east side of the park would first have to find some way to cross the Susitna River, which can not be forded, and then contend with thick willow and alder, bushwhacking their way up the ridge.

In the early 1900s, when it took two days to travel from Seward to Fairbanks, train passengers would often lay over in Curry for an extra day to climb the east side of Curry Ridge to view Mt McKinley. The small hexagonal-shaped building at Curry Lookout is still there but the cable for safe transportation across the river is long gone.

LITTLE COAL CREEK TRAIL

Little Coal Creek Trail features a well-defined path and is the easiest climb into the alpine area of Kesugi Ridge. From its trailhead just off the George Parks Hwy you emerge above the tree line in less than three miles. It's a steady climb up, especially with a backpack on, but not nearly as steep as the trek up Kesugi Ridge from Byers Lake Loop.

The trail also serves as the first leg of the Kesugi Ridge Route – a route that parallels the crest of the ridge south to reach Byers Lake State Campground in 27.4 miles or the trailhead of Troublesome Creek Trail in 36.2 miles. It's not a maintained trail, rather a worn path in some places of the tundra and little more than a series of cairns in others.

Park rangers stress that the Kesugi Ridge Route is a challenging trek which requires you to know how to use maps and a compass properly. Above the tree line, snow can reach depths of more than six feet during the winter, and often lingers into July. On the ridge, you're also exposed to foul weather and high winds that can appear quickly and last for days. Poor visibility due to whiteouts and inclement weather are common problems.

If you are unsure about your ability to traverse the entire ridge, plan to enter and leave the park from the trailhead of Little Coal Creek Trail. The trail will lead you to excellent camping areas in the alpine area but will also provide you with quick access out of the high country if foul weather moves in suddenly. Hiking and then backtracking the first two stages would be such a trek and you would end up with a 16-mile round-trip overnight trek into the alpine area that would be rated moderate in difficulty. Traversing the entire ridge is a challenging trek.

The USGS 1:63,360 series map for Little Coal Creek Trail only is *Talkeetna Mountains D-6*. For the ridge walk to Byers Lake State Campground, you'll also need *Talkeetna Mountains C-6* and *Talkeetna C-1*.

Access

The trailhead is at *Mile 163.9* of the George Parks Hwy, where there is a parking area off the highway for the Little Coal Creek Trail. In Anchorage, contact Moon Bay Express (☎ 274-6454) about van transportation to and from the trailhead. Many trekkers are dropped off at the trailhead and then picked up a few days later to continue onto Denali National Park.

Stage 1: George Parks Hwy to North Fork Birdhouse

(3.1 miles, 2-3 hours)

(Backcountry camping)

The trailhead area for Little Coal Creek Trail includes a large parking area, vault toilets and an information board with warnings, suggestions and a topographical map with the entire Kesugi Ridge route penned in. Copy the information but don't steal the map.

From here the trail immediately heads into the woods and heads for Little Coal Creek. You can hear the water rushing below you at times but you never really see it as the trail quickly swings to the south-east and remains in the forested edge above the rugged ravine. In less than a mile, the trail skirts a beaver pond and a quarter of a mile beyond that you finally emerge at an opening where it is possible to see the creek below.

From that point, or 1.8 miles from the trailhead, the trail begins to do some serious climbing. In less than half a mile, you're going to gain 1000 feet, climbing above the tree line, crossing a creek at two miles and then hiking through some thick alder. Along the way the brush will thin out and you'll be able to view Little Coal Creek and the ravine it has cut in both directions.

The climbing tops off at a 3100-foot rocky knob unofficially known as 'the Lunch Spot'. The knob is well named, the views on a clear day are excellent here and allow you to munch on lunch in view of Mt McKinley in all her glory. The knob also marks where you move from sub-alpine willow and alder into an alpine tundra setting of grassy meadows loaded with ripe blueberries in August.

The trail is still easy to recognize as it continues across the rolling meadows to the headwaters of Little Coal Creek. At 3.1 miles from Parks Hwy you reach what is referred to as the North Fork of Little Coal Creek and an area that is referred to as the North Fork Birdhouse. There is a posted topographical map where you cross the creek. If you had a late start, there are places nearby to set up a tent and spend the night.

Stage 2: North Fork Birdhouse to 8-Mile Divide

(5 miles, 3 hours)

(Backcountry camping)

What makes Kesugi Ridge such a natural route is a rolling plateau at the 3000-foot level on its western side. To reach it, you ford the North Fork of Little Coal Creek and then follow the trail as it enters an amphitheater and becomes obscured in a rock slide. Somewhere in these boulders is Little Coal Creek.

Carefully make your way across the boulders to ascend to the tundra meadow on the south side, where you'll see the South Fork of Little Coal Creek following through. You should also be able to pick up the trail here as it crosses the creek and then climbs a ridge at 3500 feet. The trick here is getting through the bog around the creek without soaking your boots.

Once you climb the ridge, the natural route along the bench is very apparent if the weather is clear. And if it is, the views will be outstanding. You'll be hypnotized by Mt McKinley and the Alaska Range to the west while seemingly lying at your feet will be the board valley of the Chulitna River and, if you look carefully, even the George Parks Hwy where the RVers look like ants scurrying for cover.

The route up here is a mix of well-beaten segments of path with other stretches merely marked by rock cairns. From the ridge you descend gently to a pair of small pools, reached 1.2 miles after crossing the North Fork, and then to a third pool which is tucked away in the base of the high alpine ridge you're skirting.

Within another mile you pass another group of alpine pools from where two creeks begin their fast journey down Kesugi Ridge into the Chulitna River. The first is labeled Horseshoe Creek on park maps. This spot, 2.3 miles from the North Fork, or 5.4 miles from the trailhead, is a good spot to set up camp for the night. You have water, magnificent views and enough flat terrain to handle a number of tents.

DENALI

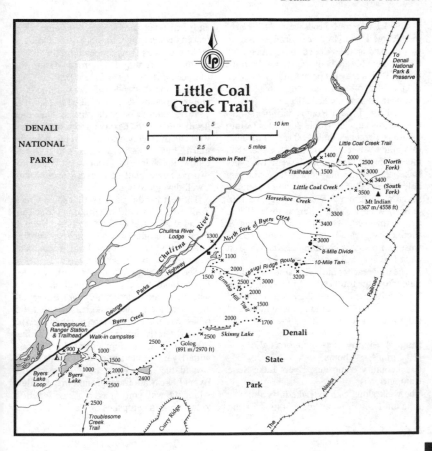

Little Coal Creek Trail

The next reliable source of water on the ridge, the North Fork of Byers Creek, is another two miles south, or 7.5 miles from the trailhead. You gently descend to cross the creek and then climb out of it on the other side to skirt a knob and descend to 8-Mile Divide. You'll find this an area of small pools and tarns where it's possible set up camp.

Stage 3: 8-Mile Divide to Skinny Lake
(9 miles, 5-7 hours)
(Backcountry camping)
From the divide, the route continues to head south, meandering across the crest of the

ridge with stunning views of the mountains to the west. Within two miles you come to a large tarn, referred to as 10-Mile Tarn, and then immediately skirt a distinctive rock formation that some people call Stonehedge.

You remain above 3000 feet for the next 2.5 miles until the trail descends to cross a stream and continues to drop off the ridge, moving into thicker willow and alder brush. At times the route will be flagged in this stretch. At 13.6 miles from the trailhead of Little Coal Creek Trail, you cross another stream where on the other side is the junction with the Ermine Hill Trail.

DENALI

This 3.1-mile route heads west a *Mile 156* of the George Parks Hwy near Ermine Lake. It was marked and developed as an emergency escape route for anybody caught on the ridge during foul weather. For the most part it's a steep descent off the ridge along a route that in many places has only been flagged.

The Kesugi Ridge Route continues south-east and also makes a rapid descent back into the forest. You descend 1000 feet in the next two miles before bottoming out. Other than the beginning and final descent to Byers Lake, this is the only other time you dip below the timber line. At this point, roughly seven miles from 8-Mile Divide, the trail crosses what is often referred to as 'Bitch Creek' (probably so-called because it can be such a boggy area) and then swings south-west and resumes climbing again. The east end of Skinny Lake is 1.5 miles away.

The trail reaches the well-named lake 17.2 miles from the trailhead of Little Coal Creek Trail and skirts its north side. You'll find old camping areas here among the willow and alder brush that border it.

Stage 4: Skinny Lake to Byers Lake
(10.2 miles, 6-8 hours)
(Backcountry campsites, Byers Lake State Campground)
The walk along Skinny Lake lasts almost a mile until you cross a stream at its west end

and then resume climbing. You climb 700 feet in the next mile, topping off at Golog, a 2970-foot peak that is labeled on the USGS topos and reached 19 miles from the trailhead of Little Coal Creek Trail.

The route descends off the south side of Golog, dropping several hundred feet to cross a stream, climbs a bit on the other side and then gently drops in the next two miles to reach the west end of an unnamed lake. At this point the trail is much more developed and easier to follow. It continues its south-west course for two more miles until it arrives at a junction with a well-developed trail.

The left-hand fork is Troublesome Creek Trail, which leads 12 miles along the stream to end at *Mile 137.6* of the highway. Keep in mind that through much of the summer this trail is often closed due to large numbers of bears feeding on the salmon run.

The right-hand fork heads north-west for Byers Lake State Campground. It begins with a very steep descent, by far the steepest anywhere along the route. In the next 1.5 miles, you'll drop 1500 feet, much of it in the first half-mile, in leaving Kesugi Ridge. Eventually you bottom out at the junction with Byers Lake Loop, a 4.8-mile walk around the lake. Head right to reach the Byers Lake State Campground in 1.5 miles. Along the way you'll pass a posted junction to the walk-in campsites on the lake.

Fairbanks

Of the three largest cities in Alaska, Fairbanks is the only one without great hiking at its doorstep. While in Anchorage and Juneau you can take a city bus to a handful of scenic treks and trails, this is not the case in Fairbanks. As Alaska's second-largest city (population 77,720) it is the gateway to the Arctic and a number of national parks and Bureau of Land Management (BLM) preserves where there are excellent trails. The problem is getting to them. Other than expensive bush-plane charters, public transportation is thin this far north. Hitchhiking is always possible but you'll find traffic is light, even by Alaskan standards, while most car rental places stipulate that their vehicles may not be driven on many of the remote dirt roads where trailheads are.

Trekking in the Fairbanks region requires time and patience and a strong desire to explore the land that borders the Arctic Circle. The logistics can be a headache at times but the trails are worth it. Very much so – the scenery is unusual, especially if you come from the Southeast or the Kenai Peninsula; the crowds found in places like Denali National Park are absent; and often at the end of the trek you can spend a day recuperating with a soak in a natural hot spring.

Of the two treks described here, Granite Tors Trail is shorter and easier to reach because Chena Hot Springs Rd, where the trailhead is located, is paved and well used by both locals and tourists visiting Chena River State Recreation Area. Van service to the trailhead can even be arranged if there are two or more of you. At the end of the trek you can continue east for a stay at Chena Hot Springs.

The other trek, Pinnell Mountain Trail, is much more difficult to reach but certainly not impossible. This three-day walk is one of the great hiking trails in Alaska, rating right up there with the Chilkoot Trail and Resurrection Pass in terms of scenery. This wonderful

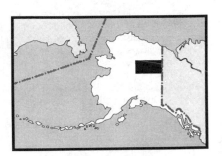

adventure is enhanced even more if you continue east along the Steese Hwy to visit the remote town of Central and soak at Circle Hot Springs.

Climate

Like the rest of the Interior, Fairbanks has excellent trekking weather during the summer. From mid-June to mid-August it is often pleasantly warm with an average temperature of 70°F and an occasional hot spell in August when the temperature breaks 90°F. The days are long with more than 20 hours of light each day from June to August, peaking at almost 23 hours on 21 June. Generally, the trails are clear of snow from June through September.

You must be prepared with rain gear and warm clothing, however, because winds in these alpine areas can be strong, sometimes exceeding 50 mph in places where there is little protection. Winds can also lower the temperature significantly during the summer. Especially on the Pinnell Mountain Trail, beware of low-lying clouds that can create white-out conditions, making travel much more challenging.

Information

The best place to get trekking information anywhere in the Fairbanks area is the Alaska Public Lands Information Center (☎ 456-0527) on Cushman St, two blocks south of the Chena River, downtown. You'll find local trail information along with brochures on state and national parks, wildlife refuges and recreation areas elsewhere in Alaska. You can also obtain shuttle-bus coupons and campground reservations at Denali National Park 21 days in advance, which can save you a big headache once you arrive at the park. Hours for the center are from 9 am to 6 pm daily during the summer.

Information on Pinnell Mountain Trail or the White Mountain trail system can also be found at the BLM office (☎ 474-2200) on the corner of Airport Way and University Ave. Practically next door to the BLM office is the Alaska Division of Parks & Outdoor Recreation (☎ 451-2695) if you want information on the Chena River State Recreation Area.

The main source of travel information is the Convention & Visitor Bureau Log Cabin (☎ 456-5774) which overlooks the Chena River near the corner of 1st Ave and Cushman St. The log cabin is open daily during the summer from 8.30 am to 8 pm. Other visitors' centers are located in the railroad depot (open before and after each train arrival) and Alaskaland (on the corner of Airport Way and Peger Rd). There's also a limited visitors' center near the baggage-claim area of the Fairbanks International Airport.

Places to Stay

Camping The only public campground in the Fairbanks area is the *Chena River State Campground* (51 sites, $12) off University Ave just north of Airport Way. The campground has tables, toilets, fireplaces and water, and being right on the river, a boat launch.

If you just want to park the van or RV and don't need facilities or a hook-up, there's *Alaskaland* (☎ 459-1087) on the corner of Airport Way and Peger Rd, where spending the night in its parking lot costs $7. Even better is the *Fred Meyers* store just west along Airport Way. It's become a common practice, since the store arrived, for RVers

and others to just spend the night in the parking lot.

Hostels The best thing to happen to Fairbanks is the arrival of backpacker's hostels that offer inexpensive, bunkroom lodging. Presently the *Fairbanks Youth Hostel* (☎ 456-4159) is a home hostel with eight beds. You reach it from College Rd by turning south on Aurora Drive and then east on Willow St. The nightly fee is $6.

Even better is *College Bunkhouse* (☎ 479-2627), three blocks south of College Rd on Westwood Way. The place is clean, provides showers, kitchen, and a small picnic and barbecue area and is near both a city bus line and a bike trail. The rate for a bunk is $16 a night. Nearby is *Billie's Backpacking Hostel* (☎ 479-2034), on Mack Rd which intersects Westwood Way. This hostel has the same facilities plus a sun deck while the rate is $15 a night. Both offer courtesy pick-up and drop-off to the airport and train station.

B&Bs Fairbanks has more than 100 B&Bs and most of them have a brochure in the visitors' center downtown. A courtesy phone there lets you check which places have a room and which are full. The Fairbanks Association of Bed & Breakfast also publishes a brochure with more than 30 members listed in it and a map showing their locations. Pick it up at the visitors' center or write in advance to the Fairbanks Association of Bed & Breakfast, PO Box 73334, Fairbanks, AK 99707.

If you're arriving by train or bus, there are several downtown places that are within easy walking distance from the depot. At Cowles St and 4th Ave, there is *Cowles Street B&B* (☎ 452-5252) and next door *Ah, Rose Marie* (☎ 456-2040). Between them they have nine rooms and will refer guests back and forth to find a bed. Both places include a full breakfast though Cowles St B&B is slightly more affordable with singles/doubles from $50/60. Further to the west is *Thompson's Bed & Breakfast* (☎ 452-5787) at 1315 Sixth Ave. Singles/doubles are $35/45 and the hosts are friendly.

Hotels Most hotel/motel rooms in Fairbanks are not as expensive as those in Anchorage but still be prepared to pay $70 per night during the summer. The few with reasonable rates are less than desirable or are a considerable distance from the city center. With the handful of places clustered downtown on the east side of Cushman St check out the room before handing over your money.

The *Tamarac Inn* (☎ 456-6406), on the north side of the Chena River at 252 Minnie St, is within easy walking distance from the railroad depot. Singles/doubles cost $62/68; some units have cooking facilities.

By heading away from the city center you can find better rates and cleaner rooms. Try *Noah's Rainbow Inn* (☎ 474-3666) at 700 Fairbanks St, reached by heading west on Geist Rd from University Ave or by jumping on the city bus Blue Line. Rooms are small but begin at $35 a night and the inn features shared baths and kitchen and has a coin-operated laundry on site. The *Golden North Motel* (☎ 479-6201 or (800) 447-1910) at 4888 Airport Way has rooms with cable TV, rolls and coffee in the office and free van service within the city. Rooms tend to be on the small side and rates in the summer begin at $69.

Circle Hot Springs From Eagle Summit, the eastern trailhead of the Pinnell Mountain Trail, it's just 20 miles along the Steese Hwy to Central and Circle Hot Springs, both colorful towns of hardcore miners. Central, at *Mile 127.5*, is the larger of the two towns (population 800 in the summer) where you'll find gasoline, groceries, a post office and the *Central Motor Inn* (☎ 520-5228). This motel has it all – rooms, campsites, showers, café and gas. Rooms cost $38 for two people and showers are $3 per person. The café is perhaps the best place to eat anywhere along the Steese Hwy.

Just beyond Central, the Circle Hot Springs Rd heads south and in six miles passes the *Ketchem Creek Campground* (seven sites, free). This BLM campground is run down and unmarked along the road but it's still the best place to pitch a tent in the area. Two miles beyond the creek is *Circle Hot Springs Resort* (☎ 520-5113). Now listed on the National Register of Historical Sites, the hotel is a classic. Rooms with shared baths begin at $45 while on the third floor are hostel accommodations for $20 a night. They also rent rustic cabins, some with no running water; the more deluxe cabins have kitchens and hot tubs.

The hot springs are piped into an Olympic-sized pool in which 139°F mineral water is pumped through at a rate of 231 gallons per minute. Spend 20 or 30 minutes soaking here and you won't have sore muscles or a care in the world. If you're camping down the road it's $7 to soak in the pool; open until midnight.

There are also two public campgrounds along the Steese Hwy before you reach the Pinnell Mountain Trail. The first is the *Upper Chatanika River State Campground* (25 sites, $6) on the river at *Mile 39*. The next campground is the *Cripple Creek BLM Campground* (21 sites, $6) at *Mile 60*.

Chena Hot Springs Chena Hot Springs Rd extends 56 miles east off the Steese Hwy to the hot springs of the same name. The road is paved and in good condition and passes several campgrounds. The first is *Rosehip State Campground* (25 sites, $6) at *Mile 27*. Its large, flat gravel pads makes it a favorite with RVers. Further to the east at *Mile 39.5* is *Tors Trail State Campground* (20 sites, $6) with large sites in a stand of spruce with a canoe launch on the Chena River. Across the highway is the trailhead for the Granite Tors Trail. Both campgrounds tend to be popular during the summer but there are many gravel turn-offs along the road for the nights when they are full.

At the end of Chena Hot Springs Rd is *Chena Hot Springs Resort* (☎ 452-7867), which recently updated its already fine facilities. The springs are at the center of a 40-sq-mile geothermal area and produce a steady stream of water that's so hot (156°F) it must be cooled before you can even think about a soak. The most popular activity is hot-tub soaking, done indoors where there are two jacuzzis, a pool and a hot (very hot) tub. The resort has hotel rooms and rustic cabins that begin at $50 per couple per night. There is also a campground, where a site costs $8 per night. The use of the hot tubs is extra for campers; $8 for an entire day, $6 after 7 pm.

Maps

You can pick up USGS topographical maps at the Public Lands Information Center but they handle primarily the larger scale 1:250,000 maps. For the 1:63,360 series for Fairbanks or anywhere in Alaska, stop by the USGS office (☎ 456-0244) in the Federal Building at 101 12th St, east of Cushman St. Hours are from 8 am to 5 pm Monday through Friday.

Equipment

By all means, stock up on your Lipton noodle dinners, instant coffee and jars of peanut butter before heading out on any trail. Fairbanks has lots of grocery stores but *Fred Meyers One Stop Shopping*, just west of Alaskaland on Airport Way, has a great selec-

tion of food and a limited selection of camping equipment. It's open to 10 pm daily. Near the downtown area head to *Carr's* on Gaffney Rd near Cushman St. It has loads of freshly baked goods, gorp, dried fruit and nuts by the pound and is open 24 hours. Right across the street is a laundromat.

For a more serious selection of backpacking gear, or for freeze-dried dinners or a windscreen for your stove (a must on the Pinnell Mountain Trail), go to *Beaver Sports* (☎ 479-2494) at 3480 College Rd on the north side of town. It's open to 7 pm Monday through Friday, until 6 pm Saturday and until 5 pm on Sunday. Downtown *Big Ray's* (☎ 452-3458) at 507 2nd Ave has outdoor equipment.

Cabins

The Pinnell Mountain Trail has two free-use shelters, strategically placed at *Mile 10* and *Mile 17* of this 27-mile trek. You should still pack a tent, however. These small four-sided shelters are designed as cooking areas or for emergency accommodations during foul weather. They should not be monopolized by two or three people trying to sleep in them.

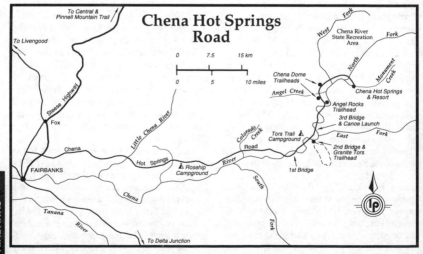

There is also a new free-use shelter halfway along the Granite Tors Trail, that was constructed in 1994.

There are no USFS cabins in the Fairbanks area but both the BLM and the Alaska Division of Parks & Outdoor Recreation have several for rent.

The BLM maintains the Fred Blixt Cabin off *Mile 62* of the Elliott Hwy, 10 miles before the junction with the Dalton Hwy. A short spur leads from the road to the cabin. Cripple Creek Cabin is an old trapper's cabin that was renovated by the BLM in 1972. It's at *Mile 60.5* of Steese Hwy and reached by a short trail. The cabin, available only from mid-August to mid-May, does not offer a truly isolated setting because Cripple Creek Campground and a Youth Conservation Corps (YCC) Camp are nearby. Still, the surrounding area is scenic.

Within the White Mountains National Recreation Area, the BLM maintains nine cabins and a trail shelter. The newest is Lee's Cabin, accessed from the Wickersham Creek Trail at *Mile 28* of the Elliott Hwy. It's a seven-mile hike through a lot of muskeg to the cabin, which features a large picture window overlooking the White Mountains, and a loft which comfortably sleeps eight people. Also in the recreation area is the Borealis-LeFevre Cabin on the banks of Beaver Creek (reached from the Summit Trail) and Moose Creek Cabin (reached from Wickersham Creek and Moose Creek trails). Keep in mind that only the Summit Trail is recommended for summer travel as the rest of the trails involve extensive stretches of wet and muddy terrain.

All cabins should be reserved in advance through the BLM office (☎ 474-2200) in Fairbanks. The rental fee is $20 per night.

Within the Chena River State Recreation Area is Angel Creek Cabin. It can be reached from *Mile 22.5* of the Chena Dome Trail by following a ridge north for 1.5 miles and descending 1900 feet. The unit costs $20 a night; reserve it by contacting Alaska Division of Parks & Outdoor Recreation (☎ (907) 451-2695), 3700 Airport Way, Fairbanks, AK 99709.

Hoary marmot

Trails

Creamer's Field Trail A self-guided, two-mile trail winds through Creamer's Field Migratory Wildlife Refuge, an old dairy farm that has since become an Audubon bird-lover's paradise, as more than 100 species of bird pass through each year. The refuge is at 1300 College Rd and the trailhead is in the parking lot adjacent to the Alaska Department of Fish & Game office (☎ 452-1531), where trail guides are available. The trail is mostly boardwalk with an observation tower along the way and lots of bugs. The flocks of geese, ducks and swans move onto nesting grounds by late May but sandhill cranes can be spotted throughout the summer.

Chena Lakes Recreation Area This facility opened in 1984 as the last phase of an Army Corps of Engineers flood control project prompted by the Chena River's flooding of Fairbanks in 1967. Two separate parks, Chena River and Chena Lakes, make up the recreational area which is 18 miles southeast from Fairbanks past North Pole, off the Laurance Rd exit of the Richardson Hwy. The Chena River park contains a 2.5-mile self-guided nature trail. Between the two parks there are three campground loops providing 78 sites ($6 per night).

FAIRBANKS

Angel Rocks Trail This 3.5-mile loop leads to Angel Rocks, large granite outcrops near the north boundary of the Chena River State Recreation Area. It's an easy day hike with the rocks less than two miles from the road. From the first set of rocks, the trail makes a moderately steep ascent of several hundred feet as it weaves through many granite tors before emerging at a rock ridge. At this point the trek follows an unimproved trail or you can scramble up the hill to an alpine ridge above the tree line for views of the Alaska Range, Chena Dome and Far Mountain. The posted trailhead is just south of a rest area at *Mile 49* of the Chena Hot Springs Rd. Practically across the street is the southern trailhead for the Chena Dome Trail (USGS quads *Big Delta D-5* and *Circle A-5*).

Chena Dome Trail Also in the Chena River State Recreation Area is this 29-mile loop that most trekkers undertake as a three-day backpacking trip. The trail circles the entire Angel Creek drainage area and for the first three miles cuts through forest and climbs to the timber line. It ends that way as well but in between, the hike follows tundra ridgetops where the route has been marked by rock cairns.

For those who enjoy romping in the alpine area, this route is a treat. Four times you reach summits that exceed 3000 feet and in between you are challenged with steep climbs and descents. Chena Dome (reached at *Mile 10.25*) is the highest point on the trail, a flat-topped ridge at 4421 feet that provides awesome views. Other inviting features of the hike are the wild flowers in July, the blueberries in August, wildlife (including bears) at anytime of year, and a public-use cabin that can be rented in advance (see Cabins, above).

If you're hiking the entire loop, it's best to begin at the trailhead at *Mile 50.5* of the Chena Hot Springs Rd. When traveling west, the trailhead is 0.7 miles past Angel Creek Bridge on the left side of the road. The other trailhead is at *Mile 49*.

Pack a stove; open fires are not permitted in the area. Also bring an extra quart of water

and then replenish it at every opportunity along the trail. For the most part water will be collected from small pools in the tundra and must be treated.

Mosquitos and gnats can be bad from June through early August so bring powerful insect repellent.

USGS quads *Big Delta D-5* and *Circle A-5* and *A-6* are needed for this trail.

Summit Trail The BLM, which maintains the Pinnell Mountain Trail, also administers the White Mountains trail network, which includes Summit Trail. This 18-mile, one-way route was especially built for summer use and has boardwalks over the wettest areas. The route winds through dense spruce forest, traverses scenic alpine ridgetops and arctic tundra, and ends at a junction with Wickersham Creek Trail. From there you can continue east for two miles to reach the Borealis-LeFevre Cabin (see Cabins, above) on scenic Beaver Creek.

Reservations often aren't necessary during the summer as the last 2.5 miles of this trail drops off the ridge line and descends into a muskeg area where hikers must ford up to four streams. Most parties end the day camping above the tree line instead of dealing with the low-lying swamp. Keep in mind that you must ford Beaver Creek to reach the cabin, a dangerous crossing when water levels are high.

Hiking in for a night at the cabin is a five-day adventure. Even stopping short of it, the hike still takes two or three days to reach the highest point along the route – the 3100-foot ridge line, 10 miles from the Elliott Hwy. The highlight of the trek is the view from the top of Wickersham Dome, which includes Mt McKinley, the White Mountains and the Alaska Range.

The trailhead is at *Mile 28* of the Elliott Hwy, 31 miles north of Fairbanks. Don't confuse the White Mountain Summit Trail (also called Summer Trail), which was made for hikers, with the Wickersham Creek Trail, that departs from the trailhead. The Wickersham Creek Trail, like most of the trail system in the White Mountains, leads

Free-use shelter, Pinnell Mountain Trail (JD)

Top Left: Overlook on the Coastal Trail, Caines Head State Recreation Area (JD)
Top Right: Flattop Mountain Trail (JD)
Bottom: Fox River, Mile 11 of the Resurrection Pass Trail (DS)

through swampy, muskeg lowlands, making hiking extremely challenging.

The BLM District Office in Fairbanks (☎ 474-2200), at 1150 University Ave, has a useful *Trip Information Planning Sheet* (TIPS) on this trail and other trails in the recreation area. You can also pick them up at the Public Lands Information Center in downtown Fairbanks (USGS quads *Livengood A-3*, *B-2* and *B-3*).

Getting There & Away
Air The Fairbanks International Airport, expanded in 1984, is almost four miles south-west of the city off Airport Way. Alaska Airlines (☎ 474-0481) provides eight daily flights between Fairbanks and Anchorage, where there are connections to the rest of the state, as well as a direct flight to Fairbanks from Seattle. The one-way standard fare (the most expensive) from Anchorage is normally around $190 but airfare wars have pushed it to as low as $55 at times. The other intrastate airline is MarkAir (☎ (800) 478-0800), though you have to wonder how long the financially troubled carrier will remain flying.

Bus Alaskon Express (☎ 452-2843) provides service to Fairbanks from Haines, Skagway, Whitehorse, Tok and Delta Junction on a run that departs from Beaver Creek Monday, Wednesday and Friday at 9 am. In Fairbanks, buses depart from the Westmark Hotel at 820 Noble St in the city center at 8 am Sunday, Tuesday and Friday during the summer for the return trip. The one-way fare to Fairbanks from Delta Junction is $49, from Tok $62 and from Haines $169.

Alaska Direct Busline (☎ (800) 770-6652) also runs from Haines Junction to Fairbanks. A bus departs at 8.45 am on Tuesday, Friday and Sunday and also passes through Beaver Creek, Tok and Delta Junction. They seem to move their pick-up point every summer so call them to find out what hotel they are presently working out of. The one-way fare from Haines is $150, from Tok $40. They also have a bus that makes the Anchorage-to-Fairbanks run, leaving Anchorage at 7 am Monday, Thursday and Saturday. The one-way fare is $65.

If you're coming up from Denali National Park, Fireweed Express (☎ 488-7928) offers van service during the summer from the national park's Visitor Access Center. The van departs from the center at 4 pm, arrives in Fairbanks at 6.30 pm and costs $25 one way.

Train The Alaska Railroad (☎ 456-4155) has an express train to Fairbanks that departs from Anchorage daily at 8.30 am from late May to mid-September, stops at Denali National Park and then reaches Fairbanks at 8.30 pm. One way costs $120; the railroad depot is at 280 North Cushman St, a short walk from the Chena River.

Getting Around
Car Rental For two or three travelers, splitting the cost of a used car is often the best and cheapest way of getting to outlying areas such as Chena Hot Springs. What the rental companies won't let you do, however, is drive the rough highways of Steese, Elliott or Dalton to visit such places as the Circle or Manly Hot Springs. In fact, you might have to search around to find anybody that will let you take a rental 'out the road'.

Rent-A-Wreck (☎ 452-1606) at 2105 Cushman St, south of Airport Way, has compacts for $38 per day with 100 free miles. Likewise AllStar (☎ 479-4229) at 4415 Airport Way, just north of the airport, has cars for the same rate and provides courtesy pick-up at major hotels. You can also check with Affordable Car Rental (☎ 452-4279) and U-Save Auto Rental, at Chevron Stations at 3245 College Rd (☎ 479-7060) and near downtown at 333 Illinois St (☎ 452-4236), before calling the expensive national companies.

PINNELL MOUNTAIN TRAIL
The first National Recreational Trail to be established in Alaska was Pinnell Mountain Trail, a three-day, 27.3-mile trek that follows a serpentine route along tree-less, alpine ridges. Located in the 1.2-million-acre

Steese National Conservation Area and managed by the BLM, this trail climbs over or around several high passes and peaks, including 4915-foot Porcupine Dome and Pinnell Mountain, the high point of the trek at 4934 feet. There are stunning views from almost every step of the way as you gaze down upon valleys and rivers or out at the White Mountains, Tanana Hills and Alaska Range on the horizon.

For many, the most outstanding sight on the trail is the midnight sun. From 18 to 25 June the sun never sets on the trail, giving hikers 24 hours of light each day. The polar phenomenon of the sun sitting above the horizon at midnight can be viewed and photographed at several high points on the trail, including the Eagle Summit trailhead. June is also an excellent time to view the wild flowers which carpet the arctic-alpine tundra slopes from late May. In August, you can feast on blueberries, low-bush cranberries and other wild berries.

About the only thing the trail lacks is numerous encounters with wildlife. By packing a pair of compact binoculars you can search the surrounding valleys and occasionally spot wolves, grizzly bears and even small groups of caribou from your high vantage point. But on the trail itself, wildlife is limited to hoary marmots, pika or 'rock rabbits', and a variety of migratory birds like Lapland longspurs, northern wheatears, lesser golden plovers and golden eagles. Rock ptarmigans are year-round residents on the alpine ridges.

The trail is well marked with both cairns and mileposts. It winds along tundra ridgetops that lie above 3500 feet and at times the trekking can be steep and rugged. The hike is a natural three-day adventure, with backpackers covering eight to 10 miles a day. There are two small shelters built by the YCC which are open to anyone, without reservations or fees. They are great places for waiting out a storm or cooking a meal on a windy evening, but you should still bring a tent with good bug netting to sleep in at night.

Expect snow cover in May (with patches remaining to June) and mid-September. These patches are good sources of water which is scarce on this trail. Bring at least

---

The Midnight Sun

Although some tour-group operators will fly you north from Fairbanks to see the Arctic Circle, the circle is actually an imaginary line that circumscribes the earth at latitude 66° 32′, parallel to the equator. This is the point where the sun does not set for an entire day (21 June or the summer solstice) and does not rise for an entire day (21 December or the winter solstice).

This is the strange polar phenomenon of the midnight sun – at the witching hour the sun is still above the horizon. Go north of the Arctic Circle to Barrow and you'll find the sun doesn't dip for 84 days, from 10 May to 2 August. That's because the earth is tilted and during the summer the northern frigid zone leans towards the sun. It doesn't make any difference where the earth is in its 24-hour rotation, north of the Arctic Circle the sun will always be shining.

Although the Pinnell Mountain Trail is south of the circle, the sun does not set on it from 18 to 25 June. This is because of the refraction of the sun's rays which is so great near the North Pole that it causes the light to linger and the sun to appear as if it hasn't set at all.

The Pinnell Mountain Trail, with its high points and open tundra, is a great place to watch the sun at midnight. Don't bother lathering on the suntan lotion – the rays strike the earth at a lower angle in Alaska and thus lose much of their intensity. Also because of the angle, the midnight sun appears to skim the horizon, never setting but never getting very high in the sky either.

But the best thing about this slanting Arctic light is the warm colors and shades it produces throughout the summer. A clear day is a photographer's dream, when every hour is like the golden hues of late afternoon elsewhere. If you're on the Pinnell Mountain Trail on a clear day, plan on burning up some film – the blue sky, white clouds, the golden tundra and the wild flowers of early summer will be painted in deep, rich colors that have never looked so good. ■

The Habits of the Hoary Marmot

Though most trekkers want to see bears, moose, dall sheep and possibly even wolves, the animal many of them get to know best is the hoary marmot. The marmot is the largest member of the squirrel family – some tip the scales at 30 pounds in midsummer. They are usually found above the tree line in mountainous areas throughout Alaska, from Barrow to Bristol Bay, including Denali National Park and the alpine trails around Fairbanks.

The marmot is so easy to encounter and watch because it's diurnal, rising at the crack of dawn and leaving its burrow to feed or to just sun itself. Marmots also naturally curious and very social animals that live in communities on rocky but open ridges.

Among the most comical things to witness is the meeting of two marmots. They often will touch muzzles and then may stage what appears to be a wrestling match with the pair tumbling down the rocky slope. Biologists believe this muzzling is used to identify members of a community while the wrestling may help to establish male dominance.

The other noticeable trait of the marmot is its whistle. Produced by internal cheek pouches, it is so loud at times that it can be heard two miles away. It's an alarm system that not only protects other marmots from approaching predators but also from other species. At times, a marmot will also bark, yip and even yell.

It's hard to sneak up on a marmot. But there is no better way to spend a warm afternoon in the mountains than watching a community of marmots feeding, sunning and wrestling each other. ∎

---

two quarts of water per person and then refill your supply at either snow patches, springs or tundra pools at every opportunity. Boil or filter all standing water from pools and slow-running springs.

The winds can be brutal in this barren region, as there are no trees to slow the gusts that can come howling over the ridges. Bring a wind screen for your camp stove, otherwise cooking dinner can become a long ordeal.

Your most serious concern, however, is foul weather that produces low-lying clouds or white-out conditions. On a clear day, it's easy to follow the trail as the next cairn or milepost is almost always in sight. But when there are low clouds, the trail is obscured and following the right route is much more challenging. If the weather is bad, don't hesitate to sit out a day, playing cards in the emergency shelter. It'll eventually improve.

Do not depend on the free trail map that the BLM publishes. Purchase and carry the proper USGS 1:63,360 series topos, *Circle B-3*, *B-4*, *C-3* and *C-4*. The trail is labeled on most of them and rated moderate in difficulty.

Access

Most hikers begin at the Eagle Summit trailhead on *Mile 107.3* of the Steese Hwy, the higher end of the trail. The western end lies at Twelvemile Summit, closer to Fairbanks at *Mile 85* of the Steese Hwy. Traffic on the Steese Hwy is light this far out of Fairbanks, but there is still a steady trickle. Hitching is possible if you are willing to give up a day getting out there and back. Even with a car, most hikers also end up hitching back to the trailhead where they began.

Check at the Fairbanks Visitor Center (☎ (907) 456-5774) to see if anybody is running transportation out to Circle Hot Springs. Another alternative is to rent a car and combine the trip with a drive to Circle Hot Springs or the wilderness town of Circle on the Yukon River. The problem with that is none of the used-car rental places will allow you to take their vehicles out the Steese Hwy. That means renting from a national company like Avis and paying $60 a day.

Stage 1: Eagle Summit to Ptarmigan Creek Shelter

(10.2 miles, 5-6 hours)
(Backcountry camping, shelter)
From the Eagle Summit parking area, you begin to climb immediately and ascend 180 feet before the trail swings to the north-west. A short spur completes the climb to the top of the 3900-foot knob from which the first of many great views along this route is enjoyed.

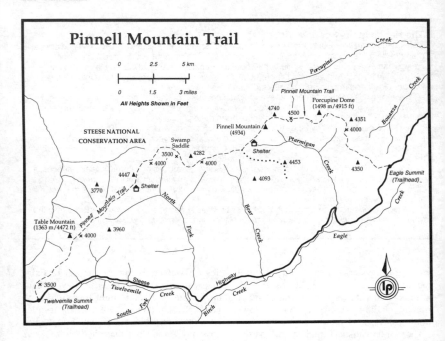

Pinnell Mountain Trail

0   2.5   5 km

0   1.5   3 miles

All Heights Shown in Feet

STEESE NATIONAL
CONSERVATION AREA

Swamp
Saddle

Pinnell Mountain
(4934)

Pinnell Mountain Trail

Porcupine Dome
(1498 m/4915 ft)

3500   4282   × 4000
× 4000

Shelter

Ptarmigan

4740   4500
▲   ×

▲ 4351
× 4000

4447 ▲

3770

Shelter

North

Fork

Pinnell Mountain Trail

Table Mountain
(1363 m/4472 ft)
▲   × 4000

▲ 3960

× 3500

Twelvemile Summit
(Trailhead)

Twelvemile

Steese

Creek

South   Fork

▲ 4093

▲ 4453

Bear

Creek

Highway

Birch   Creek

Eagle

Porcupine   Creek

Creek

Bonanza   Creek

▲
4350

Eagle Summit
(Trailhead)

Creek

The Pinnell Mountain Trail, meanwhile, descends to a pass along the ridge where it reaches *Mile 1* and then skirts the east side of a 4350-foot peak. Perched on the side of this knob you enjoy good views of the Bonanza Creek valley and Porcupine Creek in the distance. Sit for a while with a pair of high-powered binoculars and you might spot a bear or other wildlife crossing the creeks.

The trail descends to another low point in the ridge line and then reaches *Mile 3*, which marks the first steep climb of the day. In the next mile, you ascend 700 feet with the help of a series of switchbacks. Along the way you pass a huge boulder that will offer a bit of shade if it's one of those sunny, 90°F days in the Interior. You top off at the high point of 4351 feet and are immediately rewarded for all your efforts. The views are excellent. On a clear day it's possible to see in every direction, including to the Eagle Summit parking lot, your starting point four miles away. You can also gaze down on the Ptar-

migan Creek drainage area for the first time while all around you are ancient rocks perched in unusual upright positions and piles. The rocks, some of the oldest in Alaska dating back 500 billion years, look like headstones, prompting a few backpackers to refer to this as the 'graveyard stretch' of the hike.

The trail follows the high ridge line, descends sharply to another pass where it reaches *Mile 5* then climbs halfway up Porcupine Dome before it begins skirting its south side. At this point it's easy to drop the packs and scramble up the loose talus slope for the remaining 400 feet to the top of the 4915-foot peak. Along the south side, you begin 'bouldering', stepping from one large rock to the next. You pass *Mile 6*, halfway around and finally descend to a pass in the ridge line.

You bottom out at *Mile 7* and then begin the final and hardest climb of the day, actually accomplished in two stages. First you climb close to the high point of 4740 feet,

At the top of Pinnell Mountain

bouldering along its north side, from where views of Porcupine Creek are possible. The second stage, beginning at *Mile 9*, is Pinnell Mountain itself. It's a 300-foot climb along a series of rock switchbacks and, considering it's at the end of your first day out, a heart-pounder for most people. But the 4934-foot peak is a beautifully rounded dome with views everywhere, including your starting point almost 10 miles away. Stay awhile if the weather is nice, there is no need to rush down to the shelter.

The last leg of the day is the sharp descent off the peak. On the way down you'll spot the shelter in the saddle below and possibly a few tents. You pass *Mile 10* a quarter of a mile before reaching the shelter. The camping is excellent here with views off both sides. Often there are small pools of water on the south side of the pass.

Stage 2: Ptarmigan Creek Shelter to North Fork Shelter

(7.5 miles, 4-5 hours)
(Backcountry camping, shelter)
The route is marked in the pass and begins with an immediate climb up a ridge line. Once on the ridge there is a tendency to head south towards a 4595-foot knob. But the route continues to climb and then heads west along a ridge that features another set of ancient rocks. Many are pinnacles that have been carved into unusual shapes by wind, rain and other elements of nature. One, positioned just after *Mile 11*, looks like a profile of former US president Richard Nixon. There in the middle of the Alaskan wilderness, is Tricky Dick greeting you.

You skirt the high point of 4721 feet along the south side, pass *Mile 12* and then descend more then 400 feet to a low point in the ridge line. The route then begins to climb towards a 4282-foot dome but swings towards the north side before reaching the top. After bouldering around the side of the peak you emerge to the view of Swamp Saddle.

It sounds uninviting and Swamp Saddle can be in early July if the flies and other bugs overpower you. But in late summer this can be a delightful area. You descend to *Mile 14* where planking more than a mile long leads across the boggy area. The wild berries here are as thick and sweet as anywhere along the trail and include blueberries and low-bush cranberries. Small pools, within reach of the planked trail, exist through most of the summer and can be used to refill your water bottles.

The planking descends the saddle, crosses

it and then heads up a ridge on the other side, extending a short way past *Mile 15*. Eventually the planking stops and soon you top off on a ridge where the route begins a wide curve to the south-west. At *Mile 16* you make the final climb on the way to the second shelter. The first 300 feet are covered in a series of switchbacks but it is still a knee-bending climb. Gradually the route levels out, passes *Mile 17* and reaches the high point of 4447 feet.

The descent on the other side is just as hard and even more disconcerting to many backpackers when they can't see the shelter in the saddle below. That's because it's off the trail to the south. North Fork Shelter is a classic log structure pitched on the edge of the ridge with a sweeping view of its namesake river below. There are places to camp on the saddle and usually a few pools of water can be found here as well.

Stage 3: North Fork Shelter to Twelvemile Summit Trailhead

(9.6 miles, 5-6 hours)
(Backcountry camping)
Many trekkers will pass up the North Fork Shelter and continue on the trail to reduce the walk on the final day. It's two miles if you want to camp at the next saddle, and three miles to the one beyond that, where you would reduce your final trek to less than seven miles.

From the shelter, you resume climbing and then skirt the north side of a pair of 4300-foot knobs before descending to the next saddle, passing *Mile 19* on the way down. Blueberries abound here, so do the places to pitch a tent. You leave the area with a brief climb and then undertake a long descent 300 feet into the saddle at the foot of Table Mountain.

If it's still the second day, camp here. Table Mountain is a hard climb to undertake at the end of long day of trekking. You begin with a series of steep switchbacks that take you 600 feet to the top of the mountain's flat, table-like ridge line where you pass *Mile 22*.

The trail never does reach its true 4472-foot peak but instead departs from Table

Mountain from its south-east corner and begins a long descent. You'll drop more than 700 feet in the next 1.5 miles before passing *Mile 24* and climbing a 3865-foot knob. At the top you'll pass *Mile 25* and a surveyor's marker implanted in the ground. Important to many trekkers is the view of the Steese Hwy, which from here looks incredibly close.

The last leg of the journey is a climb around one more knob of 4100 feet and through another gallery of impressive rocks and stone pinnacles. Just beyond *Mile 26*, the trail begins descending and eventually curves to the south towards the highway and trailhead parking area. Much of the final mile is wet muskeg but planking makes it a pleasant end to the three-day hike.

GRANITE TORS TRAIL

What began as a rock climber's route to a series of pinnacles in the alpine area east of Fairbanks, became a backpacker's destination when the YCC constructed a trail in the early 1980s to the granite tors of Chena River State Recreation Area. Today this 15-mile loop provides easy access to the tundra world above the tree line where you can trek and camp among these unusual rock formations.

Tors are large granite outcrops that were formed million of years ago when molten rock pushed upwards and cooled before reaching the surface. When the surrounding area eroded, the large hard-rock pinnacles remained and invited rock climbers to scale them and trekkers to hike between them. The pinnacles range in size from boulders to rock outcrops up to 200-feet high. Most are above the tree line.

For the most part, Granite Tors Trail is a very well-marked and easy-to-follow trail that gains 2500 feet from Chena Hot Springs Rd to the tors. It is used much more than the Pinnell Mountain Trail, especially on any nice weekend in the summer when there's an influx of locals.

You can camp anywhere along the trail and you'll see many areas that are obviously favorites among backpackers. One of the best places to stay for the night, however, is on the descent from Flattop Ridge where a free-use shelter was erected in 1994. Like those trekkers on the Pinnell Mountain Trail, it's best to pack a tent and not count on getting sleeping space in the shelter. From here the tors are less than half a mile away. Bring a camp stove because open fires are prohibited along the trail. Also pack an extra quart of water and refill your water bottle at every opportunity; water can be tough to locate during the height of a dry summer.

The area is covered by the USGS 1:63,360 series quad *Big Delta D-5* but the trail itself is not marked on it.

Access

The trailhead is marked with an information bulletin board in the parking area of Tors Trail State Campground at *Mile 39.5* of Chena Hot Springs Rd. There is also another bulletin board with a registration book on the other side of the road. Hitchhiking is not the grand effort it is on the Steese Hwy because of the heavy summer usage of the Chena River State Recreation Area. You can also call Chena Hot Springs Resort (☎ 452-7867) which has a shuttle-van service to the end of the road; the round trip costs $55 per person (minimum of two persons per trip). Also check with GO Shuttle Service (☎ (800) 478-3847) which began limited service out to Chena Hot Springs Rd in 1994.

Stage 1: Tors Trail State Campground to Free-Use Shelter

(6.5 miles, 3-4 hours)
(Backcountry camping, shelter)
From a bulletin board in the parking area of Tors Trail State Campground, a trail heads to the highway bridge over the Chena River and uses a walkway to cross it. From here you cross Chena Hot Springs Rd and follow a levee to the river itself where there is a second bulletin board with information as well as an intentions book.

At the end of the levee, the trail splits. The left-hand fork leads off to the East Trail, the right-hand fork to the West Trail. The easiest way to hike the loop is to follow the East Trail which leads across a boardwalk

Granite Tors Trail

through black spruce and bog areas before crossing Rock Creek.

At this point the trail swings south-east and skirts the creek, heading upstream briefly through a forest of white spruce before moving into stands of birch and aspen where it begins to climb, a mile from the trailhead. For the next three miles you continue to gently climb and are occasionally rewarded with a view of the Chena River though the trees. Eventually the trail descends to a pair of saddles, resumes climbing and five miles from the campground reaches the tree line at nearly 2500 feet. At this point you reach a junction with a half-mile spur that leads left to a small group of tors, some of the few that are below the timber line.

You resume climbing to views of Chena Dome to the north and Flattop Mountain to the west along a trail that is marked by cairns. Eventually you traverse the talus slope of the Munson Ridge before descending into another saddle and arriving at the free-use shelter in an alpine meadow.

The four-sided shelter, which features a wood-burning stove, was a Boy Scout project in 1994 and is expected to be ready for the 1995 hiking season. It is reached 6.5 miles from the trailhead. From here the main group of granite tors, the Plain of Monuments, is only half a mile away. Camping spots abound in these alpine meadows above the tree line.

Stage 2: Free-Use Shelter to Tors Trail State Campground
(8.5 miles, 4-5 hours)
At this point the trail swings south-west and in half a mile, or seven miles from the trailhead, reaches the Plain of Monuments, the largest group of granite tors. Here the East Trail ends and a route through the tors

continues for two miles and is marked by wooden posts and rock cairns. The area can be a slosh through wet muskeg at times but the tors are fascinating and the views of the Alaska Range to the south are excellent from this 3000-foot vantage point.

Roughly nine miles from the trailhead, the West Trail begins when you reach a spruce and alder saddle; follow it to an open ridge-top. From there you descend to the last group of tors known as The Lizard's Eye, reached 3.5 miles from the free-use shelter.

This last group of granite pinnacles is at an elevation of 3000 feet and from here the trail drops into a sparsely wooded saddle and then, a mile from The Lizard's Eye, begins a rapid descent. You drop almost 2000 feet in the next three miles, returning to the tree line and ending in a black spruce forest on boardwalk along the upper stretches of Rock Creek.

In the final mile, the trail skirts the creek to return to the junction with the East Trail. Head left to follow the levee back to Chena Hot Springs Rd and the bridge over Chena River. You'll find the campground just on the other side.

Glossary

Alcan – Alaska Hwy (the only overland link between the state and the rest of the country)
aurora borealis – northern lights: a spectacular show on clear nights, possible at almost anytime of the year. The mystical snakes of light weave across the sky from the northern horizon in colors ranging from white to red. They are the result of gas particles colliding with solar electrons and are best viewed from the Interior between late summer and winter

backcountry camping – setting up camp in a wilderness area where there are no designated sites
backcountry campsite – a designated camping area near the trail
bidarka – a skin-covered kayak used by the Aleuts
BLM – Bureau of Land Management (although sometimes referred to as the Bureau of Logging & Mining, the BLM oversees a wide range of preserves and recreational areas, including the Pinnell Mountain Trail)
board valley – a glacially carved valley that features wide, gently sloping sides. The ridges or mountains slope away in a rounded U-shape as opposed to a river-carved valley which tends to have a sharp V-shape
boardwalk – also referred to as 'planking', these are the boards or planks used to cross a bog, *muskeg* or other wet area along a trail
bouldering hopping or scrambling across a slope of large boulders and rocks
braided stream – a stream or river with many shallow channels, broken up by bars of gravel. These are the safest places to ford a river
Bush, the – any area in the state either not connected by road to Anchorage or which does not have a State Marine Ferry dock in town

cache – a small hut or storage room built high off the ground to keep supplies and spare food away from roaming bears and wolves
cairn – a stack of rocks that indicate the direction of a route or trail (commonly used in areas above the tree line)
clear cuts – areas where loggers have cut down every tree, large and small, leaving nothing standing (they're ghastly to look at, and most travelers first view them from a state ferry in Southeast Alaska)
confluence – where two rivers or streams merge
crampons – a set of spikes attached to the bottom of boots that allow hikers and climbers to cross snowfields and glaciers

d-2 – a phase that covers the lands issue of the late 1970s, pitting environmentalists against developers over the federal government's preservation of 100 million acres of Alaskan wilderness as wildlife reserves, forests and national parks
dipnetters – anglers who use large nets to catch spawning salmon
Dolly Varden – a species of fish that resembles rainbow trout
drop-off – a steep descent along a slope, ridge or mountain

flashlight – torch
fording – crossing an unbridged river by wading through the current
fork – an alternative track leading off from a track junction
4WD track – a track used by a 4WD vehicle such as a jeep or off-road vehicle

glacial outwash – the gravel debris left behind by a retreating glacier

hemlock – a species of pine tree, native to Alaska

ice worm – a small thin, black worm that thrives in glacial ice; made famous by a Robert Service poem

internal frame – a backpack that is not attached to a rigid, tubular frame (its support is built within the pack)

Klondike stampede – the famous gold rush to the Klondike gold fields in the Yukon at the turn of the century; thousands of miners began the journey by following the Chilkoot Trail from Alaska

levee – an embankment to prevent a river from overflowing

Lower 48 – the way Alaskans describe continental USA

midnight sun – the polar phenomenon of the sun still visible at midnight

milepost – mile markers found along Alaska highways and a few hiking routes, eg the Pinnell Mountain Trail

moraine – accumulation of debris pushed into a mound by a glacier; it can be terminal, lateral or medial depending on its position within the glacial valley

muskeg – the bogs in Alaska where layers of matted plant life float on top of stagnant water (a bad place to hike or pitch a tent)

no-see-um – nickname for the tiny gnats found throughout much of the Alaska wilderness, especially in the Interior and parts of the Brooks Range

NPS – National Park Service (administers such parks as Denali and Wrangell-St Elias)

outcrop – a bare rock face or pinnacle

outside – to residents, any place that isn't Alaska

out the road – an Alaskan phrase that means 'to the end of the road'

permafrost – permanently frozen subsoil that covers two-thirds of the state

quads – quadrangle (used by trekkers in reference to a *USGS* topographical map; the quadrangle number is how each map is identified)

razorback – a sharply crested *ridge line*

ridge line – the backbone of a ridge

route – a natural direction of travel, such as along a river or *ridge line* (it is not a developed path; see *trail*)

run-off – the melted ice of a glacier

RVers – the drivers of large recreational vehicles, motorhomes or trailers pulled by cars

saddle – a low point along a *ridge line* or between two peaks

scat – any animal droppings (usually used to describe those of a bear)

scree – loose rock, usually found along steep, unstable slopes

Southeast sneakers – also known as Ketchikan tennis shoes, Sitka slippers, Petersburg pumps and a variety of other names. They are tall, reddish-brown rubber boots that Southeast residents wear when it rains (and often when it doesn't).

spur – a side trail

standing waves – a constricted stretch of a river or stream where the current forms permanent waves

summer solstice – the first day of summer on 21 June, and the longest day of the year. In the Interior and around Fairbanks, the summer solstice has from 21 to 22 hours of daylight.

switchbacks – the section of a trail that weaves back and forth, allowing you to ascend a ridge or slope in a gradual manner

taku wind – Juneau's sudden gust of wind that may exceed 100 mph in the spring and fall (in Anchorage and throughout the Interior, these sudden rushes of air over or through mountain gaps are called *williwaws*)

talus – see *scree*

tarns – small alpine lakes, often nestled in flat ridges

tent pad – a posted and elevated area to pitch a tent

topo – topographical (a term for *USGS* maps)

tors – large granite *outcrops* and pinnacles formed millions of years ago when molten rock pushed through the earth's surface and cooled

trail – a well-defined path that is often posted with trail markers and signs (see *route*)

trailhead – the beginning of a trail (usually posted or marked along the road)

traverse – to move horizontally across a slope

tree line – the point of elevation at which it is too high for trees to survive

true left – left side of a river when facing downstream

true right – right side of a river when facing downstream

tundra – vast, treeless Arctic plains

USFS – US Forest Service (the agency that oversees the national forests)
USF&WS – US Fish & Wildlife Service
USGS – US Geographical Society (the government agency that produces the *topos*)

VAC – Visitor Access Center (the new information center in Denali National Park)
vault toilet – outhouse, loo, pit toilet

williwaw – see *taku wind*

YCC – Youth Conservation Corps (the group that works with government agencies to build shelters and maintain trails)

Index

PLANET TALK
Lonely Planet's FREE quarterly newsletter

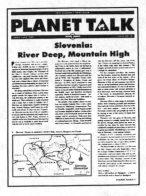

We love hearing from you and think you'd like to hear from us.

When...*is the right time to see reindeer in Finland?*
Where...*can you hear the best palm-wine music in Ghana?*
How...*do you get from Asunción to Areguá by steam train?*
What...*is the best way to see India?*

For the answer to these and many other questions read PLANET TALK.

Every issue is packed with up-to-date travel news and advice including:

- *a letter from Lonely Planet founders Tony and Maureen Wheeler*
- *travel diary from a Lonely Planet author - find out what it's really like out on the road*
- *feature article on an important and topical travel issue*
- *a selection of recent letters from our readers*
- *the latest travel news from all over the world*
- *details on Lonely Planet's new and forthcoming releases*

To join our mailing list contact any Lonely Planet office (address below).

LONELY PLANET PUBLICATIONS

Australia: PO Box 617, Hawthorn 3122, Victoria (tel: 03-819 1877)
USA: Embarcadero West, 155 Filbert St, Suite 251, Oakland, CA 94607 (tel: 510-893 8555)
TOLL FREE: (800) 275-8555
UK: 10 Barley Mow Passage, Chiswick, London W4 4PH (tel: 0181-742 3161)
France: 71 bis rue du Cardinal Lemoine – 75005 Paris (tel: 1-46 34 00 58)

Also available: Lonely Planet T-shirts. 100% heavyweight cotton (S, M, L, XL)

Guides to the Americas

Alaska – a travel survival kit
Jim DuFresne has travelled extensively through Alaska by foot, road, rail, barge and kayak, and tells how to make the most of one of the world's great wilderness areas.

Argentina, Uruguay & Paraguay – a travel survival kit
This guide gives independent travellers all the essential information on three of South America's lesser-known countries. Discover some of South America's most spectacular natural attractions in Argentina; friendly people and beautiful handicrafts in Paraguay; and Uruguay's wonderful beaches.

Baja California – a travel survival kit
For centuries, Mexico's Baja peninsula – with its beautiful coastline, raucous border towns and crumbling Spanish missions – has been a land of escapes and escapades. This book describes how and where to escape in Baja.

Bolivia – a travel survival kit
From lonely villages in the Andes to ancient ruined cities and the spectacular city of La Paz, Bolivia is a magnificent blend of everything that inspires travellers. Discover safe and intriguing travel options in this comprehensive guide.

Brazil – a travel survival kit
From the mad passion of Carnival to the Amazon – home of the richest ecosystem on earth – Brazil is a country of mythical proportions. This guide has all the essential travel information.

Canada – a travel survival kit
This comprehensive guidebook has all the facts on the USA's huge neighbour – the Rocky Mountains, Niagara Falls, ultramodern Toronto, remote villages in Nova Scotia, and much more.

Central America on a shoestring
Practical information on travel in Belize, Guatemala, Costa Rica, Honduras, El Salvador, Nicaragua and Panama. A team of experienced Lonely Planet authors reveals the secrets of this culturally rich, geographically diverse and breathtakingly beautiful region.

Chile & Easter Island – a travel survival kit
Travel in Chile is easy and safe, with possibilities as varied as the countryside. This guide also gives detailed coverage of Chile's Pacific outpost, mysterious Easter Island.

Colombia – a travel survival kit
Colombia is a land of myths – from the ancient legends of El Dorado to the modern tales of Gabriel Garcia Marquez. The reality is beauty and violence, wealth and poverty, tradition and change. This guide shows how to travel independently and safely in this exotic country.

Costa Rica – a travel survival kit
Sun-drenched beaches, steamy jungles, smoking volcanoes, rugged mountains and dazzling birds and animals – Costa Rica has it all.

Eastern Caribbean – a travel survival kit
Powdery white sands, clear turquoise waters, lush jungle rainforest, balmy weather and a laid back pace, make the islands of the Eastern Caibbean an ideal destination for divers, hikers and sun-lovers. This guide will help you to decide which islands to visit to suit your interests and includes details on inter-island travel.

Ecuador & the Galápagos Islands – a travel survival kit
Ecuador offers a wide variety of travel experiences, from the high cordilleras to the Amazon plains – and 600 miles west, the fascinating Galápagos Islands. Everything you need to know about travelling around this enchanting country.

Guatemala, Belize & Yucatán: La Ruta Maya – a travel survival kit
Climb a volcano, explore the colourful highland villages or laze your time away on coral islands and Caribbean beaches. The lands of the Maya offer a fascinating journey into the past which will enhance appreciation of their dynamic contemporary cultures. An award winning guide to this exotic fregion.

Hawaii – a travel survival kit
Share in the delights of this island paradise – and avoid its high prices – both on and off the beaten track. Full details on Hawaii's best-known attractions, plus plenty of uncrowded sights and activities.

Mexico – a travel survival kit
A unique blend of Indian and Spanish culture, fascinating history, and hospitable people, make Mexico a travellers' paradise.

Peru – a travel survival kit
The lost city of Machu Picchu, the Andean altiplano and the magnificent Amazon rainforests are just some of Peru's many attractions. All the travel facts you'll need can be found in this comprehensive guide.

South America on a shoestring
This practical guide provides concise information for budget travellers and covers South America from the Darien Gap to Tierra del Fuego.

Trekking in the Patagonian Andes
The first detailed guide to this region gives complete information on 28 walks, and lists a number of other possibilities extending from the Araucanía and Lake District regions of Argentina and Chile to the remote icy tip of South America in Tierra del Fuego.

Venezuela
Venezuela is a curious hybrid of a Western-style civilisation and a very traditional world contained within a beautiful natural setting. From the beaches along the Caribbean coast and the snow-capped peaks of the Andes to the capital, Caracas, there is much for travellers to explore. This comprehensive guide is packed with 'first-hand' tips for travel in this fascinating destination.

Also available:
Brazilian phrasebook, **Latin American Spanish** phrasebook and **Quechua** phrasebook.

Lonely Planet Guidebooks

Lonely Planet guidebooks cover every accessible part of Asia as well as Australia, the Pacific, South America, Africa, the Middle East, Europe and parts of North America. There are five series: *travel survival kits*, covering a country for a range of budgets; *shoestring guides* with compact information for low-budget travel in a major region; *walking guides*; *city guides* and *phrasebooks*.

Australia & the Pacific
Australia
Australian phrasebook
Bushwalking in Australia
Islands of Australia's Great Barrier Reef
Outback Australia
Fiji
Fijian phrasebook
Melbourne city guide
Micronesia
New Caledonia
New South Wales
New Zealand
Tramping in New Zealand
Papua New Guinea
Bushwalking in Papua New Guinea
Papua New Guinea phrasebook
Rarotonga & the Cook Islands
Samoa
Solomon Islands
Sydney city guide
Tahiti & French Polynesia
Tonga
Vanuatu
Victoria
Western Australia

South-East Asia
Bali & Lombok
Bangkok city guide
Cambodia
Indonesia
Indonesia phrasebook
Laos
Malaysia, Singapore & Brunei
Myanmar (Burma)
Burmese phrasebook
Philippines
Pilipino phrasebook
Singapore city guide
South-East Asia on a shoestring
Thailand
Thai phrasebook
Vietnam
Vietnamese phrasebook

North-East Asia
China
Beijing city guide
Cantonese phrasebook
Mandarin Chinese phrasebook
Hong Kong, Macau & Canton
Japan
Japanese phrasebook
Korea
Korean phrasebook
Mongolia
North-East Asia on a shoestring
Seoul city guide
Taiwan
Tibet
Tibet phrasebook
Tokyo city guide

Middle East
Arab Gulf States
Egypt & the Sudan
Arabic (Egyptian) phrasebook
Iran
Israel
Jordan & Syria
Middle East
Turkey
Turkish phrasebook
Trekking in Turkey
Yemen

Indian Ocean
Madagascar & Comoros
Maldives & Islands of the East Indian Ocean
Mauritius, Réunion & Seychelles

Mail Order

Lonely Planet guidebooks are distributed worldwide. They are also available by mail order from Lonely Planet, so if you have difficulty finding a title please write to us. US and Canadian residents should write to Embarcadero West, 155 Filbert St, Suite 251, Oakland CA 94607, USA; European residents should write to 10 Barley Mow Passage, Chiswick, London W4 4PH; and residents of other countries to PO Box 617, Hawthorn, Victoria 3122, Australia.

Indian Subcontinent
Bangladesh
India
Hindi/Urdu phrasebook
Trekking in the Indian Himalaya
Karakoram Highway
Kashmir, Ladakh & Zanskar
Nepal
Trekking in the Nepal Himalaya
Nepali phrasebook
Pakistan
Sri Lanka
Sri Lanka phrasebook

Africa
Africa on a shoestring
Central Africa
East Africa
Trekking in East Africa
Kenya
Swahili phrasebook
Morocco
Arabic (Moroccan) phrasebook
North Africa
South Africa, Lesotho & Swaziland
Zimbabwe, Botswana & Namibia
West Africa

Central America & the Caribbean
Baja California
Central America on a shoestring
Costa Rica
Eastern Caribbean
Guatemala, Belize & Yucatán: La Ruta Maya
Mexico

North America
Alaska
Backpacking in Alaska
Canada
Hawaii

South America
Argentina, Uruguay & Paraguay
Bolivia
Brazil
Brazilian phrasebook
Chile & Easter Island
Colombia
Ecuador & the Galápagos Islands
Latin American Spanish phrasebook
Peru
Quechua phrasebook
South America on a shoestring
Trekking in the Patagonian Andes
Venezuela

Europe
Baltic States & Kaliningrad
Britain
Central Europe on a shoestring
Central Europe phrasebook
Czech & Slovak Republics
Dublin city guide
Eastern Europe on a shoestring
Eastern Europe phrasebook
Finland
France
Greece
Hungary
Iceland, Greenland & the Faroe Islands
Ireland
Italy
Mediterranean Europe on a shoestring
Mediterranean Europe phrasebook
Poland
Prague city guide
Scandinavian & Baltic Europe on a shoestring
Scandinavian Europe phrasebook
Switzerland
Trekking in Spain
Trekking in Greece
USSR
Russian phrasebook
Vienna city guide
Western Europe on a shoestring
Western Europe phrasebook

The Lonely Planet Story

Lonely Planet published its first book in 1973 in response to the numerous 'How did you do it?' questions Maureen and Tony Wheeler were asked after driving, bussing, hitching, sailing and railing their way from England to Australia.

Written at a kitchen table and hand collated, trimmed and stapled, *Across Asia on the Cheap* became an instant local bestseller, inspiring thoughts of another book.

Eighteen months in South-East Asia resulted in their second guide, *South-East Asia on a shoestring*, which they put together in a backstreet Chinese hotel in Singapore in 1975. The 'yellow bible' as it quickly became known to backpackers around the world, soon became *the* guide to the region. It has sold well over half a million copies and is now in its 8th edition, still retaining its familiar yellow cover.

Today there are over 140 Lonely Planet titles in print – books that have that same adventurous approach to travel as those early guides; books that 'assume you know how to get your luggage off the carousel' as one reviewer put it.

Although Lonely Planet initially specialised in guides to Asia, they now cover most regions of the world, including the Pacific, South America, Africa, the Middle East and Europe. The list of *walking guides* and *phrasebooks* (for 'unusual' languages such as Quechua, Swahili, Nepali and Egyptian Arabic) is also growing rapidly.

The emphasis continues to be on travel for independent travellers. Tony and Maureen still travel for several months of each year and play an active part in the writing, updating and quality control of Lonely Planet's guides.

They have been joined by over 50 authors, 110 staff – mainly editors, cartographers & designers – at our office in Melbourne, Australia, at our US office in Oakland, California and at our European office in Paris; another five at our office in London handle sales for Britain, Europe and Africa. Travellers themselves also make a valuable contribution to the guides through the feedback we receive in thousands of letters each year.

The people at Lonely Planet strongly believe that travellers can make a positive contribution to the countries they visit, both through their appreciation of the countries' culture, wildlife and natural features, and through the money they spend. In addition, the company makes a direct contribution to the countries and regions it covers. Since 1986 a percentage of the income from each book has been donated to ventures such as famine relief in Africa; aid projects in India; agricultural projects in Central America; Greenpeace's efforts to halt French nuclear testing in the Pacific; and Amnesty International. In 1994 over $100,000 was donated to such causes.

Lonely Planet's basic travel philosophy is summed up in Tony Wheeler's comment, 'Don't worry about whether your trip will work out. Just go!'.